Finding Alpha

The Search for Alpha When Risk and Return Break Down

ERIC FALKENSTEIN

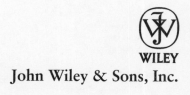

John Wiley & Sons, Inc.

Published by John Wiley & Sons, Inc., Hoboken, New Jersey.
Published simultaneously in Canada.

For general information on our other products and services or for technical support, please
contact our Customer Care Department within the United States at (800) 762-2974, outside
the United States at (317) 572-3993 or fax (317) 572-4002.

Library of Congress Cataloging-in-Publication Data

Falkenstein, Eric, 1965–
    Finding alpha : the search for alpha when risk and return break down / Eric Falkenstein.
        p. cm.
    Includes bibliographical references and index.
    ISBN 978-0-470-44590-7 (cloth)
    1. Financial risk management.   2. Rate of return.   3. Capital assets pricing model.
I. Title.
    HG4521.F315 2009
    332.63′2042–dc22

                                                                                    2008053436

Printed in the United States of America

10 9 8 7 6 5 4 3 2 1

Contents

CHAPTER 5

Investors Do Not Mind Their Utility Functions   **99**

CHAPTER 6

Is The Equity Risk Premium Zero?   **113**

CHAPTER 1

Risk Uncorrelated with Returns

In 1992, the *New York Times* noted a current *Journal of Finance* article, "Market Place; A Study Shakes Confidence in the Volatile-Stock Theory."[1] This was highly unusual, as the *Journal of Finance* is the premier academic finance journal in the world and deals with very abstract issues, but this was a highly unusual article. Prominent researchers Eugene Fama and Kenneth French had published a paper on the signature theory in empirical finance, the Capital Asset Pricing Model (CAPM).[2] It documented that the main empirical implication of that model, namely that *beta* was positively related to stock returns, was untrue. A stock's *beta* is a measure of its relative co-variance with the aggregate market, and was theoretically positively related to returns: higher betas imply higher returns, on average. Fama and French documented that beta's relation to returns was flat if not slightly negative, with high beta stocks producing no greater return than low beta stocks. It was as if Richard Dawkins wrote an article saying there is no empirical support for evolution. In 1973, Eugene Fama wrote one of the earliest and most widely cited papers supporting the CAPM, and nothing is more convincing, more necessary, perhaps, than that one of the priests had turned against the official religion. It was to be one of the most heavily cited *Journal of Finance* articles in its history. The basic model of risk and return that academics had taught for decades was shown to be empirically useless.

This finding of Fama and French, corroborated in many subsequent studies, is an example of the "omitted variables bias." Across the universe of stocks, which includes many small stocks that are hardly tradable, you see a positive relation between beta and return. But within a size grouping, say $1 to $2 billion in market capitalization, you would get the same, if not lower, return for having a high beta portfolio as you would with a low beta portfolio. The overall finding that beta was correlated with returns was totally due to the correlation between beta and size, not between beta and returns. It was as if someone noted the fact that people with longer hair were shorter than people with short hair, but this finding was merely due to ignoring the more fundamental variable, gender: the fact that women are shorter than men, and many women wear their hair longer than men do. The correlation between hair and height, when one controlled for gender, was zero, and reflected the deeper, true relationship between the variables. A similar complication was occurring between return (height), beta (hair length), and size (gender).

Economists assume that risk begets return, in the sense that risk is the price one must pay to get a higher-than-average expected return. The implication is profound, if limiting: Your investment success is solely based on whether you can tolerate risk, and dumb luck. You may be tricky at finding higher returns, but you always get only as much as implied by the risk, so when we see alpha, it is mainly sheer luck or survivorship bias. When this theory was created in the 1950s and 1960s, the profession's thought leaders pretty much assumed that the empirical corroboration would be easy. A correct theory's best friend is data, but the data have been very unkind, not just to their original financial model of risk and return (the Capital Asset Pricing Model, or CAPM), but any model purporting to capture the risk premium. When we look at risk and try to measure it directly, it is generally uncorrelated with average returns. The contrast between theory and practice is illustrated in Figure 1.1. The little dots represent observations, which are noisy estimates of reality. If you draw a line through them, on average, that line should slope upward, so that the average return is positively correlated with risk (the black dots). We see instead a bunch of dots in a cloud that, if anything, slopes downward (the white dots). Curious. A theory should *usually* work, at least approximately. If it almost always does not work, a good scientist should reject it—data are the ultimate judge of theory.

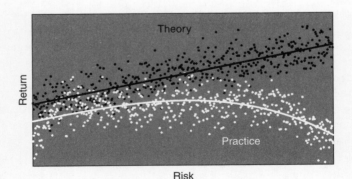

FIGURE 1.1   Risk and Return in Theory and Practice

As measures of risk are only rarely positively correlated with average returns, earnest attempts to find alpha through modern financial theory are snipe hunts, predicated on something that does not exist. However, if we accept that the empirical data on risk and return is not anomalous, but reflects an equilibrium when people are better described as envious as opposed to greedy, attempts to find alpha can be much more productive. As risk does not beget return on average, there are some strategies implied that are as obvious as the move from active mutual funds to index funds, yet offer significantly higher Sharpe ratios. Furthermore, while some alpha seeking is based on understanding portfolio theory, most of it is not. Lastly, alpha is basically private information about straightforward but detailed situations, which implies that people have a good reason to present it strategically.

The theory that risk underlies any returns not due to chance is fundamental to modern finance, and because it is also wrong presents both current confusion and considerable opportunities to those seeking alpha. The key is that risk taking and risk tolerance is not like physical courage, the ability to withstand a physical pain, but rather like intellectual courage, the ability to withstand ridicule. Physical courage is something most people agree on, and invites empathy, as when we cringe when watching someone crash his bike. In contrast, intellectual courage as it is sometimes practiced is usually seen as foolishness because risk is a deviation from what everyone else—the wisdom of crowds, the vast majority of smart people—is doing, and invites ridicule that is pointed and very hurtful.

Risk taking in financial markets is much more like intellectual risk taking than physical risk taking, though the foundations of current models are predicated on a "physical risk" premise, as when Keynes compared the risk premium to a compensation for working in a "smelly" environment. In that view, one who takes higher, nondiversifiable risk is something intuitively onerous to all but sociopaths, and indeed risk's universal recognition at some level is necessary for it to theoretically generate a return premium. Empirically, however, taking more of this kind of risk actually generates a lower return within equities, and in general, people who put a disproportionate amount of their wealth into the stock market, or take all their wealth out of the stock market, are taking similar risks, and are generally regarded as bizarre, not brave. Thus, standard models are profoundly misleading because they mischaracterize what risk taking feels like, and what to expect from taking it.

Only in the context of a life's strategy, of taking risks to discover about oneself, to invest time and effort to learn more about a very parochial problem carefully matched with one's talents, does risk taking reveal itself as a superior strategy. A good risky investment is tied to one's human capital, meaning it is highly idiosyncratic, not so much dependent on covariances with the business cycle as with one's talents.

THE RESPONSE: RETURN (RISK (RETURN))

The response of the academy was like a socialist hearing about the failure of the Soviet Union and saying that the Soviet Union was hardly a socialist state. Fama and French said that beta, the traditional sufficient measure of risk, was merely incomplete. If one looked at the things that did appear correlated with returns, *size* (that small cap firms outperform large cap firms) and *value* (low price/earnings aka P/E companies outperform high P/E companies), these were actually risk factors. Like dark matter in the universe, we don't see it directly but we do see its effects and infer it must be there because of those effects. The high returns on some characteristics must imply risk, and these are our new risk factors, which are really proxies for the risks they represent. Furthermore, they were not going to replace beta with proxies for size and value, but add proxies for size and value to the model. Size and value weren't bugs, but features of their interpretation of the risk-return theory. Fama and French proposed a new three-factor model that included variables for size, value, and beta in an attempt to save the standard theory.

Economics is the king of social sciences, but that's faint praise. In the heady 1970s, there was a consensus that economists were Worldly Philosophers, and knew what made some countries rich, as well as how to forecast if not avoid recessions.[3] Chastened, economists now focus their laser logic on why it's optimal to peel a banana from the other end (as monkeys do), why people pay too much for gym memberships they don't use, or why sumo wrestlers cheat.[4] They may not be big questions, but at least you can answer them correctly, and a right answer to a small question is better than no answer to a big question. Asset pricing related to risk, alas, is more like business cycles than peeling a banana.

Current asset pricing theory with respect to risk and return is not really a theory, but a framework. A theory is a specific testable idea, whereas a framework is a set of properties a theory must have, but still allows many, possibly infinite, expressions. An intuitive idea that has elegance, consistency, and can be mathematically elaborated becomes awesomely alluring when there are no data, sufficiently complex so that when the data start coming hard and fast, the framework is ready to handle it. The framework is nonfalsifiable because any test is not of the framework, but merely a specific theory that the framework allows.

There is no consensus on how to measure risk, and the leading candidates at any point in time are parochial, inconsistent, and changing. Originally, it was volatility, then covariance with the market, then covariance with several macroeconomic variables, and now it's a covariance against something called a *stochastic discount factor*. As Nobel laureate Robert C. Merton said about economics, "Risk is not an add-on.... It permeates the whole body of thought."[5] Indeed it does; risk is everywhere in economics as an explanation, but not as something directly measurable, at least in regard to risk relevant to expected return premiums. Risk is the economic equivalence of the ether, a substance that nineteenth-century scientists thought permeated the universe and explained how electromagnetic and gravitational forces moved through space. As no one could ever find it, however, more and more complex reasons were given as to why we could not measure it (for example, it carried a little turbulence with the mass) until Einstein created a model that did not need it. Risk is to finance what ether was to nineteenth-century physics.

But even if we can't measure risk directly, there is One True Thing about risk according to financial economists: it is positively related to expected returns. Thus, we can always work backward, find something with high returns, and say there must be a lot of risk. Even behavioral economists, who argue that many things are the result of systematic biases in human heuristics, admit that risk explains a lot, just not, say, the value effect. The problem is: the things that correlate with returns, the potential proxies for risk, tend to be parochial, inconsistent, and changing.

When risk appears to work, it is always inconsistently applied. The same equity risk that is used to explain why the stock market has higher returns than bonds is for some reason inversely correlated with returns when applied *within* equities. The same interest rate risk that is used to explain why three-year bonds have higher returns than the less volatile three-month Treasury bills is not relevant when extrapolated to the more volatile 30-year bond, where there is no further return premium. The same distress risk that explains the difference between AAA (safe) bonds and BBB (less safe) bond returns, is somehow not relevant when extrapolated to B (really unsafe) bonds. For a while, bankruptcy risk was thought by many to explain the high returns, and thus risk, of value and small cap stocks, yet when measured directly, high probability of default companies were found to have lower equity returns than low default companies. Banks, equity options, junk bonds, bankrupt bonds, mutual funds, commodities, small business owners, movies, lottery tickets, and horse races, have all failed to show any positive risk-return pattern—unless one defines risk as that which is reflected by assets with high returns.

FAILED PARADIGMS

The Ptolemaic system was a classic paradigm that seemed to explain the motions of the heavens. The basic model was that the moon, sun, and stars were affixed to spheres of various diameters, all with the earth at its center. Little spheres, called epicycles, were added to the sphere surface to allow the model to capture more complex movements, as when Venus appears to slow down, stop, and move backward in an otherwise circular path around the earth. As more observations came in and the model grew in complexity, we discovered that if we put the sun at the center and replace circles with parabolas, all those little epicycles are no longer needed. The truth is simpler than its alternatives because an incorrect theory has to add epicycles to rationalize its anomalies, and a good judge of theory is its coherence: does it need "lots" of epicycles? It seems so obvious now, but then, the jury-rigged Ptolemaic system worked pretty well in explaining the data because it was fit to the data, and further, the idea that the earth was stationary was a seemingly self-evident assumption. And so it is with our current theory on risk and return.

Academics have been studying risk for decades, and assert regular investors all price it consistently across various asset classes, yet have not been able to identify this risk factor to first order approximation. Perceiving risk must presumably be like our ability to distinguish dogs from cats, something we take for granted, yet a task too difficult for any machine using Artificial Intelligence.[6] Furthermore, most investors behave nothing like the theory implies—trading frequently, massively undiversified—but this inconsistency is supposedly inconsequential. This book documents the scope of the risk-premium failure, and what this means for the 99 percent of market participants who ignore efficient markets theory and try to find alpha anyway. Alpha seeking in financial markets is based on a risk taking rule that is good generally, but in highly competitive asset markets more like gambling than investing.

Any metric of risk used to explain one fact is inconsistent with a million other facts, and so if the higher return on the equity market is due to a risk premium, this implies that little gremlins of some other risk are then inversely correlated with the correlation between individual equities and the market as a whole, a sort of equity risk karma. So, going long the market *seems* to generate a 6 percent risk premium (return above the risk-free return on U.S. Treasuries), while going long a 1.75 beta asset and short a 0.75 beta asset—generating a zero-cost market return (that is, Beta = 1)—generates a *negative* return. A clever person can think of a neat story about why this is so, but then, the Arbitrage Pricing Theory that motivates so many factor models is built off the feasibility, nay, the active implementation, of such arbitrage on equivalent portfolios. As the anomalies have proliferated, the analogy of adding epicycles is not dramatic license. Such complexity is excusable, even attractive, if one thinks that reality is, in fact, complicated, and these models generate value to those willing to invest the time in gaining understanding of complex theories, but at some point you come up with so many auxiliary patches that the theory collapses under its own weight.

Though economists admit the CAPM or volatility is not a useful measure of risk, they have not removed it from its prominence in introducing the concept of risk and return to students. Risk is supposedly a variation on these themes, a technical detail about to be discovered that will appear as an extension to volatility or beta (which is from the CAPM). Academics who study the issue can't agree, or measure, risk to a first approximation, and prominent practitioners define it idiosyncratically: volatility, beta, correlations with inflation, yield curve slope, consumption, or exchange rates. Nonetheless, the great unwashed supposedly agree sufficiently to affect the price of things based on a conception we can't measure or model.

From a tautological perspective, volatility and return are correlated. But strictly speaking, that is the relationship between maximal returns and volatility, not expected or average returns and volatility. A highly volatile asset, like a lotto ticket, has an insanely large top return, and so to achieve such a return one must have made a highly risky bet. But generally economists are not interested in the possible, but the average, and so the degree to which volatility and *average* returns correlate is the subject of interest. Saying to get a high return, you have to take risk, or that if you take high risk, you could get a high return, is very different from saying that you should expect a higher return for taking more risk. The term *risk* is also confusing because in many cases a return is like a stated yield on a bond—it pertains to the best case or most probable scenario. As some bonds default, a stated yield and an actual yield differ by the effects of the defaults, which are usually concentrated in time around recessions. Thus when someone says a bond with a 15 percent yield has high risk, this is because we know that on average the return will certainly be much lower, as the default risks materialize and chip away at this stated return. But that is all merely amortizing expected defaults over the life of a security. The more fundamental issue is that no one has found a formulation of risk that explains the various *average* returns, the returns we expect to get over the cycle of good and bad times on a variety of investments. That is, risk as a premium for the discomfort it causes, not like the depreciation against stated yield due to random but statistically certain losses.

In contrast to the immeasurability of risk, consider physical beauty, a characteristic similar to risk in that you can rank it. Beauty is based on our preferences. Indeed, at first glance, beauty is *more* subjective than risk (no one sees a bunch of equations in *People*'s annual "Most Beautiful" issues).

Yet empirically, beauty is much easier to define than risk. Most everyone thinks that Jessica Alba and George Clooney are physically attractive. Identifying physically unattractive people is also easily agreed upon (overweight, bad skin, asymmetric facial features). In contrast, if *Forbes* had to put a list of 10 risky companies on its cover, it would not be obvious at all, because volatility and beta are actually *inversely* correlated with returns when you control for size. What does one choose? Value companies? Value companies are not risky in any obvious way, relative to growth companies, which, at high P/E multiples and higher volatility fit the more intuitive description of risky. Distressed companies? In fact, distressed companies have poor returns, so in the risk-return framework such deathbed companies have some strange low-risk characteristic. Some assets, like short term U.S. Treasuries, or AAA bonds, have very low returns, and are intuitively not risky: low volatility, correlation with the market, the business cycle, yet these characteristics do not generalize along the yield curve or within corporate returns. In ranking things from highest to lowest, why should identifying risk be infinitely more difficult than identifying beauty? One thing finance never mentioned in the early advanced textbooks on asset pricing, because they never expected this problem, is that risk as a practical matter is insanely subtle.

It is often amusing to consider how our scientific ancestors' quaint beliefs that we now know, with hindsight, are absurd, such as geocentrism, or that heavy objects fall faster than light objects. But consider the following ideas: eating fats as opposed to carbs cause obesity, steroids do not affect athletic performance, juvenile delinquents are lacking in self-esteem, stretching before an athletic performance makes you stronger, babies should sleep on their stomachs, or that primitive peoples are less violent than those in modern society. Each of these ideas was embraced by experts in their field and later found to be 180 degrees wrong, cases where the grandmother's common sense trumped her know-it-all Ph.D. grandson at Harvard. Theory is very powerful, and acts as a lens and a blinder; ultimately you can't see things right before your eyes. The more educated you are, the easier it is to confabulate an explanation for seemingly anomalous results. A step-by-step outline of the little evasions and selective omissions used in self-delusional good faith by smart, educated academics today is useful in understanding how flawed paradigms survive. Outsiders cannot judge these theories because of the jargon and specialized mathematics of this literature, other than to look at the general results.

This book tries to make a serious criticism and counterproposal to current financial theory on risk and return that is comprehensible to the average college-educated reader. Once one understands that risk-adjusting returns, in the sense of adjusting for a priced risk factor (as opposed to amortizing infrequent defaults), is a red herring, one can search for alpha more productively.

YOU MINIMIZE SOME RISKS, PAY TO TAKE OTHERS

In general, volatility and things correlated with it (covariances, uncertainty) are uncorrelated with return. However, for the highest volatilities, there is a negative correlation, such as really volatile stocks that have lower-than-average returns, and for the lowest volatility assets such as cash, Aaa bonds and Treasuries also have lower-than-average returns. There appears to be a premium people pay to acquire "sure things," and, at the other end, to buy "hope."

The key false assumption in the standard risk-return theory is that people are merely selfish. If people look at their own wealth, irrespective of others, and value the hundredth dollar less than their first dollar (declining marginal utility), you get an aversion to absolute wealth volatility that is like our aversion to smelliness. Thus, to the extent something is irreducibly volatile it must have a premium to persuade people to own this smelly stuff. In contrast, consider replacing this assumption with the assumption that people are fundamentally status seekers. Now we have a zero-sum game because status is about your rank, peers you benchmark against, and so minding to the market portfolio is risk-free because it keeps you in the same place, while taking any deviation from the market—too much or too little exposure to common factors—is risky. Merely by assuming people maximize their relative position as opposed to wealth, you get a different result, because a risk-free portfolio in a world of status seekers is different from a world of mere greed: one is doing nothing; the other is doing what everyone else is doing.

The absence of a general risk-return correlation is a non-obvious implication of this relative status assumption. In a rational equilibrium, if people care about their relative rather than absolute wealth, all risk becomes like diversifiable risk in the traditional CAPM, avoidable, and therefore unpriced. Risk taking is deviating from the consensus, the benchmark, and when you put disproportionate money on IBM, someone must be putting disproportionate money short on IBM—relative to the consensus. Such risk taking is predicated on alpha, and alpha is a zero-sum game. A zero-sum game is symmetrical, and therefore, implies that for every risk taker there is someone essentially taking the same amount of risk, just in the opposite direction, like when one is playing poker. If all risk is symmetrical, it must have the same expected return (both players can't have a positive expected return when one player is betting against another), and so arbitrage sets the returns to everyone the same, and risk has no premium.

Risk, unfortunately, has two distinct meanings within economics, and economists often confuse them. In one, it is a measure of variance, or volatility, though you can make this as complex a distribution as you desire. If the expectation has a greater-than-zero variance, it is risky. To the extent we are talking about random draws from an opaque urn, investors, and everyone else, seek to minimize it. They also need to estimate it, knowing how bad things can get (Value-at-Risk), or the value of options that are highly nonlinear functions of the payouts and necessitate knowing the state space. The other definition of risk pertains to the specific type of covariance that is priced in asset markets, as say beta represents in the Capital Asset Pricing Model, and this is the risk that is currently a mystery.

When it is priced, however, usually standard theory has a sign error! We pay for hope and for certainty, two ends of the risk spectrum. Thus, with certainty we have things like cash, short-term U.S. Treasuries, and AAA securities, whereas for hope we have casting calls, high-flying stocks, out-of-the-money options. Both sets of assets have below-average returns and because the market cannot generate an endless supply of these assets, there are barriers to entry in generating certainty and hope. We pay to take risk allied with our dreams because dreams are an unappreciated part of our reality: much of our daily thought concerns dreams. We pay for our dreams, because a life without dreams is a definition of Hell ("Abandon All Hope, Ye Who Enter Here," in Dante's *Inferno*). Many bad investments cater to our hopes but are imprudent, because in practice there is not a fine line between healthy risk taking and gambling, and the noisier the data the less obvious risk is gambling.

There are situations where alpha exists like the archetypal arbitrage, but the emphasis should not be on the risk adjustment and portfolio mathematics, but rather the parochial details about a market niche that may allow one to confidently know that alpha is really there. No matter what your position, it helps to understand how the archetypal alpha is created, because a manager who knows the source of his organization's alpha is much more effective than one who merely knows everyone's name. Even if you are not a portfolio manager creating alpha, it is essential to understand the archetypal alpha you are selling, and how it relates to the market, customers, and employees. Meanwhile, risk does permeates our actions because we often make decisions that attempt to do something better, which is like being blindfolded in a labyrinth, moving forward based on a theory as to how that labyrinth was designed, but also corrected by occasionally smacking into walls. Learning by doing often leads one to drastically refocus one's tactics or objective, as one learns of more pressing, or more feasible solutions, as those who went to California in 1849 to find gold, but then made their fortune selling shovels. Entrepreneurs, inventors, alpha seekers and others like them are trying to create value by doing something differently from how others would do it.

The goal in the search for alpha is to find what you are good at, become better at it, and do it a lot. Thus, it is more of a self-discovery process in a quest to find an edge that can become a vocation or firm value, rather than a specific trading strategy. Nothing will work for everyone, in the same way that not everyone is suited for a career in football, acting, or writing software. The value of knowing that taking a risk in almost any form is not generally rewarded is very useful, because you can then focus on what really matters, which is the expected value using a common discounting rate (for example, long-term LIBOR rates). Further, you can make sure your non-alpha investments are not in areas where investors are accepting lower-than-average return because it plays into their hopes. There is no return premium for doing something different without alpha, just as there is no return for taking systematic risk, because both risks are symmetric when people benchmark against others. If you don't understand alpha you are a sheep to be shorn, because the markets are like poker tables: They may not be efficient, but they are highly competitive.

Just as there are hundreds, if not thousands, of aspiring actors for every actor who makes a living acting, there are hundreds, if not thousands, of investors trying to be the next Warren Buffett, even though there are very few who can make the returns that compensate for the extra expense and idiosyncratic volatility entailed in trying to outwit the markets. But the key is not to stop dreaming, but to be sufficiently realistic to not take risk on the misplaced idea that any general sort of risk begets returns, and learn when to cut your losses, especially in areas that encourage the misconception that everyone has alpha in a certain domain. Knowing that you generally must *pay a premium to take risk* gives one a very different view on risk taking, because it is something you must economize on and think hard about, not something that will necessarily, on average, generate high returns. Indeed, thinking about risk as something that *necessarily* generates higher returns independent of our particular strengths leads inadvertently to gambling, a well-known investing vice. The larger-scale opportunity cost of not taking risk is even greater, though, which is why we do not mind flouting the poor average returns to financial risk taking, because we consider the broader context of intelligent risk taking in one's career.

When you know something important that's true, new, and important, the world makes more sense. Things that were previously unrelated anomalies now fit as part of a pattern, and so are easier to contemplate. For example, imagine your grandson, making the equivalent of $500K per year in current dollars, feeling depressed about his lot in life because his neighbors all make $700K a year. It's hard to fathom, yet that is precisely our condition, as the average white collar wage is near $100K, about five times as much as our grandfathers' average income, and yet surveys show that there has been no similar upward trend in happiness during this massive prosperity. This is the Easterlin Paradox, where aggregate income appears to generate no commensurate increase in happiness after only $20K per year, which is a puzzle to those who presume that happiness is a function of wealth. If we assume people are benchmarking themselves against others, this makes sense, while if their utility were merely a function of absolute comfort, it makes no sense.

If people invest on hope, some based on a search for alpha, some merely dreams, we should see assets with the greatest upside (positive skew) with lower returns, and indeed, highly volatile assets with the greatest upside tend to have the lowest average returns. The massive underdiversification of most investor portfolios (for example, more than 50 percent of them contain fewer than three stocks), makes sense only if people perceive they can pick stocks with higher-than-average returns, consistent with the alpha presumption that accompanies actual risk taking. The statistical inefficiency of these picks makes sense to these undiversified investors because, in general, one can rationalize potential alpha insights for only a limited number of situations. This preference toward volatility is why the highest volatility stocks have the lowest returns of any stocks, because they are popular for those attempting to play their alpha, and this excess demand increases their prices and lowers the future returns.

You need to know less to understand more with a correct theory, because a theory reduces the degrees of freedom necessary to explain the world, sort of like if you know $y = x^2$, you only need to know x to know y, whereas if you mistakenly think $y = x^3$, you need a story for why this isn't so for every observation of x and y. Think about true believer socialists in the mid-1980s, coming up with ever more clever explanations as to why East Germany was really more advanced than West Germany if you look solely at the ball bearings industry, or has a freedom that is less alienated, or something equally too narrow to really be a true measure. Or perhaps we should look at Albania. No, Yugoslavia. No, and so on. An untrue model leads to theories becoming more complex as more data arrive, and the empirical analysis of the data becomes more complex as well. So we see more and more anomalies to the standard final model, which gets more and more complicated because it doesn't work.

There is nothing more devastating to an intellectual than to know that much of his life's work created, refined, or elaborated is a dead end, not just an honest mistake overcome by progress, like someone making vacuum tubes shortly before silicon chips were developed, but someone working on phrenology, Marxism, or N-rays. Any serious thinker thinks about posterity, about becoming the father of some idea that is the foundation of other ideas, like the Double Helix of Watson and Crick fame, the Nash equilibrium, or the Black-Scholes options pricing model, ideas that seem to enter an *Ideas Hall of Fame,* forever esteemed by educated people. For an academic, it is the equivalent of heaven. The flip side, however, is just as strong. The thought that I am a sensible, competent person is inconsistent with the thought that I spent most of my creative energy supporting a theory that turned out to be worthless. Therefore, most intellectuals will distort their perception of the data in a tendentious direction, trying to not write off their past efforts as a sunken cost, usually by emphasizing not specific results, but the ability of the mathematical framework to accommodate the ultimate true model. Only when they die does the idea that in their youth they thought they would live forever die with them; the idea does not die first. The current experts of finance are almost surely smarter, know more math and statistics, and have examined more data, than you have. Yet they also strongly believe in something patently untenable, a strange example of when more expertise leads to a less accurate picture of the world.

Most top financial researchers see the current anomalies as just that, anomalies. Papers are presented each year, explaining how a novel conception of risk like the Fama and French three-factor model—that regular investors supposedly have applied all along—explains various anomalies, or suggest how potentially, extending the model by using facts such as non-normal distributions or parameter uncertainty, would be within-the-paradigm solutions. Statistician George E.P. Box famously said, "all models are wrong, but some are useful." The CAPM and its offshoots are not one of those useful models. It is not a useful approximation because it, as an approximation, has a sign error. It prioritizes estimating a risk discount factor, even though the collective effort after 40 years of finance professors has not generated successful models. Lastly, the current proponents of various tweaks from behavioral finance, tail risk, or downside risk do not appear to realize these refinements have been around since the inception of the status quo 50 years ago, and the lack of success of these new ideas is that they have never worked, not because they have not been tried.

Strangely, it is more useful to know that the risk-return theory is generally not true, than if it was true. If it were true, the only practical implication is to be diversified, the rest, a matter of preference along the risk-return trade-off that is fair and set by the market. You always get what you pay for. If it is generally not true, the key question is, can you trade your jealousy for greed, and then choose a low absolute risk, higher relative risk portfolio that will significantly increase your wealth? If you merely wish to maximize your Sharpe ratio relative to the passive indexes, if you are willing to bench-mark performance against the risk-free rate as opposed to the market, this is straightforward. As people generally overpay for hope, position one's port-folio to sell it. Generally, do not invest based on scenarios of massive success because on average these are bad investments; to the extent risk taking on average works, it is allied with highly specific wisdom and effort, so passive attempts to achieve your dreams are usually just lottery tickets.

It is also important to understand that, in general, alpha is concealed and distorted because it is valuable and so easy to copy. Suppose you dis-covered the momentum effect in 1980, something that is simple enough to understand, but was not well known at the time. How would you get access if you had no capital, and no contacts? What would say to your new partner that would be sufficiently convincing, yet not reveal your secret? On the other side, you have multitudes who want access to your capital and no objective way to judge their potential success. How do you choose among them given that they cannot prove they are valuable before actually letting them have access to your resources? How do you split proceeds? It is thus very important to understand the common activities in finance, the sub-terfuge, the negotiations, and the parochial situational knowledge, because these issues are endemic to alpha searchers. People invariably look at their own situation and think it is unusually unsophisticated, petty, and political, but that is the result of a world where alpha is so often misrepresented.

This book tells the story of risk from its beginnings to its current miasma, where risk now is evidenced by return as opposed to vice versa. After more than 40 years, one wonders how completely the existing paradigm must fail to generate more than a refinement to the market portfolio proxy. This book argues for replacing the old assumptions with new ones, primarily replacing greed with envy in utility functions, and, like derivative pricing, concentrate on the expected return and forget about the discounting. Finding alpha is about finding attractive expected returns, and this means exploiting one's comparative advantage, protecting, and understanding the politics inevitable when valuable ideas have little marginal cost.

CHAPTER 2

The Creation of the Standard Risk-Return Model

The story of risk is usually presented as the crowning success story of the social sciences, a manifestly human subject tamed through rigor and logic, with its canon of heroes from Markowitz to recent Nobel laureate Danny Kahneman. As MIT economist Andrew Lo says, finance is "the only part of economics that works," and within finance, risk rules.[1] The story of risk was presented in a best-seller by Peter Bernstein in *Against the Gods: The Remarkable Story of Risk,* where Bernstein chronicles the development of the Standard Model from the middle ages, and notes that:

> *By showing the world how to understand risk, measure it, and weigh its consequences, they converted risk-taking into one of the prime catalysts that drives Western society. Like Prometheus, they defied the gods and probed the darkness in search of the light that converted the future from an enemy into an opportunity.*[2]

Appropriately, there's a Rembrandt on the cover, with majestic sailors battling a tumultuous sea: just like risk managers! It's common for any specialist to think that his specialty—literature, jazz—is what separates us from preliterate savages. Experts in risk are generally pretty proud of their field's stature, as B-School enrollment affords considerable funding of research and faculty positions.

Usually, one starts in finance with the fundamental ideas of Harry Markowitz and portfolio theory and the development of the Capital Asset Pricing Model (CAPM) by William Sharpe, what is called Modern Portfolio Theory, or MPT. If you can understand the CAPM, the extensions are straightforward, and these extensions form the Arbitrage

Pricing Theory (APT) and finally to general equilibrium Stochastic Discount Factor (SDF) models, which represent the vanguard of current theoretical finance. The key concepts are absolute risk aversion and diversification, which implies that certain systematic covariances are all that matter in this paradigm.

The innovators all used extensive mathematics and abstruse notation befitting an academic when developing these concepts, but this is largely unnecessary. As Merton Miller said when discussing the theory that won him his portion of the Nobel prize in economics,

> *"Think of the company as a gigantic pizza, divided into fourths. If you cut it into eighths, [our] Theorems say you will have more pieces, but not more pizza."*
>
> *The reporter then exclaimed incredulously, "They gave you a Nobel Prize for something so obvious?"*
>
> *Miller immediately replied, "Yes, but you must remember, we proved it rigorously."*[3]

Indeed, Miller probably would not have won the Nobel prize if he had stated his argument in a 1,000-word *Newsweek* column, though anyone familiar with the Miller-Modigliani Theorem knows that is all they needed to communicate the gist of that theory.[4] Such is the rhetoric in any field, where professionals, using specialized jargon, think that any argument comprehensible to nonspecialists is insufficiently thorough. A seminal economic argument uses the tools one spends years learning in graduate school. The amenability of the CAPM to pedagogy cannot be underestimated in its success. You can develop the CAPM using basic assumptions, with each step involving neat insights, references to Founding Fathers, and elegant mathematics, perfect for a teacher who needs to create problems that are relevant and easy to evaluate. What better than a formal system of development like the CAPM, with its use of utility functions and statistics? Whatever its demerits (such as it not working), it is a teacher's dream to cover in class.

I hope my reader is somewhat familiar with the argument, as it is deep enough to require some repetition to gain a real feel for it. As with elementary statistics, I think I did not really understand it until I myself taught it several times as an instructor. Yet a rigorous or extended derivation from first principles would be a distraction, and so I am merely going to highlight the key assumptions and present the model, which is the basis for all subsequent extensions.

THE CAPM

Prior to the CAPM, there was great confusion as to the essence of profits. Some thought it was merely an implicit return to capital, or a function of monopoly power, but the bottom line is that there was no theory that implied higher risk, on average, generated higher returns on capital invested. Frank Knight's 1921 treatise, *Risk, Uncertainty, and Profits,* argued that the essence of profits was a return to uncertainty. The problem at that time was that, theoretically, profits should go to zero by way of competition, the same way arbitrage profits disappear in the market. Indeed, this was a major plank of Marx's *Das Capital,* as the fall in profit would be one of the main spurs for the upcoming socialist revolution. Yet profits seemed to be a constant portion of national income, generating a true puzzle.

In Knight's view, risk was not related to profits because risk can be diversified away. As he put it, "the busting of champagne bottles, if known to a precise probability, can be thought of as a fixed cost of storage. This is the principle of insurance."[5] Thus, risk, to the extent it is calculable, is not associated with a higher return, but rather, is merely a cost statistically amortized.

The only way people could make profits, in Knight's view, was if something prevented capital from moving too quickly into profitable areas. The uncertainty that precluded easy entry by competitors, what generated otherwise abnormal profits, were risky ventures for which there is "no valid basis of any kind for classifying instances,"[6] such as when an entrepreneur creates a new product. His conception of uncertainty has been hotly debated, as to whether the essence of how uncertainty inhibits capital may be due to moral hazard, the ability of the businessman to abuse the investor in such environments, a true uncertainty aversion, or something else. In any case, Knight sees businessmen making profits, by seizing on opportunities infused with uncertainty, as a subset of risk.

All of these explanations of profits were rather unsatisfying. The monopoly profits explanation would be tenable if larger, more politically powerful companies generated higher returns over time, but while it has always been popular to lament the greater power of the Captains of Industry, small stocks have done at least as well as large stocks since the data on these things began (see the "small cap effect"). Knight's theory, meanwhile, was inherently difficult to apply because if you could measure it, it was not risk. It was in this environment the CAPM was developed.

The key pillars of the CAPM are twofold: diversification and decreasing marginal utility. With these two assumptions, you get the essence of the CAPM, where a nondiversifiable factor generates a risk premium. Please see Figure 2.1.

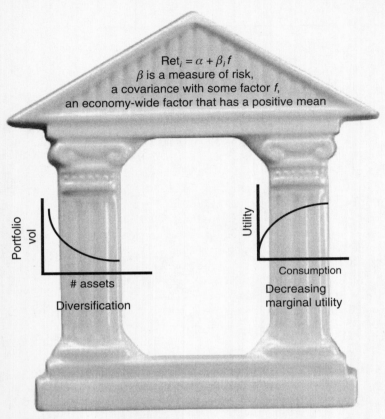

FIGURE 2.1   Asset Pricing Theory

Pillar 1: Decreasing Marginal Utility Means Risk Aversion

The idea of decreasing marginal utility really becomes fundamental in economics with the Marginal Revolution of the 1860s, when independently, Stanley Jevons in England, Carl Menger in Austria, and Leon Walras in Switzerland seized upon the concept of diminishing marginal returns to clear up many economic puzzles. For example, economists were able to explain the Diamond-water paradox: Why is a diamond worth more than water, though water is necessary for life, the other a mere bauble? They key is not to look at either as a whole, but at the margin. It is true that the total utility of water to people is tremendous because we need it to survive, yet as water is in such large supply, the marginal utility of water is low. Each additional unit of water that becomes available is applied to less urgent uses as more urgent uses for water are satisfied. Therefore, any particular unit of water becomes worth less to people as the supply of water increases. On the other hand, diamonds are in much lower supply, and their rarity brings great pleasure to those few who can wear or display them. Thus, diamonds are worth more to people.

The idea that people liked their first of anything—an apple, a glass of water, a dollar—more than the second one, and so on, is both intuitive and helps solve a lot of puzzles that beset classical economists like Smith, Ricardo, and Marx, and as it represents a rather mathematical concept (first derivative positive, second negative), it lends itself to a lot of mathematics, making it popular among economists. Applied to our wealth, we get Figure 2.2. When utility increases, but at a decreasing rate, this means we have diminishing marginal utility, and it is a crucial assumption in generating equilibrium, because otherwise, whatever product we liked best, we would spend all our money on, while in practice people have a variety of consumables, a scenario that makes sense only under the concept of diminishing marginal utility.

A not-so-obvious consequence of this fundamental assumption is that people are risk averse. They prefer, as in Figure 2.2, the certainty of receiving 50 dollars than a 50 percent chance of receiving 100 and a 50 percent chance

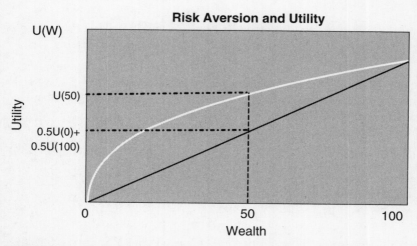

FIGURE 2.2 Diminishing Marginal Utility of Wealth Implies Risk Aversion

of receiving zero [$U(50)$] > [$0.5 \times U(100) + 0.5 \times U(0)$]. Mathematically, you can see that the expected sure thing will be on the curved line, and the average of the two extreme expectations, on the straight line. As the concave line will always lie above the straight line connecting its ends, you have risk aversion. You prefer the sure thing because of your risk aversion. In the late 1940s seminal work by Johnny von Neumann and Oscar Morgenstern (*The Theory of Games and Economic Behavior*) and Milton Friedman and Leonard J. Savage highlighted how the standard diminishing marginal returns lead to "risk aversion" which, intuitively, implies that when facing choices with comparable returns, agents tend to choose the risky alternative only if compensated.[7] Importantly, they applied the concept of utility to one's total consumption, or total wealth, independent of what others are consuming, or have. The implication is that people are volatility averse; they want to minimize risk as much as possible. This is a consequence of the diminishing marginal utility of wealth, and also seems eminently reasonable, because by then it was central to microeconomics, and passes the sniff test intuitively: the poor have to appreciate a dollar more than the rich.

The implication of such a function is our common notion of risk aversion, because if utility as a function of wealth is increasing everywhere yet increasing at a lower rate, you prefer the certain expected value to the gamble of that same expected value.

In practice, economics uses the following to represent our utility for wealth (W) in actual empirical applications:

$$U(W) = -e^{-aW}, \text{ or } U(W) = \frac{W^{1-a}}{1-a},$$

Here W is our wealth, broadly defined, and a is the coefficient of risk aversion, and the higher a is, the greater the curvature of this function, and so the greater the risk aversion. These functions are all concave and increasing in W. Average estimates for a are usually between 1 and 3, not more than 10, and economists often apply these functions to real data. You could include your present value of labor income or merely the cash in your wallet, but if we presently value our life, and call it W, the idea is that a concave function of it is appropriate.

Within the expected-utility framework, the concavity of the utility-of-wealth function is a necessary *and* sufficient to explain risk aversion. To repeat, diminishing marginal utility of absolute wealth is the *sole explanation* for risk aversion.

Pillar 2: Diversification Means Not All Risk Is the Same

The idea of diversification had been known to insurance companies for millennia. There are quotes from the Bible and Shakespeare highlighting that a diversified portfolio of assets is less risky than any one asset, and this was why Frank Knight thought risk was irrelevant to profits.[8] The key to the portfolio approach is the variance of two random variables is less than the sum of their variance. Diversification is a rare free lunch in economics, in that you get lower risk merely by holding several assets instead of one, which is costless. As the number of stocks grows, portfolio volatility asymptotes to some low, constant level.

In Figure 2.3, the total volatility of a portfolio declines to a limit equal to the total systematic risk of the portfolio. This is because the diversifiable risk cancels out, but the systematic risk stays. Mathematically,

$$\text{Portfolio Variance} = \frac{1}{N} \text{ average variance} + \left(1 - \frac{1}{N}\right) \text{ average covariance}$$

$$(2.1)$$

Equation 2.1 shows how as the number of assets N in the portfolio becomes large (for example, greater than 30), the only risk remaining is due to the covariances. If the covariances are on average zero, the portfolio variance goes to zero. *Covariance is all that matters to a large portfolio.* This is why the risks of a casino, where bettors are independently winning money from the house, generate pretty stable revenue to the house. The bettors will

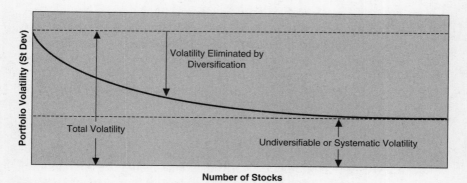

FIGURE 2.3 Diversifiable Risk as a Function of Portfolio Count

have uncorrelated, or zero covariance, to their payoffs, because card hands, or slot machine payouts, are independent. Thus a large casino has little risk from gambling payouts, excepting only when really large but improbable payouts occur.

To get from these two principles to the CAPM, you need only two major steps. First, as there is diversification, the set of feasible returns and volatilities from the infinite set of possible portfolios comprised of these securities is a convex hull. It generates what Markowitz called an "efficient frontier," where higher returns could come only via higher volatility. Indeed, much of the focus of Markowitz was on how to calculate this efficient frontier. At the time the subject seemed to his dissertation adviser, Milton Friedman, to contain a little bit too much statistics as opposed to economics, because it spent a lot of time on algorithms to determine the portfolio weights for the efficient frontier. Nothing stings like the lukewarm approval of men we respect, so in a scene surely envied by many a thesis advisee, Markowitz noted in his Nobel lecture:

> *When I defended my dissertation as a student in the Economics Department of the University of Chicago, Professor Milton Friedman argued that portfolio theory was not Economics, and that they could not award me a Ph.D. degree in Economics for a dissertation which was not in Economics. I assume that he was only half serious, since they did award me the degree without long debate. As to the merits of his arguments, at this point I am quite willing to concede: at the time I defended my dissertation, portfolio theory was not part of Economics. But now it is.[9]*

Markowitz's early work was on the nuts and bolts of generating the efficient frontier, statistical work without much intuition. It was understandable that Friedman found this focus to lack obvious relevance to economics, as with hindsight, the efficient frontier in mean-variance space has little to do with risk according to the new general equilibrium models. One could say that the efficient frontier underlies all portfolio mathematics, but really no more so than the idea that diversification is a free lunch, so the portfolio volatility should be of interest, not total volatility of an asset in isolation.

Tobin's Separation Theorem was the next step needed to get to the CAPM, and while this is an interesting model, its derivation is covered in most standard finance textbooks.[10] The basic idea is that any optimal portfolio involves two separate calculations: first, to find the optimal risky portfolio on the efficient frontier that contains only risky assets, and second, to find the combination of that portfolio, along with the risk-free rate, to reach one's highest level of utility.

With 1,000 assets, you needed to calculate 550,000 different covariances to generate an efficient frontier of portfolios so that you could find the optimal tangency portfolio. In the days before computers were common, this could simply not be done. But given Tobin's Separation Theorem, the problem for an investor turns out to be trivial. In one of those moments of simultaneous discovery that suggests the result was truly inevitable, John Lintner, William Sharpe, Jack Treynor, and Jan Mossin each independently discovered that you could merely look at an asset's correlation with the aggregate market, not each individual asset. (Sharpe published first, and won the Nobel prize. There is a lesson there. Treynor published in 1962, Sharpe in 1964, Lintner in 1965, and Mossin in 1966.[11]) Given Tobin's Separation Theorem, this is really kind of obvious for the following reasons.

Wealthier and risk-averse investors might allocate various amounts to this portfolio of risky assets, but within that risky portfolio, the composition would be exactly the same for all investors, because Tobin's Separation Theorem implies that regardless of risk preference, every rational person holds the same composition of risky assets, just in different aggregate amounts. Since equities exist in positive supply, in equilibrium, people have to hold them, and if any rational person holds them, every rational person holds them in the same proportion. Thus, prices must adjust such that everyone holds every asset is exact proportion to its supply in the market. Otherwise, people would demand more of a stock than exists, or not enough. The argument is an equilibrium result because in equilibrium, supply has to equal demand, so given that everyone holds the same proportion of risky assets, their demand must proportionately match supply, or supply does not equal demand. If the market is the efficient portfolio, it then dictates the equilibrium return for every asset.

Unlike what Knight assumed, not all risk can be diversified away, because in stressed times all assets tend to move downward together (covariances are not all zero). This residual systematic risk, because we are risk averse, is priced in the same way living next to a smelly factory is priced into a house. The risk premium in asset markets is the return of the risky portfolio above the risk free rate: the price of risk. The covariance of an asset with the market, normalized by the variance of the market, is the *beta,* and represents the amount of risk any asset has. A beta of 1.0, means it is as risky as the market, and so receives the same expected return premium as the market portfolio; a beta of 2.0 has twice the risk, and gets twice the premium. The return to the investor is linear in the amount of risk.

Mathematically, that generates the familiar CAPM equation, which underlies the Security Market Line in Figure 2.4.

Here R_f is the return on the risk-free asset, $E[R_i]$ is the expected return on asset i, and $E[R_m]$ is the expected return on the market. Beta is the "how

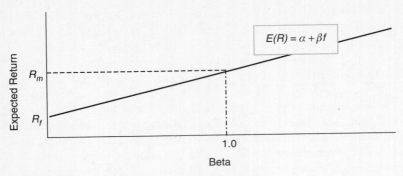

FIGURE 2.4   Security Market Line aka CAPM

much" of risk, and equal to the covariance of asset i and the market divided by the variance of the market (that is, σ^2_{im}/σ^2_m), which is basically the same as the coefficient in an ordinary least squares regression of asset returns on the stock market proxy (and as regression estimates are generally called *beta* in introductory textbooks). Idiosyncratic risk and covariance with assets other than the market portfolio are irrelevant, because presumably only the market represents the nondiversifiable variance that people must hold, yet dislike. $E[R_m - R_f]$, the equity risk premium, compensates you for your pain.

This is an equilibrium result. That is, assume it did not exist, that a security with a beta of two had the same return as the market. In that case, only a fool would hold this asset, which generated the same displeasure—in the sense of adding variance to one's utility—as two units of the market portfolio, but only generating one unit of market return, an impossibility in efficient markets. Alternatively, an asset with a beta of zero, yet the same return as the market, would be preferred by every investor relative to the market portfolio, as it generates the same return without the volatility-of-utility displeasure. But if everyone rushed to buy it and sell other securities, its price would rise, and its return would fall.

An equilibrium result in finance can also be presented as an arbitrage result. Linearity in pricing is implicit in that beta, a scalar, is multiplied times the equity risk premium to generate the expected return. Linearity in pricing implies no arbitrage, and vice versa. It's as if milk costs $2 a gallon, and then every fraction or multiple of a gallon is merely $2 times how many gallons you bought. An exposure to market risk, as reflected by beta, will give you the same return, regardless of how it's assembled: by individual stock, portfolio, or risk, such as represented by beta in the CAPM, generates a linear return; in the case of CAPM, $(R_m - R_f)$. This generalizes, or is applicable, in every other theory in asset pricing.

THE ARBITRAGE PRICING THEORY (APT)

The CAPM is a straightforward theory. You can test it. It predicts that all that is needed to estimate expected returns is the beta, which is straightforward given data on asset returns and a market proxy like the S&P500, and also an expected market premium, also called the equity premium. If you do not know the equity risk premium, you should at least be able to ordinally rank assets by their expected returns because these are positively related to beta.

But the CAPM was hardly definitive, even before one could see its empirical flaws. The basic two extensions are the Arbitrage Pricing Theory of Stephen Ross in 1976, and the general equilibrium approach, which turn out to have very similar empirical implications.[12] Unlike the CAPM, these are frameworks, not theories. There are no crucial tests of either of these approaches. The APT and general equilibrium approaches rationalize throwing the kitchen sink against an asset's return, because risk factors are only constrained by your ability to articulate an intuition for risk, which considering the cleverness of top professors, is really no constraint at all. Even Fama (1991) called these theories a "fishing license" for factors.[13]

The APT is a simple extension of the logic applied in the CAPM, only to more than one factor using the law of one price, or arbitrage. The idea was simple. Assume a stock has several risk factors, things that are priced like in the CAPM, have risk like the CAPM (nondiversifiable), and are measured like the CAPM (betas). For example, a three-factor model would have the following form:

$$E[r_i] = r_f + \beta_1 \left(E[R_1] - r_f \right) + \beta_2 \left(E[R_2] - r_f \right) + \beta_3 \left(E[R_3] - r_f \right)$$

$$(2.2)$$

A four- or five-factor model would generalize in the logical way. Thus, each factor is just like a little CAPM term, where the factor, $(R_1 - R_f)$ has a premium, an expected return over the risk-free rate, just like the market in the CAPM. Each firm has its own beta, β_1, with respect to each factor. These are determined in practice by regressing returns against these factors, so in a multifactor model the problem is more complicated than the simple ratio of the variance to the covariance, but if we accept that betas come out of regressions, and regression packages come within Microsoft Excel, it's simple enough. The fundamental result relies on the same logic in the CAPM. No matter how you achieve the amount of risk as represented by a beta, it should cost the same regardless because of arbitrage, ergo, it is the Arbitrage Pricing Theory. If exposure to a risk factor generated a different return, through individual stocks or portfolios, one would buy the cheap one, sell the expensive one, and make risk-free money. If you measure the beta correctly, it should have the same price no matter how it was constructed. Risk is all that matters, and so it is priced consistently.

Betas measure how much risk, and are a function of covariances, not volatility (though as a practical matter, equities with higher betas have higher volatility and vice versa). Risk premiums, well, where they come from is not essential to the APT; all we know is that if there is no arbitrage, whatever those priced risks are, return is linearly related to the factors through their betas.

The APT assumes some unspecified set of risk factors, but since its inception, most researchers assume the first factor is the standard CAPM market factor, plus others that are intuitive things that reflect risk: a measure of currency volatility, oil prices, inflation changes, industry risk, country or regional indexes, to name a few. Just write down these things like you would a return on the market portfolio, and regress them against a security to get the betas. These are all things where, like the stock market, changes cause us pleasure and pain, affecting our utility. Stocks that go up when we are surprised by good news are less valuable or riskier than things that go up only a little when good new arises.

An early example of the APT was Barr Rosenberg's Barra company, which estimates factors for things like value, size, industries, countries, price momentum, and various combinations (small cap growth) therein, eventually coming up with over 50 such factors. The idea is that a long or short portfolio based on size (long the small stocks, short the big stocks), proxies some risk, and so these proxy portfolios are risk factors, because they reflect the relative return on a strategy focusing on value, size, or what have you. They have been offering services since the 1970s.

Actually, one need not even specify the factor as something intuitive. *Factor analysis* allows one to boil down a stock market's volatility into statistical factors that often have no intuition at all. There are statistical techniques that generate time series of data that look like market returns, but they are really returns on portfolios that explain the variance of the constituents. There will be a factor, or set of factors (that is, returns), that explains most of the variance within the S&P500 one observes over time. In practice, this first factor is highly correlated with the equal weighted return on the portfolio. So the first factor in these approaches is somewhat of an equal-weighted market proxy. The second factor was smaller by a factor of 10 in terms of the ability to explain returns—a big dropoff—and is not intuitively obvious to anyone what this correlated with, and less so for subsequent factors.

This makes the APT more generalizable, but also less useful, because some may choose to include a risk factor for inflation, or oil, and some not. Who's to say what risk factors are priced? In the APT it is purely an empirical question, which has turned out to be much more ambiguous than expected.

THE STOCHASTIC DISCOUNT FACTOR (SDF)

General equilibrium models of asset pricing get down to Stochastic Discount Factors, which is really a different way to generate the same form as the APT, which is itself more general than the CAPM. Enthusiasts see this as the alpha and omega of finance, a unified field theory of derivatives, yield curves, equities, and so forth, because it generalizes to macroeconomic models of output and growth. The elegance and profundity of the SDF is essential in understanding the deep roots to the current paradigm in the face of its empirical failures.

The SDF approach is often called an "intertemporal general equilib-rium model," because it models both the real processes in the economy (production functions) and the preferences of individuals. This was stan-dardized into modern form by Merton (1971), expanded by Robert E. Lucas (1978), and finally Cox, Ingersoll, and Ross (1985).[14] Although it is highly mathematical, it comes to the basic implication that returns of assets are a function of some risk-free rate, plus a risk premium that is a function of the covariance of the return of that asset with the marginal utility of wealth. Things with high payoffs when the marginal utility of wealth is high, pay off when the level of wealth is low (because marginal utility de-clines with wealth). The marginal utility of wealth can be proxied by a state variable representing the state of something that affects utility. As this state changes over time—because of recessions, changes in optimism about the future—this means it is stochastic. As this affects the risk premium, it is thus a "stochastic discount factor (discount factor being the inverse of the risk premium)." Under some assumptions, this stochastic factor is merely a function of consumption or GDP, which makes it more intuitive (a hedge against recessions).

General Equilibrium modeling can involve the most abstruse math-ematics. The popularity of this approach blossomed in the 1970s, as it was deemed that the best economics tended to be rigorous, mathematical work, in theory or empirical analysis. The thought that more rigor is good, however, developed into an arms race, and so economics became much more mathematical over the decade. Most Ph.D. level research is a mathematical subject involving not just advanced statistics, but set theory, real analysis, and continuous time calculus, all well beyond what MBAs are expected to understand, and rarely used by financial practitioners.

An example of this was the explosion of *lemmas* and theorems in articles, which are mathematically proven statements. In the leading journals, these were essentially absent in the 1950s, but they grew steadily in each decade since. In grad school, we would whisper about a professor "He has his own theorem," meaning his name coupled with a theorem was known by economists, like Arrow's Impossibility Theorem, the Coase Theorem, Shepard's Lemma, or the Gibbard-Satterthwaite Theorem, and it implied that they were economic rock stars.[15] It was considered good form to emulate the strict, airtight reasoning of mathematics because it eliminated imprecision and illogical reasoning. It made the field more scientific, that the soft sciences don't have lemmas and theorems, but the hard sciences do. The thought—the hope, really—was that economics contains lots of important truths only expressible in higher level math—like physics. Sophisticated mathematics has the unfortunate property of making banal arguments seem much more profound, in the same way that bad poetry accompanied by good music can seem really deep.

The real beginning of the SDF approach was when future Nobel Prize winners Kenneth Arrow and Gerard Debreu invented the concept of a state-space security, what would later be called Arrow-Debreu Securities. These theoretical constructs would pay off a unit if the state were achieved, zero otherwise, where the *state* could be anything you could imagine, such as when stocks decline by 10 percent over the previous day and Fed Funds are above 5 percent. Such *state contingent* thinking forms the basis of the Stochastic Discount Factor.

Discount Factors allow one to translate a dollar tomorrow into a dollar today. They are stochastic, in that they change over time, depending on how nervous or prosperous the aggregate economy is. For example, a higher interest rate would increase the discount rate. Also, intuitively, discount factors should be higher when we are in good times, or there is little uncertainty about the future, or the growth in the economy is expected to be large. Thus the discount factor *should* fluctuate over time, and this fluctuation will lead to varying returns even if payoffs are constant on average. In general, think of a discount factor as being less than 1, and

$$DF = \frac{1}{1 + R_f + g} \tag{2.3}$$

Where g is the risk premium of, say, 4 percent, and R_f the riskless interest rate of 5 percent. In the absence of risk, the discount factor is merely the inverse of the gross risk-free interest rate, or $1/(1 + R_f)$: the higher the interest rate, the lower the discount rate, and vice versa. This would generate a discount factor like the following:

$$DF = \frac{1}{1 + .05 + .04} \approx 0.917 \qquad (2.4)$$

The basic idea in asset pricing is that the price of a security is worth the discounted value of its payoffs, multiplied by the probability of those payoffs, which is how they are modeled in standard utility functions.

Because good times imply we have little need for stuff, and bad times not, this implies we should affect the discount factor for things that pay off in good times versus bad times. It is higher in poor states because in those states of the world, the value of money is higher. Any asset paying off something in the future is merely the sum of the Discount Factors, *times* their payoffs, *times* their probabilities.

$$P_0 = \sum_{s=1}^{S} prob(s) \cdot P_1(s) \cdot DF(s) \qquad (2.5)$$

Here $DF(s)$ is the discounted value of a dollar in state s tomorrow, where it is supposed to be different in the different states, because money is worth different amounts, depending on, say, whether there is a recession or expansion in that period.

Dividing through by P_0, and one turns this from a relationship for prices to one on gross returns (gross returns are simply net returns $+ 1$, like 5 percent is a net return, and 1.05 is the gross return; P_1/P_0 is R), one gets:

$$1 = \sum_{s=1}^{S} prob(s) \cdot R(s) \cdot DF(s) \qquad (2.6)$$

The sum of probabilities is just an expectation, where $E[x] = \sum_{s=1}^{S} prob(s) \cdot x_s$, so we can write this as:

$$1 = E[DF \times R] \qquad (2.7)$$

Which, for some unknown reason, DF was changed to M, and thus became:

$$1 = E[MR] \qquad (2.8)$$

In the 1970s, economists began to prove mathematical properties that would be nice for the *DF*s to have. To get a flavor of this research, there was much rejoicing when Harrison and Kreps proved theoretically that the *DF*s had to be nonnegative, meaning you would never get paid to potentially receive a dollar in some future state, as if this needed proving.[16] Indeed, there is a lot of emphasis on technical issues because financial academics are very good at math (even though it is fashionable to say, "I know a famous mathematician and he says economists are very sloppy with their proofs"), and the consistency of their equations is interesting irrespective of the empirical issues. The basic paradigm develops a momentum of its own through these theoretical discoveries and extensions. Mark Rubinstein outlined the assumptions needed to reify a single consumer as a representative agent of the entire economy, and though these assumptions were insanely strong (for example, that everyone has the same beliefs about probabilities), once he outlined the assumptions, the use of a representative agent was now defensible because Rubinstein proved this was appropriate under some basic assumptions, which were not really important because most economic assumptions, like perfect information or zero transaction costs, are not technically true (this inures one to absurdities).

Most importantly in this early period, they proved that arbitrage implies cash flows will be weighted the same regardless of security. This is really like the APT, which was introduced around the same time. Clearly, the idea was in the air, that if one security has a codicil that says you get $1 if the S&P goes down 10 percent next year, that part of the security should cost the same no matter what security it is attached to because its price is independent of the portfolio it may be in. Financial assets are always priced the same regardless of context due to arbitrage. More realistically, if a security should expect to do especially poorly in the next credit crunch, that aspect of the security adds or subtracts the same to every security that has this characteristic. Linearity is in the pricing of risk, just like the CAPM and APT. Another property of this approach is that risk is taken into account in terms of covariances. The only difference is that this is the covariance with utility, not the market.

But where does the *DF* come from? Where do you get these discount factors for all these states of nature?

The answer is from the following idea. A dollar today can be transformed into X dollars tomorrow through an investment. The utility of a dollar today is the marginal utility of a dollar, based on how wealthy we are, and so on. The utility of a dollar tomorrow is the marginal utility of a dollar then, based on how wealthy we are then. Let *r* represent the rate of return on the asset. The marginal value of a dollar today equals the product of the marginal value of a dollar tomorrow, times the marginal value of a dollar tomorrow:

$$U_0' = U_1' \cdot (1 + r) \qquad (2.9)$$

Here U_0' is the marginal value of a dollar today, and U_1' the marginal value of a dollar tomorrow. Today is represented by the subscript 0, tomorrow 1, and the $'$ superscript notes that this is the derivative of utility, or marginal utility, at that time.

If the interest rate is, say, 5 percent, we can easily exchange \$1 today for \$1.05 tomorrow with this interest rate, a "transformation machine." This can only be equilibrium if people's preferences value \$1 today like they would \$1.05 tomorrow, otherwise, they would either never save, or save everything and never consume, both of which are counterfactual. Now, dividing by U_0', we get:

$$1 = \frac{U_1'}{U_0'} (1 + r) \qquad (2.10)$$

Replacing $\frac{U_1'}{U_0'}$ with M we get

$$1 = E[MR] \qquad (2.11)$$

Since $R = 1 + r$ (R being the gross interest rate). Thus we are back to the DF formulation, but now we have economic intuition for where the Discount Factor comes from, and in the literature call the discount factor M for historical reasons ($M = DF$). But though it has a more compelling origin than the APT, it works the same way: It values payouts in various states the same, regardless of the package.

The tricky thing is that since M and R are potentially random variables, they must obey this following statistical law that holds for any random variables:

$$E[MR] = E[M]E[R] + \text{cov}(M,R) \qquad (2.12)$$

As the covariance was the key to the CAPM, using some very intuitive assumptions, there's a neat sketch of a proof in the appendix of this chapter showing how this approach leads to the CAPM as a special case, that is, back to

$$E[R_i] = R_f + \beta E[R_m - R_f] \qquad (2.13)$$

This is the kind of result that scientists love, where a preliminary model is a special case of a more general model that has weaker assumptions. The way the SDF approach based on utility functions and assumptions about growth processes, connects both to the APT, which is founded merely on arbitrage, to finally the CAPM as a special case, is the kind of consistency that is very alluring to the mathematically minded. How could this be an accident? Only the truth could be so beautiful!

So the Discount Factor approach suggests we look for things that are proxies of our marginal valuation of dollars tomorrow. Utility suggests that we look for things that proxy our wealth because our aggregate wealth determines our marginal utility. Such things include the stock market, but also inflation, exchange rates, wage rates, consumption, oil prices, and so forth. Whatever you think affects people's well-being could be a factor. A positive return on a security would be worth a lot more if you lost your entire savings that same year; the covariance of an asset with these hypotheticals determines its risk. The covariance of the payout matters, though instead of tying it to the market, as in the CAPM, we now tie it to the abstruse idea of your marginal utility tomorrow, or your valuation of money tomorrow.

Yet, just as in the APT, we are left with this unspecified multifactor model, only now we have motivation for the factors: things that are related to our marginal utility. The difference between the Discount Factor and APT approach is merely in the derivation, the philosophy. One is based purely on arbitrage, the idea that whatever risks exist are priced at, they must be priced linearly according to their betas. The other, based on something more fundamental, the marginal utility of investors in various states, but the result is the same as the APT: we have risk factors (that is, the price of risk) and their betas (that is, the amount of risk).

ADDING NON-NORMALITY

The base Normal or Gaussian distribution has several nice properties that make it a very useful pedagogical device, but it is also too simple. For example, if you add a bunch of normally distributed random variables, you get a normally distributed random variable. This isn't true for most distributions, and so, if you add a lognormally distributed variable to another lognormally distributed variable, you get a kluge, and then analytic tractability is gone. The assumption of normality is convenient for someone modeling, and models are maps of reality, not reality itself. If you take the expected value of an exponential utility function, a normally distributed exponent generates a certainty equivalent closed form solution.[17] It is thus highly convenient to the modeler to assume normality, even if not true, for expositional purposes.

The CAPM can be derived under a variety of assumptions, but the normally distributed return is one of the more common assumptions used to justify this approach.

Markowitz's treatise *Portfolio Selection: Efficient Diversification of Investments* in 1959 outlines many tactical issues in empirical asset pricing. In this early work, Markowitz addressed semideviation directly as a viable alternative to regular standard deviation, and it continues to pop up as a more intuitive measure of risk that may be more empirically meaningful. Semideviation is like standard deviation, but it ignores the upside, because, intuitively, an above-average return is not risk. Other measures of risk that would capture the deviation from a non-normal distribution include: kurtosis, skewness, and clearly to the degree they exist, they could be material, and have not been neglected.

Yet it has been known since at least Mandelbrot (1963) that actual stock returns have both fatter tails than Gaussian distributions (kurtosis) and are also skewed.[18] Furthermore, everyone knows that an unexpected three standard deviation downswing is more relevant in estimating risk than a three standard deviation upswing.

In 1963, Mandelbrot used some tricky distributions, called stable-Paretian, to explain the fat tails in stock markets. In 1987, James Gleick published a best selling book, *Chaos*, which highlighted Benoit Mandelbrot's fractals, and suggested that he had a new insight that was about to revolutionize finance (in *Chaos*, anything nonlinear was about to revolutionize everything). In 1997, Mandelbrot published *Fractals and Scaling in Finance*, which was a collection of his papers. In 2006, Mandelbrot and Hudson published *The (Mis)Behavior of Markets: A Fractal View of Risk, Ruin and Reward*.[19]

After 40 years, Mandelbrot is still highly enthusiastic toward his revolutionary insights applied to finance and his adjustments to the Gaussian models. The rest of the profession, however, is not so impressed. As Mark Rubinstein states in *A History of the Theory of Investments* (2006), "In the end, the [Mandelbrot] hypothesis proved a dead end, particularly as alternative finite-variance explanations of stock returns were developed."[20]

To see why, note that chaotic systems are purely deterministic but sufficiently complex that they appear random, and through their flexibility can easily look like stock returns, even those with fat tails. These systems have large jumps, or phase shifts, reminiscent of market crashes or sudden bankruptcies. They have butterfly effects where small changes produce big differences in outcomes. Mandelbrot's alternative approach is based on new parameters that would replace the mean return and volatility of return or standard deviation. His first parameter is Alpha, derived from Pareto's Law, which is an exponent that measures how wildly prices vary. It defines how fat the tails of the price change curve are. The second one, the H Coefficient, is an exponent that measures the dependence of price changes upon past changes. Using these parameters, you can generate a time series that look a lot like actual price time series.

Unfortunately, people looking at the same data will generally estimate different parameters as Alpha and H. Using one method, you could derive Alpha and H coefficients that suggest a stock is not risky; using another method, you would reach the opposite conclusion. When you have to model, not just something that looks like IBM's stock price, but IBM's stock price itself, you are flustered. You always can fit the historical. But the degrees of freedom mean you invariably miss the future. Thus, to the extent non-normal distributions are alive in asset pricing theory, it is mainly in looking at effects of simple kurtosis (tail fatness) and skewness (asymmetries) because any specific type of non-normality tends to fail miserably. In a sense, the failure of chaos is like the failure of modern finance, in that the mere potential for a solution, after a while, is insufficient for continued use.

THE UNCERTAINTY REVIVAL

While Knightian uncertainty was one of the traditional return explanations eclipsed by the CAPM, it has undergone a robust revival of sorts, always hovering in the margins of asset pricing theory, never dead. I was a teaching assistant for Hyman Minsky while an undergrad at Washington University in St. Louis. Minsky was a leading post-Keynesian economist, and he emphasized to me that risk was the fundamental difference between his fringe Post-Keynesian school and orthodox economics. In his mind, mainstream economists trivialized risk, packed it into a hermetically sealed irrelevance, and made it a cost no different from the price of wheat. In Minsky's conception, risk was this wonderfully elusive, powerful concept.[21] He considered, of course, Keynes to be the source of his understanding of risk, which is "that which cannot be quantified." There was something indubitably right about the incalculability of real-world events such as a future for a war, or the success of a company, in contrast to explicit games of chance such as rolling a die.

As any Keynesian will tell you, Keynes actually wrote his first book on mathematics, a *Treatise on Probability* (this supposedly implies the vague algebra in his general theory has deeper roots, in the same way Fermat's bona fides suggest his eponymous theorem was more than mere conjecture).[22] In his treatise, Keynes goes on to prove all sorts of things relating to joint probabilities being less than total probabilities, or that confidence in probabilities increases our belief in them, and defining certain implications and certain exclusions with probabilities 0 and 1. It isn't helpful to define a functions endpoints, then intimate vague things about what goes on in between; you don't need algebra to do that. Mathematics should never be more precise than what it is presenting. In the end, Keynes states in 1937:

> By *"uncertain" knowledge, let me explain, I do not mean merely to distinguish what is known for certain from what is only probable. The game of roulette is not subject, in this sense, to uncertainty; nor is the prospect of a Victory bond being drawn. Or, again, the expectation of life is only slightly uncertain. Even the weather is only moderately uncertain. The sense in which I am using the term is that in which the prospect of an European war is uncertain, or the price of copper and the rate of interest twenty years hence, or the obsolescence of a new invention, or the position of private wealth-owners in the social system in 1970. About these matters their [sic] is no scientific basis on which to form any calculable probability whatever. We simply do not know.*[23]

Knight's definition is the same, that risk is measurable randomness, and uncertainty relates to unmeasurable randomness, between complete ignorance and complete information, where one has enough information to form an opinion, but not to have an objective probability. The confusion arises because opinions on the future have the same form as an explicit probability.

Richard Ellsberg discovered the following experiment in the 1960s that showed how people differed between risk and uncertainty, in an experiment now known as Ellsberg's Paradox (which was first mentioned as an assertion in Keynes's *Treatise on Probability*):

Assume two urns of balls exist, each with 100 balls.

- Urn A: There are 50 red balls, 50 blue balls
- Urn B: There are either 100 red balls, or 100 blue balls in the urn.

Now if you were to receive $1 for picking a blue ball, and you stick your hand into either urn blindfolded, most people would choose Urn A. If you offered $1 for a red ball, most people would again, choose urn A. This is "uncertainty aversion," and is very confusing to logicians, though very intuitive to most people who consider it casually. It clearly is related to the relation of uncertainty to profits outlined by Knight. It has been considered in application to equities, primarily in examinations that look at proxies for uncertainty and their relation to returns. One such proxy is trading volume because people often trade when they disagree. Another proxy is "analyst disagreement," looking at the variance of analyst expectations for things like Earnings per Share, or the degree to which a short-sales constraint is binding.

The key difference between Keynes and Knight was not their conception of *relevant* risk, but rather the implication. For Keynes and his followers, the inexactitude of risk, as opposed to probabilities, was key to business cycles. For Knight, the uncertainty of risk was the essence of profitability. Thus, even while the CAPM held supreme, other areas of economics were applying this other conceptions of risk to other major fields of research. The revival of Minsky in these times of financial crisis has brought forth the importance of this conception again among macro economists.

APPENDIX: CAPM: A SPECIAL CASE OF THE STOCHASTIC DISCOUNT FACTOR MODEL

If you like math, you might appreciate the following. Start with the basic equation of the Stochastic Discount Factor Model:

$$E[MR] = E[M]E[R] + \text{cov}(M,R) \qquad (2.14)$$

Which can be rearranged to

$$E[R] = \frac{1}{E[M]} - \frac{\text{cov}(M,R)}{E[M]} \qquad (2.15)$$

Now, here's where the algebra becomes interesting. Assume we are considering a risk-free asset. It has no variance, so no covariance (that is, covariance with anything is zero). So this nails down $E[M]$:

$$E[R_f] = R_f = \frac{1}{E[M]} \qquad (2.16)$$

The value of a dollar tomorrow is negatively correlated with the expected market return given the concavity of utility (higher wealth means we are richer, and thus value money less), the value of a dollar tomorrow is therefore negatively correlated with the return on the stock market. If the economy has a representative agent with a well-defined utility function, then the SDF is related to the marginal utility of aggregate consumption.

So replace U_1', the marginal value (aka derivative of utility) of an agent in period 1, with $-\gamma R_i$, so now:

$$M = \frac{U_1'}{U_0'} = \frac{-\gamma R_m}{U_0'} \tag{2.17}$$

Now, we already know that by definition, $M = \frac{U_1'}{U_0'}$, so replacing M with in equation (2.15) we get:

$$E[R] = R_f + \left(\frac{U_0'}{U_1'}\right)\left(\frac{\gamma \mathrm{cov}(R_i, R_m)}{U_0'}\right) \tag{2.18}$$

Or

$$E[R] = R_f + \frac{\gamma \mathrm{cov}(R_i, R_m)}{U_1'} \tag{2.19}$$

Apply this equation to the market itself, so that $R_i = R_m$

$$E[R_m] = R_f + \frac{\gamma \mathrm{cov}(R_m, R_m)}{U_1'} \tag{2.20}$$

Then the marginal value of a dollar today is worth

$$U_1' = \frac{\gamma \mathrm{var}(R_m)}{E[R_m - R_f]} \tag{2.21}$$

Replacing U_1' with $\dfrac{\gamma \mathrm{var}(R_m)}{E[R_m - R_f]}$ in equation (2.19) we have

$$E[R_i] = R_f + E[R_m - R_f]\frac{\mathrm{cov}(R_i, R_m)}{\mathrm{var}(R_m)} \tag{2.22}$$

Which, given the definition of β, is merely the CAPM equation:

$$E[R_i] = R_f + \beta E[R_m - R_f] \tag{2.23}$$

QED

CHAPTER 3

An Empirical Arc

Real theoretical advances in science do one of three things: they integrate seemingly disparate phenomena, resolve an inconsistency, or predict something new. Maxwell's equations explained light and magnetism as being fundamentally the same, driven by photons traveling the speed of light, an integration of two seemingly different phenomena. Einstein's special relativity theory explained the seeming inconsistency between Maxwell's equations and Newtonian mechanics: one implying the speed of light is constant in all inertial frames, the other not. Dirac's model of the hydrogen atom predicted the positron, which was soon discovered thereafter. The CAPM was not solving a puzzle and did not integrate two previously disparate fields; it predicted something new: that returns were related to beta and only beta, positively and linearly, through the formula

$$r_i = r_f + \beta_i \left(r_m - r_f\right)$$

Even *before* the empirical support was documented, in September 1971 *Institutional Investor* had a cover story on the CAPM, "The Beta Cult! The New Way to Measure Risk."[1] The magazine noted that investment managers were now "tossing betas around with the abandon of Ph.D.s in statistical theory." Unlike the theory of efficient markets, the theory of asset pricing and risk was popular from its inception.

The first tests of the CAPM were on mutual funds, presumably because they attempted to show that good mutual fund performance was a function of beta, not managerial expertise (what was soon to be called *alpha*). Consider the delight in some academic proving, using the mathematics in the last chapter, that a star fund manager is merely a sideshow to an incidental bet on beta. Thus, in the mid-1960s, Sharpe looked at a mere 34 funds, Jensen 115 funds, Treynor and Mazuy 57 funds.[2] These initial tests were not very supportive of the CAPM, but there was little consternation among the cognoscenti at that time: no "Beta Is Dead" articles would appear for 25 years. When scientists anticipate empirical confirmation *just around the corner,* as they did in 1970, they are really much further than they realize. Again and again, the idea is that if a bunch of smart people apply themselves to a problem that did not previously have a lot of specific attention, it is only a matter of time before it will be solved. Analogies are often made to Kennedy's exhortation to put a man on the moon, the United States's ability to increase war production in tanks and ships during World War II, or the development of a polio vaccine. Unfortunately, those are exceptions, not the rule. That the initial tests of the CAPM were not very supportive, was presumably just a data problem, though with hindsight and the now rejection of simple one-factor models, they were as doomed as a theory that purported $E = mc^3$.

George Douglas published the first remarkable empirical study of the CAPM in 1969.[3] He applied a fairly straightforward test of the CAPM. He ran a regression on 500 stocks, each with five years of data, explaining the return based on their beta, and their residual variance. With 500 different sets of betas, residual variances, and the average returns, he found that residual variance was significantly and positively correlated with returns—not beta. Lintner, one of the CAPM theoretical pioneers, also examined this, and found that residual variance and beta were both relevant in explaining cross-sectional returns.[4]

Merton Miller and Myron Scholes (1972), two economists who would later win the Nobel Prize for independent theoretical work, pointed out several flaws in Douglas's empirical work.[5] The important point to remember is that any empirical test is incomplete. That is, one does not test theories and reject them; in practice, testers tend to publish only tests that are consistent with their prior beliefs because they sincerely believe that to do otherwise would be a mistake. Scientists know that posterity belongs, not to the humble and virtuous, but for early discoverers of important truths. Thus, if you know the truth, as a scientist, your goal is to get published quickly proving that truth in some way so you can become one of the founding fathers.

Any empirical test makes assumptions. For example, it assumes certain variables are normally distributed, or independent, measured without error, or if they are measured with error, such errors are unbiased, or that x causes y as opposed to vice versa. At some level, you have to take an argument on faith. You cannot prove anything to someone sufficiently skeptical. In contrast, if the idea is less preposterous you merely ask for a few checks. If I assert that the average housing price in my city is $300,000, you may merely ask for a list of recent sales, and take this assertion on its face. If you were more skeptical, you would differentiate between stand-alone homes and townhouses, sales made in the past six months, and so on. The bottom line is that there are many legitimate issues to account for, and generally smart people who have examined this issue have different opinions, and they can choose which evidence is important, and which is misleading or irrelevant.[6] Any really important theory will have multiple, independent bits of relevant evidence, and advocates will emphasize that evidence consistent with their view is valid, and that evidence not consistent with their view is less valid, if not misleading or fraudulent. In the end, a scientist usually thinks herself right, not biased, and the real issue comes down to a preponderance of evidence—theoretical and empirical—sufficient for those forming the intellectual consensus among the leading researchers of the day.

Miller and Scholes found Douglas's effect was greatly diminished by controlling for potential biases caused by

- Changing interest rates
- Changes in volatility
- Measurement errors in beta
- Correlations between residual volatility and beta
- An inadequate proxy for the market
- Cross-sectional correlation in residual errors
- Correlation between skewness and volatility

Taking these issues into account diminished *but did not eliminate* Douglas's findings. It was inevitable that controlling for so many things diminishes any effect, because the more degrees of freedom you add to an explanation, the more you spread the effect among several variables as opposed to one.

Then, the seminal confirmations of the CAPM were provided by two works, Black, Jensen and Scholes (1972), and Fama and MacBeth (1973).[7] They both applied the following "errors in variables" correction to Douglas. They formed portfolios on the basis of earlier estimations of beta, and then estimated the beta of the resulting portfolios. This would reduce the problem that plagued the earlier tests, because previously a high beta stock (for example, beta = 2) would, on average, be overestimated. That is, if betas are normally distributed with a mean of 1.0, and measured betas are simply the true betas plus error, the highest measured betas will on average have positive errors. So, a stock with a measured beta of 2, on average has a true beta significantly lower, say 1.75. On the other side, lower-than-average estimated betas would have forward betas that were closer to 1.0, so a 0.4 estimated beta would probably be closer to 1, like 0.6, in practice.

So, grouping into portfolios, and looking at the stock returns, they found the predicted result: higher beta correlated with higher returns. Even

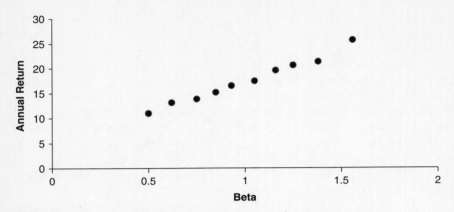

FIGURE 3.1   Returns and Betas from Black, Jensen, and Scholes (1972)

more important, idiosyncratic volatility of these portfolios was insignificant. Please see Figure 3.1.

For both Black, Jensen, and Scholes and Fama-MacBeth, the slopes were positive—higher beta, higher return—which was all everyone interested needed to know. The only mild concern was the slope, which seemed a little flatter than anticipated. For example, in Fama and MacBeth, the hypothesis that beta is uncorrelated with returns is significant only for the entire 1935-to-1968 sample; in each of the 10-year subperiods you could not reject the hypothesis that there was no effect between beta and returns.

In spite of lukewarm support, these tests had staying incredible staying power as references that the CAPM worked. The tests were not corroborated, merely cited again and again over the next few decades. Even in the 1990s popular finance textbooks cited these papers as the primary evidence of the CAPM's validity.

For a few brief years, all was right in the world. The CAPM was slick financial theory, mathematically grounded, and seemingly empirically relevant.

But notice that the major perceived flaw in Douglas's initial work was correcting for estimation error in beta. This problem should bias both residual volatility and beta similarly, yet in Douglas's work, residual risk was significant, while beta was not. The error-in-variables correction reversed this. With the benefit of hindsight, this is totally explainable. Both beta and residual variance are positively correlated with size, a stock characteristic subsequently found highly correlated with returns. Both Black, Jensen, and Scholes and Fama-MacBeth created portfolios based on initial sorts by estimates of beta, so that the resulting spread in average beta would be maximized. But this then makes the size effect show up in the betas, because sorting by beta is, in effect, sorting by size. They could have presorted by residual variance, which is also correlated with size, and the results would have been the same as found for beta, only with residual variance the explainer of returns. Presorting by betas made the spread in betas large relative to the residual variance spread, and so made the small cap effect to speak through beta, not residual variance.

Of course, that is all with hindsight, knowledge of how the size effect works, before all the work in the 1980s showing how to correct for various biases that exaggerated the size effect. Nonetheless, it was somewhat inevitable that a theory, touted as the Next Big Thing before its first real test, is tested until the right answer is generated, and everyone stops making corrections, and cites the articles prominently for the next 20 years. As we subsequently learned, there were many more corrections to make (for example, most of the size effect was measurement error), but with the right results, there was little demand for such scrutiny. Test and make corrections until you get the right answer, then stop. In some sense, this is wisdom at work because as there are an infinite number of corrections to make, if you make them all, your results must be insignificant because the resulting sample size is so small. A skeptic may argue for adding uncertainty to the parameters, and to the parameters of the parameters, and at some point one must say no. In general, we test results with reasonable thoroughness, where *reasonable* is influenced by the plausibility of our result. Thus, at the heart of even the most technical debate is common sense, because one cannot relax, or validate, every assumption. But alas, common sense is no more common among academics than among anyone else.

Einstein's General Theory of Relativity was only a few years old, yet academics were eager to put the nightmare of World War I behind them, and show the common bond of the old adversaries. Proving the German's theory correct was so desired that it suggests that scientists are as objective as the rest of us. The null hypothesis, set up by standard Newtonian Physics, was that there should be a 0.85 arc-second deflection in light from stars behind the sun, while Einstein predicted a 1.7 arc-second deflection.

In 1919, an eclipse offered a chance to measure the degree to which the sun bended the rays of light from far-off stars, a prediction of the General Relativity theory. Famous English physicist Arthur Eddington was a World War I pacifist, and so had a predisposition to mend the rift

(*Continued*)

between German and English academics. He made a trek to the island of Principe, off the coast of West Africa, one of the best locations for observing the eclipse.

Eddington did not get a clear view of the stars because it was cloudy during most of the eclipse. He used a series of complex calculations to extract the deflection estimate from the data, and came up with an estimate of 1.6 arc-seconds. Data from two spots in Brazil were for 1.98 and 0.86, but Eddington threw out the 0.86 measurement because he was concerned that heat had affected the mirror used in the photograph, and so the standard error was too large, generating an average of near 1.7, with a relatively modest standard error.

Scientists have subsequently concluded that Eddington's equipment was not sufficiently accurate to discriminate between the predicted effects of the rival gravitational theories, and his dismissal of the Brazilian measurement unwarranted (he could have equally applied his reservations to his own measurement). In other words, Eddington's standard errors were too low, and the point estimate too high. He validated a theory based as much on his preconceptions as the data. Eddington died after a life full of honors, and for decades this experiment was cited as the proof of the General Theory, yet even in the 1960s, when they tried to redo the experiment given a similar eclipse and methodology, they found they could not. The tools and the event were simply too primitive to allow the kind of accuracy needed to prove general relativity.

In the late 1960s, using radio frequencies as opposed to pictures from an eclipse, Eddington's *results* were, ultimately, confirmed. It is important to have correct prejudices.

Around 1980, Merrill Lynch printed large beta books, showing the beta for every stock. In 1990, William Sharpe, and Harry Markowitz won the Nobel Prize for their work in developing the MPT, which the Nobel Committee considered to be the "backbone of modern price theory for financial markets."

THE BEGINNING OF THE END OF CAPM

The initial tests in the early 1970s were positive, yet more like Keynesian economics than any theory of physics: it had a consensus, but was also empirically questionable to anyone in the know, and practitioners generally ignored it.

One of the early issues was technical in nature, having to do with sequentially estimating betas and returns. A big part of this was mere computing power. Before 1980, running a regression was difficult, and running Maximum Likelihood functions nearly impossible. These more complex functions, which are a mainstay of empirical research today, use a hill-climbing algorithm that involves a lot of steps. It is not a closed-form solution that involves a fixed set of steps as in matrix algebra in Ordinary Least Squares. So, researchers satisfied with empirical work that had issues that in hindsight are more primitive than anything one can do today in an Excel spreadsheet. Once computing got cheap, people tended to look again at early empirical work and found it could be improved by more modern techniques that were superior. For example, early work on default models used discriminate analysis because in binary modeling (default or no-default) this merely involved inverting a matrix. Logit estimation made much more reasonable technical assumptions, not requiring the errors to be both Gaussian and equal in size in both groupings. But logit requires solving a maximum likelihood, so only when the 386 PCs with their fancy built-in math coprocessors became popular was this approach feasible. Today, no one does discriminate analysis anymore except in introductory statistics classes.

A maximum likelihood approach avoided several technical problems in BJS and F&M by simultaneously estimating betas, intercepts, and slopes. Shanken (1985) , Gibbons (1982), and Gibbons, Ross, and Shanken (1989) applied maximum likelihood techniques that rectified several technical issues in BJS and F&M, testing the heart of the CAPM by whether or not the market is mean-variance efficient (as implied by Tobin and Sharpe).[8] While Shanken and Gibbons got respect for their cleverness, and rejected the CAPM at the 0.1 percent level, no one really cared about the substance of their results, because given any sufficiently powerful test, all theories are wrong. For example, Newton's ideas don't work if we measure things to the tenth decimal place, but they still work. Powerful tests on whether the CAPM was true were publishable, but everyone knew it was an almost impossibly stern standard. Such findings were published in the top journals and useful references, and probably primarily responsible for these researchers getting tenure at top research universities, but I doubt anyone was convinced as to the CAPM's practical value through these tests.

The harsh tests of Gibbons and Shanken were largely motivated by a curious result discovered by Richard Roll in 1977, when he published his famous Roll Critique.[9] Roll proved that *any* mean-variance efficient portfolio would necessarily be linearly related to stock returns. It implied that to the CAPM's main implication, therefore, was merely whether or not the market was mean-variance efficient. Roll then added, given the relevance of the present value of labor income and real estate in a person's portfolio, the stock market was clearly not the market, clearly not mean-variance efficient, and therefore the CAPM was untestable. This might seem devastating, but Stambaugh (1982) found that inferences are not sensitive to the error in the proxy when viewed as the measure of the market portfolio, and thus while a theoretical possibility, this is not an empirical problem.[10] Shanken (1987) found that as long as the proxy between the true market was above 70 percent, then rejecting the measured market portfolio would also imply rejecting the true market portfolio.[11] So if you thought the market index, any one of them, was highly correlated with the true market, the CAPM was testable as a practical matter.

The Roll critique was constantly invoked to motivate the APT, in that because the CAPM necessitated the market return, and we can't measure the market, and it could explain the zero relationship between beta and return, well, an APT approach would solve this problem. When the CAPM was being sullied in the 1990s, Roll and Ross (1994) and Kandel and Stambaugh (1996) resurrected this argument and addressed the issue of to what degree an inefficient portfolio can generate a zero beta-return correlation, which by then was accepted as fact.[12] That is, is it possible that beta is uncorrelated with the S&P500 or whatever index is being used, even though it works perfectly with the true market index? In Roll and Ross's words, if you mismeasure the expected return of the market index by 0.22 percent (easily 10 percent of one standard deviation away), it *could* imply a measured zero correlation with the market return.

This sounds devastating to tests purporting to reject the CAPM, but to generate such a null result with an almost efficient index proxy, one needs many negative correlations among assets, and lots of returns that are one hundred fold the volatility of other assets. In other words, a very efficient, but not perfectly efficient, market proxy *can* make beta meaningless—but only in a fairy tale world where many stocks have 100 times the volatility of other stocks, and correlations are frequently negative. Now average stock volatilities range from 10 percent to 300 percent, most between 20 percent and 60 percent annualized. Betas, prospectively, as a practical matter, are never negative.

Existence proof such as these are generally crutches for desperate promoters. It is fun to prove that there exists an equilibrium where, say, raising prices leads to more demand (a Giffen good), or where greater individual savings lowers aggregate savings (the paradox of thrift), or where protecting infant industries increases domestic productivity. These are all possible, and you can prove it rigorously given various assumptions, but they are generally untrue, because they take a lot of strange assumptions more implausible than the main assumption that drives the basic result, and they are empirically counterfactual. Nonetheless, many people jump on these results, and using the logic similar to the idea that since I may get hit by a meteor or I may not implies that I should buy meteor insurance—suggests that existence proves these possibilities are probable. But if this is one possibility out of many, it is hardly credible. In this case, the fact that the market is not mean-variance efficient *could* imply a zero beta-expected return, cross-sectional relationship, but this would be highly implausible because it would imply many large negative correlations between stocks. Those who take great interest in what is possible, or impossible, are generally making unempirical statements because any real empirical issue is about probabilities, not possibilities. All the really interesting debates are about degrees of probability, not whether things are impossible or certain (in which case things are usually tautologies).[13]

The big counterfactuals to the CAPM were two anomalies discovered around 1980: the size anomaly and the value anomaly. Small cap (that is, low market cap) stocks had higher returns than large stocks, while value stocks (that is, low price-to-earnings, high book value-to-market value, high dividend ratios) outperformed their opposite. Black, Jensen, and Scholes reported beta deciles with returns that had about a 12 percent annualized difference between the highest and lowest beta stocks. But for size, estimates of the difference in returns between the bottom and top size deciles was an eye-popping 15 to 24 percent.[14] While the betas were positively correlated with size, that was insufficient to explain this big return differential. Something very strange was going on, and it started the hornets' nest buzzing. Within a year of the finding of the size effect, there was a special issue in the *Journal of Financial Economics* on this issue.[15]

Over the next decade, several adjustments were made, and the size effect was drastically reduced, down from initial estimates of 15 to 24 percent to around 3 percent, annually, for the difference between the smallest and lowest capitalization stocks. Many of the biases were technical, but no less real, and affect many historical findings. The first tip-off that something was rotten in the size effect was that 50 percent of it was in January, 25 percent in the first five days of the year. What economic risk factor is so seasonal? What was to become known as the *January Effect,* where small stocks outperformed large stocks in the month of January, was soon found to be highly influenced by the error caused by averaging daily returns. For example, if you average daily returns, and add them up, you get a very different result from if you cumulate daily returns, and average them. If you have a very small cap stock, and its price moves from, say, its bid of 0.5 to its ask of 1.0 and back again, every day, its arithmetic return is thus +100 percent, −50 percent, +100 percent, and −50 percent, for an average daily return of 25 percent. But in reality, its return is zero, which you would get by taking the geometric sum and dividing by the number of days. Averaging daily return for a portfolio assumes one is rebalancing a portfolio to equal-weighted starting values every day, highly impractical given one generally buys at the ask (high), and sells at the bid (lower). This arithmetic averaging issue arises quite a bit in finance. Blume and Stambaugh (1983) found this bias cut the size effect in half.[16]

Another big technical adjustment was discovered by Tyler Shumway, who noted that delisted stocks often have "N/A" on the month they delist, and these delisting months are actually quite devastating: down 55 percent on average![17] As small stocks delist much more frequently than large stocks, this bias overstates the return on small stock portfolios. Delisted stocks tend to overstate their actual returns because they systematically do not state these large, negative returns when they leave the database used by most researchers. The effect was almost 50 percent of the size premium. The current effect of the size effect is now around 3 percent, and even that is driven by outliers, in that if one excludes the extreme, 1 percent movers, it goes away completely.[18]

Size is clearly a correlated grouping, a factor, in that small cap companies are more correlated with one another than large cap companies. Many investment portfolios now make distinctions for size (micro cap, small cap, and large cap), which initially was thought to generate a big return premium, but now, it's more like a factor people like to add to their portfolio, classic diversification, as opposed to easy money. But the return premium for the smallest cap group is only a couple of percent per year, an order of magnitude lower than what was originally discovered around 1980. The key question today is whether this factor is a true risk factor—something priced by the market, with special correlations—or whether it is survivorship bias in an unconscious research fishing expedition, or whether it's a factor that reflects risk, or possibly a return premium from behavior biases (a "small stock aversion" effect).

In contrast, the value effect is considered stronger than the size effect, though its discovery was much more inauspicious. Initial estimates by Basu (1977) estimated that the low price-to-earnings (aka P/E) stocks outperformed the highest quintile P/E stocks by 6 percent annually, which is close to the current estimate of what the premium to a value over growth portfolio should be.[19] Subsequent work played on this factor in various guises. Bhandari (1988) found that high debt-equity ratios (book value of debt over the market value of equity, a measure of leverage) are associated with returns that are too high relative to their market betas.[20] Stattman (1980) documented that stocks with high book-to-market equity ratios (B/M, the ratio of the book value of a common stock to its market value) have high average returns that are not captured by their betas.[21] P/E, book/market, and dividend yield are all highly correlated ratios that relate a market price to some metric of fundamental value, such as book value or earnings. For some reason, the beat-up stocks, those with low earnings but even lower prices, tend to outperform. Unlike the size effect, this was not concentrated in January. Though never as popular as the size effect in the 1980s, the value effect has been more successful than the size effect over the past 30 years (size-oriented funds were started in the 1980s, while value and growth funds became popular only in the 1990s).

But one had to see size and value anomalies in context. In economics, or really any field of reporting, there is a premium on what is new, ergo, *news*. Anomalies get published because they are potentially interesting and useful corrections to conventional wisdom, while confirmations of existing theory are not news. But if 1,000 finance professors are trying to get published, and apply a test that, assuming the base theory is correct, still rejects the correct theory 5 percent of the time (the standard statistical metric of *significant*), then 50 articles are presented to journal editors with statistically significant results, and the editor is faced with either publishing noise or missing out on the next big thing. The bottom line is, there have been many ephemeral results that are published: the weekend effect, the end-of-month effect, the low-price stock effect (remember low-priced stock funds?). Even today, I find that the very anomalous Internet bubble of the late 1990s was correlated with many things: high growth rates, large R&D. Anything correlated with Internet stocks will, using the past 20 years of data, generate a huge return effect merely because of this huge bubble. One can't help but be skeptical seeing all these new anomalies, and so be more partial to theory than data. Theory is more convincing than data because data without theory are biased by its peculiarity. Knowing why is much more important than knowing what, because if you have the *why* correct, you can predict; the *what* merely describes.

Bill Schwert wrote in a 1983 review of the size effect: "I believe that the 'size effect' will join the 'weekend effect' . . . as an empirical anomaly," highlighting the confusing nature of popular anomalies.[22] The weekend effect was part of the collection of seasonal anomalies very prominent in the early 1980s. As mentioned earlier, there is the January effect, whereby small stocks outperform large stocks, the September effect (the worst month of the year), the Monday effect (worst day of the week), the Friday effect (best day of the week), and the belief that days before holidays tend to be good. In the mid-1980s, Werner De Bondt and Richard Thaler got a lot of mileage out of their documentation of mean reversion in stock prices over period of three years—this finding was essentially reversed a decade later through a much stronger momentum effect over one year, and there has been very little corroboration of the three-year reversal finding. Fischer Black remarked that

"I find theory to be far more powerful than data,"[23] after being burned in this field by false leads so many times, and Bill Sharpe noted that "I have concluded that I may never see an empirical result that will convince me that it disconfirms any theory."[24] Understandable, but there's an unhealthy nihilism there.

The weekend effect, like the other seasonal anomalies, has disappeared. So, like the latest miracle diet or ab machine, the latest anomaly is treated skeptically by your average economist for good reason, because most are dead ends based on selection biases and just bad data.

APT TESTS

In the 1970s, before the full development of the Arbitrage Pricing Theory (APT), Barr Rosenberg (1974) suggested that portfolios demarcated by firm characteristics could likely serve as factors.[25] Tests of the APT started in the Eighties, many pointing to the Roll critique in that the APT is inherently more susceptible to empirical validation than the CAPM, but the APT and the SDF both gave sufficient justification for doing the same thing, basically, to find some time series and use that to explain returns. If you think of the time series of stock returns, you merely need a set of equivalent time series to regress this against. But the basic approach has three distinct alternatives: the macro factor approach (oil, dollar, S&P500), the characteristic approach (size, value), and the latent factor approach (statistical constructs based on factor analysis).

In 1986, an initial test of the APT by Chen, Roll, and Ross seemed to show that the APT worked pretty well using some obvious macroeconomic factors.[26] They used the factors representing Industrial Production, the yield between low and high risk bonds (actually, between BBB and AAA bonds, which are both pretty low risk), between short- and long-term bonds (the slope of the yield curve), unanticipated inflation, expected inflation, and finally, the market (as in the simple CAPM). These were all reasonable variables to try because they were all correlated with either the yield curve, or things investors care about. Now, given that Ross was the creator of this model, it should come as no surprise that they found these factors explained a lot of return variation. But only a few factors seemed priced, that is, you may find that stocks are highly correlated with a factor, such as the market, but on average stocks with a greater loading on this factor did not generate higher returns, the risk premium or the price of risk may be zero. This is what we mean when we say some risks are not priced (common risks that are not priced include industry risk, which clearly affects sets of stocks, though on average no industry, by itself, generates superior returns).

While this finding was promising, it was not a lot better than the CAPM in regard to its ability to explain returns, and did not explain the perplexing value or size anomalies that were confounding academics in the 1980s. More troublingly, in future tests of the APT, no one championed this particular set of factors except as a comparison, so you have people comparing an APT test using oil, employment growth, and the S&P, and another using the dollar, investment growth, and corporate spreads. As novelty is a big part of getting published, and there were no restrictions on what is allowed, the multiplicity of models examined in the literature was inevitable.

While the Chen, Roll, and Ross approach was intuitive—you could understand the factors they were suggesting—a new approach was being forged that seemed more promising: The idea that risk factors were statistical constructs, called *latent factors* because they were statistically implicit, not clearly identifiable by words. These are very statistical constructs that appealed to finance professors familiar with the matrix mathematics of eigenvectors and eigenvalues, a branch of mathematics that is both deep and has proven quite practical in other applications.

If we think about the original mean-variance optimization objective of investors, the latent factor approach actually makes the most sense. If one is minimizing portfolio volatility and cross-sectional volatility comes from several factors, all significant factors need to be addressed. One could come up with intuitive factors that span this space, but there are methods that are more powerful than mere intuition. Yet the first factor, which explains about 90 percent of the total factor variance, is about 99 percent correlated with the equal-weighted stock index (Connor and Koraczyk, 2008; Christopher Jones, 2001).[27] This alone suggests that latent factors were not a good alternative. Consider that many researchers use the equal or value weighted stock index as a proxy for the market, both using eminently reasonable justification. For example, the value-weighted market proxy was used as the market by some researchers, while others used the equal-weighted market, and some used both.[28] You can argue the value-weighted proxy is more like the market because it weights stocks by their actual dollar size, giving more weight to Microsoft than some $50 million Internet start-up from Utah. On the other hand, the equal-weighted proxy weighs small firms more, and these firms might be more representative of smaller, unlisted companies that make up the true market portfolio. The bottom line is, if either worked considerably better, we would have a story for why it should be the market proxy, and researchers would have stuck with one over the other. Neither works better than the other (their betas do not explain average returns), so it really doesn't matter. Now, if 90 percent of the latent factor approach is indistinguishable in power to the CAPM, and there isn't a big difference between the value- and equal-weighted index, it is improbable this approach is going to bear fruit.

But even if the latent factor approach was empirically successful, it has another large problem. Most researchers assumed there were around three to five factors, all declining rapidly in statistical relevance. But while factor 1 looked a lot like the equal-weighted index, the other factors were not intuitive at all. They were not correlated with anything you can put your finger on. Furthermore, many stocks had negative loadings on these secondary factors, so whereas the loading on the first factor, as in the CAPM, were almost all positive, these other strange factors, with no intuition, had 60 percent with positive loadings, and 40 percent with negative loadings. You could not explain exactly what the factor was, but sometimes it generated a risk premium, sometimes you were presumably paying for its insurance like properties—even though no one had enough intuition to figure out what this provided insurance against. Consider a broker suggesting that a stock is a good addition to the portfolio because it has a negative loading on the fourth factor, which no one really knows what it is, but one should be eager to earn 1 percent less because it will pay off big in some scenario when this fourth factor is really low. I am certain that this sales pitch has never happened, and considering that asset pricing theory is based on the assumption that people are in generally investing this way, is cause for skepticism.

Empirically, both of these APT approaches generated at most a modest improvement to the CAPM, and a slightly better ability to explain the perplexing size effect better. Generally, if something is true, and in the data, someone will find it, and the APT was a license to throw the kitchen sink at returns. It was rather surprising that this approach was so unfruitful.

FAMA AND FRENCH PUT A FORK IN THE CAPM

The debate changed dramatically when Fama and French published their paper in 1992. While I disagree with their diagnosis of the CAPM's problems, their work is to be admired because it is unequaled in academic finance for its readability. Clarity and common sense are as rare among scientists as almost anyone, so when Fama and French win their Nobel Prize, as I expect they will, it will be richly deserved. Too many researchers tell you they are going to test some theory, and that it offers a rich and dynamic way to explain the post World War II data, and after reading it you have no idea what was tested or how you would use it, though the wealth of information is, indeed, rich. Fama and French don't hide the substance of what they are doing behind abstruse mathematics; they prioritize and highlight their findings, which are often obviously relevant. When I was in graduate school, I remember my more technical professors considered Fama to be somewhat unsophisticated, good at turning a phrase ("efficient markets") but not doing serious research, which then were extensions of Gibbons and Shanken, in empirical work, or Banach Space extensions as suggested by the APT. I'm sure, given Fama and French's current stature, they don't remember thinking that way, in the same way few people recall being against civil rights in the 1960s.

The key finding was not so much showing value and size generate large returns in the U.S. data, it was in showing that whatever success beta had, it was *completely* explained by the size effect. "Our tests do not support the central production of the [CAPM], that average stock returns are positively related to beta." That is, if you remember the earlier (Figure 3.1), now we have Figure 3.2.

Shanken and Gibbons proved the CAPM wasn't perfect; Fama and French showed it was not even useful. It's not even an approximation; it's not insufficiently linear, or insufficiently positive, its point estimate has the wrong sign! Stephen Ross (1993) noted that in practice "the long-run *average* return on the stock, however, will not be higher or lower simply because it has a higher or lower beta."[29] The previous single measure of expected return was accepted now as not being *useful* even as an incomplete measure of risk.

Such an empirical rejection would seem to be fatal, but this highlights the non-Popperian nature of real science. In Karl Popper's construct, theories produce falsifiable hypotheses. If these hypotheses are falsified, the theory is then rejected. The CAPM predicted that beta was linearly and positively related to stock returns: the actual relation was zero. End of story? It would be naïve to think that after 25 years, a simple fact would cause so many finance professors to abandon an idea that was the backbone of their

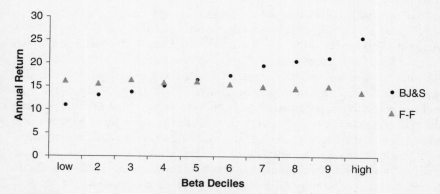

FIGURE 3.2 Returns and Betas from Black, Jensen, and Scholes (1972) to Fama and French (1992)

research papers, and formed the basis for lectures they had given for a decade, would be snuffed out like runt on a farm. In Thomas Kuhn's paradigms, researchers see the seminal anomaly explained with a new theory, and then create a new theory in the new paradigm. But the Fama-French approach was clearly a "mend, don't end" approach to the CAPM. The paradigm would continue, just as the APT (or SDF), but now, a three-factor model, the now ubiquitous three-factor F-F model

$$r_i = r_f + \beta \left(r_M - r_f\right) + \beta_{SMB} \left(r_S - r_B\right) + \beta_{HML} \left(r_H - r_L\right)$$

where: r_m = market return
r_S = small cap return
r_B = big cap return
r_H = high book/market return
r_L = low book/market return

Note that this approach is really just the CAPM equation with two extra terms. The first term, $\beta(r_M - r_f)$, is the return on the market above the risk-free rate, and this, plus the risk-free rate, is the CAPM. The next term, $\beta_{SMB}(r_S - r_B)$, is the return on the small cap portfolio minus the big cap portfolio. As small cap firms outperform big cap companies, this average is positive, suggesting this has a positive price, that is, it is a priced-risk factor. The loading on this factor, β_{SMB}, represents the sensitivity of an asset to this factor, as measured by the beta on this factor from a regression. The final term, $\beta_{HML} (r_H - r_L)$, is the return on the high book to market (aka value companies, low P/E companies) portfolio minus the return on the low book to market (aka growth companies, high P/E companies).

This approach is totally consistent with the APT and SDF, in that either of these motivate the addition of the value and size factors as risk factors, because they are factors that explain a lot of cross-sectional volatility and they are on average positive, suggesting they are priced and thus reflect some state variable that affects our utility. Working backward, since only risk generates average returns, the anomalies imply some kind of risk. As the APT says, it really does not matter what or where these factors came from, all that matters is they must be priced linearly, and so the beta terms representing their loading tell us how much of these factors are being used. This is known as *atheoretical risk factor identification,* because it comes from returns, not something more basic. The Kuhnian paradigm was not shifted; an epicycle was added.

Saving the Standard Model

Generally, better empirical data and testing generates greater support for the correct theory over its incorrect rival. Correct theories get clearer as the data refine them. In the case of finance, the data has spawned the correlate to superstring's multiple universes (now, 10^{500} potential solutions), and the past is unconsciously rewritten so that a young researcher would think there has been a consistent, asymptotic trend toward the truth.

Currently, the three-factor Fama-French model remains perhaps the most popular model for benchmarking equity returns by academics, although it has a significant number of detractors. The main puzzle to the Fama-French model is what kind of risk factors do the value and size represent? Small stocks have higher betas, and are more volatile, but as these characteristics themselves are not positively correlated with returns, we can't say that small stocks outperform large stocks because of their volatility, or covariance with the market. Value stocks actually have betas that are higher in booms, and lower in busts, suggesting a win-win approach to investing that is decidedly not risky. So in what way are small size, and high-book-to-market (low P/E) stocks risky?

Early on in the size effect, people were at a loss to figure out what kind of risk that size, outside of beta, captured? Remember, the obvious risk, residual risk from these very small stocks, was diversifiable, and so not risk. Fama and French came upon the idea that both the value premium and the small stock premium were related to some sort of distress factor, that is, value stocks, whose price was beaten down by pessimists, and small stocks, which had less access to capital markets, probably had more risk of defaulting, or going bust, if the economy faltered. It may not show up in correlations or covariances, but that's merely because such risks are very episodic, like the risk of a heart attack: The first symptom of a heart attack is a heart attack.

There were two problems with this interpretation. First, as Daniel and Titman documented, it was the characteristic, rather than the factor, that generated the value and size effects.[30] They did an ingenious study in that they took all the small stocks, and then separated them into those stocks that were correlated with the statistical size factor Fama and French constructed, and those that weren't. That is, of all the small stocks, some were merely small, and weren't correlated with the size factor of Fama-French, and the same is true for some high book-to-market stocks. Remember, in risk it is only the covariance of a stock to some factor that counts. Daniel and Titman found that the pure characteristic of being small, or having a high book-to-market ratio, was sufficient to generate the return anomaly, totally independent of their loading on the factor proxy. In the APT or SDF, the covariance in the return with something is what makes it risky. In practice, it is the mere characteristic that generates the return lift. Fama and French shot back that their approach did work better on the early, smaller sample, and more survivorship biased 1933-to-1960 period, but that implies at best that size and value seem the essence of characteristics, not factors, over the more recent and better documented 1963-to-2000 period.[31]

In a similar vein, Todd Houge and Tim Loughran (2006) find mutual funds with the highest loadings on the value factor reported no return premium over the same 1975-to-2002 period, even though the value factor generated a 6.2 percent average annual return over the same period.[32] Loading on the factor, per se, did not generate a return premium.

This suggests that size and value are not risk factors, just things correlated with high stock returns cross-sectionally. This could be an accident of historical data mining, as when people find that some county in some state always votes for the correct president, which is inevitable given a large sample, but ultimately meaningless. Alternatively, these findings could be proxies for overreaction. People sell small stocks too much, sell value stocks too much, and a low price leads to them to being both small cap and having a high book-to-market ratio. But this overshoot sows the seeds for an eventual correction. This effect works the opposite way for large cap and low book-to-market ratio stocks, where the prices shoot too high. Lakonishok, Shleifer, and Vishny proposed just such a model in 1994, and this is the standard behaviorist interpretation of the size and value effect: They capture systematic biases, specifically, our tendency to extrapolate trends too much to ignore the reversion to the mean.[33]

Another problem with the distress risk story was that, when you measure distress directly, as opposed to inferring it from size or book value, these distressed stocks have delivered anomalously low returns, patently inconsistent with value and size effects as compensation for the risk of financial distress. Around 2000, when I was working for Moody's, I found this to be true using Moody's proprietary ratings data. Moody's had a unique, large historical database of credit quality going back to 1980, and I found that if you formed stock portfolios based on the credit rating of the equity's debt, there was a perfect relationship from 1980 to 2000: the lowest-rated credits (C) had the lowest returns, followed by the next lowest-rated companies (B), then Ba, and so on, to AAA with the highest return. Better credit and lower default risk implied higher future stock returns. As not many people had Moody's ratings data, I thought this was a very interesting finding. I presented this finding as an aside at a National Bureau of Economic Research conference, which was primarily about debt models, and I was surprised when the crowd of esteemed professors, including Andy Lo,

Robert Hodrick, and Kent Daniel, thought I had to be wrong. It is a strange thing when people you respect, and are excited to apprise of a new finding, respond by telling you that you made a mistake. They did not even have the data, but they were certain I was wrong. It was on one level frustrating, but on another encouraging, because it suggested just how valuable my fact was. That is, one thing any good idea has is novelty, and clearly this fact was novel in that no one believed it.

Like any empirical fact, other people found it as well. Ilya Dichev had documented this back in 1998, but this finding could be brushed off because he presumably had a poor default model (he used the Altman Model). But then several others documented a similar result, and finally Campbell, Hilscher, and Szilagyi (2006) find the distress factor can hardly explain the size and book or market factors; in fact, it merely creates another anomaly because the returns are significantly in the wrong direction.[34] Distressed firms have much higher volatility, market betas, and loadings on value and small cap risk factors than stocks with a low risk of failure; furthermore, they have much worse performance in recessions.[35] These patterns hold in all size quintiles but are particularly strong in smaller stocks. Distress was not a risk factor that generated a return premium, as suggested by theory, but rather a symptom of a high default rate, high bond and equity volatility, high bond and equity beta, and low equity return.[36]

Finally, there is the issue of what the market is doing in the three-factor model. That is, why include the market if it does not explain equity returns? Simple, Fama and French respond. If you also include government bonds, you need the market factor to explain why the stock indexes appear to rise more than bonds do, as the factors for size and value—whatever they represent—cannot explain the aggregate difference in return between stocks and bonds. The market factor, which Fama and French admit is not relevant for distinguishing *within* equities, is necessary to distinguish *between* equities as a whole and bonds. And so it is with most models, as currency models find factors built off such proxy portfolios that help explain the returns on various currencies, but they only work in explaining currency returns. The same holds for yield curve models, where risk models are a function of those points on the yield curve that generate positive expected returns, and thus explain the yield curve by way of this risk factor. None of these factors apply outside their parochial asset class, though; they just explain their anomalies. If these were truly risk factors, and represented things that paid off in bad states of the world, it should hold across all asset classes, so that, say, a set of risk factors used to explain, say, equities, would be applicable toward currencies and the yield curve.

In the end, we have atheoretical risk factors, each of which was chosen to solve a parochial problem recursively, so that return is a function of risk, which is a function of return, and so on. Value and size, longstanding anomalies, were simply rechristened as risk factors, and then used to explain, well, themselves. Fama and French said it worked out of sample by testing it on strategies sorted by P/E ratios, but the P/E ratio is so correlated with the B/M ratio that this is hardly out of sample. Furthermore, the inability of the market to explain cross-sectional returns of stocks within the market, did not hurts its importance in explaining why the market explains the differential return between it and the bond market, even though, again, this is tautological: The higher return of equities over bonds is explained by the return of equities over bonds (called the *equity risk premium*). If it is a risk factor, why does it apply only to itself, that is, the market, and not to individual equities? In sum, it seems a lot more like a description of anomalies rather than a theory, because it does not generalize to assets it was not created from, and value and size are still factors without any intuition.

It did not take long for researchers to jump on this bandwagon. A new anomaly, momentum, published in 1992 by Jegadeesh and Titman, as past winners over the last 3 to 18 months tended to continue over the next 3 to 18 months.[37] They did not even propose a risk motivation for this finding, and even Fama and French are reluctant to jump on that one, which would lay bare the factor fishing strategy at work. Mark Carhart was the first to then add momentum (a long winners–short losers portfolio) to the F-F three-factor model and create a four-factor model in a 1996 study.[38] At the very least, it captured things that a naïve investor would make money on, which was useful in Carhart's case because in examining mutual fund returns, to the extent a fund is relying on a simple strategy that rides on momentum, size, or value, it seems relevant to how much pure alpha they had (although one could argue that implementing a momentum strategy before academics prove it exists involves alpha). That is, if you can explain a fund's returns through momentum, that seems important in understanding funds. Whether it is a true risk factor is a separate issue, but the Fama-French model seems useful in explaining it irrespective of whether its factors are related to risk, or are predictive.

SERIAL CHANGES TO APT

The striking fact about multifactor models applied to cross-sectional equities is that there is no consensus on the factors. The APT and SDF approaches have slightly different emphasis in empirical tests, and the APT testers generally have more intuitive results, whereas the SDF approach generates more statistically powerful, but less compelling results, but generally it all comes down to identifying factors and using them to explain returns.[39] Which returns? Well, after Fama and French, everyone tried to explain, which really means to correlate, a model with the returns of portfolios that are created by cross-tabbing book-to-market and size, two characteristics that are historically related to returns for some reason. That is, each month, you sort stocks into quintiles by size, and then sort within each quintile by book or market. You get 25 portfolios after the 5 by 5 sort. Many of the proposed models seem to do a good job explaining these portfolio returns as well as the three-factor Fama-French model, but it is an embarrassment of riches. Reviewing the literature, there are many solutions to the Fama-French set of size-value return, but there is little convergence on this issue. This is especially true given the great variety of factor models that seem to work, many of which have very little in common with each other.

For example, Chen, Roll, and Ross (1986) assert six factors as the market return, inflation (expected and actual), industrial production, Baa-Aaa spread, and yield curve innovations; Sharpe (1992) suggests a 12-factor model, while Connor and Korajczyk (1993) argue there are "one to six" factors in U.S. equity markets using principal components analysis.[40] Ravi Jagannathan and Zhenyu Wang (1993) assert human capital and the market portfolio are the two factors because a metric of human capital is needed to capture the total market; they later argue (1996) that time-varying betas can explain much of the failure in CAPM.[41] Lettau and Ludvigson (2000) use the consumption-wealth ratio in a vector autoregressive model to explain cross-sectional returns.[42] Jacobs and Kevin Wang (2001) argue idiosyncratic consumption risk and aggregate consumption risk; and Jagannathan and Yong Wang (2007) have year-over-year fourth quarter consumption growth.[43] This research is vibrant and ongoing, but the diverse approaches extant suggest they have not begun to converge, even within the prolific Jagannathan/Wang community. The bottom line is that unlike the value, momentum, or size, no one has created an online index of these more abstract factors because they change so frequently; there is no single such factor that would be of interest to general researchers.

The problem is that 25 portfolios sorted by factors that were found to be correlated with returns makes for an easy target for statistical explanation. In data mining, you throw a bunch of time series against a bunch of data until a high correlation is found, and then, poof, an explanation. It's derisively known as "survival of the fittest," meaning the set of explanatory data with the highest R^2 or statistical fit is the answer, and given enough data to throw at these poor 25 portfolios, one set of these will have an R^2 this will be rather high. The key point to remember is the hot alternative in 1994 looks nothing like the alternative in 2000, which looks nothing like the current alternative. These solutions invariably explain the 25 Fama-French portfolios sorted on value and size, and then do horribly on different tests, and the best evidence of this is the ephemeral nature of these solutions; a correct solution would draw emulators, but mere statistical correlates are one-shot publications. Fama and French created a standard for getting published that is good for just that, getting a publication, and then, extensions are null results, uninteresting, and so everyone moves on.

Another issue is that with financial time series, many patterns are cyclical but not predictable. That is, if you look at the past time series for the value and size factor proxies, you will see that if you could merely predict their major swoons and booms, you will be able to explain a lot of the spread between size and book- or market-sorted portfolios. Given that these turning points are so important, and there are only a handful of them, what other time series have similar turning points? Any such series would be found to explain stock returns. Small cap stocks did poorly from 1969 through 1974, rebounded through 1983, trailed through 2000, but then rebounded smartly. Value stocks did poorly in the Internet bubble, but also rebounded nicely. With thousands of economic and financial time series, some combination will generate similar turning points merely by chance. Thus, you look at consumption growth, and if that doesn't work, take real consumption growth, then real consumption growth per capita, and if that doesn't work, use year-over-year (as opposed to quarterly seasonally adjusted) consumption growth, and then one can deduct expenditures on durable goods, or use only durable goods. The U.S. Department of Commerce's National Income and Product Accounts shows hundreds of variations on expenditures and consumables; all you need is one them to turn on the correct dates, which one eventually will, and all are, on first glance, plausible proxies for the SDF. The key is when these valuable proxies are found sequentially, they lose all their statistical properties because they are not random samples. Yet, this bias is often not conscious but merely the result of a process that publishes only significant results, and so these biases are often totally unintentional. Please see Figure 3.3.

In Figure 3.3, a roughly noisy set of data are presented in dots. A linear best fit line has only two degrees of freedom, an intercept and slope, whereas the curvy line is a fifth-order polynomial and has six degrees of freedom. Although the polynomial function passes through each data point, and the line passes through none, the line is a better fit because if the function that created these dots was extrapolated, one should expect the polynomial model that exactly fit the data would do much worse out of sample. Overfitting is related to the wisdom of Occam's razor, which says simpler is better. We all want to explain the data better, but there's a trade-off where at some point it hurts our ability to predict. This is very nonintuitive because people generally find that more information always adds to one's confidence in a

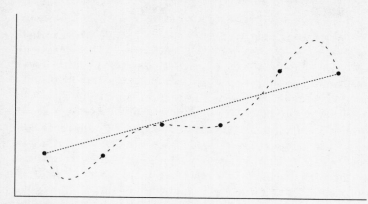

FIGURE 3.3   Overfit Models Extrapolate Poorly

subject. That is, most people would consider 13 reasons for some proposition is better than 7 reasons. However, statistically, a model with 13 parameters often does worse at prediction, largely because the correlation between the regressors causes the standard error of the forecast to blow up. For example, in a simple model with two explanatory bits of data, x_1 and x_2, the standard errors are proportional to $1/(1 - \text{corr}(x_1, x_2))$, so the higher the correlation with existing information, the higher the standard errors for the individual coefficients, which implies a more precarious out-of-sample performance. This generalizes to more variables in a straightforward way.

Thus, the number of turning points for a model explains the data, which is about 10. A couple of hundred really smart Ph.D.s do research, each trying to explain the 25 Fama-French portfolios, and a couple do. Seems great! Each individual researcher is probably not biased, but the collective process is. The problem is that no one knows the number of degrees of freedom in *a* model, because that is implicit in a process of an unknown number of unpublished approaches.

SKEWNESS

Recent research on distributional adjustments has been intriguing, but not compelling. For example, Harvey and Siddique (2000) found that a firm's marginal contribution to negative skew, coskewness, can do as well as the Fama-French three-factor model.[44] Yet, the data seem fragile. They calculate skew using 60 months of data for each stock, and this biases the data set because it excludes about 40 percent of the sample. Ang, Chen, and

Xing (2002) find that downside beta, which is like negative coskewness, is positively related to returns for all but the highly volatile stocks, where the correlation with returns is negative.[45] Furthermore, value and small companies that have high returns, have positive skewness.[46] Thus, skewness may be at work, but as a general measure of risk, it is quite fragile.

One major problem with this research is that, prospectively, all stocks have positive skew. A stock with negative skew is rare, if only because for any stock, the upside is unlimited, but they can all go to only zero. Furthermore, stocks with the greatest downside have the greatest upside, so you cannot simply say the risk of failure is a sign of skew: these companies invariably have the greatest chance of both massive success and total failure. Thus, in looking for a preference for skew within equities, this is like evaluating the claim that height explains basketball prowess among NBA players. Clearly, being tall is helpful in being a good basketball player, yet, conditional upon being in the NBA, the effect is weak at best.

Interestingly, individual stocks are on average positively skewed, while portfolio returns are negatively skewed because correlations between stocks increase in market downturns.[47] Thus, if anything, the risk is greater for a portfolio of stocks by this measure than for individual stocks, and we do see some evidence of a risk premium for stocks in aggregate, as opposed to cross-sectionally.

The real world is much more complicated than any model, but models are about compression. Pattern prediction is strangely seductive, as a method for generating a pattern like something is often mistaken as a specific prediction. But my ability to generate a time series that *looks like* a price series from the New York Stock Exchange from a glance at a graph and matching mean, variance and skew, does not mean this is valuable. The key is, can we identify some of these parameters as more or less risky, and do they correlate with future average returns? No, which is why theories like chaos are not used 40 years after their discovery.

Yet despite the long history of looking at higher moments of variable distributions, such as skew and kurtosis, its anemic results and therefore relatively small empirical examination can make it appear unexamined. I have been in meetings many times where someone proposes ignoring upside variance as a measure of risk, as it seems intuitive and rarely used, so I would venture hundreds of times every day, worldwide, people in finance independently generate this hypothesis. But a really high return tends to give information relevant to whether there will be a large drawdown, because 100 percent returns suggest a high probability of a 50 percent drawdown, just as much as a previous 50 percent drawdown does. Thus, as a forward looking metric of risk, the semi-deviation generally does worse than metrics that use all the information. The bottom line is that adjustments to the normal distribution were there at the beginning, presented as a solution every so often (see Kraus and Litzenberger (1976), and Post and van Vliet (2004)), and if it worked, these would be a canonical non-normal model by now.[48]

Initial theoretical work by Rubinstein (1973) showed how one could add skewness and kurtosis with the CAPM.[49] The idea is that sometimes people prefer positive skew, as in preferences for lottery tickets, and for negative skew, as when people appear to overinvest in investments with large but infrequent losses. The *Journal of Portfolio Management* online list of abstracts mentions *skewness* in no fewer than 66 articles and *kurtosis* in 44. Why do these intuitive corrections seem to always be talked about, but never make it to the status of, say, the Fama-French value or size factors? Because the results are so weak and nuanced.

ANALOGY TO BUSINESS CYCLE FORECASTING

The empirical arc, from optimism that we had a useful model of asset return, to pessimism that we do not, has happened before in economics. The intuition is that real data follow patterns like the tides, the motion of the planets, or the distribution of fauna along a riverbank. If you take something big and important, like the stock market, and say, we have finally generated comprehensive data on it, many smart people will assume there is a pattern there just waiting to be discovered.

So it is no coincidence that the initial development of the CAPM was the early 1960s, which coincided with the creation of the Center for Research in Security Prices (CRSP). At the behest of Merrill Lynch, two professors at the University of Chicago, James H. Lorie and Lawrence Fisher, created what was to become the preeminent database on stocks in the United States. In 1964, their database was complete, and they successfully demonstrated the capabilities of computers by analyzing total return—dividends received as well as changes in capital as a result of price changes—of all common stocks listed on the NYSE from January 30, 1926, to the present. A seminal article by Lorie and Fisher in the *Journal of Business* reported the results. The article proclaimed that the average of the rates of return on common stocks listed on the NYSE was 9 percent. The front page of the *New York Times* financial section heralded the pair's findings.[50]

Researchers had data, just in time to merge with the new theory. For a researcher used to picking apart dog-eared books where many have treaded before, this truly was exciting. In a statement that can only be understood by financial quants, Rex Sinquefeld, now CEO of the quantitative equity management firm Dimensional Fund Advisors, noted, "If I had to rank events, I would say this one (the original CRSP Master File) is probably slightly more significant than the creation of the universe."[51] Virgin data, important data, and theory, imply one is like Kepler looking at Brache's data on the positions of the planets—new laws are about to be confirmed, or discovered. The initial researchers would be *Founding Fathers* of this new field of scientific finance!

Alas, not everything moves in patterns like the planets. A similar life cycle of untempered optimism, adding epicycles to explain anomalies, and then manifest failure, could be applied to macroeconomics and its study of business cycles. In the 1930s, you had Simon Kuznets and Jan Tinbergen creating vast accounting systems for the entire nation, what was to become Gross National Product and National Income and Product Accounts. As Keynes was developing the first macro theory at that time that explained the dynamics of a macroeconomy from such building blocks as investment, consumption, and so on, it was thought that one would finally see everything in front of them and know how to steer. As Keynes wrote in 1940 contemplating the arrival of national income accounting data, "We are in a new era of joy through statistics."[52] The idea was that if we can see where we are and where we have been, we know where we are going. Keynesian theory would allow us to adjust the economy, so that unlike before when we would sail, hit an iceberg, sail again, repeat, it would simply be smooth sailing.

Jan Tinbergen won the first economic Nobel prize for this work, and over the next 10 years several Nobel prizes were bestowed on researchers in this area, because it was important and seemed obvious that given our ability to measure, and the application of sophisticated mathematics, the ability to manage was *just around the corner*. Paul Samuelson's first paper in 1939 was to apply mathematics to the new theory of macroeconomic dynamics, in this case a second-order difference equation, and the optimism was palpable.[53] Macroeconomic experts were about to wander in the desert for 40 years.

But a generation of failure is not apparent in real time, only with the benefit of hindsight a generation later. By the early 1970s, macroeconomic modeling had missed many economic turning points, but still many were jumping into the field and saw a bright future in macroeconomic forecasting. After all, it is easy to explain away prior failures, and as business cycles happen only once every 5 to 10 years, it was not like these failures were happening all the time. There was the oft-repeated joke "He predicted seven of the last four recessions," in full confidence that it was just a matter of time. By the late 1970s, macroeconomics was being assaulted by an unanticipated increase in interest rates, and the unanticipated simultaneously high levels of unemployment and inflation, and leading edge researchers were seeing a crisis. The models were breaking down, becoming obviously wrong to the casual user. But practical reputation follows achievement with a lag. In the 1980s, I worked with economists who worked for the Bank of America in the mid-1970s, and they talked of a whole floor of economists, forecasting at various industry and regional levels (Modesto, California, Retail Sales employment growth, for example). The chief economist then was very charismatic, and had a conspicuous trophy wife he took to corporate functions.

Right out of college, having been a teaching assistant for the macro-economist Hyman Minsky, I was excited to be an economist myself. I got a job at First Interstate, a major bank in Los Angeles, in the economics department, making very little money doing very mundane analyst work, but seemingly learning from priests who knew what was true and important. I could not have been happier. The first thing I discovered was that we had no ability to forecast the future, and our explanations of the past were lame. No one had a clue why inflation was falling so fast at that time, the main financial trend of 1986. No one really understood why oil prices were falling so low (then down to $13 from $30), why the stock market crashed in 1987, or whether the net effect on the United States would be positive (low inflation) or negative (wealth effects on spending). We had lots of forecasts for all sorts of variables, often to the second decimal place, and followed the rule to "forecast early and often," so that by the time data arrive, the reader is comparing them to the latest revision, which given the inertia in time series, allows one to get close with the most recent forecast. The key is to overload your reader with data so they will have misplaced the forecast from last year, or worse, three years ago, and just look at the latest paper when the actual number comes out. Nothing imprints as strongly as learning as a young man, something you strongly believed turned out mistaken.

It became clear to me we were not fooling anyone because economics departments were shrinking. Nothing speaks louder than declining employment in a field. My enthusiasm for macroeconomics was clearly not shared by market participants. When I got back into banking after graduate school around 1994, the large regional bank I worked for had over 10,000 employees and 1 economist, whose main job was public relations, not advising internal decision making, and this was a typical use for an economist. A few years later, they got rid of him.

In the macroeconomic equivalent to the Fama-French paper, in 1980, Chris Simms showed that a simple Vector Autoregression (VAR) could do as well as a hundred equation macro model.[54] That is, instead of modeling the economy as a complex set of subroutines that operate in a giant feedback loop based on optimizing behavior of firms and consumers, just regress past changes in GDP on past changes in GDP and investment growth. Such an atheoretical approach worked just as well (or badly) in terms of predicting the future as the more theoretical models derived from first principles, and embodying the monetarist and Keynesian pet theories. When such a simple approach dominates a much more complicated approach, there is always soul searching.

But hope always springs anew. In the late 1980s, one of my Northwestern professors, Mark Watson, tried to create a better leading economic indicator.[55] The Leading Economic Indicators was created in the 1950s, before computers, and a wealth of econometric methods. It seemed obvious that the top professors in the field could easily improve upon this indicator, because fundamentally there was no "rational expectation" reason why forecasting recessions, over the next six months, should be so intrinsically difficult. That is, you can say that no matter how much information and processing power, the stock market is hard to predict because every day we predict the next day and this involves predicting how we will predict the next day, so we are predicting predictions. To the extent something is predictable, it gets into prices now, not in some foreseeable lump in the future. But that argument doesn't apply so much to business cycles, which are based, not on expectations, but real activity. So it seemed that predicting GDP growth was theoretically possible, and from a pure technology and technique perspective, an obvious trade-up from the naïve rules created in the 1950s that became the Leading Economic Indicators (LEI).

The standard LEI averaged 10 indicators thought predictive of the economy. Other than normalizing each indicator to make its volatility equivalent, they were simply added together in the late 1960s. In contrast, Stock and Watson developed a fancy Kalman filter approach and applied to state spaces in a Markov to create a new and improved LEI in 1989. This different approach seemed to make the Sims critique irrelevant, because those macro modelers were using too much theory, and not enough statistics. After all, the Kalman filter was actually being used to guide rockets, and, as we all know, rocket scientists are the gold standard of modeling stochastic processes. They subsequently went on a whirlwind tour of major central banks with their state-of-the-art forecasting device. The LEI was a simple sum of interesting variables that was created in 1950, the Kalman filter was cutting edge econometrics, and tested on data from 1919 to 1985, dominated the naïve LEI in backtesting. It was like the difference between my cell phone and two cans with a string attached to their ends. Or so it seemed.

The problem is that there is much less data there than you think, because the data are cyclical. With cyclical data, if you can call the peaks and troughs, you explain a lot of the data. So really, there were only eight recessions after World War II, and God knows how many iterations of the Stock and Watson model before development. As any good economist who knows the data really well, the data used in her model become *in sample* rather unconsciously, in that anyone looking at historical time series of macroeconomics for 10 years has seen how various indexes relate to one another, and as the data change modestly each year, the data to be explained are pretty much static—until the next recession.

Unfortunately, the *real-time performance* of the Stock and Watson approach has been no better than the original, naïve Leading Economic Indicators index. In 1990, the difference was that the dollar was strengthening and the yield curve was steepening, meaning that monetary policy was not particularly tight immediately before the recession, in contrast to the prior recession. In 1993, the then head of the American Economic Association remarked at the annual meeting, that regarding the 1991 recession, "established models are unhelpful in understanding *this* recession."[56] The Stock-Watson model failed to predict the 1990–1991 recession, and an updated version of the model (one that would have caught the 1990 recession) then failed to predict the 2001 recession. Stock and Watson (2003) discuss, with admirable honesty and clarity, this failure and argue that it is hard to predict recessions because each is caused by a unique set of factors. For instance, housing and durable goods consumption was strong preceding and throughout the 2001 recession, and the decline was focused on high technology manufacturing. By contrast, in the 1990–1991 recessions, housing and durable goods spending slowed considerably. As Stock and Watson say, "Without knowing these shocks in advance, it is unclear how a forecaster would have decided in 1999 which of the many promising leading indicators would perform well over the next few years and which would not."[57] Indeed.

All recessions have key differences in their origins and emphasis, because businessmen and politicians tend not to repeat the exact same mistakes, other than that a large minority of them will have overinvested in *something* that, with hindsight, was bound to fail. Thus, in 1990, the key losers were hotels, in 2000, telecoms, and in 2008, the primary losers were mortgage lenders. There is little relation to the overbuilding and overpricing in hotels, telecoms, and housing other than they subsequently contracted, and so were at abnormal peaks when viewed with hindsight at the peak of the expansion.

When a field has new data and theory, there is a natural belief that some basic laws will be discovered or confirmed. It is as if one expects there to be higher level patterns from a bunch of lower level decisions, because we know that most patterns, at a lower level, cannot be seen. The idea of stepping outside one's little universe, like the two-dimensional man in flatland seeing his universe from the third dimension, is incredibly alluring, seems like you should see more. Further, advances in statistics and computing imply that patterns previously unseen should now be revealed. Alas, sometimes a lot of data just highlight that we do not have any good theories.

SUMMARY

The CAPM started with a tepid confirmation, and while there was much whistling past the graveyard, and hopes that warts like the size and value effect would go away, it turned out they merely focused researchers on questions they should have asked at the very beginning. The seeming correlation between beta and returns was mainly due to the correlation with the size effect, and this, in turn, was mainly due to measurement errors. The best cross-sectional predictor of equity returns is momentum and book-to-market, neither of which have an intuitive risk rationale. Tweaks to the model have been conspicuous in their ephemeral nature, always popping up in different guises.

"In the end," notes Fischer Black, "A theory is accepted not because it is confirmed by conventional empirical tests, but because researchers persuade one another that the theory is correct and relevant."[58] This is a very postmodern interpretation of finance, accurate in the short run, but not in the long run.

CHAPTER 4

Volatility, Risk, and Returns

The problem in attacking a framework, as opposed to a theory, is that there is no definitive test. The CAPM was a simple model with an unambiguous implication, and has been rejected so thoroughly it is now indefensible, yet still, strangely, prominent in the MBA curriculum. But the APT and general equilibrium (SDF) framework are healthy in academia because they can never be disproven, as any test of that theory is merely a test of one person's guess as to how to reify risk. Any single bit of evidence, such as the low return to highly volatile stocks, in isolation, is just an anomaly, and may merely suggest a new risk proxy. Yet fundamentally, the theory of risk premiums is based on the idea that we do not like things that covary with our wealth, broadly defined, because they increase our net wealth volatility, broadly defined. It seems reasonable to presume, therefore, that priced risk is somehow positively correlated with volatility or betas.

Thus, the most damning evidence is the scope of the volatility-return failure across many asset classes. This evidence has never been presented as an argument for the failure of the conventional theory because as this theory cuts across several asset classes, each with their own measurement and stochastic characteristics, a neat statistical amalgamation test is difficult if not impossible. But the welter of data is broad, and examples of a positive volatility-return relation are the anomalies, rather than the observation that volatile securities have lower returns in a particular asset class.

Even an incorrect framework should be moderately consistent with reality. Whatever the true risk factor is in the current models, it should be somewhat positively related to volatility, or be positively correlated with the business cycle (risk should be greater in bear markets). These are basic, intuitive properties about risk, present at the creation of our conception of risk aversion, and the definition of risk, related to both our dislike of wealth variance, and our relative dislike for things that go bad when everything goes bad. As a first approximation, we should see vague, general evidence consistent with this view of risk if the standard theory is correct, because if risk is

totally uncorrelated with volatility or the business cycle, the as-yet unidentified risk factor makes little sense. After all, markets are presumably aggregating risk preferences, and if risk is related to something uncorrelated with the
business cycle, and the stock market, and total volatility, it defies credulity
that this is what people really think of as risk. In most prominent venues
of risk and return we can imagine, the things that are volatile, that seem
to do worst in recessions, do not have higher returns. Indeed, more often
than not, they have lower-than-average returns. Let us consider the various
venues where researchers have looked at how risk and return are correlated.

TOTAL VOLATILITY AND CROSS-SECTIONAL RETURNS

In 1992, when I was looking for a dissertation topic, I found that volatility
was negatively correlated with returns. The key bias obscuring this fact was
the size effect. If you controlled for size, you saw volatility negatively related
to returns. My dissertation in 1994 was on documenting this finding, and
arguing that it was relevant to the belief that mutual funds showed a preference toward highly volatile stocks—investors were buying hope, based on
overconfidence, the amenability of volatile stocks to a sales pitch, and trying
to take advantage of the highly nonlinear fund inflows from doing very well.[1]

Why this was so incredible is that idiosyncratic variance should pick
up mismeasured factor loadings, and mismeasured factor loadings should
help explain the poor performance of factor models such as the APT.[2] For
example, as mentioned, Stephen Ross and Richard Roll point out that it
is possible—though not probable—inefficient estimates of the market portfolio are uncorrelated with returns, yet then residuals should still show a
positive correlation with returns.[3] That is, if some factor is misestimated,
the measure of beta is not perfect because of imperfections in the risk proxy.
But then the residual variance in such an equation should be positively correlated with returns. Furthermore, early in asset pricing, residual risk was
thought to capture risk because of naïve investors failing to distinguish between systematic volatility and diversifiable volatility, seeing only a very
volatile stock.[4] Because many investors are not highly diversified, being undiversified in volatile stocks is more unpleasant than being undiversified in
a low volatility stock. For both of these reasons, residual risk *should* be
positively correlated with return, yet in fact the correlation for residual risk
goes the wrong way.

I figured that knowing that low volatility stocks had lower returns than
high volatility stocks, adjusted for size, had first-order implications for any
strategy maximizing a Sharpe ratio, because the denominator in a Sharpe

ratio, the variance, would be lower for the low volatility strategy, and returns would be higher. I was in the economics department, and most of the finance professors at Northwestern considered this finding uninteresting, my story *ad hoc*. Though worthy of a dissertation, I did not get much positive feedback on my asset return finding, though my mutual fund finding related to this became the basis of a *Journal of Finance* article.[5] It did not bother me because I figured that the investment world would love this result, and I liked the idea of becoming a portfolio manager as opposed to an academic.

As with any fact that really exists, others discovered this finding, too. Most notably, a paper by Ang, Hodrick, Xing, and Zhang in 2006 documented the relationship between idiosyncratic variance and returns cross-sectionally, and followed this up with another paper documenting it internationally.[6] Please see Figure 4.1. While I was at Northwestern, Bob Hodrick was head of the Northwestern finance faculty, and when I was looking for thesis advisers, he was uninterested in my findings. Hodrick was a Chicago school, efficient markets type, who saw a risk factor or spurious result whenever someone saw an anomaly and my anomaly seemed no different.

But facts catch up with everyone, and it's a testament to the true scientific nature of finance that researchers eventually acknowledge the facts in a way that politicians or soft sciences do not. So now Hodrick was a co-author on a finding I found 10 years earlier. They found that stocks with higher volatility had significantly lower returns, and this held constant:

- Book to Market
- Leverage
- Liquidity
- Volume

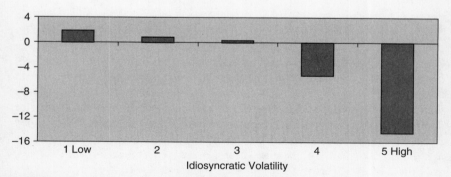

FIGURE 4.1   Annual Excess Returns for G-7 Equities
From Ang, Hodrick, Xing, and Zhang 2007, Table 7. Returns are annualized from 1963 to 2003.

- Turnover
- Bid-Ask Spread
- Coskewness (when returns go up, more positive skew)
- Analysts' dispersion

That is a lot of things to control for, a pretty consistent finding. The results are in Figure 4.1, and I think the essence of any real finding is that it shows up in a simple-to-read graph, and the negative excess returns are very large. These are the average annual returns for quintiles sorted by idiosyncratic volatility. As is customary in academic studies, they only present excess returns, which are like the alpha in a market model that includes factors, in this case, the four-factor Fama-French factors. You take the total returns, and subtract the factor returns, because the excess return is that which is unexplained by the Fama-French factors. Because these factors are generally positively correlated to variance, which merely increases the alpha, the total volatility and beta are positively correlated, meaning highly volatile stocks have a higher beta and higher expected return. But that's all a distraction in this case, because the excess returns are ridiculously large—15 percent annually for the highest volatility stocks. The following year, they documented this effect in 23 developed country markets and leave this finding as a global puzzle.

Like any result, you could find earlier premonitions in the literature. Most notably, Robert Haugen documented the low return to volatility and financial leverage back in the 1990s in a series of papers and a book. But this effect was somewhat hidden because it was given equal weight with several other independent explanatory variables, and so was not given prominence. The negative cross-sectional return to high volatility stocks is indisputable; the question is why.

BETA-SORTED PORTFOLIOS

When I found while researching my dissertation that volatility was negatively correlated with returns, I found that beta was also negatively correlated with returns at the high end. Yet I had to focus on idiosyncratic volatility because the idea that beta was actually slightly negatively correlated with returns was so preposterous, I would lose all credibility for even broaching the idea. My dissertation was consequently titled "Mutual Funds, *Idiosyncratic* Variance, and Asset Returns." We also see that Ang et al. focused on *idiosyncratic* volatility. But the truth of the matter is that firms with higher betas have higher idiosyncratic volatility and vice versa. Indeed, the return by beta, when cross-tabbed with size, was reported as negative by Fama and French (1992), but that was presumably measurement error. The gist reported was that beta was uncorrelated with returns.

It is one thing to say beta does not work, but quite another to say that it is *negatively* correlated with returns. There had been too much work generating stories, anecdotes, and so forth to help explain beta to the great unwashed B-schoolers and their ilk, to now say—sign error! Best to say, beta is incomplete, and perhaps there's a risk gremlin lurking in low idiosyncratic risk. But actually, the returns to beta are worse than anyone expected.

I constructed beta portfolios using only those stocks with sufficient market capitalization to be investable. As an institutional investor has great difficulty investing in stocks with market caps below $500MM, this is in the 20th percentile of the New York Stock Exchange companies today. As these NYSE stocks are generally larger than those listed on the American Stock Exchange, or the Nasdaq, applying this cut-off backward in time is a nice way of focusing on those stocks that are truly investable, which is important in these types of tests because really small stocks tend to dominate the extremums of beta or volatility tests. No ETFs, REITs, closed-end funds, and so on. All common stocks. Next, I simply calculated the beta of each stock against the value-weighted NYSE-AMEX market return using the prior 36 to 60 months of data. The top 100 were high beta stocks, and the bottom 100 were low beta stocks. Please see Figure 4.2.

Figure 4.2 shows that historically, the cumulative return of low beta stocks significantly outperforms the high beta stocks. While the Internet bubble brought them back to an even performance, this was an aberration, and their subsequent performance in the Internet bust and the recent market cataclysm generates a net annualized 4.6 percent premium to low beta stocks. Like the tortoise and the hare, slow and steady wins the race. High betas are risky in the sense they have much higher volatility, and covary directly with the business, or market, cycle. Please see Table 4.1.

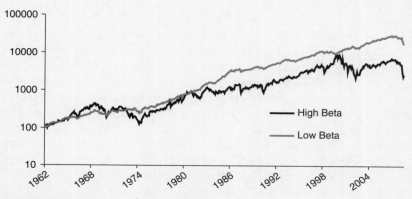

FIGURE 4.2 Total Return to Beta Portfolios

TABLE 4.1 High and Low Beta Portfolios Formed
Semi-Annually in the United States

	Beta High	Beta Low
Arithmetic Ann Ret	11.0%	11.9%
Geo Ann Ret	7.3%	11.88%
Std Dev	28.0%	11.0%
Beta	1.62	0.50

Data from July 1962 through December 31, 2008.

We can see that much of the poor performance from the high beta portfolio comes from the effect of geometric averaging, because the high beta stocks have such a higher volatility. Remember that the geometric average is a buy-and-hold return, whereas the arithmetic average assumes one can true up one's position daily, and the difference is the variance divided by two. Indeed, calculating the geometric return by way of a total return index, and applying the formula, generates about the same result. For the high beta portfolio, this adjustment lowers returns by 3.9 percent annually, whereas for the low beta portfolio, it is more like a 0.6 percent adjustment (it does not show up in the actual geometric returns because there is some positive autocorrelation in the low beta return). Considering the differences in beta, you could put on a negative beta portfolio at a premium (long low beta, short high beta), and then go long the aggregate market—which supposedly also generates a positive return—and generate a significantly positive zero beta portfolio.

It is striking that as prominent as beta is in financial pedagogy, there are no portfolios grouped by beta one can look up online or in Bloomberg, while value, size, and even momentum have a variety of different indexes and fund groupings. If beta is on par with these atheoretical factors, why is it not monitored the way these are? Because the high beta stocks have lower returns than low beta stocks once one merely controls for size, and so the beta factor proxy constructed in the way that the size and value factors are constructed would give it a negative price, which would turn the most fundamental parameter of finance (the equity premium) on its head. Nonetheless, today it is a dirty little secret, something all good equity quants know, but it is rarely addressed directly. It makes absolutely no sense in the conventional theoretic framework, and strikes at the very core of what is meant by risk, because if beta is inversely related to risk, then the standard theory is irredeemable. Thus, much prominence is given to Ang et al.'s piece on *idiosyncratic* variance, but the same result applied to beta would simply be too hard to square with the vast array of examples of how beta should work.

CALL OPTIONS

Theoretically, beta—or any covariance with the elusive risk factor—
measures the "how much" of risk, and so if risk is priced, higher options
with higher strike prices (that is, more out-of-the-money) have higher beta(s),
which implies a higher average return. Therefore, far out-of-the-money call
options should offer extremely high expected returns. As underlying stocks
always, in practice, have positive betas against the market, all calls will have
positive betas that exceed the beta of the underlying stock, and call betas
will increase in the strike price as the calls get further out of the money.
Hence, all calls will have positive expected returns and the expected returns
will be larger for greater strike prices, because the betas, as a function of the
call price, increase as you go out of the money.

For example, say you have a stock with a price of 100, and buy a call
with a strike price of 120, expiring in three months. If the stock price rises to
110 over the next month, the call option will rise about 120 percent, while
a long stock position rises only 10 percent. This is the implicit leverage in
an option, that is, it is like being able to borrow 10 times one's capital and
invest in the market. It is exactly the same bet as an equity position, just
higher powered. This is why greedy retail investors with inside information
prefer options: You get the most bang for your buck in options if you know
where stock prices are going.

Coval and Shumway (2001) prove that expected European call returns
must be positive and increasing in the strike price provided only that investor
utility functions are increasing and concave and stock returns are positively
correlated with aggregate wealth. They then document that this does not,
indeed, happen.[7] Please see Figure 4.3.

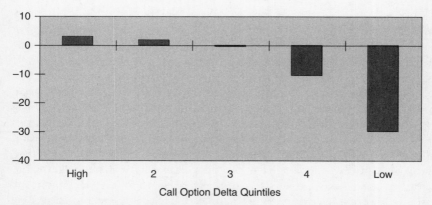

FIGURE 4.3 Monthly Returns, Betas for Call Options Ranked by Delta

Sophie Ni (2007) looked at data from 1996 through 2005, and found that the highest out-of-the-money calls, with one month to expiration, have average returns of −37 percent over a month![8] Figure 4.3 shows that if you bucket call options into groups based on their deltas, you find that call options, indeed, are indeed highly levered stock positions. Lower deltas mean the call option is less sensitive, in dollar terms, to a stock moving, but more sensitive, in percentage terms. Thus, an at-the-money call option with a delta of 0.5 moves 0.5 dollars for every 1 dollar move in the underlying, while an out-of-the-money option may have a delta of 0.08. On a percentage basis, since the at-the-money option has a price of around 5, while the out-of-the-money option a price of 0.25, the percentage change in price for the low delta option is much greater. The key to remember is that the average stock has a beta of 1.0. and betas on their call options range from 4 to 15—giving one 4 to 15 times the juice of the daily return. An option's beta is the beta of the stock, times the omega, which is a measure of the percentage return in the option price given a 1 percent change in the stock price. If the omega on a Ford call option is calculated to be 3.6, then for every 1 percent change in the price of Ford, the price of the call option will rise by 3.6 percent.

Not only is the average return negative for call options, these returns get worse the more implicitly levered, and the riskier the options become, in contrast to what the weak assumption is as described by Coval and Shumway. Returns are negatively correlated with the betas. Call options have several times more risk, whatever that is, than their underlying stocks, yet negative average returns. Investors basically are overpaying for lottery tickets when they buy options, and just like the lottery, the average payout is worse the more risk one takes. If there's a risk premium in equities, it certainly is not amplified in options in any way, because you lose money, on average, buying leverage market positions by way of call options.

SMALL BUSINESS

Entrepreneurial investment, such as in small proprietorships (S corps and private LLCs) is generally a highly undiversified investment for most entrepreneurs. The reasons are straightforward, in that when one person has a significant effect on the business through his effort and competence, it is natural that he should have the most "skin in the game." This is a classic issue of moral hazard because a business manager, who has significant upside and, without ownership, no downside, is motivated to take wild risks on the theory of heads I win, tails the banker loses. However, if the manager is the majority owner, his failure should affect his net wealth too. About 75 percent of all private equity is owned by households for whom it constitutes at least

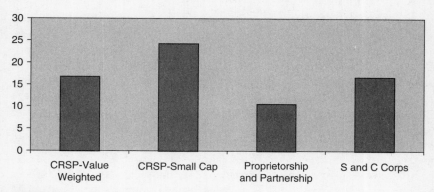

FIGURE 4.4 Annual Returns, 1990–1998

half of their total net worth. Furthermore, households with entrepreneurial equity invest on average more than 70 percent of their private holdings in a single private company in which they have an active management interest. Despite this dramatic lack of diversification, private equity returns are on average no higher than the market return on all publicly traded equity.[9] Figure 4.4 shows the basic results, that over an 8-year period, if anything returns to private business, be it partnerships, proprietorships, S corps, C corps, and two entirely different sets of data, there is no demonstrable premium. Given an investor can invest in a diversified, and liquid equity portfolio, it is puzzling why households willingly invest substantial amounts in an asset with an equivalent return, but much higher volatility, including a positive correlation with the market.

The forced nondiversification of a private equity investment, from a pure portfolio perspective, implies a requisite higher return. How much higher than the average public equity return would we expect the average private equity return to be? Using standard utility models to calibrate the hurdle rate that would make a household indifferent between investing in a portfolio of a single private firm, a public equity index, and T-bills, or a portfolio of just the public equity index and T-bills, researchers estimate that private equity risk generates a hurdle rate of about 10 percent higher the public equity return.[10] You should receive a huge premium for the large idiosyncratic risk you are taking, risk that unlike idiosyncratic risk in the market, is impossible to diversify away. Entrepreneurs appear to be taking extra risk, for no extra return.

Leverage

The Miller-Modigliani theorem states that regardless of the debt and equity proportions, the value of the firm is the same. As a firm increases its leverage using more debt, its equity concentrates the variable returns of the business on a smaller and smaller base, making them both riskier: the equity's beta and volatility will increase, the debt will have a higher chance of defaulting. The implication is that highly levered firms should have lower rated debt (junk), and more volatile equity, but because debt has a lower return than equity, the net, total return to all a company's securities (debt and equity) is a constant. That is the theory. But as was just shown, levering up the equity does not appear to increase returns in the case of options, which are merely levered equity positions, and equity option betas were shown to be highly negatively related to returns. Please see Figure 4.5.

In Figure 4.5, we see that leverage is, anomalously, clearly negatively correlated with returns.[11] These researchers held constant size and book/market, so that this market leverage should not pick up these well-known anomalies. Higher leverage implies lower returns for equity even though this should increase risk of that equity, and thus should increase returns. There have been only a handful of studies on this, which is understandable because no one likes to generate results that do not support well-established theories, and researchers tend to think the theory is correct, and so the analysis is probably wrong.[12] Indeed, perhaps the biggest implication is from the dog that is not barking here. There have been no papers linking how leverage is positively related to expected returns, even though this result would have been consistent with a Nobel Prize–winning theory. Empirically supporting Nobel-winning theory for the first time is worthy of a publication in a top journal, and for academics, this is their number one priority. The absence of a positive finding in this context is perhaps more powerful than the handful of negative results.

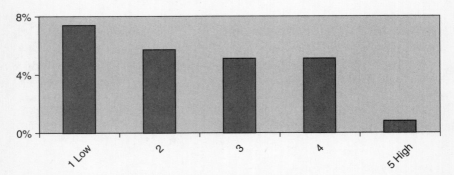

FIGURE 4.5   Annual Return to Portfolios Sorted by Market Leverage (Debt/Market Cap) Adjusted for Book/Market and Size Exposure
Source: Penman, Richardson, and Tuna, 2007, Table 1.

MUTUAL FUNDS

The original tests of the CAPM were on mutual fund returns, hoping to show that mutual fund performance would be explained by the new risk factor.[13] That is, wouldn't it be neat if economists could explain the returns, not as managerial expertise, but beta? Early work by Jensen looked at the value add of mutual fund managers, and denoted their abnormal performance *alpha,* a term that has stayed with us.[14] Subsequent work found no relationship between a stock's return and its beta, and it was sufficiently uninteresting that in more recent work, the relation between beta and returns is addressed only as an aside in Malkiel (1995), who notes that a fund manager's beta is uncorrelated with his fund's average return.[15]

As with leverage studies, the absence of any volatility or beta correlation with mutual fund returns is most relevant here, because it highlights an absence of confirmation in an area examined since the very beginnings of asset pricing theory. Absence of evidence is evidence of absence, not proof, but suggestive, especially when you know there has been a systematic, thoughtful search for such evidence.[16] Carhart's 1997 study of mutual funds is most well known for introducing momentum as a factor, akin to Fama and French's value and size factors, but it was also notable for the manifest irrelevance of beta in his analysis.[17] Good or bad, a mutual fund's beta was never an issue in explaining the results, and so that paper hardly mentioned the null results, and instead centered on the importance of momentum as a factor that explained the positive one-year persistence. Later studies of mutual funds by Russ Wermers (2000) don't even address beta.[18] The problem is not a lack of attention to this issue, but the absence of any empirical relevance of beta to average mutual fund returns, leading researchers to focus on factors that are correlated with return, which are then rationalized as risk.

If you look at Morningstar's detailed analysis of mutual funds on their splash pages for particular funds, they note the degree to which the fund is in value versus growth, or in large versus small cap, the asset turnover, expense ratio, and the tracking error. No beta. Correlation with the market, or any risk factor, is left as an exercise for the reader. This highlights the situation that in practice no one cares about beta when investing in mutual funds, nor has there been any evidence that they should. People just want funds that generate high returns.

FUTURES

Futures are derivative securities, bilateral agreements, one side to buy, the other to sell, at a future date, a spot commodity at a prespecified price.

Futures returns are not driven by lower expected spot prices because such prices are reflected in a low current futures price.[19] Unexpected deviations from the expected future spot price are by definition unpredictable, and should average out to zero over time for an investor in futures, unless the investor has the ability to correctly time the market.

What return can an investor in futures expect to earn if he does not benefit from expected spot price movements, and is unable to outsmart the market? The difference between the *current* futures price and the *expected* future spot price. Assume the current futures price is below the current spot price. This usually implies the expected spot price is above the futures price (we don't truly observe the actual expected futures price, but this is generally true). On average, going long the futures makes money when it is below the current spot price because the futures price rises to the eventual spot price. At maturity, while the spot price may have fallen, the futures price has risen too. This is called *normal backwardization* because if you put the futures prices out like a yield curve, the more distant futures prices are below the current price. Please see Figure 4.6.

Figure 4.6 shows the term structure of futures for gold and copper in August 2008. Copper is in backwardization, while gold is in *contango,* a fun name that means the opposite. Historically, gold is always in contango, meaning, if you are long gold futures, you lose money on average as it rolls to maturity. Other commodities flop around, sometimes flat, sometimes in normal backwardization, and sometimes in contango. Harvey and Erb (2007) find that copper, heating oil, and live cattle were on average in backwardization, while corn, wheat, silver, gold, and coffee were in contango, on average.[20]

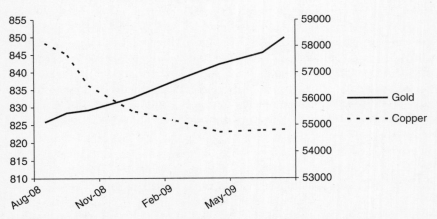

FIGURE 4.6   Term Structure of Futures for Gold and Copper: August 2008

Now, on average, this term structure relating futures prices to maturity dates predicts future returns fairly well, so that a commodity in normal backwardization generates a predictable positive return for being long, whereas a commodity in contango generates a predictable positive return for being short. The question, obviously, is why are some futures in contango, and others in normal backwardization, from a risk perspective? A prominent early explanation put forth by none other than John Maynard Keynes, on why futures generate risk premium from being long, is that farmers grow wheat, say, and wish to hedge it by selling now, rather than waiting until the season is over. So a speculator buys the wheat now, and takes on the price risk, for which he must be compensated.

Futures allow operating companies to hedge their commodity price exposure, and since hedging is a form of insurance, hedgers must offer long-only commodity futures investors an insurance premium. Normal backwardization suggests that, in a world with risk-averse hedgers and investors, the excess return from a long commodity investment should be viewed as an insurance risk premium. It is easy to expand this to the other side, by focusing not on the producer of a commodity, but the purchaser. Say you are Boeing, and buy a lot of aluminum to build airplanes. If you hedge, you buy a futures today, locking in a price. Thus, whether you hedge by buying if you are a consumer, or selling if you are a producer, futures have an insurance-like characteristic. The key is knowing, between consumers and producers, who dominates the futures contracts. One explanation of the futures returns is that for some commodities, producers dominate the demand for insurance, and thus futures, in the other, consumers dominate.

In a diversified worldwide market, however, this reasoning does not work in explaining equilibrium returns. Asset pricing theory tells us that returns are a function of risk. And as most investors are not aluminum consumers, or corn suppliers, the net covariance with the risk factor should be at work. For example, the needs of a company, its preferences, are unrelated to its returns, which are a function of the change in the expectation of a company's cash flows in relation to these other things we care about (for example, the S&P500). This is due to arbitrage, and because asset prices are set by supply and demand, where investors should be allocating capital in a way so that the price of risk, from any source, is the same whether it comes from futures or equities. If one can get the benefits of the futures roll and not be involved in the futures commodity—as most investors are not—this should be like idiosyncratic risk is, the CAPM: diversifiable, and so unpriced. And the expected roll returns (so-called because the futures prices *rolls* to the current spot price over time), based on the current relation of the futures to the spot, are uncorrelated with the prominent risk factors for equities (that is, the market, value, and size factors) or for corporate bonds (that is, the Baa-Aaa yield spread). Changes in inflation adversely affects the roll returns from normal backwardization, while adversely affecting the roll returns for contango.[21]

In sum, there are predictable returns in futures returns, primarily from the movement in the futures price as the maturity date moves closer to the present, which is foreseen in the current relation of the futures price to the spot price. But what drives this, from a risk perspective, is a mystery.

CURRENCIES

A currency is not just a medium of exchange, but an asset with a return like a stock. The interest rate is like a dividend, the change in spot price, the capital appreciation. One would expect the return of currencies to be related to risk.

Uncovered Interest Rate Parity is a theory that connects current to future spot rates. This theory states that you have two ways of investing, which should be equal. First, you can invest in your home country at the riskless rate. So if the U.S. interest rate is 5 percent, you can make a 5 percent return in one year, in U.S. dollars (USD). Alternatively, you can buy, say, yen, invest at the yen interest rate (each currency has a different risk-free rate), and then convert back to USD when your riskless security matures. For this to be equal, you need something like

$$r_{USD} = r_{yen} + \text{\% change in yen}$$

Where r_{USD} is the U.S. interest rate, and so on. So, if you make 5 percent in USD, an U.S. investor should receive that same return in yen, by way of the interest rate in yen, plus the expected appreciation or depreciation in the yen against the dollar. If the interest rate in yen is 1 percent, this means one expects the yen to appreciate by 4 percent. When the foreign interest rate is higher than the U.S. interest rate, risk-neutral and rational U.S. investors should expect the foreign currency to depreciate against the dollar by the difference between the two interest rates. This way, investors are indifferent between borrowing at home and lending abroad, or the converse. This is known as the *uncovered interest rate parity condition,* and it is violated in the data except in the case of very high inflation currencies. In practice, higher foreign interest rates predict that foreign currencies *appreciate* against the dollar, making investing in higher interest rate countries a win-win: You get *appreciation* on your currency, and higher riskless interest rates while in that currency.

Now the rates of expected return through the two investment paths can differ according to risk, of course. So one can imagine, looking at the yen, or the dollar, or various European currencies in the 1970s, and so on, trying to tie each to some measure of a home currency's risk factor: consumption, or the stock market and so forth.

Like high returns to low volatility stocks, it is difficult, but not theoretically impossible, to make sense of this. Robert Hodrick wrote a magisterial technical overview of the theory and evidence of currency markets in 1987.[22] He summed up his findings:

> *We have found a rich set of empirical results. We do not yet have a model of expected returns that fit the data. International finance is no worse off in this respect than more traditional areas of finance.*

That is seeing the glass half full, such as a book of models, trying to find something that would intuitively relate to a risk factor that predicts the perverse finding that futures curves predict currency movements. Indeed, Hodrick looked at CAPM models, latent variable models, conditional variance models, models that use expenditures on durables, or nondurables and services, and Kalman filters. None outperformed the spot rate as a predictor of future currency prices. Hodrick leaves off with the idea that "simple models may not work well." Indeed this is true, and I think is the ultimate hope of these researchers that a little more math will uncover a solution that is merely complicated.

And so it continued for the next 20 years, and many hedge funds specialized in the carry trade, which was as simple as it was successful: lend capital to high interest rate currencies, enjoy the high riskless rates and currency appreciation on the spot rate; borrow capital at the low interest rate currency, and make money on the depreciation of this debt over time. Thus, in 2008, researchers took a different tack, and noted:

> *Overall, we argue that our findings call for new theoretical macroeconomic models in which risk premia are affected by funding and liquidity constraints, not just shocks to productivity, output, or the utility function.*[23]

By "our findings" they mean the carry trade continued to work 30 years after being identified by Farber and Fama (1979), and it has continued as a puzzle because no reasonable risk factor can explain it. Thus, they are looking at new conceptions, in this case, based on negative skew, because liquidity constraints is an academic euphemism for downside risk (and thus blowing through one's capital).

Lotteries

The annual per capita lottery expenditure in the United States is about $170, and the rate of return is about −47 percent per dollar played. It clearly presents a challenge to the idea that people are looking at these games on a risk-return continuum, but they are in some sense risky decisions at their most basic level. These investments clearly cater to what is commonly called those seeking risk, or positive skew, in particular. There are two primary characteristics of lotteries. First, poor people play them more, in both relative and absolute terms, than wealthy people. A St. Louis Fed article finds that those with household income of less than $25,000 spent $575 on lotteries on a per capita basis. This spending was substantially more than spending by those with a household income over $100,000 ($196).[24] The people who can least afford it, buy the most of it.

A study of the popularity (sales) of lotteries found that average payout (expected return) or variance did not matter, but the size of the top prize was highly significant.[25] In other words, the $100 million Super Lotto has the most sales even though the probability of winning is so small it basically is outside the realm of intuition (1 in 150 million). Indeed, such lotteries are the only ones I play. People who bet seem to prefer those bets that offer the worst odds, but the greatest payout. Gambling seems to be totally outside the assumptions of risk aversion that underlie the risk-return assumption, and is one of the motivators of Prospect Theory, though all this theory does is say that when little sums are involved, people are risk loving, which is not so much a theory as a description of small stakes gambling.

Movies

A paradox in the movies is that their rate of return is around 4 percent and the risk is higher than most industries. Art DeVany (2003) found that between 1986 and 1999, G-rated movies generated lower volatility and higher returns than R-rated movies, though there was a clear preference toward R-rated movies (over 1,000 R-rated movies and only 60 G-rated ones).[26] But movies have a strong Pareto distribution, where the mean is much higher than the median or mode. It seems everyone is betting on the next *Titanic,* because the very highest grossing movies are R-rated. Furthermore, the R-rated genre is more artsy, and so has reputational aspects to those involved that go beyond mere revenues.

WORLD COUNTRY RETURNS

The risk premium is an expectation, and returns are a realization. To the extent a return is high, it is never clear whether this return was expected or rather just random luck. Nevertheless, one would expect that over the long run, or for lots of cases, the average return equals the expected return. If not, what is the point of an expectation?

Thus, it is interesting that among country equity returns, there is no clear risk premium. The United States had about the same average top line return relative to short-term debt from 1900 to 2005 compared to 17 other developed countries worldwide, about 5 percent.[27] There is no clear return either within developed countries, or between developed and undeveloped countries. Erb, Harvey, and Viskanta (1995) show similar returns between developed and underdeveloped countries, using data from 1979 to 1992.[28] As the arithmetic returns are much higher than the geometric returns, he highlights those monthly returns for displaying a risk premium based on the volatility, but if you look at the geometric returns, they are about the same as the developed country data (13.5 percent for developing, 12.3 percent for developed). Using a more updated set of data from 1989 through 2000, Bansal and Dahlquist (2002) report approximately similar arithmetic returns (15.8 percent versus 16.1 percent), but then using annualized geometric returns, the return for the developed countries was 13.8 percent versus 6.7 percent for the developing countries.[29]

Intuitively, investing in Nepal would seemingly be taking on extra risk, but in practice there is no risk premium for such forays historically. It is strange that there is not a pattern among their returns in regard to its volatility, because intuitively, those countries where the stock market index is especially volatile, would have a higher risk premium, as foreigners would not be able to invest sufficiently because of tax and institutional reasons, and eliminate the risk premium for this idiosyncratic risk. One can look for global risk factors that explain this, and the usual ones (for example, a world stock market index) do not work.

CORPORATE BONDS

The conventional corporate bond puzzle is that spreads are too high. The most conspicuous bond index captures U.S. Baa and Aaa bond yields going back to 1919, which generates enough data to make it *the* corporate spread measure, especially when looking at correlations with business cycles. Yet Baa bonds are still investment grade, and have only a 4.7 percent 10-year cumulative default rate after their initial rating. As the recovery rate on defaulted bonds is around 50 percent, this annualizes to a mere 0.23 percent annualized loss rate. Since the spread between Baa and Aaa bonds has averaged around 1.2 percent since 1919, this generates an approximate 0.97 percent annualized excess return compared to the riskless Aaa yield, creating the puzzle that spreads are too high for the risk incurred.

In the 1980s, Michael Milken was the point man for leading a revolution in finance, where firms with a 5 percent annualized default rate would have an active market, and firms could even issue bonds at this grade. As the old saw goes, banks only lend to firms that can pay them back, and so the probability of default, historically, for investment grade companies is well below 1 percent annualized. B and BB rated bonds have default rates of 6 percent and 1.5 percent, respectively, and before 1987, the market for these bonds was very illiquid, and all these bonds were "fallen angels," bonds initially issued at investment grade whose ratings have fallen because of adverse financial performance.

There was a spirited debate as to what the actual default rate, and return, on junk bonds was during the 1980s, as Michael Milken and his firm Drexel Lambert were getting rich promoting these bonds, while others, like Warren Buffett and Ben Stein were saying these bonds had horrible returns. There simply were not a lot of data, so the debate was rather limited. My friend and former Moody's colleague, Jerry Fons, wrote his dissertation on this market in 1985, and actually received payments from his university from people asking for copies of his dissertation because there was so little empirical data in this area.[30] Not a lot of money, but a fun distinction, because most dissertations are not only never published, they are rarely read by anyone but one's advisers.

Altman and Bana (2004) and Kozhemiakin (2007) note there is no premium to high yield portfolios relative to investment grade portfolios, a set of bonds with a 3.84 percent average annual default rate from 1970 to 2005.[31] Furthermore, Altman (2006) notes that a bankrupt bond portfolio underperforms investment grade bonds.[32] Both high yield and bankrupt bonds have more volatility and cyclicality than investment grade bonds, and do their worst when returns are most valued, in bad times. Junk bonds are intuitively, and academically, risky. Data from the Merrill Lynch High Yield Index show a 6.77 percent annualized return relative to the 7.18 percent return of their investment grade index from 1987 through December 2008. The risk premium is a negative 0.41 percent in these indexes, which seems odd given that high yield debt has greater volatility, and more cyclicality. This might be seen as mild support for the idea that risk begets return, but it assumes one can buy the index using closing prices during this period.

Yet the indexes are really an overstatement because such indexes have a systematic bias when portraying illiquid or unaudited asset classes. Even today, many times a junk bond's bid-ask spreads is five points wide, and this transaction cost is implicit in the fact that for a set of mutual high yield mutual funds that currently exist (that is, *with* obvious survivorship bias), their total annualized return from 1987 through 2008 was 3.44 percent, whereas the Merrill High Yield Index rose 6.77 percent (see Figure 4.7) annually. Investment grade funds underperformed their index by much less,

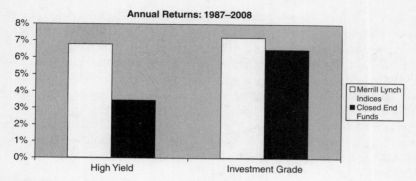

FIGURE 4.7 Annual Returns: 1987–2008
Data from 27 high yield closed-end funds, 12 investment grade funds.
December 31, 1987 through December 2008.

in that the index return was 7.18 percent compared to fund returns of 6.48 percent. The simple idea is that illiquid assets have higher transaction costs, including higher management fees, that cause actual performance to be lower than that of an index. If it cost 5 percent to buy an asset (commissions, bid-ask spread, trade impact), given average turnover, this will diminish your returns by 5 percent, amortized over the average holding period in one's portfolio. If your average holding is 3 years, over 30 years that's not 10 trades, but 20, because you buy and sell each trade. Thus the closing prices of illiquid assets, such as in an index, will be a biased proxy for real returns if based merely on closing prices. If you take a couple percent off the high yield index due to price impact, commissions, and the bid-ask spread, there is no premium to these risky assets.

Illiquid and highly volatile assets often have this problem, and there's a clear bias by data providers to ignore this risk in computing indexes. For example, Malkiel and Saha (2005) found that no hedge fund database providers had the last year of Long Term Capital Management in their data set, the –92 percent return, and so the indexes exclude the very risks that make hedge fund investors nervous.[33] Malkiel and Saha estimate this bias adds approximately 6 percent to the annualized returns. Who creates these indexes? Usually groups that are allied with the product one is examining. For example, the Credit Suisse/Tremont Index that monitors hedge fund returns is maintained by the following:

> *The joint venture, Credit Suisse Tremont Index LLC, combines the considerable expertise of Credit Suisse, one of the world's leading global investment banking firms, and the data research group of Tremont Capital Management, Inc., a full-service hedge fund of funds investment management firm.*

It is an inevitable conflict of interest where those most knowledgeable, and have access to the best data, who provide data generally used by researchers, will be advocates of this field—one does not become extensively knowledgeable in something one thinks is irrelevant, inefficient, or fraudulent. There is oftentimes an arm's length separation between the index provider and the portfolio managers, but there is no way they can be indifferent: without the market thriving, seeming to offer a good opportunity, their service will not have a long life. After all, it was conventional wisdom that active portfolio managers outperformed passive indexes until the 1980s—for several generations!—because the evidence was generally held and presented by the active managers and their industry groups. There are always good reasons why a certain investment should not be included in a database, and for someone with a rooting interest, these will tend to be poorly performing investments. So asset indexes are often biased, but little is done to note such biases because the index makers are advocates.

Therefore, the excess corporate risk premium puzzle pertains to one portion of the risk spectrum the difference between a 0.03 percent and a 0.3 percent annualized default rate, a distinction without a difference to most people. When one goes from a 0.3 percent to a 15 percent default rate, as one does when you go from BBB- to C rated bonds, there is no return premium at all. Given reasonable expectations of transaction costs, and the actual difference between the high yield indexes and actual high yield returns, it seem probable that people extend into higher credit risk with a lower average return. It is difficult to see how the little risk is priced, the big one not, if risk is to have any consistent meaning. If the corporate spread is a function of risk at one end, why is it not at the other, more intuitive end?

THE LONG END OF THE YIELD CURVE

The general shape of the yield curve is as follows. It rises about 1% until about three years, then flattens out. But this is deceiving, because bonds have positive convexity, and so their returns are very non-normal at annual frequencies. Furthermore, the higher maturity bonds have higher volatility, and this subtracts from their cumulative returns through the geometric averaging adjustment where we subtract the variance divided by two from arithmetic returns. We should expect long bond holders to have long frequencies, and so this adjustment on monthly data is important.

Thus, I took data on the U.S. government bond yield since 1958 through 2008 and constructed a set of annualized returns based on a buy-and-hold strategy. Each monthly return subtracted the Fed Funds rate, and included

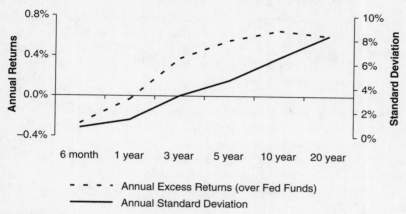

FIGURE 4.8 U.S. Interest Rate Date: 1958–2008
Data from Federal Reserve H. 15 Report.

both the monthly price appreciation plus the coupon yield. These data are presented in Figure 4.8.

As we can see, the returns to a funded position in bonds, an excess return, is very close to zero over this period. Indeed, buying six-month T-bills funded at the Fed Funds rate was a money loser, and for the one-year bond, about a zero return.[34] But returns are increasing over maturity. Yet, the increase in yield from 5 years to 10 years is miniscule, from 0.55 percent to 0.65 percent, and it actually declines to 0.60 percent for the 20-year bonds. It is fair to say the returns to yield curve extensions past five years are basically zero. The price volatility, meanwhile, increases consistently as maturity increases, and thus the Sharpe ratio, the ratio of the return on the bond minus a risk-free rate, falls as the maturity increases beyond five years. Why would anyone hold long-term bonds, because you get the same yield (and return) but must take on more price volatility?

One explanation is that many investors have a specific time horizon they are interested in, say 10 years. It is merely a difference in perspective, the nominal payout in 10 years is fixed as least risky if you are fixated on consumption in 10 years, as compared to a security that rolls over the short rate many times. But now the theory is at a stand-off. For someone who needs a fixed payment in 10 years, the 10-year fixed rate bond is risk free. Changes in yield cause it to have price variability, which is no concern to the person with a fixed payment in 10 years. On the other hand, some people buy assets, and don't know when they will need it, or want its valuation to remain stable, as in the early naïve approaches to modeling bond risk. A risk-free asset in this context would be an asset such as a floating coupon that reset every month, and a fixed price. So the issue is, what is risky: a fixed payment in N years and a floating current price, or a fixed current price and a floating terminal payment as the yield curve changes? In this framework, risk is as justifiable as one's favorite color, because everyone has different investing horizons.

But even with the degrees of freedom implied by this reasoning, we face a puzzle. Why does the return, and thus risk, rise, and then flatten? Thus, using the aforementioned reasoning on fixed versus floating bonds, the two-year bond is riskier than the three-month bond because of its price volatility. But after three years, the price volatility does not matter. This cannot be because people are indifferent to a fixed payment in 20 years or 5 years, because if you assume five years, then the 20-year bond is much riskier, and vice versa if you assume people prefer fixed payments in 20 years.

The yield curve is usually used to demonstrate a risk-return premium by comparing two points on the yield curve, either the 1-year versus the 30-year, or the 1 month versus the 10-year. The key is, you span the 1- to 3-year fulcrum where the yield curve flattens out. Indeed, the six-month T-bill dominates the three-month T-bill in the sense that it generally gives one 20 basis points more return at immeasurably small levels of interest rate risk; the shorter end of the curve is a free lunch for investors who use the Sharpe ratio. But the returns to bonds and bills are often noted as proof of a risk premium, usually by merely noting that one has higher return and higher volatility. Price volatility, however, is clearly not the driver, because volatility continues to rise long after a return premium disappears, and no one thinks volatility as applied to stocks is related to risk any more.

One clever answer is that we observe nominal bonds, and to the extent there is an inflation risk premium that increases as maturities increase, because if there is really high inflation, like in the 1970s, where the real returns on long-term bonds were negative, the more so the longer the maturity. Short-term T-bills were able to keep pace with inflation because one continually rolled them over. Therefore, if one has a demand for a fixed, real, future payment, then not a nominal fixed payment, but rather, the short-term rollover strategy is preferred. Thus, after three years, there is an exact canceling out between the inflation hedging properties of the shorter-term bond (which can be rolled over at higher rates in high inflation times), which preserves future value, and the low risk that comes from a fixed nominal payment of a longer maturity bond. A clever set of assumptions about the nature of inflation versus real interest rate risk could get this to work.

Yet looking at the inflation indexed Treasuries, TIPS, which started around and in data collected since 2004, these show that the 5-to-20 year spread is virtually identical to the nominal Treasury spread over that period.

That is, the difference between the 20-year and the 5-year, when 2 percent nominally, was 2 percent for the TIPS. The yield curve for TIPS out two years looks just like the regular U.S. bond yield curve, just shifted downward. When the yield spread between short- and long-term bonds was near zero nominally for U.S. bonds, it was near zero for the TIPS. It would appear that inflation risk premia are not relevant to shape of the yield curve. The real Sharpe ratio declines for TIPS as one moves out in maturity just as for nominal Treasuries.

The bottom line is that an explanation has to explain the really low returns to the short end of the yield curve while explaining why price volatility and inflation risk do not matter, or cancel out after a certain point. This is impossible, so modern interest rate models are based on latent factors, yields as a function of their yields, and so they are atheoretical tautologies like saying value stocks outperform growth stocks because of the value risk factor.[35] If the 10-year forward rate is above the current rate, you can say that that is because of inflation expectations, an expected increase in the real interest rate, and a risk premium. You cannot prove this is not true, but then you are taking a lot on faith. The specific reason why the expected return rises, or falls, or rises and then falls, is totally flexible, because the current yield is a function of itself, though suitably rationalized.

DISTRESS RISK

As mentioned in Chapter 3, distress risk, or the risk of financial default, was at one time thought responsible for both the size and value effect. Several studies subsequently documented that when measured directly, firms with higher distress risk have much lower returns, and so this explanation is no longer feasible. Indeed, while I was at Moody's in 2000, I was able to use their database of ratings back to 1975 and find that the rate of return lined up almost perfectly with the rating, with AAA having the highest return and C the lowest. I updated those data using S&P ratings, and used the rating in June to form a portfolio over the following 12 months, a very straightforward strategy. I used 1987 as the starting point because before this, junk bonds, those with a rating below investment grade, were small in number, as there was a structural shift in the junk market in the late 1980s when these instruments started to have good pricing data. Please see Figure 4.9.

The returns are pretty constant until you get to the signature junk bonds, the Bs, and then it falls precipitously, and the Cs are even worse. Thus, the equity returns to firms with low financial strength are low, and their debt does not seem to compensate either. High risk, from a financial distress

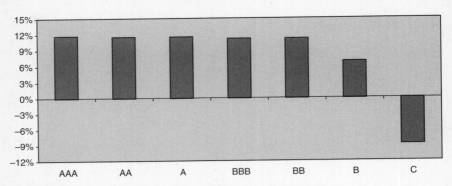

FIGURE 4.9   Annual U.S. Equity Stock Returns: 1988–2008
Source: Moody's, S&P, Compustat.

perspective, appears generally flat, but then for the highest default risk companies, a strong negative relation to returns for agency-rated companies. When combined with the flat returns for the highest default risk bonds, it seems that the expected return on risky firms—debt and equities—is net lower than for less risky firms.

SPORTS BOOKS

Bets on high probability–low payoff gambles have high expected value and low probability–high payoff gambles have low expected value. For example, a 1-to-10 horse having more than a 90 percent chance of winning has an expected value of about $1.03 (for every $1 bet), whereas a 100-to-1 horse has an expected value of about 14 cents per dollar invested.[36]

This bias has appeared across many years and across all sizes of race track betting pools. The effect of these biases is that for a given fixed amount of money bet, the expected return varies with the odds level. For bets on extreme favorites, there is a positive expected return. For all other bets, the expected return is negative. The favorite long-shot bias is monotone across odds and the drop in expected value is especially large for the lower probability horses.[37]

Interestingly, sports like baseball and hockey, where the favorite odds are rarely greater than four to one, show no such bias. It seems the bias arises only in the extreme odds that are prevalent in horse racing, but absent in most sports. That is, even a bad team has a one in four chance of winning in baseball, whereas a bad horse's chance will be more like 1 in 50. People appear to pay for an opportunity for positive skew, big payoffs, but this is not risk aversion, but rather risk-loving, and only for the extreme odds.

TOTAL VOLATILITY AND EXPECTED EQUITY INDEX RETURNS

Thus far we have looked mainly at cross-sectional risk and return. This is because it is often simpler to look at one asset class, such as equities, that presumably have a similar relevant risk factor. If we compare bonds and equities, or bonds and houses, the differences make relative ranking of risk difficult, because their returns have different distributions; their data sources are different. But there is another prominent manifestation of risk and return: a time series. The stock market has what is known as serially correlated volatility: high volatility months follow high volatility months, low volatility follows low volatility. Unlike stock returns, volatility of assets is very predictable: I can predict when assets will have higher volatility tomorrow. Of course it isn't perfect, but statistically, a big move in either direction today, implies a big move tomorrow.

The most basic risk models assume that the expected return on an asset is proportional to the expected nondiversifiable variance of the asset: the higher the variance, the higher the expected return. Modern models tend to focus on some abstract thing we don't like, like declines in consumption, wealth, or output, but those bad states are generally coincident with higher volatility, as volatility increases when the economy is doing poorly. And so what do we see? Some research documents a null relationship between volatility and future returns, and some find a negative relationship.[38]

Implied option volatilities are forward looking. They are market predictions of volatility, and thus, are true expectations. One may think these volatilities are biased, as they are driven by market supply and demand considerations, but if they were biased, it would be easy to make money arbitraging the difference by forming an arbitrage portfolio of the option and the underlying, and exploiting the difference. Indeed, in the late 1980s, many traders would buy yen options and hedge them with futures, because on average the implied volatilities were low. Please see Figure 4.10.

Using daily data from 1986 through 2007, I took all 5,300 observations from the VIX, which is a weighted measure of the implied volatility of liquid stock at the money put-and-call options. I then compared this to the stock market return over the next 12 months. I then grouped these observations into deciles based on implied volatility, and looked at the resulting average future stock returns. Figure 4.10 shows that there is definitely no positive correlation between expected volatility and future returns. If theory

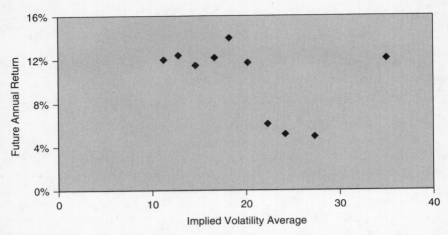

FIGURE 4.10 Implied Volatilities Are Not Correlated with Future Stock Index Returns S&P500 1986–2007. Data sorted into deciles by volatility

suggested the opposite, one would probably see papers suggesting that the pattern is significant, but because there's no theory for this, researchers don't make such interpretations.

Steve Sharpe and Gene Amromin actually looked at survey data, and found that investor expectations were totally inconsistent with this assumption.[39] They found that when investors have a more favorable assessment of macroeconomic conditions, they tend to expect higher returns. Second, they found that the expectation of more favorable economic conditions has a strong negative effect on expected stock market volatility. Another example is a Gallup poll put out by Paine Webber.[40] In 1998, at the beginning of the stock market boom, they surveyed an expected return of 13 percent from investors. After back-to-back 20 percent-plus returns, when the Nasdaq doubled, investors raised their expectations to 18 percent in February of 2000, right before the peak. Two years later, after a 50 percent correction, and a 50 percent rise in the VIX (a measure of expected volatilities), they anticipated only a 7 percent expected return. So from a Sharpe ratio perspective, when investors expect a high numerator, they expected a low denominator! Win-win. They expect good times to be high returns and low risk, and bad times to be low returns and high volatility. Investors do not see risk and return as a trade-off, but rather, as Warren Buffett has articulated, low risk means a good return for many investors, in that if you think an asset will rise 20 percent, as opposed to 10 percent, it has less risk of returning less than zero.

This flies in the face of the axiom that stock market returns should compensate investors for exposure to anticipated macroeconomic risks: when times look good, people expect good returns, and when times look bad, people expect bad returns. Intuitive at some level, but counter to theory that at some level, risk implies a higher expected return.

UNCERTAINTY AND RETURNS

Keynes's and Knight's writings on this have generated a lot of intuition and excitement because there is something profound about their idea that the risks we take are distinct from the risks in lotteries or roulette tables, with their explicit *a priori* odds, but they have not generated any concrete models in terms of risk conceptions that are priced. A recent attempt to apply this concept was Harvard economist Martin Weitzman, who uses some impressive mathematics to show that uncertainty in parameter estimates can explain the seemingly large equity risk premium.[41] While in practice the distribution of future growth rates has its mean and variance calibrated to past sample averages, Weitzman shows that proper Bayesian estimation of uncertain growth parameters adds an irreducible fat-tailed background layer of uncertainty that can explain the seemingly large equity risk premium. In effect, the 17 percent annualized volatility of the stock market *feels* two or three times that because of the fat tails implicit in a nonergodic process like the stock market.[42] But while this might get the equity risk premium into standard utility models, it also then implies that systematic volatility should be positively correlated with future aggregate returns using those same utility functions, which Figure 4.10 shows is not the case. That is, if uncertainty is positively correlated with volatility, which it almost certainly is, why is volatility, if anything, negatively correlated with returns across most assets? Why is aggregate volatility uncorrelated with future returns for an asset class like equities? Why is analyst disagreement *negatively* correlated with returns?

Differences of opinion should proxy for parameter uncertainty, a perhaps better estimate of risk.[43] Using analysts' earnings forecasts as a proxy for differences of opinion among investors, Karl Diether et al. (2002) find the quintile of stocks with the greatest opinion dispersions underperformed a portfolio of otherwise similar stocks.[44]

Each month, they take stocks and sort them into five groups based on size (market cap), and then within these groups, sort again into quintiles on the basis of analyst forecast dispersion, as measured by the ratio of the standard deviation of analyst current fiscal year annual earnings per share forecasts to the absolute value of the mean forecast. They find that the stocks with the higher dispersion in analysts' earnings forecasts earn significantly lower returns than otherwise similar stocks. Specifically, the highest dispersion group had a 9.5 percent annual return deficit over the 1980-to-2002 period.

Diether et al. note higher estimate dispersion is positively related to beta, volatility, and earnings variability, yet, because the returns go the wrong way (lower return for higher volatility), they note "our results clearly reject the notion that dispersion in forecasts can be viewed as a proxy of risk." Thus, in spite of being correlated with all things intuitively risky, like beta, volatility, and size, but uncorrelated with value or momentum, the correlation with returns proves it is not correlated with risk, because the one thing we know about risk is that it is positively correlated with returns.

IPOs

An initial public offering has a great deal of uncertainty, especially for an economist wishing to apply a factor sensitivity to it, because there is no time series. One usually applies a factor based on its characteristics, such as size, book or market, and perhaps industry. But without a track record, these assignments are highly uncertain in the Keynesian/Knightian/Ellsbergian sense. One would expect, given uncertainty aversion, for these stocks to have higher than average returns to compensate for this risk.

Jay Ritter at the University of Florida has a wonderful web site with data and articles on this issue going back 20 years.[45] These data ignore the first day increase, because this one-day pop is only available to insiders with access to IPOs at the issuance price, a favor usually doled out by the big brokerages to their favorite customers. You simply cannot buy an IPO at the issuance price unless you are already paying a brokerage a lot of money in commissions or have in some way "paid" them a favor, so the relevant return for investors is from the close of the first day of issuance is used. Examining IPOs from 1970 to 2008, the geometric annual average return for these IPOs five years after issuance are 3.7 percent below size-matched firms.[46] People who buy IPOs pay a premium, perhaps on the hope of buying the next Yahoo! or Google.

TRADING VOLUME

Another metric of disagreement is the amount of trading volume in a stock, normalized by its stock volume. A stock may turn over 50 percent of its stock a day, suggesting it is a useful factor proxy or there is a lot of disagreement about its prospects. On average, if disagreement leads to more buys and sells, we should see a higher return to these stocks. We do not, of course.

In the United States, since 1997, I created an index of stocks in the top 1,500 that had the highest trading volume, or shares, outstanding, every six months. The annualized geometric return for these high volume stocks was 1.6 percent, versus 9.7 percent for the low volume stocks.

VOLATILITY AS SHORTHAND FOR RISK

Introductory texts on risk and return, such as Brealey, Myers, and Allen's popular MBA finance textbook, give the following examples as *prima fascia* proof that risk generates return (Table 4.2).[47]

This is a typical overview, as Malkiel's *Random Walk down Wall Street* has a similar exposition. The implication, not mentioned explicitly but clearly implied, is that things that have higher volatility have higher risk, and *thus* higher returns. In Brealey, Myers, and Allen, the explanation is merely that "portfolio performance coincides with our intuitive risk ranking," though they do put the standard deviation numbers up there with the inevitable implication that risk and volatility are one and the same, or at the very least correlated. Malkiel mentions that higher returning stocks are "more variable."

As we saw in Chapter 3, the excess return generated by small stocks is a fact, but it is not clear in what sense it is risky. Small stocks have greater volatility and a greater beta than regular stocks, but volatility and beta are not measures of risk, because if they were, there would be a massive arbitrage opportunity in many areas where systematic and idiosyncratic volatility actually generates negative return premiums. As to the very short end of the yield curve, the very high quality corporate bonds, to the extent these are proof of risk begetting return, fail to generalize within their own asset class. More highly volatile bonds, either because of increased default risk, or duration, do not generate higher average returns when extrapolated

TABLE 4.2 Typical Misleading Presentation of Risk and Return

	Return	Volatility
Small Stocks	17.3%	33.4
Stocks	13.0	20.2
Corporate Bonds	6.0	8.7
Government Bonds	5.7%	9.4
T-bills	3.9%	3.2

Data from Brealey, Myers, and Allen's MBA finance textbook (p. 154).

to B-rated, or 30-year bonds. The authors seem to be aware of this: They very conspicuously avoid saying directly that risk is volatility, because they know risk is not volatility or beta *per se*. That these three prominent researchers are involved in this sort of deception suggests a massive amount of cognitive dissonance. The intuitive description of risk is volatility, and this describes Table 4.2 pretty well, but when you dig deep, you see academics running from volatility as a metric of risk like the plague, although they don't mind using it at the introductory level.

In the 1980s, you might see standard deviation and risk used inter-changeably, as this followed directly from the graphs generated in the con-struction of the CAPM, and the efficient frontier. Return was on the vertical axis, standard deviation on the other. But now researchers are aware that the CAPM is an empirical failure of the first order, and so, while the standard deviation (*vol*) is often used as shorthand for risk, serious researchers know this is not the measure of risk relevant to expected returns.

If one's education was unaware of utility functions, or Modern Port-folio Theory, one would have to look at these data and say that volatility is inversely correlated with returns. The theory that metrics of risk such as volatility or covariance is positively correlated with average returns fails spectacularly when applied to cross-sectional equities, movies, beta, devel-oping country equities, U.S. time-varying equity returns, gambling, lotteries, options, financial leverage, financial distress, currencies, mutual funds, small businesses, analyst forecast dispersion, IPOs, and futures. These are not minor lacunae, but the heart of the risk-return theory. As a first approxima-tion, volatility, distress, or covariance with the market should be generally positively correlated with returns if risk is to have any meaning in an asset pricing theory. As Richard Feynman stated: "It doesn't matter how beautiful your theory is, it doesn't matter how smart you are. If it doesn't agree with the experiment, it's wrong!"

CHAPTER 5

Investors Do Not Mind
Their Utility Functions

The concave utility function that is both necessary and sufficient for the risk premium has implications for more than mere asset returns. Most fundamentally, it has implications about behavior and happiness. For example, people should be minimizing risk when they can, and they should be happier when they have more money. But even in these dimensions, the theory has been known to fail miserably, yet this failure is often seen as immaterial. Yet, given the failure of the pricing implication, it is not as if we can ignore this failure, because it gives us further evidence to suggest the foundation is seriously flawed, as opposed to imperfect.

Economists are used to dealing with what appears to many as absurd assumptions, because they often don't matter. In Milton Friedman's essay, *The Methodology of Positive Economics* he explains that assumptions should be judged by their consequences alone.[1] He discusses the example of how the expert billiard player makes shots as if "he knew the complicated mathematical formulas that would give the optimum directions of travel, could estimate accurately by eye the angles, and so forth, describing the location of the balls, could make lightning calculations from the formulas, and could then make the balls travel in the direction indicated by the formulas. Our confidence in this hypothesis is not based on the belief that billiard players, even expert ones, can or do go through the process described." In sum, if the assumptions work in predicting things, good enough for scientists.

As the implications, the predictions, of the risk-return theory do not work in general, the assumptions are fair game for examination. That is, perhaps we have had a bad century, and should believe in the theory because, fundamentally, the assumption and logic are correct, only the empirical implications counterfactual. Surely someone intelligent, someone thinking ahead, should be biased toward the theory, not data, because we know theories only work on average, and perhaps our sample is not sufficiently large, or is biased. But, in face of bad evidence, an examination of the assumptions is appropriate. The common assumption that people are rational is often criticized because one can always find many examples of irrational behavior.

The assumption that people act as if they were rational generates lots of testable assumptions that seem to work: people buy more when prices are relatively low, and less when prices are relatively high, there are very few examples of arbitrage opportunities because others exploit them to make money, and so on. The alternative to rationality cannot be unspecified irrationality, but rather, a specific type of irrationality and here's where irrationality falters. Generally, irrationality deviates from rationality in an unbiased way, with just as many overconfident as timid, or those who underweight base-rate information versus those who overweight it. The burden is on those in favor of irrationality to show in what circumstances it is too much or too little.

Furthermore, heroic assumptions about zero transaction costs, no taxes, limitless borrowing, and perfect information, allow economists to isolate the main drivers of an idea by a model showing the bare logic of the theory presented, hopefully allowing one to test it, to identify how the violations of the theory cause deviations. A classic example is the Miller-Modigliani Theorem, which says that the debt-equity ratio does not affect the firm's value. In practice, the debt-equity ratio is very important for a company and everyone knew that, and so the Miller-Modigliani Theorem highlights the specific assumptions needed to generate this effect (often, asymmetric information, taxes, and so forth). Ideally, a model becomes not just a metaphor, but when parameterized, a realistic description of some interesting phenomena.

For these reasons, we can understand why the unrealistic assumptions of the CAPM, and the utility function that underlay it, were not seen as necessarily fatal. But the assumptions of the CAPM are truly in a class of their own. Sharpe's seminal paper on the CAPM that was to win him the Nobel Prize was initially rejected because of this very assumption. Dudley Luckett, the editor at the *Journal of Finance,* informed Sharpe that his assumption that all investors had the same expectations was so preposterous as to make his conclusions uninteresting. A new editor came in, and Sharpe's paper was published in 1964.[2]

Jason Zweig wrote a book about investing called *Your Money & Your Brain,* and he recounts a story about Harry Markowitz, who was then working at the RAND Corporation and trying to figure out how to allocate his retirement account. He knew what he should do: "I should have computed the historical covariances of the asset classes and drawn an efficient frontier." But, he said, "I visualized my grief if the stock market went way up and I wasn't in it—or if it went way down and I was completely in it. So I split my contributions fifty-fifty between stocks and bonds." So even the originator of the MPT did not follow its implications back in the day when he created the efficient frontier, and was thinking instead about his relative performance.

And how was it even possible for investors to know about all those betas (implicitly, the covariances)? Arbitrage was from buying 1.5 beta stocks and shorting 0.5 beta stocks, creating a zero-cost 1.0 beta portfolio. How could they do this if, in the days before computers, they didn't have the ability to calculate betas? Presumably they intuited the betas, on average, and the wisdom of crowds generates such insights. The concept of *emergence* is the paradoxical ability of a swarm to exhibit greater intelligence than the individuals that make it up. Emergent behavior is evident in several natural realms, including ant colonies, brain cells, and city neighborhoods. All these systems solve problems by drawing on masses of individually stupid elements, rather than a single, intelligent executive branch. Thus, the market is, in theory, a prominent emergent thing, created by a bunch of semi-smart, semi-stupid individuals, to create what is commonly referred to as a hypersmart individual, a representative, rational, agent creating arbitrage portfolios.

But in economics you find that when someone proves that something can exist, others take this as a license for assuming they do. Assumptions are not expected to be true, so as long as there exist some assumptions that work, that is good enough. Tractability of the modeling, the usefulness of the assumptions, is in practice more important than the realism of the assumptions.

Those are assumptions whose violations are curious, but hardly fatal, because it is plausible these deviations from theory do cancel out. However, these are not merely pricing implications for the MPT, but behavioral implications, and these fail massively. Most theories are designed to explain some particular thing, but if they are describing reality, there will be other implications. False theories are actually best figured out through these incidental implications, because usually the theory was created post hoc, so it will explain the data very well on one issue. The MPT as originally constructed was not a post hoc theory explaining the data, it predicted a relationship that was not obvious. Only after its failure was documented, did it morph into a series of parochial, ephemeral, risk factors under the rationalization of the general equilibrium approach.

Let us consider the main behavior failures one by one.

BEHAVIORAL VIOLATION 1: INVESTORS TRADE TOO MUCH

In theory, investors buy efficient portfolios, and adjust their weightings based on different preferences, wealth, and so on. They do not buy and sell stock based on bullish and bearish views on individual securities, because they all agree on the expected returns, and covariances, of those securities.

Thus, even those models that allow for asymmetries in information across traders, the volume of trade is mainly affected by unanticipated liquidity and portfolio rebalancing needs of investors. However, these motives would seem to be far too small to account for the tens of trillions of dollars of trade observed in the real world.[3] The turnover of a passive fund is around 10 percent a year—and passive funds are what investors should buy, according to standard theory. In contrast, the average annual turnover rate on the New York Stock Exchange is currently around 100 percent, which implies that people are not buying factor proxies and rebalancing as their risk preferences change, but rather, reading the news and trying to get in front, or out of the way, of the next big move. This dissonance has led even the most ardent defenders of the traditional pricing models to acknowledge that the bulk of volume must come from something else—for example, differences in prior beliefs that lead traders to disagree about the value of a stock even when they have access to the same information sets. Nonetheless, being off by a factor of 10 on trading volume suggests the canonical model is missing something fundamental.

BEHAVIORAL VIOLATION 2: TOO MANY FUNDS

In the CAPM, there is the One-Fund Separation Theorem, which states that everyone invests in the same risky portfolio, which is the market portfolio. From this fact, the linearity of return in beta is a function of arbitrage. For the APT, this argument is generalized to a handful of factors that are unspecified—maybe oil, the dollar, and so on. The driver is the same idea, that investors merely want access to a factor proxy. In contrast, there are *thousands* of funds available, and new ETFs, or stocks representing passive indexes, are created every day, 1,000 times as many as implied by theory. One could argue that there should be more than one fund for each factor on institutional grounds, that some marketing issues are important, but when theory says, "five" and reality says, "13,000," this is a material miss.

BEHAVIORAL VIOLATION 3: UNDERDIVERSIFICATION

William Goetzmann and Alok Kumar (2005) document extreme underdiversification among investors using more than 40,000 equity investment accounts.[4] More than 25 percent of investor portfolios contained only one stock; more than 50 percent of them contained fewer than three stocks. This is massively irrational nondiversification in the CAPM context, as people appear to be assuming diversifiable risk when they do not have to. From a Sharpe ratio perspective, this can only be justified if these investors generate large returns above the market, when in fact evidence suggests traders are, on average, worse than average.

Alternatively, one potential explanation for underdiversification is that investors may consciously choose to remain underdiversified so they can increase the likelihood of extreme positive returns, or in other words, to capture higher levels of positive skewness in their portfolios. If investors have a preference for skewness, they prefer positive skewness in return distributions. Diversification then is a two-edged sword: it eliminates undesired variance in return distributions, and also eliminates desired skewness. Consequently, portfolios that are efficient in a mean-variance-skewness framework only appear to be inefficient when evaluated using a mean-variance framework.

BEHAVIORAL VIOLATION 4: NO FUNDAMENTAL ANALYSIS

Asset pricing theories generally assume investors are all agreeing about returns on stocks, and no one is doing any fundamental analysis on cash flows. Eugene Fama says fundamental analysis is a waste, in that markets are pretty efficient, at least sufficiently so that merely reading about a firm's financial statements is useless, and given the lame results of analyst recommendations or mutual fund returns, this seems rather obvious. There are not any obvious examples where a group of investors are outperforming passive investors: mutual funds, retail trader, equity analysts, so when one argues that some investors pay for more information and therefore garner higher returns because of it, no one has identified such information, other than material trade secrets that are illegal in most markets. When asked for evidence that such professionals have value, one is usually greeted with anecdotes: Warren Buffett, Peter Lynch, and so on. But these anecdotes prove nothing; they are, at best, exceptions to the rule.

Theory and evidence argue for the futility of fundamental analysis, yet it flourishes. There is a large economy built on feeding the demand for fundamental analysis, and people spending time, money, and exposing themselves to idiosyncratic variance based on the idea that the more research you do, the more you listen to analysts discussing companies on TV, the more money you will make. Your average broker has a large set of tools and experts aimed at meeting this demand, which seems, in aggregate, irrational, because in aggregate there is no evidence that it delivers value.

BEHAVIORAL VIOLATION 5: BUY RECOMMENDATIONS EXCLUDE FIRMS WITH *MERELY* LOW RISK

In the CAPM world there should be many situations in which a lower-than-average-risk stock will be expected to outperform on a risk-adjusted basis, but not an absolute basis, yet you will never see a brokerage tout a buy or strong buy recommendation that has a lower-than-average market return.[5] If people are simply maximizing their *risk-adjusted* returns, why are there *never* any recommended stocks that are expected to underperform the market, though at sufficiently low risk to be attractive? If we go outside of brokerages, the less-sophisticated Internet touts of bizarre investment schemes all have one common characteristic: They all promise greater-than-average returns. That lower-than-average return recommendations are absent suggests people only take risk if they expect an absolute greater-than-average return, which would seem to exclude half of all assets.

BEHAVIORAL VIOLATION 6: AGENTS DO NOT AGREE

The assumption that agents agree on asset return, variances, and covariances, is rather absurd, and indeed, was why Sharpe's initial submission of what was to be called the CAPM was rejected. But for some reason this did not seem a big deal after a while. Rubinstein's Aggregation Theorem, in 1974, outlined the assumptions necessary to represent the economy as a single representative agent. It is common to model the consumer for the United States as a single person, which makes models tractable. The assumptions necessary for this, however, are rather severe. In essence, Rubinstein says that if everyone has the same beliefs and preferences, wealth, patience, and there are complete markets, you can caricaturize them as a single person. The CAPM assumes investors have identical beliefs, too. While this can get very technical, at some level it is rather obvious: If everyone is the same, you can model an economy as a large, single person.

But in practice this is quite obviously violated, as disagreements on stock prospects are a staple of financial journalism. Wealth and preferences, also, are quite different from person to person. Ed Miller postulated a simple idea, that if we prohibit short selling, then the greater the disagreement for a particular stock, the greater the price. This is because if you assume expectations are normally distributed around a mean, the greater dispersion means the most optimistic will be very optimistic, and these optimists will set the price. That is, say there is an asset with a mean price of 100, but people have a distribution of standard deviation of 10 points around that. If the top 15 percent set the price, its price is 115. But if the standard deviation is 20, the top 15 percent would set a price of 130. This higher price means a lower future return, so several researchers have looked at opinion dispersion to predict returns using that as a model, but its success has been disappointing.

Several researchers have recently used the Miller model to motivate using opinion dispersion, or even raw uncertainty, as explaining returns, especially in empirical examinations of the effect of analyst disagreement and returns. The key is that models can be very elegant and consistent, but inevitably they have extremely unrealistic assumptions—like the CAPM or general equilibrium models with a representative agent, or they can be rather ad hoc, such as Miller's, which are more intuitive but less rigorous.[6] The problem is that economics has big problems modeling different beliefs, because under standard assumptions, it is irrational to agree to disagree. Of course, if the Miller model worked, it would bring forth many troublesome implications because disagreement measures are generally correlated with volatility, so it would imply that higher volatility is correlated with lower returns. But, leading researchers invoke the Miller hypothesis because it seems to explain a rather obvious pattern, that highly volatile assets have lower returns than average. Economics likes rigor, but over time, a simple story like Miller's, inconsistency with standard theory notwithstanding, will be accepted if it works.

BEHAVIORAL VIOLATION 7: THE HOME BIAS

One of the easier ways to reduce portfolio volatility is to invest in more than one's own home country. Further, if covariance between the market portfolio and aggregate consumption growth are correlated in a particular country, the move to other countries would reduce this correlation as well. It has long been known that, despite the gains from cross-border diversification and the increased integration of financial markets worldwide, the strong investor preference for domestic firms is pervasive in international financial markets. This home bias phenomenon is ubiquitous across developed and developing markets, that is, worldwide. In a more recent study based on worldwide equity fund holdings data in 1999 and 2000, Chan, Covrig, and Ng (2005)[7] document the existence of home bias in every single country in their sample of 48 countries around the world. Plausible explanations for the investor strong preference for domestic equities include the existence of cross-border boundaries that give rise to exchange rate risk, variation in regulation, taxation, accounting standards, corporate governance, and transaction costs, among others, information asymmetries, and more recently, investor behavioral factors (familiarity, culture, language, and geographic proximity).

THE ROTTEN CORE: THE UTILITY FUNCTION

The genesis of the risk premium is based on the standard utility function, which is concave in wealth, broadly defined. It generates some reasonable implications, in that faced with a random payout worth $50 on average, most people prefer the average value, the $50. But clearly, this should imply volatility of some nature would be positively correlated with returns, and here the theory fails. Economists postulate that people maximize utility and that utility is whatever people like "Consumer's market behavior is explained in terms of preferences, which in turn are defined only by behavior."[8] Thus, considering the behavior and pricing anomalies discussed earlier, this suggests something is wrong. Looking further at utility, we see this might be the basis of our problem.

ABSURD EXTRAPOLATIONS

Matthew Rabin of the University of California at Berkeley notes that a consumer who from any initial wealth level turns down gambles where she loses $100 or gains $110, each with 50 percent probability will turn down 50-50 bets of losing $1,000 or gaining any sum of money. Mathematically, you can extrapolate this using the pure logic from the concavity of a utility function that generates this property, to find that this implies you would reject an offer to gain $1 billion dollars and lose $1,000. Any utility function that is strictly concave, that would imply you do not like modest gambles, implies that you are extremely averse to really favorable gambles with 10 times the exposure—in other words, an absurdity.[9]

The major solution to the problem is the one proposed by Prospect Theory, where outcomes are considered relative to a reference point (usually the status quo), rather than to consider only the final wealth. This theory was championed by Nobel Prize winners Kahneman and Tversky in 1979.[10] The essence of the approach is to put a strange wiggle in utility curves right around the current wealth level. Please see Figure 5.1.

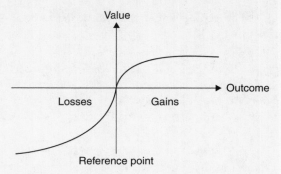

FIGURE 5.1   The Utility Function in Prospect Theory

The utility curve tries to capture three stylized facts:

1. Risk-averse behavior in gains (concave for right-hand side)
2. Risk-loving toward losses (convex for left-hand side)
3. Enjoy gains less than dislike of losses

This is an explanation for the fact that people simultaneously buy lottery tickets and insurance, but still their invest money conservatively. Lottery tickets are small average losses, and people are risk seeking here. Insurance is against big losses, and people are very risk averse here. Gains are also treated with moderate risk aversion. Indeed, Milton Friedman and Leonard Savage wrote about the first two points back in 1948, trying to explain why people buy lottery tickets, and also insurance, but noting the utility curve had an inflection point that allowed gambling, basically, the utility curve discussed earlier.

The main observation of Prospect Theory is that people tend to think of possible outcomes relative to a reference point rather than absolute wealth, a phenomenon which is called a framing effect. What affects the reference point? Researchers have suggested many things related to a person's recent history or the cross-sectional averages. When losses are looked at differently from gains, but only for certain-sized bets, theory begins to look more like an explanation of various choices—sometimes risk seeking, sometimes risk averse, depending on the data.

In 1952, Harry Markowitz tried to build on the Friedman-Savage model with a thrice-inflected utility of wealth function and argued that whenever an individual's wealth was at its customary level, it would be at the second inflection point.[11] The problem with the Markowitz model was well explained by Alchian in 1953:

> *Markowitz recognized that until an unambiguous procedure is discovered for determining when and to what extent current income deviated from customary income, the hypothesis will remain nonverifiable because it is not capable of denying any observed behavior.*

It is not clear at all how to make a general equilibrium model, where everyone has a quirky utility functions, some risk averse, some risk seeking, depending on whether they are buying or selling the bet in question. Since Kahneman received his Nobel Prize in 2002, many have noted the potential for behavioral finance to explain anomalies because it encompasses real people, who are often irrational, as opposed to *homo economicus*. The problem, however, is an embarrassment of riches. By allowing people to selectively apply risk aversion or risk seeking, by way of prospect theory, and various reference points therein, the "risk must be compensated by return" story clearly is qualified to a degree that makes it unrecognizable.

Way back in 1951, Nobel laureate George Stigler noted "each decade, for the past nine or ten decades, economists have read widely in the then-current psychological literature. These explorers have published their findings, and others in the field have found them wanting—wanting in useful hypotheses about economic behavior."[12] And so it is with behavioral finance, which attempts to apply, selectively, risk loving and risk aversion, or anchoring and extrapolation, at various problems. The problem with this general approach is like the problems with specific non-normal distributions: they explain too much, because they predict biases exist in opposite directions, depending on the data. As Eugene Fama notes in his essay *Market Efficiency, Long-Term Returns, and Market Efficiency,* in an efficient market, deviations from efficiency will be half overreaction, half underreaction, which is about what the behavioralists have applied to finance. While I agree that the current paradigm is flawed, an alternative must be somewhat specific.

EASTERLIN'S PARADOX

The fundamental assumption of risk aversion is a concave utility function over more wealth. Increases in wealth increase our utility (aka happiness, or satisfaction) though at lower rates the higher it goes. Concavity of utility is a necessary and sufficient condition for risk aversion, and thus, risk premiums: risk should beget an additional return. This basic assumption is challenged by the well documented finding that while in any given society the rich are, on average, happier than the poor, the trend in individual happiness is more or less flat once society passes a threshold of perhaps $20,000.

Richard Easterlin's original work in this area, published in 1974, discovered what is now known at the Easterlin Paradox: as economic wealth doubled after World War II in the United States, surveyed happiness was the same.[13] Initially, this reality was thought to apply only to developed countries, but recent research suggests that the paradox holds true for a large sample of much poorer countries as well. In both cases, wealthier people are, on average, happier than poor people are *within* the same country. *Across* countries or over time, however, there is a very weak correlation—if any—between average income levels and happiness.

Happiness data consists primarily of responses to a survey in which people are asked "In general, how happy would you say that you are—very happy, fairly happy, or not very happy?" Using self-reports to measure happiness immediately raises the question of comparability. But generally most people's concerns are about making a living and matters of family life, and these concerns seem about as pressing as they have always been. In a detailed analysis of data from 45 surveys covering data from 1950 through 1977 in the United States, happiness is basically unchanged over time. Local area surveys yield similar results; for example, a study of the Detroit area reports that there was no change in satisfaction among Detroit-area wives between 1955 and 1971 even though median family income rose 40 percent.[14]

Trends in life satisfaction in nine European countries from 1973 to 1989 are much like that for happiness in the United States. Satisfaction drifts upward in some countries and downward in others. The overall pattern shows little or no trend in a period when real GDP per capita rose between 25 and 50 percent.[15]

Japan provides the most stark data point. Between 1958 and 1987 real per capita income in Japan multiplied fivefold. Washing machines, refrigerators, and television sets went from being extremely rare to universal, and car ownership soared from 1 to 60 percent of the people. And just like in the West, there was no improvement in average subjective well-being. The utility function implied by this fact is clearly not increasing in wealth.[16]

But that is merely the past 50 years. Utility functions are even more absurd in light of what has happened since Adam Smith created economics as a discipline.

The increase in wealth in the past century raises some very fundamental question about assuming that utility is a function of absolute wealth. In the nineteenth century, life was comparatively nasty, brutish, and short. People existed on about 1,000 fewer calories per day than today in the West, and so your average person was a runt: about 10 centimeters shorter than today in Western countries, and about 50 percent lighter in weight. Malnutrition was a fact of life, as deficiencies in niacin, thiamine, vitamin D, which were common and not understood, led to higher rates of chronic conditions that not only increased mortality but affected the quality of life. People had higher rates of diarrhea, heart disease, and circulatory problems, among other inconveniences.[17]

In 1880, the average worker worked 64 hours a week, with seven holidays. In 1995, the average workweek was about 37 hours a week, with 28 vacation days. Real GDP per capita was $5,000 in the United States in 1900, and about seven times higher, $37,000, in 2007. But this actually understates our wealth increase, because things like computers, the Internet, videos, and e-mail are all available to us now, and would have been simply inconceivable to our great-great grandparents. Clean water, available publicly everywhere, and ubiquitous air conditioning, are things we take for granted. We are all very rich in the context of human history, yet while reading a nineteenth-century novel, I feel like people then had the same concerns, anxieties, and happiness that I feel now. I do not feel like a very rich man reading about impoverished people, which, in a pure logic of my material comfort and options available, I objectively am.

Furthermore, it should be noted that while inequality persists, today's poor have benefited far more than the rich. The typical home owned by the poor is a three-bedroom house with one-and-a-half baths. Some 73 percent of poor households own a car or truck; nearly a third own two or more cars or trucks. Eighty percent have air conditioning; by contrast, in 1970, only 36 percent of the general U.S. population had air conditioning. Nearly 9 in 10 poor households own microwave ovens; more than a third have automatic dishwashers. Back in Napoleonic times, the poor were about five inches shorter than those in the leisure class—today the heights are almost equal.[18]

Poor households are well equipped with modern entertainment technology. Nearly all poor households have color TVs, but more than half actually own two or more color televisions. One-quarter own large-screen televisions, 78 percent have a VCR or DVD player, and almost two-thirds have cable or satellite TV reception. Needless to say, even the rich of 100 years ago did not have these conveniences. The fact that obesity is more common among the poor basically tells the story: Poverty is not what it used to be.

We always think we are a 20 percent increase in wealth away from true happiness, but that is because we define happiness relative to a moving target. Like our definition of what is warm is a function of what we are used to—Minnesotans would find 40 degrees warm in January while in

Florida it would be considered cold—happiness is generally a function of what we are used to, though, at the extremes this clearly breaks down (just as −20 degrees is considered cold to both Minnesotans and Floridians). Thus the paradox of flat happiness in the face of rising wealth is explained as ever increasing aspirations. The idea that there is a paradox inherent in the drive for affluence is one of the key arguments for contemporary skeptics on economic growth. Many of the most influential books on the topic even have the word in their titles. In the past decade there has been Gregg Easterbrook's *The Progress Paradox,* David Myers's *The American Paradox,* and Barry Schwartz's *The Paradox of Choice.* In Richard Layard's *Happiness: Lessons from a New Science,* the opening paragraph states, "There is a paradox at the heart of our lives. Most people want more income and strive for it. Yet as Western societies have got richer, their people have become no happier."

A measurement issue is that, if you look cross-sectionally at status and happiness, those with higher-than-average status will be happier than those with lower-than-average status. But there is a bias to this reporting, because at any one time, those with higher-than-average status will have recently experienced positive shocks to their status, and so the short-run effect can be conflated with the relative position, so the empirical issue is whether happiness is more affected by recent gains in wealth (habituation) or the mere relative status.

Evidence in favor of the relative-to-consensus theory comes from several sources, and is considered to be greater than the habituation. A novel paper dealing with social comparisons is Knight, Song and Gunatilaka (2008).[19] This paper appeals to cross-sectional information on 9,200 households in China, and thus refers to an economy that is very different from the Europe–North America nexus that has dominated the literature. The authors are not only able to identify which villages their respondents came from, but also confirm that 70 percent of individuals indeed saw their village as their reference group by simply asking them to whom they compare themselves, making their rural sample well-suited to the question of how important reference groups really are. Controlling for their own income and for village income, those respondents who said that their income was much higher than the village average reported much higher levels of happiness than those who said their income was much below the village average. Relative income was the most important right-hand-side variable.

Another result comes from surveys of hypothetical questions. *Homo economicus* should care about his absolute income independent of others. But given a choice between two hypothetical worlds, one in which he earns $100,000 a year in perpetuity while others earned $90,000, and another world in which he would earn $110,000 while others earned $200,000, almost everyone prefers the world which is, in aggregate, poorer, because they would be relatively richer.[20] Or to take a more tangible example, as anyone with children can attest, one sure way to make Son One throw a fit, is to let Son Two watch TV and not let Son One. If you do not let either watch TV, there will be much less unhappiness, but kids are hypersensitive to their relative privileges.

In general, researchers find that relative income matters more than absolute income.[21] That is, quantitatively, changes in relative income have much larger effects on happiness than do changes in absolute income.

SUMMARY

It is not merely the risk-return implications of the risk-return theory that are violated, but other implications of the utility function that generates this result. This implication that people should merely buy the market in various degrees of leverage has always been known to be wrong as a description of the typical investor, who often buys highly undiversified portfolios based on reading about company fundamentals and cash flows, a futile gesture that is costly, time consuming, and generates excessive volatility. The implication that people's happiness is a concave positive function of wealth is not merely a prediction, but an assumption of this work and it too is empirically violated. This is often waived away by the notice that even though there is a lot of irrational activity, the market is pretty efficient, and so, the behavioral anomalies cancel out with respect to pricing (and thus returns).

Regardless of the market anomalies presented in the data, it is also clear that it is not easy to become rich in the market, and so on that basis, the rational expectations assumption thrives. The failed assumptions in the risk premium framework have no compensating empirical successes. To fix the theory of risk, one needs to fix the utility function.

CHAPTER 6

Is The Equity Risk Premium Zero?

The equity premium, which is the average return to stocks over Treasury bills, has appeared to be about 6 percent in the United States over the past century. This number is too big for theory according to the standard utility functions, and there are many papers produced each year trying to solve this puzzle. The excessive risk premium is in contrast to the lack of any equity premium one finds *within* equities or anywhere else, in that here we see too high a risk premium, where almost everywhere else we see none, if not a negative premium. Thus, it is a somewhat comforting puzzle for financial researchers: Here is a price of risk that makes some intuitive sense, even if too high, and it applies to the signature risk asset in the economy, the stock market.

I argue that the equity risk premium is like the Beardstown Ladies' putative investment success. The women had claimed that their investment club had earned an average annual return of 23.4 percent from 1984 to 1994, and published five folksy books that mingled recipes like five-hour stew with investment tips. In 1998, an article in Chicago magazine asserted that the group's stated returns had included the new investments made by its members, and that when computed in conventional fashion, their annual rate of return was actually 9.1 percent, well below the 17.2 percent return of the aggregate market over the same period. Such are the vagaries of investing, as all sorts of biases inflate returns, and the source of returns usually has little incentive in meticulously adding up all those expenses, because for many the psychic benefits of thinking they are outperforming the indexes is worth a couple percent a year in actual returns.

To recap the equity premium puzzle, in 1985 Mehra and Prescott documented that for any value of the preference parameters that generate an expected real return to Treasury bills of less than 4 percent (very likely), the risk premium is less than 0.35 percent annually.[1] Given standard estimates of consumption volatility and growth, 0.35 percent is, in practice, empirically indistinguishable from zero percent, so my assertion that the equity risk premium is zero is really not so radical as a mere numerical estimate, in that the common observation that the equity premium is 6.0 percent is about as many standard deviations from my null hypothesis, as the standard null hypothesis is within Mehra and Prescott and their considerable legacy. But there is a major difference, in that those working within the standard approach seek a solution, a revised theoretical estimate, within the system that rises to something intuitive like 3 to 6 percent, whereas my approach argues no hope for raising the real expected risk premium.

This equity premium was my main block, why I could not explain the simultaneous absence of a risk premium within equities and an equity risk premium. A free lunch seemed to exist, whereby one could get beta returns simply by going long a 0.5 beta stock, shorting a 1.5 beta stock, generating a beta of negative 1, which since 1962 has generated a zero return. Thus if we add this position to one long the market, which has a beta of 1, you have a market return at zero beta! If the equity premium is positive, you make positive expected return at zero risk. Why wouldn't everyone do this? Well, maybe they should, but there are many slips between cup and lip.

Mehra and Prescott's seminal paper on the equity premium puzzle estimated a U.S. risk premium of 6.2 percent using 1889–1978 U.S. data. The 1996 edition of the popular Brealey, Myers, and Allen finance textbook presented an 8.4 percent risk premium, but by 2001 Ivo Welch surveyed academic financial economists and found the average equity premium was 7.0 percent in 2000, and 5.5 percent in 2001. In 2002, the American Institute for Management and Research sponsored a forum on the equity risk premium with several well-known researchers of this issue, and those offering a forward-looking premium generally estimated a mean of 3.0 percent.[2] This is in line with the real-model generated estimates of Fama-French (2002) and Blanchard (1993), of around 3.5 percent. As the top-line return on the S&P500 was basically zero from August 1998 through January 2009, the equity return premium is sure to be revised downward by this group yet again. Thus, in the past 20 years the equity premium has been cut in half, and so my proposal that it is actually zero is in line with previous adjustments in this number.

The specific drivers that would lead us to zero are several, and to my knowledge no empirical researcher has addressed all of them simultaneously, making them highly probable in theory. But my interest in this adjustment is highly influenced by personal experience. In 1987, the Friday before Black Monday, in my first securities purchase ever, I bought a put on the most out-of-the-money put option I could find on the S&P100 index. I had noted that interest rates were climbing, and the Fed was staying tough, trying to defend the dollar, and after listening to Hyman Minsky keep telling me that we are always on the brink of a market collapse, especially when the Fed is tightening, I figured it was a good investment. After the biggest 1-day drop in history, my insanely fortunate market timing had turned my $3,000 nest egg into $44,000. I was rich! I then imagined using my investing savvy to become independently wealthy right away.

I figured, big picture calls were good, but I could make them even better by looking at individual stocks, where presumably there is even more inefficiency.[3] So I bought Value-Line's listing of stocks, which ranked them from one to five. I then figured, since the Fed had eased, following Minsky logic, no Depression, in fact, the market should rebound. I then put all my money into out-of-the-money calls. The problem was, I was taxed about 40 percent on my windfall, so I had only $25,000 left the next year. I proceeded to buy calls on individual stocks, and even as the general market rose 27 percent in 1988, I lost most of the money left, primarily crossing the bid-ask spread in these illiquid equity option transactions. The market makers in the equity option pits skinned me alive, as I would buy a call for $1^3/_4$ and sell it for $1^1/_4$ (they quoted in fourths then), a round trip that over time guaranteed failure. The net effect of taxes and transaction costs through a naïve understanding of trade execution, gave me close to a cumulative zero percent return, even though my big picture forecast was spot on during the most extreme event in stock market history, and my arithmetic return was still well over 500 percent.

I had a large amount of good fortune in that span, but still generated a modest return. Yet, such costs are rarely mentioned, let alone prioritized. Ignoring these issues seemed like, well, looking at your pre-tax top line revenue as if it were money in the bank.

GEOMETRIC VERSUS ARITHMETIC AVERAGING

Remember, the size effect, initially, was found to be on the order of 20 percent between the smallest and largest stocks using daily data. Yet, it was quickly discovered that if you merely used monthly data, that then cumulated the returns as they bounced up 100 percent and down 50 percent every day, cutting this effect by more than half.[4] De Bondt and Thaler prominently discovered that stocks tended to mean-revert, using the past three years' return as the explanatory variable.[5] Yet, the past three years' losers invariably had such low prices, the difference between the arithmetic and geometric average explained this result.[6] Finally, it should be noted that the infamous hedge fund Long-Term Capital Management had an arithmetic annual return of slightly above zero in their four-year existence, but they are widely noted as a failure, more consistent with their −93 percent cumulative return, or a −47 percent geometric annual average.[7] All numbers are correct, but the geometric is clearly more meaningful.

It has already been mentioned that the geometric average return is the buy-and-hold return, where the arithmetic average assumes one rebalances a portfolio at the frequency of the return data. Thus, the common use of monthly returns is an overstatement to the extent monthly returns are used to present data. Since stock index returns have an annual standard deviation of about 20 percent internationally, the predicted difference is variance divided by two, which in this case would be $0.2^2/2 = 0.02$, or 2 percent.

This closely matches the difference in the geometric versus arithmetic return internationally over the past 100 years as documented by Dimson et al. (2006), a 2 percent reduction for geometric averaging.[8] This is a lower bound, because as most investors are highly undiversified—they do not invest, their volatility is at least 50 percent higher, implying a 4.5 percent adjustment.

SURVIVORSHIP BIAS

There is a bias of using one of the most diversified and successful equity markets in the world, the United States, where most of the leading financial academics work. Brown, Goetzmann, and Ross (1995) claim that survival of the series imparts a bias to ex post returns.[9] For example, in countries such as Czechoslovakia, Hungary, Poland, Russia, and China equity investors at some point lost 100 percent of their equity investment, a data point that significantly affects geometric averages. They show that an ex ante equity premium of zero can generate a high ex post positive premium by simply conditioning upon the market surviving an absorbing lower bound over the course of a century.

Jorion and Goetzmann (1999) address this issue by expanding the sample by collecting additional cross-sectional data.[10] Using real return data for 39 countries over much of the twentieth century, they include not only markets that survived, but also those that experienced both temporary and permanent interruptions. This approach generates a reduction in the risk premium of 350 basis points compared to using the U.S. time series alone.

A different look at similar data gives a very different answer, however. Dimson, Staunton, and Marsh (2006) estimate the survivorship bias by looking at the entire world portfolio and value-weight the returns by country. This approach generates an estimate around 20 basis points because the size of the better-performing countries was generally larger, and the average of annual returns across the world is less volatile, and thus has a higher geometric mean than the averages of more highly variable time-series returns for individual countries. Thus, survivorship bias can be interpreted as trivial or large, depending on whether one thinks we should consider each country as a data point with equal weight (3 percent), or look at the globe as a giant market portfolio (0.2 percent); whether we equal weight, or value weight the world portfolios. Reasonable people can disagree as to which adjustment is most appropriate, generating a meaningfully different estimate looking at the same data.

PESO PROBLEMS

The Peso problem is related to survivorship bias, but different because it tries to address the estimate of the probability of a large collapse by merely calibrating the probability of such a collapse that would explain the equity premium of, say, 3 percent. It turns out that this probability need only be very small, so small it is quite probable that it would not be observed in sample. Rietz (1998) calls this a "Peso problem" in that it represents a small probability of a large catastrophe, like when the Mexican peso fell 75 percent in 1982, and caught most investors completely off guard.[11] If a market has a 2 percent chance annually of falling 75 percent, you might not see this in a century, but it affects your geometric expected return by 3.13 percent. If you looked at the historical price variability of the peso, this was a statistical improbability so small as to be inconceivable, but such are the real-life vagaries of financial time-series, the fat tails. Major disruptions have afflicted nearly all the markets in their sample, with the conspicuous exception of the United States, which is often used to represent the market.

This approach relies on small probability events that make it difficult to quantify, however, and an assumption about whether catastrophe generally involves debt and equity going to zero (as in Russia), or just equity generating severe declines as in the Great Depression (see Mehra and Prescott [1988]).[12] Robert Barro (2006) argues a correct probability of a significant catastrophe explains much of the equity premium, about 300 basis points.[13] When you are arguing about events that are expected to happen once every 100 years, given our limited data, you can expect they are somewhat irrefutable, and thus also somewhat unconvincing, because one can't prove that an actual 1-in-100 year event should be considered a 1-in-200 year event, or a 1-in-50 year event, though the difference is material.

ONE-TIME EFFECT OF AN ANOMALOUS POST-DEPRESSION PERIOD

A significant portion of the previous century was due to an increase in valuation ratios that cannot be expected to repeat. For example, if a 10-year bond moves from a 10 percent yield to a 5 percent yield in one year, it will generate a significant price appreciation and thus a greater-than-10 percent return. Prospectively, however, the yield is diminished to 5 percent, and its historical one-year return is clearly a bias of its future expected return. The post–World War II U.S. period dominates the data. In the 1930-to-1955 period with the Great Depression, World War II, and the fear of another great depression, the survival of the capitalistic system was in doubt, and by 2000 these fears were largely gone. The dividend yield (dividend divided by the price) was 7.18 percent in 1951, and only 1.2 percent in 2000.[14]

Using fundamentals to estimate expected stock returns can get around this bias. That is, one can assume the return on stocks is from the dividend yield, and growth in the dividend. This gets around issues of expected capital gains from reductions in the equity premium that could be biased in our post–World War II sample. This approach generates forward-looking returns around 3.5 percent lower than what is in the historical twentieth-century data for an equity premium.[15]

ASYMMETRIC TAX EFFECTS

In the United States, the average long-term capital gain tax rate has been around 25 percent, while short-term tax rates are then just like one's marginal tax rates, and the top marginal tax rates in the United States since 1926 has been around 60 percent.

Investors care about their after-tax return, not pretax, and this is relevant because the tax rate will compress an equity premium. That is, consider a risk-free rate of 5 percent, and an equity return of 11 percent. At a tax rate of 40 percent, the risk-free rate becomes 3 percent and the equity return 6.6 percent, reducing the equity premium from 6 percent to 3.6 percent.

Different countries have different policies, and they generally change a lot over time, so that it is difficult to generalize as to what tax regime the average investor faced in the twentieth century. Furthermore, the demographics of the marginal investor, be he the middle-income investor to whom the tax-loss carry-forward is significant, or the large investor for whom the tax-loss carry-forward is irrelevant, is unclear. Lastly, the volatility of one's investment strategy is relevant, because if you invest in a risk-free asset, you can ignore the asymmetries between gains and losses, whereas if the volatility is sufficiently large, proportionately more of the upside goes to the government (you do not get a rebate check for your investment losses).

Given the multidimensional matrix of inputs changing over time, we can only estimate the average effect of taxes on the after-tax return. Jeremy Siegel differentiates between long-term and short-term gains, and the differing tax rate on dividends.[16] He assumes a very modest 5 percent average annual turnover, which I find extremely conservative, given that the average mutual fund has a 100 percent turnover. He calculates that from 1926 through 1997, taxes reduced the equity premium above U.S. Treasury bonds from 5.2 percent to 4.0 percent for the top bracket, and 4.7 percent for the lowest tax bracket, which is a reduction of 0.5 percent to 1.2 percent from the pretax equity premium.

Niall Gannon and Michael Blum modeled the after-tax returns more meticulously. They modeled a portfolio that began in 1961 and saw identical returns to the S&P 500 Index, and assumed a 20 percent annual turnover, on which it paid long-term capital gains tax at the highest rate.[17] The model portfolio also received annual dividends, based on the dividend yield of the index, on which it paid taxes at the highest rate. This generated a 6.72 percent annual return, a 5.28 percent reduction compared to the CRSP NYSE-AMEX market-weighted index as calculated by Kenneth French. During the same time period studied, the Long-Term Municipal Bond Buyer Index had a straight-line average return of 6.14 percent, with about one-third the volatility. That is, the equity premium was reduced to 58 basis points by taxes.

The interesting point here is that this assumed a 20 percent annual turnover. The average stock with a market cap over $100 million trades at about a 200 percent turnover. Now, some of this is by programs, and so a short-timer with a 1,000 percent turnover, averaged with a long-term investor with a 10 percent turnover, averages out to a 55 percent average annual turnover over investors, because the short-term investor will max out his capital gains. Odean and Barber (2000) find that the average individual retail investor turns over his portfolio 60 percent each year.[18] Furthermore, as most equity investors are undiversified, their volatility will be higher than the market, leading to greater losses. Thus, I think Siegel is a lower bound for the marginal retail investor.

MARKET TIMING

In analyzing the returns of stock investors from 1950 to 2002, researchers typically refer to an average buy-and-hold return for some widely used stock index like the Standard and Poor's 500. But consider a different measure of returns, one that weights time periods by how much money was at work. That is, suppose you have a stock that goes from a price of 100, to 200, to 100. The geometric average return is 0 ([(1 + 100%)(1 − 50%)]² − 1 = 0), which makes sense because we started at 100 and ended at 100. But think of an investor buying one share each period. He makes 100 percent on his $100 investment in Period One, but then loses 50 percent on $200 new investment in Period Two, and loses 50 percent on the 100 percent he invested initially. This strategy basically buys too much when the market is high, and too little when the market is low. To the extent market inflows tend to crowd around market peaks, the average return experienced by investors will be less than if we equal weight the periods.

The Internal Rate of Return is defined as the number that when applied to a bunch of cash flows, makes the sum equal zero. In general:

$$NPV = \sum_{t=0}^{N} \frac{C_t}{(1 + r)^t} = 0$$

So in this example, we have

$$-100 - 200(1 + r)^{-1} + 200(1 + r)^{-2} = 0$$

Solving for r, you get −27 percent. Thus, if people tend to invest more after a cycle has run its course, and less after a cycle has run through a significant drawback, this suggests this adjustment will lower the estimated return to investors (as opposed to the return to stocks). To the extent one tends to invest at peaks, dollar cost averaging is a useful discipline to avoid this problem, because by putting in a fixed dollar amount each period, you avoid bunching up your investments around periods that have, historically, been investment peaks. If you invest a fixed amount of dollars per year, you avoid the bias. Unfortunately, people do not invest that way in practice.

We know that equity capital tends to flow into the market after superior past returns and preceding poor future returns (Tim Loughran and Jay R. Ritter, 1995; Malcolm Baker and Jeffrey Wurgler, 2000) and the reverse holds for equity outflows (David Ikenberry et al., 1995).[19] Thus it should be no surprise to learn that when you adjust for the inflows and outflows, the return estimated for investors is significantly less than for stock indexes.

Ilia Dichev performed empirical tests concentrated on aggregate national-market specifications to provide a comprehensive investigation of dollar-weighting effects in the United States and around the world over the full available history of stock returns.[20] The results revealed that dollar-weighted returns are systematically lower than buy-and-hold returns. The return differential is 1.3 percent for the NYSE/AMEX market over the 1926-to-2002 period, 5.3 percent for Nasdaq over the 1973-to-2002 period, and an average of 1.5 percent for 19 major international stock markets over the 1973-to-2004 period, all highly statistically significant.

TRANSACTION COSTS

Transaction costs include commissions, bid-ask spread, and trade impact. There is a tradeoff whereby small traders with low trade impact generally have higher commissions, and always cross the bid-ask spread to transact, buying at the ask, and selling at the bid. Large institutions, meanwhile, get volume discounts on their commissions, and have the incentive to invest in systems and personnel that trade in a more patient manner. Algorithmic trading optimizes the size, frequency, and limit order specifications, currently done through a computer-based execution of equity orders by way of direct market-access channels, and these strategies can be optimized through extensive trial-and-error.[21] However, as the institutions generally trade large size, their trade impact—actually moving prices by their volume—is much greater than for individuals. Thus, for both small and large investors, there are unavoidable costs in trading stock.

Brokers make money off all three components of trading costs, and it should not be surprising that they maximize their income given various institutional constraints. Furthermore, brokers mingle opportunities, such as access to IPOs, with commissions, so that an investor has to look at a very broad spectrum when considering his total costs and benefits in any broker relationship. As some brokers advertise $0 commissions, you can be sure they are making money off their customers somehow. The AMEX Broker/Dealer equity index rose at over twice the annualized rate of the S&P500 from 1993 (XBD Index) through 2004, and the price of a NYSE seat has also risen at a faster rate than the S&P500 since 1993. Brokers and floor specialists have figured out a way to squeeze money out of their trading flow even as both average commissions and bid-ask spreads have fallen by about half over this period, a period that included the reappearance of odd-eights quotes for Nasdaq in 1994, and introduction of decimalization in 2002.[22] Clearly a model that supposes explicit commissions and bid-ask spreads are proportional to total costs to traders, and revenue to brokers, is incorrect as a first approximation.

The effect of trade-impact by brokers gaming the system is evident in the mutual fund timing scandal of 2004. It was documented that a minority of savvy traders would take advantage of an institutional quirk whereby one could buy a fund at its closing price after the close that day. For institutional funds especially, this means one could buy a Japanese fund when the U.S. market was up a lot, at yesterday's closing price, even though the odds the Nikkei would open up were much greater than 50 percent. Many people played this game with their 401(k) retirement accounts, but hedge funds jumped in too, giving a fund complex, say $100 million, with the understanding that they could engage in this practice, a clear quid pro quo at the expense of those ignorant of this dilution. Even some of the mutual fund managers were doing this on their own portfolios with their personal money, a blatant breach of fiduciary duty, under the hope that you can spread a scam like this around and no one is the wiser. Zitzewitz (2006) concluded that dilution can cost investors in international stock funds 1 to 2 percent of their assets a year. This arbitrage was from the timers—who knew exactly what they were doing—at the expense of existing fund owners, in the form of dilution. The costs were not explicit for mutual fund owners, because most were probably ignorant of them, but the costs were no less real. Such is the nature of the trade impact and bid-ask transaction costs, as they show up only if you do some work estimating them. Most investors are blissfully unaware of these costs, often merely focusing on the commissions. Indeed, as an institutional investor I have dealt with major investment banks offering algorithms that benchmark against the value-weighted average price (VWAP). When I asked about the price impact, they had no idea what I was talking about. But an algorithm must address both costs, and some beat VWAP by pushing the price so much the total efficiency is worse than with naïve trading. As these investment banks served a large number of institutional clients, I can only conclude most institutional investors do not monitor trade impact.

Kenneth French discussed trading costs in his 2008 American Finance Association Presidential Address, and estimated them to be 0.67 percent of market value, based on average mutual fund expense ratios and adding up revenues of all securities companies registered by the SEC. This method of evaluation excludes many of the issues I address, such as taxes, adverse timing, and peso problems, but the trading costs he estimates, 0.11 percent in 2006, are simply implausible. At Deephaven I was involved with some high-frequency equity strategies (investment horizons less than one month). We had to estimate the trading costs, because on a long/short portfolio, trading every week generates 208 trades a year, meaning a 0.2 percent trading cost annualizes to a 41.6 percent drag on a strategy. Using thousands of transactions, and comparing my fill amount with the price at open when I traded against by fill price, I was able to estimate both a VWAP miss and a price impact, and these varied by the amount we were trading, whether it was a long or a short, whether we were initiating or closing a position, and so on. But our 0.2 percent cost was for someone whose full-time job involves minimizing this cost, using sophisticated algorithms refined via a large database that is impossible for your average retail investor to create, and direct market access software that retail investors do not have, so hearing that your average trader experienced a fraction of that cost is preposterous. Most traders, especially retail traders, are not measuring, and so cannot minimize this cost, and it is probably an order of magnitude higher for retail traders as brokers play bait and switch with commissions, trade impact, the bid-ask spread, funding costs, and other fees.

The effect of trade impact for large investors is paramount, much greater than commissions or bid-ask spreads. In trade impact, consider a broker who front runs his clients. That is, if I am a broker for a large fund, and note they started to sell out of a stock on Tuesday, given the size of their fund, if they want that position to go to zero they have a lot of selling to do. This is valuable information, and whether I trade in front of it myself (risking detection) or send subtle signals to a friend in an unspoken quid pro quo, it is rare that such valuable information is not exploited to its maximum, at the expense of the institutional trader. Such schemes are virtually impossible to detect.

Odean (1999) and Barber and Odean (2000) used brokerage data to estimate annual turnover at 112 percent and 75 percent, respectively.[23] These same sources estimate commission costs between 1.5 percent and 2.5 percent. This implies a direct cost of between 1.5 percent and 2.5 percent in commissions. Trade impact costs for larger traders probably offset any potential volume discount available to the larger institutions, and many individuals are probably subjected to large phantom costs for their larger trades by savvy brokers, and Carhart (1997)[24] estimates 0.95 percent costs for a buy-sell decision in a mutual fund, which is in the same ballpark.

Barber and Odean (2000) compared investment club actual returns to returns calibrated on closing prices, and estimated that the net effect of these costs was 2.3 to 2.9 percent annually over the period from 1991 to 1997. As large-cap equity funds underperform passive indexes by about 2.0 percent per year (Malkiel, 2003),[25] this is consistent with the idea that collectively, a group without any edge churns through 2.0 percent in costs through all of their trading costs and management fees. If management fees are around 0.7 percent, then trading costs were around 1.3 percent for these institutions, but the 0.7 percent in management fees could be thought of as the cost of accessing the sophisticated trading algorithms of an experienced trader. Total trade impact costs of between 2 and 3 percent seem reasonable for the average investor.

While currently, the lowest-cost passive mutual funds actually have negative costs because they are able to reap the benefits of lending out their long positions in stock loan transactions, these are the exception, the bleeding edge of low-cost stock access. Historically, and for the average investor, the costs have been considerably greater.

SUMMARY

When Dimson et al. published a new estimate of equity returns in 2005, revising the equity premium to a mere 3.5 percent, I e-mailed him and asked about some of these other adjustments that would lower it further. He was quick to respond that some funds actually generate a slight (for example, 20 basis points per year) premium because they are large, and have an ability to make money lending out shares with some market power. That is, a handful of cutting-edge passive funds imply that many of these risks are irrelevant. While true, my point was not that a sufficiently sophisticated investor could not capture most of the observed equity premium by avoiding active investing tactics of all sorts, but rather, that on average an equity investor has encountered these costs, and so in the process has not fared anywhere near as well as the indexes that are supposed to reflect equity investor performance. The equity risk premium is perhaps the most important parameter in finance, because it is our one estimate of the price of risk that can then be extrapolated and interpolated by risk factors. It is the base on which the cost of capital estimates are made, and its seemingly high value suggests to many economists that, while risk measurement within asset classes, or across diverse asset classes, is seemingly impossible, the large equity premium is proof positive that risk begets return, on average.

The return on the stock market is a little like the payout on slot machines in Las Vegas. If you play optimally, your losses are only 0.4 percent in blackjack, if you count cards, slightly negative! But the average person loses 3 percent per hand because they get distracted and do not bet optimally, and tend to gamble longer and more capriciously after they have won. Similarly, if we take a return of 6 percent on U.S. equities as the naïve estimate, we have the total list of adjustments listed in Table 6.1.

These are all reasonable estimates, and they add up to an adjustment to the effective equity risk premium well below zero, using reasonable estimates for each of these issues. Most papers address one of these issues and then note that such issues (peso problem, taxes, and so forth) can explain much of the equity premium. An unrecognized implication is that considering *all* of them simultaneously can explain the equity premium a couple of times over, turning the puzzle that it is too large into a puzzle that it is too negative. Like the evidence against O.J. Simpson in his murder case, you can throw out half, any half, of the evidence, and still get the same result: The

TABLE 6.1 Adjustment to Top-Line Equity Risk Premium

Geometric versus Arithmetic Averaging	3.0%
Survivorship Bias–Peso Problems	3.0%
Post–WWII Reduction in Eq. Premium	3.0%
Taxes	2.0%
Adverse Market Timing	2.0%
Transaction Costs	2.0%
Sum	15.0%

practical equity risk premium is zero for the typical retail investor. It seems likely that while the efficient investor may be able to play the Vanguard 500 mutual fund and capture much of the equity premium, such an investor is the exception. The median investor loses money in the stock market, after paying for advice, transaction help, sneaky brokers, the government, and his own poor timing.

CHAPTER 7

Undiminished Praise of a Vacuous Theory

The CAPM is still considered a first-order intellectual achievement, in spite of the current thought leaders also describing it as being "empirically vacuous" (Fama and French, 2006) or that "having a low, middle or high beta does not matter; the expected return is the same" (Ross, 1993).[1] Indeed, I would say the situation is worse, as volatility and beta are generally negatively correlated with returns.

Its extensions have proven equally impoverished. There's clearly a greater truth at work in this case, the greater truth is that *some* asset pricing model will work, and it should have the neat CAPM properties of being linear in risk factors, not include residual risk, and include something very like the market as one of the prominent factors. The theory has little equal by way of praise from economists, who see the success of derivatives as proving the risk-reward portion of academic finance as manifestly fruitful. I doubt even Keynesianism had such high approval ratings at its apex. But the flaw of the CAPM isn't that it is not perfect, but rather does not predict relative returns, even slightly, quite different from the flaws of Newtonian mechanics, which become apparent near the speed of light.

The golden age of the CAPM was from 1972 to 1992, from Fama's initial confirmation of the theory to his rejection of it. Not that it ever really worked, or that portfolio managers ever mainly relied on beta in constructing portfolios. No, it was that among experts, the belief was that the CAPM was an innovation in our abstract understanding that would stand the test of time like Euclid's Elements. Refined, extended, to be sure, but never junked. The concurrent development of the APT, and the general equilibrium SDF approach, were merely extensions. To the extent CAPM had difficulties; these more general approaches would fix them, but the basic ideas of the CAPM were paramount: linearity in pricing, and the positive premium of some systematic risk factors. It was further assumed that the main factor would be the market, and so a multifactor approach would merely add second order terms, in a very consistent way.

Today, beta is generally recognized as a risk factor for many investments, in that any good hedge fund wishes to have a low beta; yet for stocks, or funds, that perforce have positive beta, it is an afterthought. In a Bloomberg screen, it is listed inconspicuously with 10 other stock characteristics like P/E. In Morningstar's reports, you can't even find the beta for stocks or funds, because they replace this with a bevy of idiosyncratic ratios and subjective ratings (for example, "four stars out of five"). Academics, meanwhile, would never assume that merely controlling for beta controls for risk, unless they are explaining risk in MBA texts.

But this did not diminish the praise for this line of research, an intellectual achievement that was supposedly practical and profound, intuitive and elegant. The shadow cast by the initial apparent success of the theory created a strange longing for a time of order, even if that order was based on ignorance. As prominent finance professor John Cochrane wrote, the CAPM "proved stunningly successful in a quarter century of empirical work," meaning it seemed to explain the data pretty well, until we found out this was merely due to beta picking up the size effect, which itself was mainly measurement errors.[2]

This longing for a prior sense of ignorance, when a popular theory *appeared* to be working, is a rather bizarre stance for an economist. It's like saying how fun Christmas was when we believed in Santa Claus. True, but that's harmless fun, not science. The CAPM was never a benign conspiracy of professors to create joy in MBAs, but a serious hypothesis about the way the world works. In a similar vein, Paul Samuelson stated about Karl Marx in his 1995 edition of *Economics,* after the fall of the Berlin Wall reduced the allocation of his text on Marxism to a footnote: "Marx was wrong about many things—notably the superiority of socialism as an economic system—but that does not diminish his stature as an important economist."[3]

Ah, the "being wrong" part—never mind!—Marx was popular and inspirational. Clearly, economists see theories in context larger than falsifiable predictions. Any idea that generates a large literature, supposedly, is good. The thought that an idea was edifying, even if wrong, is comforting to academics who often investigate unproven ideas. I disagree. There are an infinite number of bad ideas, so eliminating many of them puts hardly a dent in the shelf from which bad ideas are drawn. This is especially true when an error merely postpones an inevitable education with reality, like saying drinking and driving was a great idea until I hit a school bus. The fact that economists as preeminent as Cochrane and Samuelson adopt the same stance toward what constitutes a successful theory (ephemeral popularity among scientists), highlights the strange power of any idea that spawns a large literature.

Peter Bernstein wrote the best-seller *Capital Ideas,* which presents the modern finance architects as heroes and mavericks; one can almost hear the "Ride of the Valkyries" as one reads his firsthand account of their achievements. Even books that note the CAPM, or the APT, were empirically vacuous, paying homage to the standard theory in obligatory fashion; harping on its flaws was like criticizing Newton for not accounting for special relativity. Derivatives pioneer Mark Rubinstein's 2002 homage to Markowitz noted that

> *Near the end of his reign in 14 AD, the Roman emperor Augustus could boast that he had found Rome a city of brick and left it a city of marble. Markowitz can boast that he found the field of finance awash in the imprecision of English and left it with the scientific precision and insight made possible only by mathematics.*[4]

Subsequent honors on the creators of the current theory have never been moderated, which is often the case for findings that create a field. For example, Carson's *Silent Spring,* Mead's *Coming of Age in Samoa,* or Kinsey's *Sexual Behavior and the Human Male* are now found to be seriously flawed to the point of being really manifestations of the author's prejudices, yet, they remain canonical works nonetheless.[5] A recent survey by Ivo Welch of finance professors noted that 75 percent would recommend using the CAPM for capital budgeting, 10 percent the Fama-French model, and 5 percent some unspecified APT.[6] So, the CAPM is holding up pretty well in spite of its failures, if only because the alternatives have little intuition and no consensus. A set of video lectures on the history of finance had four videos as of 2007, and two were from Sharpe and Markowitz. In short, they are still the fathers of academic finance for their work on what became the CAPM, which is the basis for current asset pricing theory. But it strikes me as odd, because I don't see it as merely patronizing niceness, or being nice to old men because it's better to be polite than honest; I see it as a genuine belief by this cohort that the insights created in the development of the CAPM will survive like the insights of quantum theory from the 1920s. They praise the developers of the CAPM, not because their theory works, not because its refinements work, but because there is faith that a solution will be found that is a consistent extension of the CAPM.

As the mind is very good at explaining reality, if not predicting it, financial economists are quick to make sloppy analogies to support the idea that risk, as economists understand it, is important. But there is a problem, which is that the risk that is important is very unlike the risk relevant to expected return in theory. For example, Cecchetti's textbook *Money, Banking, and Financial Markets,* immediately presents the seemingly straightforward example of how bonds with higher default rates have higher yields: Risk and return go together.[7] Yet, this is purely an anticipation of the default rates, and so is not risk in the sense of something priced. As noted, BBB bonds have, over time, about the same total return as B rated bonds. One must subtract the expected defaults and the resulting losses from a stated yield regardless of one's risk tolerance. The essential, and largely successful and ubiquitous usage of one flavor of risk—the mere statistical volatility and loss estimation—does not imply the second flavor of risk relating to a priced factor affecting future returns as also ubiquitous and essential. As the distinction between or default risk by itself and priced risk is a fundamental distinction in modern risk-return theory, the common usage of default risks when it generates an intuitive support at 30,000 feet suggests that financial professionals have a strong, perhaps unconscious, bias toward the big idea: Risk begets higher returns.

Another misplaced example of success is derivatives, which are obviously very important and useful. The really innovative portion of the Black-Scholes–Merton discovery about options was not the general formula itself, which had been published 10 years earlier by several authors. They proved that, because of arbitrage, an option can be priced as if it were a claim on a risk-neutral asset. The risk premium was irrelevant because of a dynamic hedging argument. With the price of risk out of the derivatives picture, you could generate derivative pricing models like Black-Scholes using just the probability distribution, because in this case, in a state-contingent pricing perspective, the risk premiums are all zero. This leaves a classic engineering problem, complex but soluble, and no different from the naïve expected value problem using risk-free interest rates.

Derivative pricing models are the crowning success of finance, which is the most successful field within economics, which is the most successful social science. Yet the success of the risk modeling in derivatives is really just the success of using expected value, assuming no price of risk. That is, though theoretically the SDF approach encompasses a really complex set of DFs, in practice all the DFs were the same because arbitrage implies the price of risk is irrelevant. The DFs were indexed only by time, not by states of nature. Nevertheless, SDF proponents never fail note the spectacular success of their approach in the real world of derivatives, even though the price of risk is turned off, and all it is is payoffs weighted by their probability. It's like ascribing Watson and Crick's double helix modeling success to Darwin, plausible at a superficial level—isn't everything in biology related to Darwin at some level?—but really misleading.

Around 1840, Macaulay wrote a grand history of England, and noted that doctors had historically recounted their field's successes with an obvious lack of detachment:

> *The history of our country during the last hundred and sixty years is eminently the history of physical, moral, and intellectual improvement. And this is the way the history of medicine used to be written, principally by doctors in their retirement, as a form of ancestor-worship (no doubt in the hope that they, too, would become ancestors worthy of worship). In this version, the history of medicine was that of the smooth and triumphant ascent of knowledge and technique, to our current state of unprecedented enlightenment ... [but] it is clear that for centuries it possessed no knowledge or skill that could have helped its patients, rather the reverse.*[8]

This was before anesthesia and the theory of germs, a time when visiting a medical doctor was about as useful as visiting a witch doctor.[9] Just as macroeconomics bestowed many Nobel Prizes on its macroeconomists before acknowledging they really had no clue what caused growth or business cycles, so too has the Nobel academy bestowed prizes on economists for truly impressive work, yet work that is hardly useful for an investor. The financial academy presents itself as having a strong foundation, seemingly measuring progress by the amount of papers allocated to its issues.[10] But the fundamental point, that no one can define a risk metric that is intuitive, and explains returns, is not a deficiency that history will remember well about these last 50 years.

A field will be considered fruitful regardless of empirical evidence if there is hope that a solution is possible within the paradigm. When a field's empirical success stagnates, a framework replaces a theory, and it becomes increasingly mathematical, it is on the wrong path. In this way, modern theorists are like lottery ticket buyers, or people who invest in volatile stocks, operating on hope. The key is the beauty, the mathematical elegance, of the framework. For example, in 1885, Johann Balmer found a straightforward formula that contained all the known frequencies of the spectral lines of hydrogen: each frequency could be written as one fundamental frequency multiplied by the difference between the inverse squares of two whole numbers. The formula's simplicity in accounting for so varied a set of numbers was intriguing. Then, in 1913, Niels Bohr presented a model that explained the stability of the atom by applying Balmer's formula for the frequencies of light from hydrogen by adding the notion of quantum leaps from photons hitting or leaving electrons in orbit, altering the mechanical energy of electrons going around the nucleus. An abstract, elegant (no improper fractions!) mathematical solution was found not merely descriptive, but real.

The lesson of twentieth-century physics, which guides so much mathematical theorizing as a template, is that common sense and intuition is secondary to mathematical beauty and consistency in modeling the real world. Beauty implies truth, and truth, beauty. String theory currently dominates high-level physics research, but has been criticized because it is untestable.

Nevertheless, string theorists in academia keep flourishing. Juan Maldacena is an accomplished young string theorist, currently at the famous Institute for Advanced Study in Princeton, New Jersey. In an interview in Big Ideas, he was asked, "Have you ever thought your ideas may be wrong?" He replied,

> *Yeah, this is possible. However, the mathematical structure is probably going to be useful for whatever theory is the correct theory. And, what we do ... at least is generate good interesting mathematics that is useful for other things in physics, and I think if it's not string theory, it will be probably something similar to it.*[11]

And so it is with modern finance, which fully expects the yet unknown risk solution to be built out of the mathematical edifice already created, because the elegance and power of what has been created seems not just capable, but necessary to be any reasonable solution. In the words of leading researcher John Campbell, giving his overview of the state of finance at the millennium, "Precisely because the conditions for the existence of a stochastic discount factor are so general, they place almost no restrictions on financial data."[12] The effect of a good theory is to make an accurate view of the world less complicated, not more, but instead modern researchers focus on the framework's potential as opposed to its predictive power. The stochastic discount factor approach encapsulating CAPM is surely not a coincidence to these researchers, it merely highlights that while currently wrong, it will be able to encompass the ultimate true theory. As Mark Rubinstein says about the CAPM:

> *More empirical effort may have been put into testing the CAPM equation than any other result in finance. The results are quite mixed and in many ways discouraging. ... At bottom ... the central message of the CAPM is this: Ceteris paribus, the prices of securities should be higher (or lower) to the extent their payoffs are slanted toward states in which aggregate consumption or aggregate wealth is low (or high). ... The true pricing equation may not take the*

exact form of the CAPM, but the enduring belief of many financial economists is that, whatever form it takes, it will at least embody this principle.[13]

The problem is, as the data have become clearer, the theory has become less clear. This is not a sign of a successful theory. Risk started out as merely volatility, and now volatile assets presumably have low risk through some spooky risk factor, and behavioral biases are applied piecemeal to various anomalies.

CHAPTER 8

Why Relative Utility Generates Zero-Risk Premiums

The model in Table 8.1 shows the basis of how a concern for a relative measure of wealth generates the equivalent riskiness to low and high beta assets. Assume there are two assets, X and Y, and two states of nature, 1 and 2. An investor faced with asset X or Y can see the following payoffs.

Y is considered riskier in standard theory, as shown in Table 8.1, with a 40-point range, versus a 20-point range for X. Yet on a relative basis, each asset generates identical risk. In State 1, X is a +5 outperformer, in State 2, X is a −5 underperformer, and vice versa for asset Y. In *relative* return space, the higher absolute volatility asset is not riskier, and the careful reader can check this for any example where the two assets have the same mean payout. If X and Y are the only two assets in the economy, relative risk can be achieved, equivalently, by taking on an undiversified bet on X or Y. Buying the market, or allocating half of each, meanwhile, generates zero risk relative to the mean portfolio.

The absence of a risk-return relation flows from this simple insight, and while one can prove this various ways using sophisticated mathematics, it really is a simple idea from assumption to implication. The idea that people benchmark is the key driver, because ubiquitous benchmarking is the same thing as having a relative utility function. When relative portfolio wealth is the argument in the utility function, any relevant volatility is symmetrical, because the complement to any portfolio subset will necessarily have identical—though opposite signed—*relative* volatility. You can prove, using utility functions or arbitrage, that if people care about their relative return, the risk premium is zero. The arguments are no simpler, and use no fewer assumptions, than what is necessary and sufficient to generate the traditional risk premiums. Simply replace the utility function argument of wealth, with relative wealth, and no risk premium. The driver of the result is driven

TABLE 8.1   Relative Risk Is Symmetrical

| | Total Return | | | Relative Return | |
	X	Y	Avg.	X	Y
State 1	0	−10	−5	5	−5
State 2	20	30	25	−5	5

by the logic described here, because like idiosyncratic risk in the traditional theory, anything that can be arbitraged, either will be arbitraged (in arbitrage theory, by assumption), or is implicitly arbitraged (in utility, an equilibrium exists only when there are no gains from trade remaining).

Furthermore, note the symmetry of risk. The *sine qua non* of particle physics is symmetry, and I'm not saying this necessarily implies truth, but symmetry is an attractive quality by itself.[1] Risk is symmetrical because risk is betting against the consensus, and that implies someone thinking the exact opposite. Thus, my risk to buy X cannot have a risk premium because my complement's position—to sell X, has just as much risk, but is on the other side. Ergo, there can't be a risk premium. If they were both risky, then you could create a portfolio of equally risky positions, long and short for the same security in the same amount, generating a positive return. This is an absurdity because it means you get a positive return for having a net zero position, in regard to both cost and volatility.

An important point is that for idiosyncratic risk, the results will be identical to the orthodox approach. That is, a chance to win the lottery, or bet on a horse race, or experience a car crash, is independent of what most everyone else is doing, and thus is just as risky, and unpriced (other than its expected value). Thus, a general aversion to uncertainty, or volatility, is implied in this approach just as the standard approach, because idiosyncratic volatility lowers utility when compared to a benchmark, or when merely applied to one's nest egg alone.

BENCHMARK RISK

Even the main champions of the standard model in effect acknowledge that as a practical matter, risk is relative to a benchmark. Bill Sharpe consults for pension funds evaluating asset managers and states that his first objective is "I want a product to be defined relative to a benchmark."[2] Fund Manager

Kenneth Fisher's book *Only Three Questions That Count,* in the index next to *Risk*, has "see Benchmarking."[3] When asked about the nature of risk in small stocks, Eugene Fama noted that in the 1980s, "small stocks were in a depression," and Merton Miller noted the underperformance of the Dimensional Fund Advisors small cap portfolio against the S&P500 for six or seven years in a row was evidence of its risk.[4] But the smallest 30 percent of stocks actually had a higher return in the 1980s compared to the 1970s; it was only relative to the indexes that they had negative returns. Eugene Fama notes that "Most investors are probably sensitive to the risk of being different from the market, even if overall variability is no higher. Value stocks do not outperform market portfolios regularly or predictably—if they did, they would not be riskier."[5] This is exactly my point. It seems reasonable to presume that for these investment professionals and academics, risk, intuitively, is a return relative to a benchmark, often a passive index. If all investors, and academics, act as if they are benchmarking to aggregate indexes, risk will not be priced in equilibrium.

For modern investors, portable alpha is the idea that alpha should be separated from beta risk, so that a fund manager with alpha may provide both alpha and beta risk (the beta risk being his risk of being long the stock market). You pay a premium for the alpha, but as beta is available at very low cost through passive funds if not futures, and you should not pay for that risk. Furthermore, to the extent your portfolio optimization algorithm has a slot for stock market beta, it would be nice if portfolio managers would all set their betas on conventional asset classes to zero, just to make the problem, and the costs of management, easier to evaluate. The net result, however, is alpha managers all being beta neutral, and so, defining risk as any deviation from a beta of 1 in their asset class. Thus, a convertible bond manager with a beta of 0.5, and one with a beta of 1.5, both have the same beta risk. In general, one does not appreciate these deviations; they only add complexity to the overall portfolio problem. There is little evidence that market timing is a large part of anyone's alpha, and so these bets are viewed much more skeptically.

WHY RELATIVE RISK LEADS TO NO RISK PREMIUM

We can also see how this result holds through arbitrage if investors are concerned about relative performance. Assume an economy with risky assets that are a function of a market factor, r_m. For any investor i who chooses an asset with a specific beta β_i, returns are generated by the factor model

$$r_i = \mu_{\beta_i} + \beta_i r_m \tag{8.1}$$

where μ_{β_i} is a constant for an asset with the specific beta β_i, and $r_m \sim N(\mu_m, \sigma_m^2)$. We will assume no idiosyncratic risk from assets, because the gist of this approach is better uncluttered by the extra notation.

The return on the risk-free asset is the constant r_f. The market price of all assets, risky or risk-free, is assumed equal to 1, so we are solving for a r_f, μ_{β_i} and μ_m such that this is an equilibrium.

The market return in this model is the benchmark to which investors compare themselves, just as mutual fund managers typically try to outperform their benchmark. Their objective is to maximize their outperformance, subject to minimizing its variance. Define r_{out}^i, which is the relative performance of investor i to the market return

$$r_{out}^i = r_i - r_m \tag{8.2}$$

Here r_i is the return on the investor's portfolio with its particular factor loading β_i, and r_m is the return on the market. Investors all have the simple objective of maximizing r_{out}^i while minimizing a proportion of its variance, as in

$$\text{Max } r_{out}^i - {}^a\!/_2 \sigma_i^2 \tag{8.3}$$

Where $\sigma_i^2 = \text{Var}(r_i - r_m)$. Substituting equation (8.1) into (8.2) generates

$$r_{out}^i = \mu_{\beta_i} + (\beta_i - 1) r_m \tag{8.4}$$

Since r_m is the only random variable, the variance of outperformance is just

$$\sigma_i^2 = (\beta_i - 1)^2 \sigma_m^2 \tag{8.5}$$

We can replicate the relevant risk of a stock with a beta of β_i, σ_i^2, through a portfolio consisting of β_i units of the market portfolio, and borrowing $(1 - \beta_i)$ units of the risk-free asset (cost is $\beta_i - (1 - \beta_i) = 1$, the same as for the stock, because all assets have a price of 1 by assumption). Arbitrage then implies that these have the same expected returns, so

$$E(\beta_i r_m + (1 - \beta_i) r_f) = E(\mu_{\beta_i} + \beta_i r_m) \tag{8.6}$$

The LHS of equation (8.6) is the market portfolio levered β_i times by borrowing $(1 - \beta_i)$ in the risk-free asset in financing, while the RHS is the unlevered β_i asset portfolio by equation (8.1). They have the same factor exposure, and cost the same, so they should have the same return in equilibrium. Thus equation (8.6) implies

$$\mu_{\beta_i} = (1 - \beta_i) r_f \tag{8.7}$$

This allows us to replace the μ_{β_i} with $(1 - \beta_i) r_f$ in equation (8.4) and leads to the factor model

$$r_{out}^i = (1 - \beta_i) r_f + (\beta_i - 1) r_m \tag{8.8}$$

If the degree of risk of relevance to investors is their outperformance, σ_i^2, the expected return for assets with $\beta = x$ should be the same as those with $\beta = 2 - x$, because they have the same risk in this environment: $(x - 1)^2 \sigma_m^2 = ((2 - x) - 1)^2 \sigma_m^2$. The risk of a $\beta = 2$ asset is identical in magnitude to a $\beta = 0$ asset, so the expected returns must be the same

$$E\left(r_{out}^i \mid \beta = x\right) = E\left(r_{out}^i \mid \beta = 2 - x\right) \tag{8.9}$$

Using equation (8.8) and applying the expectations operator to equation (8.9), we have

$$(1 - x) r_f + (x - 1) E(r_m) = (1 - (2 - x)) r_f + ((2 - x) - 1) E(r_m) \tag{8.10}$$

The LHS of equation (8.10) is the expected return on the $\beta = x$ asset, and the RHS is the expected return on the $\beta = 2 - x$ asset. Solving for $E(r_m)$ we get

$$E(r_m) = r_f \tag{8.11}$$

Equations (8.1), (8.7), and (8.11) imply

$$\begin{aligned} r_i &= r_f + \beta_i (r_m - r_f) \\ r_m &\sim N(r_f, \sigma_m) \end{aligned} \tag{8.12}$$

Thus no arbitrage, in the sense things equivalent in risk are priced the same (as risk is defined here), generates the traditional CAPM with the significant difference that the expected market return is equivalent to the risk-free rate. Just as the equilibrium model in the prior section implies, the expected return on all assets is the same, because $E\beta(r_m - r_f) = 0 \forall \beta$.

In contrast, a traditional arbitrage model would take from the arbitrage equation (8.7), and, combined with the market model equation (8.1), generate the standard factor model

$$r_i = r_f + \beta_i(r_m - r_f) \tag{8.13}$$

But now the maximization function reflects the fact that the investor only cares about absolute volatility, not volatility relative to some benchmark.

$$\underset{\beta_i}{\text{Max}} \; r_i - {}^a/_2\beta_i^2\sigma_m^2 \tag{8.14}$$

Substituting equation (8.13) for r_i, the first order condition on equation (8.14) generates the familiar equation

$$\beta_i = \frac{E(r_i - r_f)}{a\sigma_m^2} \tag{8.15}$$

So investor i's optimal β_i will be equal to the risk premium over the risk aversion coefficient times the market variance. Assuming a representative investor, conventional parameters for this approach of 6 percent for the risk premium, 1.5 for a risk coefficient, and 20 percent for market volatility, this implies an equilibrium beta choice of 1, consistent with an equilibrium where the representative investor holds the market basket. But if, as argued here, the market premium is in effect zero, the β_i choice will be zero, which is not an equilibrium, because on average the market beta is 1 by definition and in positive net supply. In the traditional approach, a positive market premium is necessary for investors to hold the market in equilibrium, whereas in a relative risk model, combining equations (8.3) and (8.8), we get

$$\underset{\beta_i}{\text{Max}} \, (1 - \beta_i)\, r_f + (\beta_i - 1)\, r_m - {}^a/_2(\beta_i - 1)^2\sigma_m^2 \tag{8.16}$$

$$\beta_i = \frac{E(r_m - r_f)}{a\sigma_m^2} + 1 \tag{8.17}$$

Here, the optimal choice of β_i is 1 only if the risk premium is zero (that is, $E[r_m] = r_f$), because risk is uncompensated by arbitrage; risk can be avoided in this model by choosing a beta of 1. A positive risk premium would induce a desired optimal beta greater than 1, which would then not be in equilibrium.

While this is a simple model, it has at its essence no more simplicity than what generates traditional risk premiums. The only difference is whether one puts relative as opposed to absolute wealth in the utility function. Both the absolute and relative risk approach generate the familiar factor pricing model, but in the relative risk approach, the risk premium is zero in equilibrium, whereas in the absolute risk approach, the risk premium must be positive.

CHAPTER 9

Why We Are Inveterate
Benchmarkers

The typical economic assumption is that people maximize the present discounted value of their consumption. I had a friend who took an MBA course at the University of Chicago, and the professor would begin every class with the question: "Why do we work?" And the class was expected to reply in unison: "To consume!" This was the key principle, that everything was about total consumption. Nonetheless, after certain basic needs for warmth, nourishment, and safety are met, what drives someone's behavior? Is it calculating a maximized expected consumption path or maximizing relative performance or rank in the community?

A relative utility function would explain the absence of a general risk premium, Easterlin's Paradox, and also why people prefer more to less, and are averse to idiosyncratic volatility. Yet it would be nice to get some independent evidence that it works in spite of passing the as-if test.

Economics' essence is methodological individualism introduced by Adam Smith in *The Wealth of Nations*, to see what happens when we assume individuals act in their own self-interest is indeed the economic method. Usually, assuming that people are maximizing their income, or wealth, is sufficient when you are looking at parochial issues like rent control, or farmers responding to an influx of imports. Assume a relative-status utility function would generate similar implications as the standard economic assumption in most cases, because an extra dollar, unrelated to anyone else, is good in both an absolute and relative sense.

Adam Smith emphasized a self-interest that also recognized social position and regard for society as a whole, but this was well before anyone thought of writing down a utility function, taking a stand on precisely what self-interest means.[1] Indeed, this is one of the benefits of mathematical representation of theories, because it forces one to be clear. But if self interest is evolutionarily based, success for an individual is primarily relative, because individuals compete more within their species for access to mates than with other species for access to resources, so to the extent one uses evolution to motivate a utility function, it would seem a relative utility function is appropriate.[2] No matter how rich a society is, mates are like oceanfront property, a positional good in fixed supply.

In Charles Darwin's *The Descent of Man,* he noted that if humans had evolved as bees had, "there can be hardly a doubt that our unmarried females would, like the worker bees, think it a sacred duty to kill their brothers, and mothers would strive to kill their fertile daughters; and no one would think of interfering."[3] Bees are haploid/diploid, so from a gene perspective, such behavior is optimal in a Darwinian sense for their selfish genes (males are unfertilized eggs, getting all their genes from the female Queen, females descend from the male and female, but as males are haploid, their male genetic endowment is identical among sisters). The point is, what is highly endogenous cannot be considered *all* bad, because to assume such instincts did not exist would imply many other things about current life would go away, too. As humans are just animals, natural selection has shaped not only our bodies but our very beliefs, our fundamental sense of right and wrong. This is sociobiology, and explains basic urges for the four F's (feed, fight, flee, and mate).

Consider revenge, a motive that is ubiquitous, yet considered stupid, evil, and an anachronism by many. Lions do not have this concept. So, following Darwinian logic, a new alpha male first kills all the cubs in his pride, causing all the females to go into estrus, where he can get busy creating his progeny. If lionesses held grudges against their children's killer, male lions would not do this. Nature is what it is, but I'm glad people believe in revenge to some degree, because I imagine there would be a lot more violence otherwise (for example, "Gee, you killed my boyfriend, which was mean, but I guess I'm no longer busy Friday night, and I don't hold grudges, so sure, I'll go out with you").

The key to understanding our unconscious motivation is to realize that its circuits were not designed to solve the day-to-day problems of a modern U.S. resident—they were designed to solve the day-to-day problems of our ancestors who lived without the benefits of regular productivity growth.[4] In a zero-sum world that existed until 1750, and probably currently exists in much of the Third World, increases in per capita wealth through invention, investment, and extended economic exchange were rare. More for you was less for me. Therefore, if anyone managed to acquire a great deal more than anyone else suggested there was a stash of gains, acquired by cheating, stealing, raw force, or sheer luck. With the average income constant, wealth is merely about redistribution. Anyone with conspicuous wealth would be asking for a coalition of the less wealthy to expropriate it. If actions are basically redistributive, it is hard to develop an instinct for thinking solely on one's own wealth, independent of others.

Neurologically, since humans are quintessentially social animals, much of the brain is given over to processing social information, including in-group status. Biologists Thomas Insel and Russell Fernald (2004) argue that because information about social status is essential for reproduction and survival, specialized neural mechanisms have evolved to process social information, making status orientation hardwired into our brains as a consequence of evolutionary selection (mates are the ultimate status good).[5] Indeed, one set of such cells are mirror neurons, which solve the ancient philosophical problem of how we instinctively know other people are conscious, even though we cannot *know* that others' consciousness is exactly like ours. When you see a woman grinning broadly, how do you know she is happy? Not through some abstract reasoning process that analyzes the visual information coming from her face and makes a logical inference that her expression is associated with happiness. Instead, you instantly activate mirror neurons in your brain that are active when you are happy. You may even make subtle, unconscious muscle movements to imitate her expression. They fire just as when you smile, making your recognition of her emotion effortless, requiring no logical calculations. The brain appears to reuse its complex machinery designed for taking action, feeling emotions, and perceiving objects for the purpose of understanding what other people are doing, feeling, and saying. The human mirror neuron system is now thought to be involved not only in the execution and observation of movement, but also in higher cognitive processes—being able to imitate and learn from others' actions, or decode their intentions and empathize with their pain. Autistic children tend to be mind blind, that is, they have trouble seeing others as beings with intentionality and feelings, causing them to behave antisocially, and they have been found to have deficiencies in their mirror neurons.[6] Without the hard wiring, understanding, even recognizing people, is very difficult, as artificial intelligence researchers have discovered.

The key is that recognizing other individuals, for healthy people, is hardwired, and makes us intrinsically socially conscious. Just as only animals with self-awareness, a higher-form consciousness, recognize themselves when they look into a mirror, seeing one's self in others is a part of higher consciousness.[7] "The self and the other are just two sides of the same coin. To understand myself, I must recognize myself in other people," says Marco Iacoboni, a leading researcher in this field.[8] Awareness of others is integral to our thoughts as awareness of our own feelings.

In a book titled *Human Universals,* published in 1991, professor of anthropology Donald Brown listed hundreds of human universals in an effort to emphasize the fundamental cognitive commonality between members of the human species. Some of these human universals include incest avoid-ance, child care, pretend play, envy, and many more.[9] A concern for relative status was a human universal, and relative status is a nice way of saying people have envy and desire power.

FROM A JANUARY 22, 2008, *NEW YORK TIMES* ARTICLE TITLED "POLITICAL ANIMALS (YES, ANIMALS)"

Monkey Status

Dario Maestripieri, a primatologist at the University of Chicago, has observed the social foibles of the rhesus monkey, a close relative to humans.

He notes that "throughout human history, you see that the worst problems for people almost always come from other people, and it's the same for the monkeys. You can put them anywhere, but their main problem is always going to be other rhesus monkeys."

"Individuals don't fight for food, space or resources; they fight for power." With power and status, he added, "they'll have control over everything else."

"Fighting is never something that occurs between two individuals. Others get involved all the time, and your chances of success depend on how many allies you have, how wide is your network of support."

Monkeys cultivate relationships by sitting close to their friends, grooming them at every possible opportunity and going to their aid—at least, when the photo op is right.

"Rhesus males are quintessential opportunists," Dr. Maestripieri said. "They pretend they're helping others, but they only help adults, not infants. They only help those who are higher in rank than they are, not lower. They intervene in fights where they know they're going to win anyway and where the risk of being injured is small."[10]

TYPICAL ECONOMIC ASSUMPTIONS

Our terms *status-seeking* and *status symbols* emanate from Weber's classic *Class, Status and Party*. Weber's novel concept of *status groups* proved to be both more flexible and more penetrating psychologically than Marx's dichotomy of the class struggle.[11] For Weber, status was like class for Marx, but it was more a function of wealth, which could be earned and was unrelated to mere birthright. Many of the bourgeoisie become radical, and many poor people become management. Weber's writing directly influenced author Thomas Wolfe, who noted that many parts of status took things unrelated to money, such as courage and skill. Consider what a navy aviator does in climbing what Wolfe called the "ziggurat of status" in his classic book *The Right Stuff,* where the very small niche of aviators had their own highly specific criteria of accomplishment and respect.[12]

Status as a motivator is well known by economists. In economics theory, all the big names generate interesting quotes about the relevance of status. Not merely Karl Marx, but Thorstein Veblen (1899) and his notice of conspicuous consumption, focused on status, the societal relative position, as a motivating force in individual lives.[13] This has been addressed in theoretical economics models in more recent research by Pesendorfer (1995) and Rayo and Becker (2006), where status seeking is modeled as a successful way to signal quality or evaluate one's productivity.[14] Behavioralists like Dan Ariely (2008) have noted that the complexity of calculations leads many people to borrow from the wisdom of crowds, and use peers for benchmarking.[15]

Economists have shown an incorporation of a concern for social context that alters results of traditional growth models, tax policy, public goods, social norms, charity, health insurance, and repeated interactions.[16] The hedonic treadmill of Phillip Brickman and Donald Campbell (1971) considers humans as on a treadmill having to run faster merely to stay in the same place, because the benchmark keeps moving forward.[17] This has been applied to the equity premium puzzle (see Chapter 6) in formal models such as George Constantinides's habit formation model (1990), and the keeping-up-with-the-Joneses utility function of Andrew Abel (1990).[18]

These approaches, ones that are generally based on past consumption as a reference point, are not enough. They merely move the consumption, or wealth level basically back to zero as the economy grows, exaggerating the relative volatility of wealth in each prospective period. You still get risk premiums related to volatility in consumption, or wealth, or whatever it is that makes up the SDF, in utility functions based on past consumption. Thus, it can explain the Easterlin Paradox, and perhaps the equity premium puzzle, but then not the general absence of risk-return relations within all the asset classes. The fact that highly volatile equities, which have the highest covariances with the market, and consumption, do worse than low volatility equities remains the important counterfactual to these solutions.

Virtue of Selfishness

The prisoner's dilemma is the famous game, referred to in the movie *A Beautiful Mind* about John Nash, where two people choose whether to cooperate or not cooperate, without knowing what the other party will do. In the one-period game, the Nash equilibrium is for both to not cooperate—the bad outcome. But in repeated games, people generally cooperate and get to the optimal equilibrium.[19] One can think of reciprocal altruism as the nice strategy one plays in a repeated prisoner's dilemma game, all with the goal of maximizing one's selfish payout over a long sequence of prisoner dilemma games. Economist Robert Axelrod showed how a tit-for-tat algorithm bested a variety of complicated algorithms in repeated prisoner's dilemma tournaments, and suggested a rather moral strategy: be nice, be provocative (tit-for-tat), and be forgiving (one tit per tat).[20] Evolutionary biologist Robert Trivers noted that reciprocal altruism could be a dominant strategy for a selfish gene, noting the value of forming positive sum alliances.[21]

Much of the logic of reciprocal altruism is described in Robert Wright's book *Nonzero,* where he argues that the fact that interactions can be positive sum, and requires some intelligence to implement correctly (one must keep track of how others cooperate), this is an argument for the inevitable evolution of intelligence. An example of reciprocal altruism is blood-sharing in the vampire bat, in which bats feed regurgitated blood to those who have not collected much blood themselves knowing that they themselves may someday benefit from this same donation; cheaters are remembered by the colony and ousted from this collaboration. This gives rise to complicated game theoretical issues of an abstract nature, but also, all the petty emotions and tactics of a high school social circle: moralistic aggression, gratitude, guilt, subtle cheating, and coalitions. Thus, reciprocal altruism is self-interested behavior, and it is more complex in real life because invariably the state space is not as simple as the prisoner's dilemma, and involves remembering how people behave, who they are friends with, their cues. Reciprocal altruism acts as a counter to mere continual, shortsighted selfishness because such people will not be successful in benefiting from these positive-sum interactions that allow an individual to reap the benefits of mutual gains from trade.

One must remember that the selfish behavior initially described by Adam Smith was seen as antithetical to a good society, and socialists and syndicalists tried to argue that people were not that Machiavellian. Opportunists used Marxism as a pretext for simple oppression, and the systems they built based on incorrect premises—even if merely pretexts—were doomed to fail. The Invisible Hand implies the natural competitive equilibria of individuals acting in their own self-interest are socially desirable, while reciprocal altruism makes us empathetic and compassionate. It is not obvious, but selfless animals are hardly nice. Ants are selfless, surrendering themselves to the greater good of the colony without hesitation, yet they are also the most warlike animals, nasty neighbors. Selfishness is consistent with morality because if you don't value yourself, how can you value others?

Rational self-interest can even lead to a variety of emotions. Robert Frank's book *Passions Within Reason* argues that there are emotional rewards to helping those who deserve our aid and hurting others who deserve our ire.[22] He notes our emotions precommit us to keeping our promises and carrying out our threats, so that we gain in the long run by not being able to make the dispassionate calculation. In effect, we have internal mechanisms that make us good borrowers in a game of reciprocal altruism—built-in incentive structures to pay back. We gain because others will trust our promises and respect our threats. It's costly for me to lie to you if I feel shame, sympathy, and guilt. Preferences that might seem petty may be necessary for an efficient resolution to a competitive or cooperative circumstance, allowing us to credibly signal we will not renege.

Why Envy Is Virtuous

Simple self-interest has moved from a Machiavellian vice to something that generates a social optimum (the Invisible Hand), to something natural (through evolutionary biology), to something morally good (reciprocal altruism is enlightened self-interest). Economists take a pleasure in knowing that something other disciplines considered a vice, something to exterminate in society, underlies the relative success in economics relative to the other soft sciences. The premise of selfish behavior seems more robust, empirically, than the wishful thinking of sociology, anthropology, or the prurient drives of Freudian psychology. The desire for power, the envy, the *schadenfreude*, within a relative status maximizer, however, would be starting all over in a sense, trying to rehabilitate envy the way it did with greed (which took 200 years, after all).

In the traditional model of empathy, I care about your happiness, and both your happiness and my happiness is a traditional one that increases in wealth. In that case, however, I should not care about the relative poverty in the developed world, because the poor in the United States, in relation to the history of man and the current world, are materially rich.

In contrast, in a status-oriented utility function, my caring about you means not only do I want you to not be poor in absolute wealth, I do not want you to be poor in relative wealth. I care about the poor in the United States even though they are rich in material terms relative to most of human history. Envy is necessary for compassion in a developed economy. Our empathy for others' envy makes people better neighbors, better salesmen. It is more enjoyable to talk to someone who takes a sincere interest in your concerns, and those concerns involve relative status.

Francois de la Rochefoucauld noted that "we all have the strength to withstand the suffering of others," and while a superficially sad observation, it is clearly useful that we care more about ourselves than anyone else, because ant hives and bee colonies make Orwell's 1984 seem like a 1960s commune (though if I were haploid, I'd think differently). But that we care about the relative status of others, to some degree, is probably essential too. Empathy combined with mere selfishness leads to a great amount of indifference because most people suffering the slings and arrows of modern misfortune can be mocked as mere whiners. Yet the United States produces many well-received books about how inequality is bad and getting worse, and how we need to do something now, just as it always has. Most people care about the poor in the United States, even if their strategies for alleviating their suffering differ, in spite of the fact that they are rich in the context of human history.

Why Economists Dislike Envy in General

Assume people are ranked in status from 1 to 100. Now anything that changes their rank order, makes the one who moved down, worse, the one who moved up higher, or better, this situation is ambiguous. Furthermore, a solution that makes everyone richer, keeping the rank order that same, does not make them better. While maybe true, this is not something one thinks should be true. I was surprised when an economist who looked at my approach to risk and return by a relative status function replied that it does not make sense because it implied that the aggregate wealth in the economy did not matter. It was inconceivable for him to think that a United States with 50 percent more GDP is no happier than the current United States, even though Easterlin's Paradox suggests this will be the case. If we are basically envious, not greedy, creatures, my great-grandchildren will have material comforts beyond my dreams, but still suffer the same amounts of pleasure and pain. I think this is a good forecast, even if I send them a time capsule telling them how hard life was when I was born (I used to change my own channel on the TV—by hand!).

Looking at the difference between the developed and undeveloped countries, which magnifies small differences in growth rates over generations, we see the advantages in social welfare, the arts, the sciences, from having greater wealth. Also, the mores and customs of societies that grow are more compatible with my values than those of a static society, as rates of violent death have decreased considerably since the industrial revolution, probably because the value of life is so much higher. Further, the endemic hypocritical rent seeking and free riding in egalitarian schemes have a much less salutary effect on individuals than mere greediness, and top-down policies to generate equality generally do not get rid of inequality; rather, they push it into political power or market wealth. Thus, I am a libertarian who thinks people should generally be left alone, and redistribution should be kept to a minimum. Yet I also think it probable that people in the West will be just as happy after a century of growth as they are today. While I may be indifferent to my status when I'm freezing or starving, the situation is much different when those basic needs are met.

The naturalistic fallacy moves from descriptions of how things are to statements of how things ought to be. The moralistic fallacy moves from statements about how things ought to be to statements about how things are; it assumes that the world is as it should be. This, sadly, is a fallacy; sometimes things aren't as they ought to be. It may be we are status maximizers, and that, sadly, this implies economic growth will not lead to a happier society, and bickering over growth-retarding redistribution is the optimal strategy for individuals, and also that maximizing GDP has ambiguous effects on social welfare. This is somewhat depressing and it is interesting to see smart people fall prey to the moralistic fallacy, that *ought* proscribes *is*. For example, libertarians are quick to highlight the latest paper that finds contrary results to the Easterlin Paradox as if it completely refutes decades of research.[23] Economists like the thought that, with rational self-interest, positive and normative theory are generally the same: What people actually do is what they should be doing. If people are relative status maximizers, their lectures on people merely trying to maximize consumption and the implication that aggregate growth is therefore the priority, one cannot help but think they are like missionaries telling the natives what their morals are.

This whole chapter may be considered a merely abstruse way of saying we are inveterate benchmarkers, motivated more by envy than by greed, though these are often consistent with each other. Many highly esteemed economists have applied this parochially to various issues. All I am proposing is to apply this more broadly. Such a proposal does not explain everything—for instance, why risk takers are generally overly optimistic, or why people have an inordinate desire for very safe assets—but it is a necessary assumption for explaining why, year after year, the most highly volatile assets tend to have no risk premium.

CHAPTER 10

Alpha, Risk, and Hope

The basic stylized facts are as follows:

1. In general, measures of risk—volatility, beta, covariances—are uncorrelated with average returns. There has yet to be identified a risk factor that works much of the time, let alone most of the time.
2. For extremely volatile investments, returns tend to be below average.
3. For extremely safe assets, returns tend to be below average.
4. Investors are overconfident: They trade too much, and diversify too little.

The current theory is that as-yet unidentified risk factors, plus some acknowledgment of behavioral biases account for the last item (number 4). Yet the stake in the heart of this approach is that if a risk factor explains the low return on safe assets (number 3), that it is generally absent when explaining most assets (number 1), and seems negatively correlated with volatility at extreme levels (number 2), will require a great deal of implausible rationalization. The fact that risk factors generally cancel out, or are inversely related to intuitive definitions of risk, makes a solution within this paradigm impossible.

My explanation involves three independent assertions:

1. People benchmark against the consensus, that is, each other; so all risk is like idiosyncratic risk in the conventional model: unnecessary, and so is not priced
2. A safe asset is a necessary part of every portfolio
3. Actual risk-taking is based on hope, and follows a rational rule, not a rational act, for maximizing one's success

These assumptions can explain the data we see. Thus the question should be, are they true? This chapter is primarily about pillar 3. The first pillar, that people benchmark against others, was Chapter 9. Let us dispense with the second assertion.

THE SEARCH FOR SAFETY

People crave certainty in some measure when it exists as one alternative. Consider the fact that in financial crises, correlations tend to all go to 1, or −1, whatever hurts your portfolio most. It is nice to think there is some asset—gold, cash, T-bills—that will not go to zero in such a situation, so you can pay your mortgage, and buy food and necessities. Safe assets are like a lifeboat for tough times, and we all eventually need a lifeboat. A modest allocation to some sure thing is very comforting, because while we can all manage adversity, most investors consider bankruptcy something that should be safeguarded against if possible, and pay a premium in terms of lower return. Having money stuffed under one's mattress is like a life insurance policy, an insurance against an improbable event that will allow one to get back on one's feet.

The number of assets considered safe is relatively small, and there are huge barriers to entry, so that supply is limited. A government, like Switzerland, has developed a reputation for a stable currency, whereas Brazil would have to show several decades of unseen behavior to reach that status. But in every situation, there is some asset that acts as the best, and most reliable, and generally, people's perceptions of these assets is log-linear. That is, when I was at Moody's, I noted that the agency ratings started out as a mere ordinal ranking, from very safe AAA, to safe AA, and so on. Then, in the late 1980s, Moody's and S&P started putting out data on the actual default rates of these securities, and they turned from an intuitive classification to a more quantitative one. Interestingly, initially even Moody's analysts were not sure what the default rates were for each grade. I saw an internal report circa 1989, and it noted that B-rated bonds were very risky, with estimated default rates greater than 15 percent (it's actually more like 6 percent annually). But interestingly, the scale was almost *linear* in logarithmic space (which means exponential in raw default rates). Please see Figure 10.1.

So, the default rate actually rises exponentially, which if you have worked in credit risk management at a bank, you see all the time. Bucketing of risks generates exponential losses as one moves down the intuitive buckets one ranks risks into. When people rank order things, they tend to be in log space. Many things are in log space, such as decibels and the Richter scale. Benford's law, the finding that most numbers of real things has a power law distribution, is based on the fact that so many things have logarithmic distributions. Thus, nature, and our intuition, is built on a logarithmic sensibility.

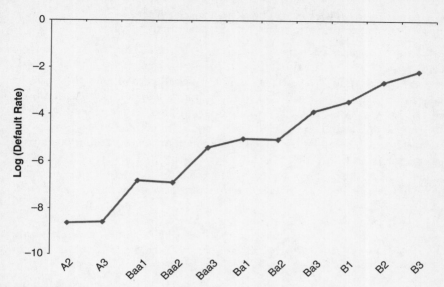

FIGURE 10.1   Default Rates Log-Linear Moody's Default Rates by Notch: 1983–2005

Fechner's Law, articulated in 1860, states that humans sense stimuli differences at a logarithmic scale, so that the proportionality of a difference is the limit of human sensation, as opposed to a computer, which might use an absolute difference, or Euclidean difference.[1] Our number intuition is logarithmic, not linear. More recently researchers have found that babies first learn that numbers are different at a ratio level: 4 or 16 is different from 8 by a factor of 2, and it is this ratio, not an additive difference, that initially develops from intuition.[2]

The point is that if we have a log sense of risk, and safe means extremely little risk, the safest assets are insanely unique. It must be 100 times safer than something merely pretty safe, and when you have to give someone credibility that something is that safe, it basically implies there must be decades of proven safety. This necessarily leaves very few assets, so supply cannot take advantage of this cheap funding. Supply is necessarily constrained by this requirement, and keeps the price of safety assets high, and their returns low.

The desire for a little haven of indestructible wealth amid a portfolio of benchmarks is one of the little takeaways from the famous Kelly Criterion, by which one is trying to maximize geometric wealth by the end of a given time. One of the basic principles of this criterion is to make sure the probability that total wealth goes to zero, is zero, because after wealth goes to zero you have nothing to make money with in the future.

MOST FINANCIAL RISK TAKERS ARE FOOLISH

Investors, in aggregate, appear to be quite foolish. That investment is in aggregate uncompensated was a theme of Keynes's *General Theory*, which noted, "If the animal spirits are dimmed and the spontaneous optimism falters, leaving us to depend on nothing but a mathematical expectation, enterprise will fade and die."[3] As someone familiar with financial markets, Keynes was no doubt aware that it was not so much the investors who get rich off finance, but the brokers. Adding up their expenses, their undiversified gambles, generally produced a weak return for the average investor, as argued in Chapter 6. A major puzzle in economics is gambling, where the expected return is actually negative, and the payoff random, seemingly a two-fer for badness.

It all starts with the behavior of retail investors, who trade too much (which is costly), do not pick winners better than random picks, and are massively undiversified relative to alternatives such as index funds.[4] And, it only gets worse from there, as research shows that financial overconfidence increases with age, experience, and success, ensuring that hubris offsets any extra skill acquired.[5] The sad thing is that this implies a Peter Principle in Alpha: People will stretch their alpha until it is gone, making all individual alpha ephemeral, and thus any positive alpha of questionable relevance prospectively. Thus, mutual fund managers deviate from the passive benchmarks, adding risk, and underperforming almost exactly equal to their transaction expenses.[6]

Contemporary psychologists agree that "on nearly any dimension that is both *subjective* and *socially desirable,* most people see themselves as better than average."[7] Thus, we don't mind being inadequate in something parochial, like math or ping pong, but in something generally esteemed like wit or courage, people generally think they are above average. Overconfidence invites people to deviate from the norm—to take risk—because they think they know some fact or theory most other people do not sufficiently appreciate. Yet this appears massively irrational, objectively.

TWO TYPES OF PRICED RISK

If someone would assume all your financial risks in health, home, auto, and other such areas, most people would pay some price for this transfer of risk. The ability of a large group to assume such risks and charge a price slightly above the statistical expected value of these risks is generally presented as the prototype of risk and return: the power of diversification, and the fact that people prefer to pay to avoid it. But it is rarely recognized there are many other types of random events about which we would do the opposite: pay to retain. To have these risks eliminated would eliminate our hopes and dreams. The distinction is hope, in that the one thing a good risk has is that it plays into our dreams, whereas the bad risk is an annoyance we minimize or transfer.

Hope applies only to something we do not have, a favored anticipation of something uncertain. There must be a chance of it not happening to call in hope, otherwise, it is merely reality, which one may like or dislike. Thus hope requires uncertainty, volatility, or risk. Hope is related to our dreams because it refers to an uncertain outcome we highly desire, something that mere contemplation makes us feel energized about, alive.

There have been previous assertions of two types of risk in the past. The popularity of these approaches highlights the intuitive appeal standard approaches of turning risk into a probability problem, like solving for the expected value of an option price, is insufficient. Thus with behavioral economics, we have two types of risk: those occurring in the risk-loving portion of one's utility curve, and risks occurring outside of that portion. With post-Keynesians we also have two types of risk: those with Knightian or Keynesian uncertainty, and those without it. But the problem of the risk-loving theory is that it is all post hoc, or descriptive. The problem with the Knightian uncertainty is that as uncertainty is positively correlated with risk, one should still see a positive volatility or covariance relation with returns, which we do not see. For the most volatile assets, which almost always have the most uncertainty, their returns are below average, which makes the distinction unhelpful.

UNCERTAINTY IN INNOVATION

Alpha creators look at the world as if everything needs fixing. Inventors are constantly criticizing, extending, and simplifying, which leads to the design of new things. The successful inventor needs a lot of highly specific knowledge of the state of the art, so his ideas are not duplicative, and the state of the market, so he can know a user's unmet needs. But looking at the current set of risk reports, portfolios, or capital structures that one might improve upon presents problems because these things currently work—however well—in a particular configuration, at a particular scale, in a particular context. Trying to find the essence of something that works is hardly straightforward; just think about the varied contradictory reasons given for why the United States is a relatively prosperous nation.

Risk taking predicated on the hope that one has an edge, is about a competitive advantage, alpha. The idea that you have a special skill in investing, or some special insight in measuring risk, or hedging, or selling home-made jewelry, is something that takes knowledge, but also a little chutzpah. You can go into an organization and follow your boss's lead, and there is a need for people with sheer competence. Yet many people think of starting their own thing, creating their own project, if not company, based on their ideas. This necessarily involves uncertainty because any good idea is novel, a step into the unknown. This is the essence of Keynes's observation that most real-world decisions are not unlike the uncertainty of a roulette wheel.

An attempt to innovate is like navigating a labyrinth in the dark. We have some idea of what to expect, but we also know that we will have to adjust our path as we occasionally smack into things. To try to estimate the risks in such ventures is like trying to foresee which trends continue (for example, Moore's law), and which do not (for example, housing prices). Success takes actually doing something, because one does not learn the essential details until one actually tries something.

WHY RISK TAKING HURTS

Jean-Claude Killy noted that "to win, you have to risk loss," but for most of us, it is not the physical courage of a downhill skier or a warrior, but rather the intellectual courage needed to stand up to colleagues who dismiss our new ideas. Though much more subtle than physical courage, intellectual courage is considerably more difficult, as researchers have found that emotional pain is more stressful, more lasting, than any physical pain.[8] To seriously try to dance with flair or wear a really eye-catching new outfit invites the scorn, the ridicule, of failing so bad, the joke is not the failure, but your mind-numbingly-clueless thought that you are John Travolta or Jennifer Lopez. If you have objectively low alpha in some area, your willingness to attempt to ply it will not be seen positively by your status group. If you fail, there is a chance that this will be more than a localized failure because of the implied obtuseness in such an objectively doomed risk-taking. Courage is therefore not viewed in isolation, because if it is rash or excessive, it is considered merely foolhardy, not admirable, as when Graham and Dodd deride gamblers.

The easiest way for a putatively innovative person to avoid humiliation is to extend an existing line of reasoning by trying something logically implied yet untried because it is insanely difficult. This is what most academics do, as they try to patch an existing theory through inside-the-paradigm puzzle solving, what Thomas Kuhn called mopping up. To apply top-level mathematics to extend a particular result is considered world-class economic theorizing, regardless of whether the result was already well known (see Debreu's *Theory of Value*). Academics generate a lot of hair splitting, but this is because their extensions tend to be merely extending the current ideas in obvious but tedious directions, because academics are good at difficult but straightforward problems, and are as risk-averse as anyone else.

In standard models of risk, there is a price of risk, and if sufficiently diversified, one gets what one pays for. There should be little regret for an unfortunate risk, any more than one bemoans the fact that their lottery ticket did not win. You took the risk, you knew the odds, and there you are. Say you offered me a bet where if it does not rain in Phoenix, Arizona, on June 21 of next year, you pay me $100, but if it rains, I pay you $100. I would take that bet because the probability of it raining are well below 50 percent, and if I end up losing the bet, I will dislike losing, but not regret the bet because the bet was better than fair. Yet, in practice, risk taking generates a lot of anxiety. With the benefit of hindsight, many risks reveal themselves to have been doomed from the start, because knowing how things worked out, it is all so obvious, and we were fools for thinking otherwise. The absence of anxiety in traditional risk models is a prominent data point against it, because this misses a prominent part of actual risk.

The key point about searching for alpha is that when testing whether one is good at something, invariably this can only occur after some expertise in the area is acquired. Learning to finger an instrument or solve math problems is difficult and time consuming, but straightforward. Eventually, however, if you wish to apply alpha and demonstrate true excellence, you need to apply that expertise in a novel way. Thus, a sufficiently self-aware person realizes the quantum gulf between, say, being able to play a song correctly and play it well, or more importantly to write a good new song. Failure is thus not inconsequential, because you cannot be in a position to make a serious effort here without developing colleagues and mentors in the field, and it is their collective judgment that will evaluate your efforts. Such feedback is stressful, because life is finite, and if this effort does not work out one then has to start anew at something else. Further, failure suggests a clueless optimism about one's actual abilities, which can be pathetic, and has reputational effects. Starting over and accepting failure with dignity without losing one's enthusiasm for life are extremely important and take intellectual courage, mainly because doing so is so emotionally stressful. This is why the only way initiatives are shut down in large organizations is when the control is taken away from the founders. It is rare one can kill their creation without using force.

Intellectual courage is only admired *ex post* for those who were successful doing something unorthodox, deviating from the consensus and being right. For example, we consider Galileo a courageous innovator, yet if we were to assess current scientists with similarly unpopular views today, most of us would think they are not courageous, but rather foolish. A scientist who believes in intelligent design or cold fusion is an outcast for good reason. Intellectual courage in real time—when the decision is made but before the outcome—means the average respectable person will lessen his estimation of you. It is easy to forget that Galileo's famous observation that all objects accelerate at the same speed was not so obvious. For example, if you push something faster, it accelerates—a heavy weight pushes harder on your hand, ergo, it should push downward faster. Add to that the observation that leaves fall to the ground more slowly than rocks, and I could see why people would assume weight is positively correlated with acceleration. Around the same time, Tycho Brahe, the man whose measurements allowed Kepler to formulate his laws of motion, did not accept the heliocentric model of the solar system, in spite of his very good data and good-natured persuasion from Kepler—is it not obvious that we are at rest? In contrast, there were many theories less outside the consensus that have shown themselves to be embarrassingly wrong: lobotomies, communism, Microsoft Bob, the Oedipus complex. If you failed, you were not merely unfortunate, but wrong, with hindsight.

CONFUSION OF RISK AND GAMBLING

Gambling has a long history of being criticized by value gurus Graham and Dodd, and their disciple Warren Buffett, as pure folly, the number one mistake of investors. We know people scoring lower on cognitive tests choose the higher expected value lottery less frequently, and that lower socioeconomic status is correlated with greater lottery play, and lower IQ.[9] Evaluating probabilistic payoffs is something that less intelligent, less educated people do less well, and hope leads them astray.

When Bernard Baruch suggested an investment to J. P. Morgan, and noted "It's a good gamble," J. P. cut him short and said, "I don't gamble." Baruch lamented using the phrase, knowing it was a deal breaker, but clearly even famous investors do not appreciate the difference. In a sense, gambling is just a word for "taking on volatility without a positive expected return," but this presumes everyone agrees on both the returns, the odds, and the nature of randomness—many people believe in luck, that somehow good karma will give them a special deal in drawing from the urn of chance.

Thus, many people think they are risk takers, but are actually gamblers, like the little ladies with a bucket of nickels playing the slots in a casino. It's all electronic. The odds are against them. The longer they play, the more they will lose, statistically. It would be easy to say, simply, don't invest on the basis of hope, and gambling appears objectively foolish, based on miscalibrated hope. Yet there is a continuum between gambling and investing based on hopes and dreams that make this difficult in practice.

FROM THE MOVIE *DUMB AND DUMBER:*

Lloyd: What are the chances of a girl like you and a guy like me ... ending up together?

Mary: Well, that's pretty difficult to say.

Lloyd: Hit me with it! I've come a long way to see you, Mary. The least you can do is level with me. What are my chances?

Mary: Not good.

Lloyd: You mean, not good like one out of a hundred?

Mary: I'd say more like one out of a million.

[pause]

Lloyd: So you're telling me there's a chance!

It is common to overemphasize the possible merely because we want it so very much. Some people's hopes are based on objective gambling, especially when the winning payout is especially large, as in lottery tickets. While these are objectively poorly returning investments, they are still based on hope, a belief in numerology or fate. If I could vet people's investment strategies, I suspect that I would be like Simon Cowell on the TV show *American Idol,* telling 95 percent of these people they are deluded if they think they will succeed with their current proposal, and to start over; too much hope, not enough alpha. The market will offer alternatives, and after looking in the Investments section of your local bookstore, you will find books instructing you on how to make money in a variety of venues where the odds for a retail investor are so low it defies credulity: how to succeed in penny stocks, options, or day trading. I would estimate that half of the shelf space in these sections encourages gambling based only on hope disguised as investing. Invariably, they have the disarming story about how, before they made their fortune, many esteemed doubters told them they would never succeed.

And those dismissing the experts have a point, because the experts are often horribly wrong. Lord Kelvin, a man prominent in nineteenth-century physics, stated that "heavier-than-air flying machines are impossible." A Yale management professor gave Fred Smith a grade of "C" for his business proposal that became FedEx. Several companies took a pass on what was to become the revolutionary Apple computer, and the founders of Google offered themselves to Yahoo! for a mere $1 million. A music executive at Decca Recording Company rejected the Beatles in 1962. The list of such mistakes is endless, and gives everyone who faces skepticism hope. It is not restricted to business, as I have often seen posters with Einstein's quote "Great spirits have always found violent opposition from mediocrities" on the wall of scientists, a motivation for times of lack of support.

In addition to experts missing good ideas, there is the issue of over-confidence for probabilities. Researchers have asked people questions like, "Which magazine had the largest circulation in 1970, *Playboy* or *Time?*" A respondent would then say, *"Time,"* with a probability of 99.9 percent, or odds of 1,000 to 1, for example. But when people's odds were incredibly extreme, as when they reported million-to-one odds of being right, these odds were actually more like 20 to 1 of being correct.[10] So, poor Lloyd in *Dumb and Dumber* perhaps was not so dumb (indeed, the actors started dating after the movie).

Thus, every bad idea actually has a chance that it too, is like those previous successes that were dismissed by the Establishment, and those previous million-to-one certainties, those expert skeptics, were wrong. Everything has got a chance, in that sense. The problem is that gambling is a lot *like* alpha-based risk taking, and a poor analogy is at the bottom of all bad ideas. The more objective alpha in the risky decision, the greater chance of success. But any case will be highly parochial, the assessment of alpha highly subjective, and evaluation is rarely disinterested, especially when you evaluate yourself.

There is no list of great *ex ante* investments, because most of us consider a person's reasons why a risk went wrong as special pleading, spurious argumentation where one tendentiously highlights some reasons and excludes others. Profits, however, speak for themselves. As Norman Mailer put it: "In the middle classes, the remark, 'He made a lot of money' ends the conversation. If you persist, if you try to point out that that money was made by digging through his grandmother's grave to look for oil, you are met with a middle-class shrug."[11]

Just as unethical decisions tend to acquire a gloss, stupid gambles that pay off are often viewed uncritically. How many millionaires who sold out at the height of the Internet bubble, selling a business for millions that soon would be bankrupt, are still considered savvy businessmen, even though objectively it would be more accurate to call them lucky? That their existence depended upon a bizarre period of irrational exuberance does not really diminish their status. I have never met a wealthy portfolio manager who considered his success *primarily* due to luck, and these are the people who form anecdotes and analogies for others making business decisions. This conflation encourages gambling, because many successful gamblers of the past are so often presented as savvy businessmen or investors.

STANDARD ALPHA CONTRADICTION

Most presentations on maximizing alpha assume one has a bunch of data that allows one to apply mean variance optimization. That is, assume a set of potential investments, they could be assets, or asset classes, or portfolio managers with alpha. This gives one a set of expected returns, volatilities, and correlations. The implied set of portfolio weights is now strictly a math problem that is straightforward and soluble.

The assumption that alpha exists in this form is a contradiction. Remember, alpha, as originally introduced by Jensen in 1968, is from an equation

$$r_i = \alpha + r_f + \beta(r_m - r_f)$$

This particular equation assumes the CAPM, but it generalizes to other factors by merely adding more betas (β), applied to more priced risk factors ($r_m - r_f$). The key is, alpha is a free lunch and if it were incontrovertible, it would not be there. Most excess returns are hotly contested debates about whether it implies a market inefficiency or a potentially misspecified market model, whereas I think the argument should center on the returns, whether they accurately reflect expected returns.

A good example of this is in mutual funds, where for decades mutual fund managers asserted that they had alpha, and they seemed to make their clients money. Many people assumed the returns on their accounts came from alpha (they did not call it that, as Jensen introduced the term in 1968). But in fact, the mutual fund managers have historically underperformed the passive indexes representing the set of stocks they chose from, the returns were merely from beta. They appeared to deliver, but only because investors did not have the right model: They did not include the market factor in the evaluation; they had a misspecified model.

This might seem quaint, but how often have you heard that investing in a strategy that is uncorrelated with the relevant benchmark by some manager with an impressive set of credentials, has alpha. Yet, his strategy is vague ("We seek value while maintaining a disciplined focus on capital preservation using a combined seventy-eight years of capital markets experience"), his track record is not obvious—it is often allied with a group he was part of (for example, "He used to work at Goldman Sachs"), and we cannot be sure it is merely survivorship bias. Nonetheless, with this information, we too assume some positive alpha. Why should we believe him? This usually comes down to the idea that a smart, wealthy guy with experience in the field should outperform a passive index. This is the mistake equity mutual fund investors made for decades, and is no less incorrect because of its long popularity (after all, bloodletting was a common cure for ailments for centuries, even though this killed far more patients than it saved). Expected returns, volatilities, and correlations really beg the question, because it presumes the hardest part of investing—figuring out expected return—has been reduced to a problem already solved (portfolio optimization). Any asset or manager's particular alpha necessarily implies most people do not agree with you about the expected return, properly amortized over the business cycle.

As much stock investing is highly undiversified, many people believe they understand the fundamentals of some company's business model (for example, the Peter Lynch principle of investing in what you know, such as firms where relatives work, or places you shop), and so believe it is undervalued. They believe the stock is worth $20, even though it's trading at $10. Indeed, using this kind of thinking, Warren Buffett considers risk and return to be inversely correlated: A stock he considers worth $30 trading at $10, has both higher expected return, and lower risk, than a stock he considers worth $20 trading at $10. But for everyone but Buffett, why should they believe they know better than the market?

Economists do not really know what to do with situations where people agree to disagree. It seems irrational. To the extent you value an asset for $20, and I value it at $10, your assessment of my valuation, and my symmetric rationality should cause you to cut your price, and similarly, I should lower my price. Game theorists have examined this extensively, and deduced that two rational people, even with different information, should eventually come to agree on some number between $10 and $20, because of complex reasoning involving the hypothetical "If I were you and thought it was worth $20, then I must know X" whereas your counterpart does the same, until you agree, at which point you no longer wish to trade because the price equals your valuation. This is the Groucho Marx Theorem of Trade: You should not join a club that would have you as a member.[12] An example of how fundamentally incorrect economists have this situation, most models of how information gets into prices assumes that, to the extent someone gathers information that is useful, it must have a cost. If information was costless and useful, it would provide arbitrage profits for everyone and thus you do not have an equilibrium. Thus, models by Grossman and Stiglitz (1980), or Kyle (1985), always have an informed agent making money, *after* paying for information, whereas the uninformed accept a lower gross return, but the same net return, as the informed investor. The problem is that no one has identified a set of informed investors.[13] Certainly not stock analysts or mutual fund managers, who have no alpha, but clearly are spending a lot of their time and effort acquiring information. Thus, standard models have a rotten core as to why people trade, which is empirically false at the micro level, as well as for its implications.

A neat recent solution to this paradox about the irrationality of agreeing to disagree was a paper that noted that if we consider the number of facts people know, the number of *combinations* of those facts rises exponentially.[14] Thus the state space blows up, and it is impossible to reverse engineer what combination of facts someone else is using to form their opinion in finite time, even if you know their facts, because there are so many combinations of facts that may be the driving distinction. If you disagree, you simply cannot reverse engineer your different assumptions.

In a similar way, even after trying to supplement your formal analysis of why a strategy is a good investment with words that articulate your reasons, the connections between your data and your final alpha estimation are simply too convoluted for others to fully grasp, and so we often agree to disagree. No test is definitive, because judgment calls are inevitable. Did the analysis control for non-normality? Are the data on interest rates from before leaving the gold standard relevant for the behavior of interest rates after we left the gold standard? Are data from mortgage defaults relevant to credit card charge-offs? Many of these issues are considered either irrelevant, or of essential importance, depending on the individual, for reasons too complex to ever fully delineate. The alpha you propose is necessarily risky, a statement about your judgment, and while it is good to apply mean variance to your final estimates of means and covariances with your portfolio, the latter tactic is trivial compared to the alpha judgment call.

WHY WE TAKE RISK ANYWAY

People do not apply a sharp distinction to financial risks versus the risks they take every day, attempting a joke, arguing for a plan based on an analogy. Most decisions we make about our education, including informal education such as learning a skill useful for planning parties, or building our own deck, involve an investment of time and money, and have an uncertain outcome. Investing in stocks is just part of that continuum.

The rewards of risk taking must be seen as based on an optimal rule, not an optimal act. An example of this rule approach is the ultimatum game where two players interact to decide how to divide $100 that is given to them. The first player proposes how to divide the sum between themselves, and the second player can either accept or reject this proposal. If the second player rejects, neither player receives anything. If the second player accepts, the money is split according to the proposal. The game is played only once, and anonymously, so that reciprocation is not an issue. Rationally, the second player should accept anything above zero, because there are no reputational effects by construction, and $1 is worth more than nothing. Offers of less than $20 were generally rejected.[15]

Nobel laureate Robert Aumann argues that this is an example of *rule rationality* over *act rationality*. One is following the rule not to be a chump, because to do so has negative reputational effects. That people follow this rule in this game, in his opinion is irrational—the second player should take the $10—but this is completely understandable because people have evolved some intuitive strategic rules ("Don't be a pushover"). The application of the rule may be irrational in any one case, but when trying to describe actual behavior, the rule rationality dominates act rationality. It seems reasonable that such a rule would arise over time, because such a rule can dominate the alternative, having to calculate the rationality of every specific act separately. So people adopt rules that work on average because the lost opportunities are small relative to the cost of having to evaluate every act without a rule.

The rule of taking risk, in spite of naysayers, skepticism, a lack of objective evidence, is a good one. As Ray Bradbury says, "You've got to jump off cliffs all the time and build your wings on the way down." You have to take risk to build those wings, because only real-life risk generates the incentives and feedback needed to become an expert at something related to the initial objective, and the payoffs are often serendipitous. For example, many baseball coaches were former minor league players who never achieved their original goal, but only through this experience could they learn how to be good managers. Consider that Jacques Morali and Leonard Bernstein wanted to be famous classical composers, and fretted about their inadequacy in this quest their entire lives, yet they gave us the song "YMCA" and the score to *West Side Story*, not quite their dreams, but spectacular successes nonetheless. The lure is often impractical—our dreams usually are—but these dreams, in combination with hard work and feedback can generate objective success. Having dreams, and more important, actually acting on them, motivates us to succeed, often in ways we never could have expected.

When I was putting together a risk management project for a regional bank in the 1990s, I had to purchase some software to calculate various value-at-risk statistics, and it was better to buy it than build it from scratch. I bought one product because it had the greatest scope of products and could accommodate a variety of risk metrics: parametric value at risk, a Monte Carlo value at risk, stress tests, arbitrary scenarios and so forth. Interestingly, the company was run by a man who centered his initial pitch based on a "patented optimization algorithm" within the software. His primary motivation for building this tool was that this optimization algorithm would allow someone to allocate capital, and hedge risks, more efficiently, as he had built his capital stake on the basis of creating a way for a firm to replicate an index using a subset of that index. He thought, similarly, his algorithm had a more general application to almost any large, complex

trading operation, not just one trying to replicate an index return most efficiently. Yet for a trading desk, general optimization algorithms are not very
useful, in that most traders hedged their trades adequately, and they were
not about to transfer any of their responsibilities to staffers in risk management. Furthermore, proprietary hill-climbing techniques in optimization are
a dime a dozen. But the software was good at the problem we wanted to
solve. He developed a useful solution for a more prosaic problem incidentally, while failing at his primary objective targeting a much sexier objective,
and his company is now tremendously successful. His incorrect estimation
of his alpha and prioritization of the high-profile solution was necessary to
finding his more prosaic niche.

A life filled with hope connects you to the future with optimism, and
optimistic people are happier, and more fun to be around. People who hold
positive illusions about themselves, their abilities, and their future prospects
are mentally healthier, happier, and better liked than people who lack such
illusions.[16] Taking risk is essential to fulfilling one's potential, finding your
best fit in a complex society that has lots of parochial niches that little
children do not esteem or understand. Taking no risk, taking the first sure
thing job, date, or investment that came along, implies we probably could
have found a better fit if we actually took some risks, even if we failed at first.

There are many who say one must experience risk taking to fully appreciate it, as in the famous line about how explaining investing to someone
who has not invested is like explaining sex to a virgin. Yet, taking risk is not
nearly as foreign as sex, because the anxieties and insecurities in attempting
to ply alpha is something everyone can relate to, especially during the insecure adolescent years, when we were very sensitive to how our peers viewed
our individuality. Financial risk taking is about appearing foolish, not bold.
If everyone thinks what you are doing is merely bold, not foolish, you are
not taking risk, in contrast to what standard theory implies.

The hope that underlies risk taking is good or bad only to the degree
it helps us become better people, or more successful. Dreams often serve as
goals to arrange our priorities, and affect short-term goals, such as finishing a
project, or long-term goals, such as choosing a major in college. Each dream
requires small steps and these practical steps build a strong foundation for
success. People like their dreams, and these dreams often make them better
people. Like Darwinian evolution, this path of discovery is not random
experimentation, but experimentation guided by selection, and so it is not
so much having a dream, but acting on them wisely: choosing intelligent
tactics, responding to feedback, and sometimes giving up and starting over.
The best way to have a good idea is to have a lot of them, and actually
implement them.

You have to see alpha-based risk taking as generating two paths. In
one, you learn you have no alpha and are merely gambling, and upon this

recognition, alter your strategy or change your objective. In the other, you find you have alpha, and play again and again. This is the hope present in alpha, because if you have some alpha, you can leverage this in many ways, over time, through repetition, borrowing. The result is decidedly nonlinear, so the initial risk is really a sampler. Consider if you play blackjack. If you have no alpha, but merely play the optimal strategy, you lose 0.5 percent per hand. The more you sit, the more certain you lose, as the law of large numbers catches up to you. After reading Ed Thorpe's *Beat the Dealer*, if you *can* count cards sufficiently, you can make 1.5 percent per hand and have yourself a new career. But until you take risk, until you actually try it, you don't know if it's feasible. Is it worth three hours sitting at a blackjack table to try? For a few, yes; for most people, no.

People take risk based on hope, and hope is a function of one's dreams. In 1961, Walter Gutman noted that "growth stocks might better be called dream stocks," and that "dreams are real—we have them every day. It's a big mistake to think dreams are unreal and what is called real life is real."[17] This is a simple, profound, model of the value effect, where stodgy, low beta firms without much upside generate a higher return than stocks that can be classified by some as the next Yahoo! Dreams, in moderation, of course, are paradoxically as real as anything, and assets that embolden dreams have extra value for investors, and they are willing to accept a lower average return because in taking risk, they are already ignoring the skepticism of the consensus.

Just as we tell our kids that as long as they try their best, they should hold their heads up high, so, too, adults should try their best, learn, and then either modify one's strategy or goals—or both. As a rule, having dreams, taking risk based on hope is part of a healthy attitude, and in general it is good for finding one's comparative advantage, a vocation, or avocation, that has high returns relative to merely following the flow. Nonetheless, it drives the irrational behavior we see, where investments with the greatest uncertainty, the highest risk have the lowest average returns, the lack of diversification, the overtrading. Like gambling, much investing is based on too much hope, a misapplication of the risk-taking rule to a game only introduced within too short of time for it to affect the hardwired intuition we have for risk taking. They are the result of a risk-taking rule that is great in general, but not appropriate for financial markets. Most people should focus their risk capital in areas less well trodden than merely buying stocks.

EXPERIMENTS, RISK, AND ALPHA

Many economists studying risk and the risk premium are not even concerned with finance. *The Journal of Risk and Uncertainty* plainly states they do not address asset pricing. The idea that risk does not beget a return premium, however, would seem preposterous to them, in that people buy insurance all the time as a way to avoid risk, so people pay a premium, that is, more than the amortized expected cost, to avoid this. Consider the various types of experiments.

- *Introspection.* Beginning with the St. Petersburg Paradox, people have framed questions that lent themselves to obvious answers. Other famous examples include Allais's Paradox and the Ellsberg Paradox.
- *Laboratory experiments.* In these cases, people take undergraduates and present them with gambles. Gamble A might be a 50–50 chance for $2 versus $1.60 versus Gamble B of a 50–50 chance for $3.85 versus $0.10. Vary the probabilities and payouts, and look at when people choose A over B, and where the cutoff is.[18]
- *Data from television game show participants.* The benefit of this approach is, unlike experiments funded by grants, these contain very large payoffs. For example, some economists examined the Mexican version of *Deal or No Deal,* where participants choose briefcases opened by attractive ladies that can lead to winning $1 million.[19] Most of these game shows are purely random, while some, like choosing how much to bet in Final Jeopardy, involve some skill.[20]
- *Hypothetical survey questions,* which can involve choices between random outcomes.[21] A typical question would be to ask people to consider a fair lottery in which you can double your yearly income with a 50 percent chance while you can lose a percentage, say x percent of your income in the other 50 percent cases. What is the highest loss x that you would be willing to incur to accept playing this lottery? The average answer is $x = 23$ percent.
- *Data drawn from market decisions,* such as whether or not to pay the high or low deductible on an insurance policy, where a high deductible generates a lower cost, but exposes one to more small losses. Or they might look at a decision to buy the extended warranty when purchasing expensive electronics.

Research in this area gets pretty involved. For example, consider this from the 2007 *Journal of Risk and Uncertainty:*

> We use survey data on income and experimental data on bet choice in a risk game to calculate rural Paraguayans' coefficients of relative risk aversion. . . . We surveyed 223 rural households in Paraguay in 2002. All households who participated in the survey were invited to send one household member to participate in economic

experiments and 188 chose to do so. The rules of the risk game were as follows: The player was given 8,000 guaranies (two-thirds of a day's wages) and could choose to bet nothing, 2,000, 4,000, 6,000, or all 8,000 guaranies. The experimenter then rolled a die to determine the player's payoffs.[22]

Now, the thought of earnest economists traveling to rural Paraguay to observe locals playing dice is kind of amusing, as if the exoticness of the situation makes it a more authentic measurement of risk preferences. But such is experimental work, for which Vernon Smith won the Nobel Prize in 2002.

These experiments lack the essence of real financial markets for all the reasons I argue are essential. First, a game hardly presents a benchmark relevant to a peer group one is interested in. Making money relative to a group of fellow experiment participants is not the same as losing 10 percent when the market goes up 10 percent. Experiments are inevitably idiosyncratic risk. Furthermore, there is no need for certainty, because there is no chance these experiments will bankrupt them. Lastly, there is trivial hope in these games, so no lure from dreams, because there is no option value from discovering that one has alpha in these games, as they are one-off little gambles, with payoffs too small to generate dreams.

Choosing my preferences for lotteries, with their explicit randomness, is quite different from choosing my preferences for engaging in actual activity that is partly a function of skill, effort, and luck, at least in regard to market activity like investment or occupational choice, because people self-select into arenas where they have reason to believe their odds are better than average, and take risks there. One's desire, or aversion, is totally different when facing random volatility I cannot control, than in cases where I think I may have alpha. In this way, risk is like sex: In one context, you might pay for it, and in another pay to avoid it (implicitly, of course). It might be the same activity, but because of the context and the resulting effect on my preference toward it, they are alike only to a mind-blind robot.

Peter Bossaerts has done a lot of empirical work in this vein, where he sets up simulated markets and observes the market prices, and he describes the situation as follows:

A number of subjects are endowed with a set of securities whose liquidation values depend on the realization of a state that is randomly drawn with commonly known probabilities (usually equal likelihood). The subjects are allowed to trade securities during certain periods before the state is drawn and liquidation values are observed.[23]

And indeed Bossaerts's experiments find that people try to maximize their Sharpe ratio (return divided by volatility) as the equilibrium, consistent with standard theory. But in the real world, most trading is based on risk-taking, in which deviations from the CAPM are predicated on perceived alpha, which is generally an undiversified bet on something. The fact that the CAPM results when you remove alpha and generate idiosyncratic risks to participants, merely highlights the importance of alpha and context to actual risk taking. Yet this is what financial economists presume, and that's why asset pricing is so sterile. The stock market contains a wide variety of dreams, and is a benchmark for investors. An experiment with known expected returns and covariances is not a benchmark, nor does it plausibly contain any alpha. The results are merely relevant for those types of risk, like those of insuring against a car accident.

Most risk taking is a combination of hope and uncertainty, and so the fact that the objective odds are against them is of little relevance, because taking risk is about bucking the odds. If you thought you were relevant to the unconditional data, you would not be taking the risk, but your hope is based on some reason to think you are special. Thus, in equilibrium, highly volatile assets generate lower-than-average returns, because the averages are like conventional wisdom, which is necessarily ignored in risk taking.

The three assumptions presented are a model of asset pricing, far more parsimonious than the alternative. It generates strong falsifiable implications: that risk metrics will generally (that is, usually), be uncorrelated with return because benchmarking implies risk is symmetric, and therefore not priced; that really safe, and really risky, assets will have lower-than-average returns, the first because it satisfies a craving for certainty, the latter because it plays into our hopes. The standard current explanation is that ultimately, returns are a function of risk and luck, though there are no robust measures of risks, merely a collection of anomalies, some of which are rebranded as risk factors. Furthermore, the obvious inefficiency of most portfolios—too much trading, too little diversification—must be explained by overconfidence in any theory, but my approach notes the consistency of overconfidence in investing with the approach people take toward all risky decisions.

Your average investor has many choices to make, whether to invest in stocks or bonds, or which stocks to buy. One way to look at this decision, the economist's way, is to assume the decision maker knows only what everyone else knows, and then calculate an optimal portfolio for himself. In contrast, risky decisions are an intrinsic part of life, where one is on a personal journey to find one's comparative advantage. This causes many people to approach risk taking in securities markets like they view the risks they take every day, defying skepticism of people like myself, and relying on hope and moxie to make something successful. Thus the demand for highly undiversified bets that have, on average, a poor return. These decisions are irrational when looked at in isolation, but they follow a rational rule. Wisdom benefits any risk taker, and understanding which risks are gambles, and which potentially have alpha, is why wisdom and hard work is correlated with market success, because having good ideas, and getting feedback by actually doing things, makes for better decisions.

CHAPTER 11

Examples of Alpha

The data in Chapter 4 highlight that higher volatility or uncertainty is generally correlated with lower returns. These are the returns *unconditional* on alpha. There is always the hope that one is like Warren Buffett, so expected returns might actually be positive for them. This generates a hope premium in wildly volatile assets, an expected return biased above the average return for these assets based on a delusion. Yet, no matter how risky my attempt to create new fall fashions, or design a new theory in physics, they would fail with certainty because I have no conceivable alpha in these objectives. More risk without alpha is a really bad idea, because markets are competitive and unless we have good reason to think we are above average, we are merely gambling in a casino that regularly plays and wins money on investor hopes. The risks that correlate positively with return have a unique synergy with your individual strengths, by acquiring insights that are not obvious, that one can then leverage this edge—take advantage of the risk-return positive correlation that exists, conditional upon you having some edge.

Lots of investment advice is more about objectives than tactics. That's easy: We all want higher return and lower risk (how many times have you read the day trader rule "don't lose money"?). And how do you estimate future returns? Presumably, first you estimate risk, and then you apply the premise that risk premia underlie all predictable returns. But there is no risk premium for most of the investment spectrum, so you can and should safely ignore this, and focus on the expected return. The expected return is generally highly case specific, and often requires tactics such as complementary market-making activity not available to the average investor.

This mistake of seeing risk as fundamentally some uber-factor that, objectively identified, generates above-average returns, is a fundamental error in finance. For example, in William Bernstein's book *The Four Pillars of Investing,* he says, "Whether you invest in stocks, bonds, or for that matter real estate or any other kind of capital asset, you are rewarded mainly for your exposure to only one thing: risk." The implication is to first understand risk, which is objective because priced risk pertains to a small set of priced-risk factors, those assets or products with certain covariances with aggregate measures of societal welfare such as the overall market or inflation. Then, choose how much of such risk one wants, which implies a specific level of expected return, noting the trade-off. Everything else is window dressing: effort, skill, and wisdom.

The main problem with this view is that there are no agreed-upon measures of risk that tend to generate higher returns. Bernstein suggests investing with a small-cap and value slant because these have had higher returns in the academic literature, even though there is no one who has identified any risk measure that fundamentally explains their risk. Indeed, as Chapter 3 noted, value firms seem, if anything, less risky than growth (lower betas, less cyclical). Thus, Bernstein is essentially saying only risk matters, but then recommends investing in assets based on characteristics associated with higher-than-average returns. But here's the rub: if the excess returns of small cap and value stocks are a function of risk, one should not highlight them as attractive. Growth (antivalue) and large cap stocks, presumably, have the same reward-to-risk ratio, properly defined. But he, like everyone else, cannot fathom what that risk would be, or know anyone who cares, so he highlights value and size because he does know people care about returns. The same inconsistency is present in Dimensional Fund Advisors, set up by the kings of Risk as an explanation of everything, Eugene Fama, Rex Sinquefeld, and Kenneth French: it started with small cap funds, and branched into value funds—why target the lower-returning growth stocks? They understand people want strategies with higher returns. It's the kind of inconsistency that drives me crazy, because the risk-begets-reward pillar is put out as this wonderful theoretical principle that explains everything, yet everyone knows that no one wants to buy a stock that will prospectively earn a lower-than-average return because it has less risk, though theoretically it should happen all the time.

Another problem with this mindset is that it neglects alpha, which is really what most financial professionals are trying to generate and capture, because investors do not pay big fees for access to beta risk. The risks that pay off to an individual, however, are of a very particular type, consistent with one's particular interests and abilities. Risk is thus like education, in that more is only better after a certain point when it is highly tailored to an individual. Some people would benefit greatly from calculus, most are wasting their time; some would benefit from learning French, most would never use it. The value of education and risk involve individuals evaluating their skills and the market need for those skills, so it is the right kind. Only individuals are motivated and informed to take the right risks, and to put someone into a volatile stock, or a new franchise, is risky, but also a certain waste if this was not the choice of the individual after looking at his various opportunities and skill set.

Successful alpha implies risk taking, but this is nothing like the risk as defined in financial models, assets with merely certain covariance characteristics. Thus, in trying to relate risk to return as a general rule, one must say something about the type of risk, which relates to the type of alpha, and this must be consistent with an individual's ability to capitalize on it.

Consider the success of John Nash. While at Princeton, Nash suggested a new physical theory to Albert Einstein concerning "gravity, friction, and radiation," and spent an hour in Einstein's office drawing equations on his blackboard. Einstein, who was then the most famous scientist alive, corrected the brash young Nash, and told him he needed to "study some more physics."[1] In contrast, without any training in economics, he discovered the concept of an equilibrium in zero-sum games that has been a workhorse for economists. What was really impressive in this result, was his application of a fixed-point theorem to this problem, as it was not obvious this type of mathematics is relevant, sort of like saying Fermat's Last Theorem can solve the traveling salesman problem in operations research. Clearly, Nash was unconventional, a risk taker who overreached on occasion. Reaching into physics was not fruitful because one needs to learn the state of the art, which in physics at this time was substantial. But game theory was really just starting, and so someone with merely a deep knowledge of math could discover a very useful result. To say Nash benefited from risk taking obscures that it was the right risk taking: the right time (early in game theory), and targeting the right subject (a problem amenable to mathematics) as defined by a person's particular strengths (Nash's excellence in math). How do we find the right risk taking for us?

FINDING THE RIGHT ALPHA

In 1972, Philip Anderson, who won the Nobel prize in physics for his work on superconductivity, wrote an article titled "More Is Different," and contended that particle physics, and indeed all reductionist approaches, have limited ability to explain the world. Reality has a hierarchical structure, but that does not mean one should always try to explain one layer from deeper layers.

> *At each stage entirely new laws, concepts, and generalizations are necessary, requiring inspiration and creativity to just as great a degree as in the previous one. Psychology is not applied biology, nor is biology applied chemistry.*

No collective organizational phenomenon, such as crystallization and magnetism, has ever been deduced from its lower-level parts.[2] Yet there is a desire to find reductionist laws based on cascading implications, and these laws tend to be very mathematical, and also tend to be frameworks so they can encapsulate the general phenomena to be explained, leaving the specifics as an exercise for the reader. Thus, the attractiveness of Chaos theory, with a basic equation generating layer after layer of ordered complexity, general consistency, but no specific model. The richness of these models is both their attractiveness and their downfall, because at the level of practicality all predictability is lost. Emergent phenomenona render reductionist views irrelevant for explaining phenomena at that level—it is unhelpful to try to understand cancer through mere chemistry, or worse, particle physics. But that does not mean that chemistry, or particle physics, is uninteresting, just, at one level, not so much. Similarly, most useful insights in finance are best described with only a level or two of greater depth than the data they are applied to. Going down to some fundamental risk explanation is not helpful, because at the broad level, it does not work, but more prosaically it pooh-poohs the importance of detailed knowledge combined with finding coalitions to successfully apply an insight.

I was once at an investors and customer conference sponsored by Northern Trust, which manages money, mainly serving wealthy clients. Most of the conference attendees were lawyers and tax accountants, the primary private wealth consultants who worked with Northern Trust. By revealed preference of customers, the most important person to speak with if you have over $5 million, is not a financial expert, but a legal and tax expert, because not optimizing over these constraints is much more important than not having the right exposure to small cap stocks. You might say that "other than tax and legal issues," the ideas from Modern Portfolio Theory are front and center, but that too is simply untrue, as you will find very few successful finance professionals who understand risk factors as described in modern financial theory.

To be a good trader, investor, or broker takes a skill set that does not necessarily require some single finance principle. To start a career in finance, and think alpha is necessarily a function of estimating returns through a market model of risk, is to constrain one's probabilities of success enormously, because very few investors make decisions this way and more importantly, because alpha is usually found far outside this approach. Not that this is never fruitful, but of all the ways to succeed, this is one very narrow path. As risk does not beget return on average, the market in practice happily ignores those who have a narrow but deep understanding of Stochastic Discount Factors.

If your job is allocating money to portfolio managers, or as an editor at a journal, you do not create the content, but you make important decisions as to what is alpha: meta alpha. One could get into semantics, and say any edge is an alpha, broadly defined. Alpha can be intrinsic to a strategy, person, group, or brand. While related to an abnormal return, it is part of a continuum of comparative advantages relative to a benchmark, what the unimaginative, or intellectually meek person would do. We take risks when we choose majors, change careers, and of course when we write checks to invest in something. There is the way everyone else does it as you perceive it, and when you deviate from this, you take a risk. You take a risk to make your life better by finding a better way of doing something.

The key to succeeding in anything is first knowing your relative strengths, because you should gravitate toward those kinds of alphas where your skills—contacts, emotional intelligence, math, computers, and so on—have the highest relative value. But you must avoid the streetlight phenomenon, where the drunk looks for the car keys under the streetlight even though he lost them somewhere else merely because that is the only place he can see. Every so often you must evaluate the field you are in, because it is easier to succeed in a field that is growing. But there is a trade-off, because your value is a function of your ability in the field, your experience in the field, and the field's viability itself. Thus, you may optimize in a stagnant field, given your abilities and contacts. In any case, you must be optimizing your alpha, and it helps to have some intuition of what kinds of things have worked in the past, because although past is not prologue, historical examples are instructive as to what we can expect going forward.

The list of good alpha ideas is highly parochial in practice because a good idea is an improvement on the state of the art, which is peculiar to a specific art. Someone in software development would benefit from business books by software engineers; someone in advertising will profit from that genre's innovators. Similarly, traders would focus on technical constraints in the institutional nature of the limited number of trading platforms, and game theoretic issues in disguising intentions and inferring trade flow, are looking at finance from an almost entirely different playbook compared to a retail investor or the head of a large pension fund. One should think about finding alpha, like finding success in an ecosystem where you get to pick your species. You can be the equivalent of a large carnivore or a tiny microbe; there's competition at every level, but you pick the domain you compete in, which require very different skills. The key is that you do not have to compete directly with everyone the way you do in school where there are a handful of subjects and sports, and everyone is graded by the same handful of teachers and coaches. In life, there are so many different occupations, you can be happily indifferent to your relative weakness in a large set of skills. Most of the alpha in finance, something people truly appreciate, is unrelated to skills in portfolio optimization.

Like school, one needs to choose well in advance activities where one is best suited to proceed, because any field has a considerable learning curve, and it is harder to get opportunities to climb such a curve as one gets older. To create alpha requires you to take a risk, and the first risk is investing time becoming an expert on the state of the art, which may turn out to be the greatest investment you ever made, or like my years learning the clarinet, or time spent learning the proofs in Stokey and Lucas's *Recursive Methods in Economic Dynamics,* a waste of time so complete I cannot think about it less. The costs include the opportunity cost, combined with the fixed cost one must pay in time and effort in getting the knowledge, credibility, and contacts in a new field, a process that could take a decade.

Thus, the first decision for an alpha seeker is building the largest skill set that leaves the largest set of areas to move into as one gains insight into opportunities. There is clearly some kind of hierarchy of knowledge in finance, understanding present valuation, statistics, option value, but also basics in computing so you can do things on your own, especially when you start and don't have minions to flush out your vague premonitions. While understanding risk in the sense of diversification of idiosyncratic risk, or taking advantage of correlations, is a fundamental concept in finance, understanding risk defined as a kind of uncertainty that is priced in the market, is not fundamental, or even useful. As there are no agreed-upon risk factors that are priced, the essential knowledge is not an abstruse concept like the SDF, but simply, looking for excess returns, conventionally defined, just as the momentum, size, and value effects were discovered.

I will focus on alpha related to finance because this is mainly a book about finance, yet it is important to remember our intuition and instincts about risk taking comes from its general application to daily life, whenever we attempt to create, do, or say something novel and present it to others. By seeing famous, conspicuous examples of alpha created, or discovered, in finance one can get a better sense of what it looks like if they create or discover it, as it generally looks nothing like Jensen's alpha, where an expected return dot is above the Security Market Line. The ideas that make you happy do not change much from century to century, but ideas that can make you rich rarely last more than 10 years. This is because a really good idea, an idea with alpha, involves a lot of institutional detail that is always changing. These details do not obscure the opportunities; they are characteristic of such opportunities. Alpha exists in many forms, each with its own set of details that makes it unique, and one must master such details if one is to truly find alpha.

ARBITRAGING PUT-CALL PARITY

One should start at the very basic alpha in finance, the arbitrage profit. This is arbitrage, seeing that you can buy a widget for $10 here, and sell it for $11 there, making an instant, riskless, profit.

Consider that in the early days of options, one could make a comfortable living merely by buying and selling options with different implied volatilities. Andy Redleaf, now CEO of the hedge fund Whitebox Capital, notes that in 1978, when he was a 20-year-old trading options on the exchange, he made a six-figure income for himself by merely arbitraging the puts and calls traded.[3] That is, using put-call parity, one could put on a riskless trade, selling a call and buying a put at the same strike price, which creates a synthetic short forward position at the expiration date, then going long the stock (or the reverse, shorting the stock and buying a call and selling a put). The combined position generates a zero-risk portfolio. If the premium on the call is greater than that on the put, you have made money at no risk. By 1982, this game was basically over, as market makers could get financing on their stock positions and do this themselves.

The arbitrage existed because he was looking at calls, and comparing them to puts, whereas most investors would merely see that these are ways to take a leveraged bullish or bearish position, because if you know which way a stock is going, options offer the greatest payout. That is, if you gave me the *Wall Street Journal* from next year, as a retail investor I would maximize my wealth by taking option positions in those biggest movers with the most out-of-the-money options available. Redleaf was looking at the problem at a higher level, the way an expert chess player looks at the problem several moves ahead of the novice, and noticed a connection between puts, calls, and the stock independent of his views on the stock's general direction, so that there was a connection between a single call, and a basket of the stock and put. It was somewhat sophisticated, but even then put-call parity was well known in standard option treatises at the time, so it is not like he had to derive this from first principles, though usually ideas like this are independently discovered by many.

CONVEXITY TRADE IN FUTURES AND SWAPS

Such instant arbitrage is relatively rare, and confined to those with special low-cost access. The following is kind of a subtle mathematical logic that is the provenance of investing *quants*. The arbitrage worked like this. Eurodollar futures mark your profit or loss, daily, to an account based on a constant times $(F_t - X_t)$, where F_t is the current Eurodollar future for time t, and X_t is the futures price at which you bought or sold the contract. The futures price at time t will be settled at the then current LIBOR three-month rate. The daily profit is a linear function of the current Eurodollar futures price for time t. A *forward* is the exact same thing, only they are not marked to market daily. Thus, you take those same profits, $(F_t - X_t)$, but they are only paid at time t, which may be 5 or 10 years from today. There is a real subtlety here, because when F_t is low, your discount rate of the payout, $(F_t - X_t)$, is high, and when F_t is high, your discount rate of that payout is low. This asymmetry leads to convexity in the present value of forward contracts, in contrast to the linear nature of futures. A forward rate contract is convex because its price rises more for a downward move in forward rates than its price declines for an equal upward move in forward rates.

In both markets, one is taking a bet on a forward rate, but with an interest rate swap, which is a set of forwards, cash changes hands only as each leg of the swap matures, often far in the future. In contrast, a strip of Eurodollar futures is market to market, and the profit and loss is booked daily. Like much of financial engineering, the general idea is straightforward, but the specifics depend on a lot of parochial details about instrument conventions, whether they are quoted in yield or price space, and so forth. The key driver is that the present value of gains and losses are asymmetric, in that futures rates falling are discounted at a lower rate, necessarily, than when future rates rise; as the futures prices are market to market while the swap is not, this asymmetry creates arbitrage.

Figure 11.1 shows how the profit and loss of these two contracts, forwards and futures, varies as a function of the forward rate. The convexity, or upward curvature, of the forward is the key difference with the futures profit.

Now, the curvature is very slight at the scale of daily changes, so that the difference in the effect on profits for forwards versus futures is only about 1 percent difference for changes in rates of 10 basis points. Only a true quant would have seen this, because graphically, on a daily basis, it is not obvious—you have to do the math, guided by the logic. With estimates of future variability of those rates, one can estimate the present value of this convexity on swaps versus futures.

This convexity in swaps, but not Eurodollars, means that to preclude arbitrage, the futures prices should have a higher implied forward rate to compensate for its lower convexity. If future and forward rates were equivalent, one could buy fixed-receive swaps and short Eurodollar futures, and the daily mark to market of the Eurodollars versus the present value mark to market of the swap would allow one to lock in a sure thing. The effect

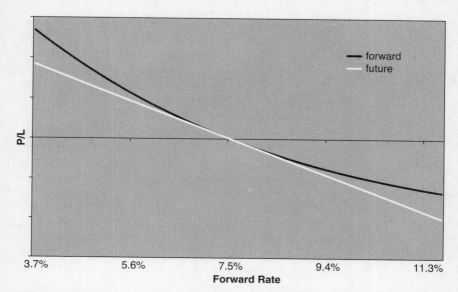

FIGURE 11.1 Forward and Futures P/L as a Function of Forward Rates: 10 Year Forward, Struck at 7.5 Percent, Flat Forward Curve

added up to 15 basis points in present value if done with 5-year swaps, and 40 basis point for a 10-year swap.

I knew an executive who worked at UBS in the 1990s who said they made tens of millions of dollars on this strategy. He was surprised when I told him that the trade was outlined very clearly in *Risk* magazine in 1990 because he was certain UBS figured the trade out themselves after that.[4] Indeed, a handful, but only a handful, of large *institutions* made a lot of money, for perhaps five years, on this trade.[5] Its demise coincided with several published papers examining this strategy in detail around 1995, outlining very methodically how it works.[6] One needed to be large to trade swaps of a long duration and offset this risk with futures, because this involves effectively cross-margining, where the gains and losses from one product, in this case swaps, is netted against the gains and losses of a different product, in this case futures. Individuals usually cannot receive cross margining from their broker, often by regulatory fiat, making this a game only the big guys can profit from.

Also, because the edge was so thin, large financial institutions could layer this tactic onto their normal market-making business in a way that made this trade viable when others could not. This is an important subtlety

to many successful trading strategies, and why as a retail trader, trading like
an institution or floor trader is not sophisticated, but rather quite stupid. The
main job of the market maker is to make money off the flow of buys and
sells he gets, while keeping the residual positions he incidentally acquires
small. If he posts a bid-ask of 10 to 11, and acquires a large short position,
he should adjust his bid-ask downward for two reasons. First, the market
is saying people value this at less than 10, and they are therefore selling to
him at 10. Second, his position now exposes him to delta risk, that is, risk
in his portfolio, which is not something he really has a view on (*delta risk
is the risk from a change in the price of a security on a portfolio*). He is
busy posting bids and offers and keeping them fresh, not trying to figure
out if the latest statements by the Federal Reserve are good or bad for his
asset. Over the intervals he evaluates stocks, his view on fundamental value
is really irrelevant, and he needs to focus on keeping his bid-ask fresh, not
worrying about his long-term opinion on the securities he is trading.

However, if a large group at a higher level of aggregation monitors these
positions, and decides that, say, being long IBM, or Eurodollars, is good,
they might tolerate an acquisition of these positions, and not move their bid-
ask so quickly as to make this portfolio go away. One can acquire positions
based on market making at a negative cost, in a sense, thereby making a
strategy with a slim expected return viable, but only in combination with
the low, if not negative cost of its implementation. Retail traders pay the
bid-ask to put on a position, whereas floor traders receive the bid-ask to
put on the position—though they have to wait until the right flow comes by
for this happy fortunate accident to occur. The key is that a strategy with a
very small edge might be feasible for a trading operation, but infeasible for
someone without the complimentary market maker function.

Another subtle statistical trade was the volatility dispersion trade.
Volatility dispersion strategy involves sophisticated analytics, especially as
a practical matter, but the gist is fairly straightforward. Consider that if
two stocks are independent (correlation is zero), and volatilities of 100 percent, the portfolio volatility of these two stocks is about 71 percent; if the
correlation is 1, the portfolio volatility is 100 percent. There is a mathematical function that relates the volatility of the options to the volatility of
the index based on the covariance (look up $cov(x+y)$, which is in an introductory statistics textbook). The arbitrage arises because index volatility
has historically traded rich on occasion relative to the basket of individual
stock volatilities and their correlations. Thus, the dispersion strategy allows
traders to profit from price differences using index options and offsetting
options on individual stocks.

The dispersion strategy typically consists of selling options on a stock index while simultaneously buying options on the component stocks, meaning

one is short correlation, or long dispersion. The reverse dispersion strategy consists of buying options on a stock index and selling options on the component stocks. Clearly, given the bid-ask of options, and the many options one needed to trade, having direct access as an adjunct to some other function such as market making was essential at making this a real value-add.

In 2002 and 2003, as the market was crashing, then rebounding, there were many opportunities in this trade. I received several calls from head-hunters around that time, desperately looking for quants to join teams that were going to implement these types of trades. One large hedge fund hired several teams to independently implement this strategy, thinking that a little internal competition might be the best way to make sure it is being done correctly. But by 2004, so many people were doing it that there was no edge in this trade, especially at large scale.[7] The fund that hired several teams to implement this kind of arbitrage let these groups go rather quickly and quietly.

At the end of a good strategy, and sometimes the beginning, only those acting in concert with market makers—those with the lowest transaction costs—will be plying it profitably, which creates a lot of confusion, because hucksters love to sell strategies as "the same as those exploited by the big banks," as if it is attractive merely because these players are in-the-know. It is a *combination* of being knowledgeable, and having the lowest cost access, that is essential for many alpha strategies. One sure sign of a strategy's demise occurs when a sufficient number of people know about it and have forced out of the last bits of profit left in the strategy, write books about how trading "like a turtle" or some such strategy can make you rich, like it did for these successful traders or institutions. These are symptomatic of rules that used to work, but no longer do, especially without having extremely low transaction costs.

PAIRS AND MEAN REVERSION

Arbitraging assets by finding connections is one way of finding arbitrage, but another is finding patterns. That is, the sequence, 1, 1, 2, 3, 5, 8 is the start of the well-known Fibonacci sequence, which underlies the population growth of rabbits, and, for some, markets. If you know Fibonacci formula, and the data indeed follow this formula, you can predict the next number. Predicting the next price, given a sequence of prices, is not the same as arbitrage, though, because there is nothing forcing one asset to equal another at some future date, or that cash flows are always constant as market values change. You merely anticipate future changes based on patterns, and hopefully, you have discovered some tendency in the data such that you go long things that rise, short things that fall, and on average make money in bull or bear markets because you are hedged. It requires faith that the future will be like the past.

The most famous pattern in markets is pairs trading. When I came in 2001 to Deephaven, a hedge fund in Minnesota, there were a lot of pairs traders there, and many of them had made money for years trading this strategy. I later learned that many large stat-arb (statistical arbitrage) shops on Wall Street, such as Princeton Newport, D.E. Shaw, and Morgan Stanley, all worked this basic idea, and many traders there became multimillionaires exploiting this pattern throughout the 1990s. The idea is simple. You find a pair of similar companies, such as Coca-Cola and Pepsi. You can find these using just correlations, or from fundamental analysis, looking at the industry and noting firms that have very similar market capitalization and product mixes. Now say Coke rises 5 percent, whereas Pepsi does not move for over a week. On average, if you shorted Coke, and went long Pepsi, you generally made money over the next week, as the initial move was generally overdone for the stock that jumped whereas the other half of the pair would move in sympathy, perhaps as traders recognized the fact that similar risks or fortunes were present in the pair asset.

What is really interesting about pairs is the sheer simplicity of the trade. While it started by trading pairs, so the trader would be hedged, the real edge in the trade came from the mean reversion in the big mover. Thus, the basic idea was to go short the big movers up, and go long the big movers down, and this was the basic ingredient in statistical arbitrage that was so successful in the 1990s. I knew some Ph.D.s implementing various nuances of this strategy, but generally their refinements were second order, somewhat inevitable whenever you give a bunch of smart people a lot of data and a basic model. Stat arb sounds very complicated, and one would often see computer scientists and mathematicians from the greatest schools in the world doing this, but it's a bit like hiring Eddie Van Halen to play *Smoke on the Water*. In their defense, people were making a lot of money, and if you are really rich, you can afford to hire overqualified people to do things just to be safe.

Andrew Lo and Craig MacKinlay wrote about this in 1988, noting that variance ratio bounds tests implied that stocks were mean-reverting at high frequencies.[8] That is, if a stock has a pure random walk (that is, big movers did not mean revert), the ratio of its five-day return variance over its one-day return variance should be five; the ratio of the 10-day variance to the 1-day, 10, and so on. In practice, the variance from daily returns was more than proportional to the monthly variance adjusted for the number of days in a month, and so implied that stocks were not a random walk, but exhibited some mean reversion that diminished their volatility over long horizons, relative to the baseline random walk. As the essence of pairs trading, or stat arb, is mean reversion at high frequencies (for example, weekly or daily), it was really all there in Lo and MacKinlay's 1988 paper, meaning that they figured it out in 1986. A paper written in 1998 showed how the profitability of a simulation of a pairs strategy worked over time, and found that the profitability of the trade decreased significantly around 1990.[9]

In 2007, Lo wrote about the decline of the stat-arb strategy of going long losers and short winners, and showed how it declined in profitability over time. His construction of the strategy weighted each position every day by the degree to which it was above or below the average return, so that it was on average neutral to the market. In practice, there are many different ways to implement the general pattern, say by concentrating solely on the extremums, ignoring companies that had substantitive news like actual earnings releases, looking at volume as well, and so forth. But while the nuances helped, they often hurt, and Lo's general trend holds for the strategy. Figure 11.2 shows how profits declined as this strategy declined over the past decade.

By 2003, you see the profitability of the strategy has fallen significantly, especially compared to the early 1990s period, and Deephaven got rid of

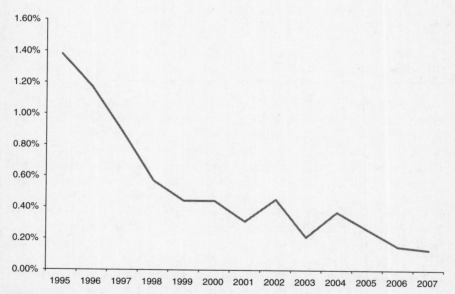

FIGURE 11.2 Daily Returns to Long Losers and Short Winners
Source: Andrew W. Lo and Amir E. Khandani, "What Happened to the Quants in August 2007?" (Cambridge, MA: MIT, 2007).

their pairs trading. Web sites advertising pairs arose around that time, and commercials on CNBC highlighted trading pairs as a great way to escape the rat race. This is surely a good sign that profits in a strategy are zero after modest transaction costs. I know a handful of pairs traders who are able to make a decent living doing this, yet it is not nearly as scalable and easy as it was. If I had a time machine that took me back to 1990, this is the easiest strategy for someone small to exploit.

In 2008, I ran into Andy Lo at a conference and asked if he regretted not taking advantage of this, given that he discovered it when it had at least another decade of incredible returns. He replied that he thought the real key to the strategy was implementing it at the lowest cost, so his edge was really not so great, his missed opportunity not so much. It is really an unfair question, because with hindsight there are many decisions one would do over, but I think he underestimated his alpha in this trade, because a good trade idea always needs more than just a strategy, so the strategy is not worthless merely because it is not worth so much in isolation. For example, any good idea needs capital, but clearly capital needs good ideas; so both are necessary and can haggle over the share of the proceeds. He needed someone with low-cost access to trading, but there were many people with low-cost access to trading who could have used such a strategy. If he found a match, even splitting the profits generously would have made him an immense fortune.

FUND INNOVATIONS

The Cowles Commission for Research in Economics was founded in 1932. Alfred Cowles, president of an investment counseling firm, initiated some inquiries into the accuracy of professional stock market forecasters over the period from 1928 to 1932. This aroused his interest in fundamental economic research, which led him to offer his financial support toward the establishment of the Cowles Commission. The first Cowles Commission product to attract widespread attention, from both businessmen and professional economists, and still one of the best known of its publications, was a paper by Cowles titled "Can Stock Market Forecasters Forecast?," published in *Econometrica* in 1933. A three-word abstract of this paper runs as follows: "It is doubtful." Cowles began his investigation with the suspicion that many forecasters had no real skill and were in effect simply guessing, and he set out to test this hypothesis. He charted the weekly individual stock purchase recommendations of sixteen established financial services from 1928 to 1932, and found that if an investor had followed all of them, with equal initial amounts of capital allotted to each purchase of a stock, he would have come out making about one and a half per cent per year less than if he had invested in the stock market as a whole. He then checked the common stock investment records of 20 large fire insurance companies for the same period, and found that on the average they fell behind the market by slightly more than one per cent per year. He then charted the forecasts of stock market level made by 24 financial publications from 1928 to 1932 and found that if an investor had followed all of them, again with equal amounts of initial capital allotted to each, he would have fallen behind the market average by about 4 percent per year. The expert's forecasts of the markets were not even better than chance.

This is the first major empirical study of the Efficient Markets Hypothesis, and has held up quite nicely. Fundamental analysis, either of stock analyst recommendations or in mutual fund management, does not outperform naïve alternative such as buying a diversified portfolio. Yet, mutual funds got away with 8.5 percent up-front commissions and 2 percent annual expense ratios until well into the 1980s. Even today, the vast majority of equity funds are actively managed (about 90 percent). Investment advisers have held themselves out for generations to be providing value through the outperformance of their picks, when everyone with data knew this is not only untrue today, it has always been untrue.

In 1940, after a horrible stretch for stocks, Wall Street veteran Fred Schwed wrote a book titled *Where Are the Customer's Yachts?* The title refers to an old joke about a visitor to New York who admired the yachts that the bankers and brokers had in the harbor. Naively, he then asked where the customers' yachts were. Naturally, there were no customers' yachts. Schwed's book outlines all the nefarious tendencies that bedevil investors out of their savings, mainly from overtrading based on hopes that were based on little more than possibilities. Though he describes the brokers as being sincere in their advice, it was generally unwise for the investor, and as the brokers made money regardless of the net return to investors, they had no incentives to become aware of their poor advice—it worked for them. In such a scenario, the easiest way to create alpha is not to devise a better stock-picking strategy, but to merely cut costs, because if a monkey throwing darts does as well as an active mutual fund manager, surely a mechanical monkey proxy is cheaper, and this advantage should add up over time.

By the early 1970s, the Efficient Markets Hypothesis had been formalized, which popularized the idea that it is difficult, if not impossible, to make money in financial markets. Paul Samuelson proved that unbiased expectations implied prices fluctuated randomly, which is either a tautology, or striking, depending on how geeky you are. Thus, there was a theory for why stock prices appear to follow Brownian motion. Applied to mutual funds, it suggested that these managers were not adding value, merely adding volatility and expense. In 1973, Malkiel's *Random Walk Down Wall Street* appeared, preaching to retail investors that they should not try to outperform the market, and in 1974, Samuelson wrote an article applying these concepts to portfolio managers, arguing for passive portfolio management.[10]

Thus, the idea was in the air, and independently, John McQuown and David Booth at Wells Fargo, and Rex Sinquefield at American National Bank in Chicago, both established the first passive Index Funds in 1973. These were portfolios targeted at institutions. Interestingly, the Wells Fargo fund was initially an equal-weighted fund on all the stocks on the NYSE, which, given the large number of small stocks, and the fact that a price decline meant you should buy more, and at a price increase sell more, proved to be an implementation nightmare. It was replaced with a value-weighted index fund of the S&P500 in 1976, which eliminates this problem. Another misstep was clearly not targeting the retail investor early, which turned out to be where the real money was. Rex Sinquefield started Dimensional Fund Advisors in 1981, in part to address this deficiency. Sinquefield was also hooked into the University of Chicago, which had Eugene Fama as its head of research. As the size effect was the hot thing at that time, DFA had several small cap portfolios at the outset to take advantage of this anomaly. Unfortunately, the size effect disappeared in the 1980s, but Dimensional was able to survive this setback admirably. Thus, even a great, simple idea like an index fund, has a learning curve in practice.

In 1951, the anecdotal evidence John Bogle assembled in his Princeton University senior thesis on the then-minuscule mutual fund industry led him to write that mutual funds "can make no claim to superiority to the market averages." How joyous it must be to quote oneself from such inauspicious beginnings to explain one's success. But another driver was that in 1975, his company, Vanguard, was a shareholder-owned mutual fund group—the company was owned by the mutual fund investors—so low-cost fund administration was not taking money from owners, it was giving money to them. In contrast, the idea of an index fund would have hardly appealed to a high-cost fund complex whose very revenue depended on the conviction that active management did add value, at least, in their particular case. In his pitch to the Vanguard board for starting an index fund, he brought some of his own data on the performance of mutual fund managers, suggesting that they underperformed by about the same amount as their expenses, and some references to recent articles by Samuelson and Charles Ellis.[11] So, blessed with some good intuition from Bogle, the rising popularity of the idea in the academy, timing, and good incentives from Vanguard, they had both the opportunity and the motive to create the first retail index fund, which is now the largest index fund in the world, and Vanguard, the second-largest fund family. By the next summer, the fund was launched with about $11 million.

At the time these funds were being introduced, the whole idea seemed stupid to most non-economists. It was dubbed "Bogle's folly," and described as unpatriotic, on the premise that any red-blooded U.S. citizen has investing alpha. Indeed, a sure sign you are taking risk is that most people, especially the experts, think you are a fool. While Samuelson sneered from his perch in his weekly Newsweek column, the hoi polloi continued investing in active managers, because index funds were a trivial portion of equity investments until the late 1980s.[12] "Sure, we considered indexing, but we rejected it—why settle for mediocrity," said an investor in *Business Week* in 1984.[13] A Forbes article about the same time made the standard argument against indexing:

> To buy an index fund is to accept mediocrity. Such a decision is hard to justify in the stock market where several great investors—the likes of John Templeton and Warren Buffett and Philip Carret—have shown that it is possible to beat the market over three-decade stretches.[14]

Note that in reciting the obvious success stories, it is the same handful of names—Buffett, Graham, Lynch, Neff, Templeton—that prove the statement "The average fund manager is average before costs" is incorrect. Why not say, many people have won the lottery, so it is hard to accept that it cannot be done? The fact that some can, and they are, generally, smart people, suggests there is a chance for someone with alpha regardless of the odds. Economists may find such hope-based investing as foolish, but remember, many an economist points to an "existence theorem" to support their views on some practical matter even if the theorem, merely implies something is possible, not probable. The key is, if it is possible, there is hope.

Russ Wermers estimated that equity mutual funds outperform the market by 1.3 percent per year, although expenses and transaction costs reduce this benefit to essentially zero. His conclusion: "Funds pick stocks well enough to cover their costs."[15] But that ignores their higher annual volatility for most funds relative to broad indexes, which perhaps is not priced risk, but surely annoying. John Bogle illustrates that an index fund has a 350-basis-point advantage over the average equity mutual fund because of management expenses, brokerage costs, sales charges, and tax advantages.[16] Arnott, Berkin, and Ye (2000) find that the Vanguard 500 Index Fund outperforms the average equity mutual fund and the effect is amplified when taxes are considered.[17] Burton Malkiel notes that over the past 25 years, about 70 percent of active equity managers have been outperformed by the S&P 500 Stock Index.[18]

Elton, Gruber, and Blake ask the relevant question: "Given that there are sufficient index funds to span most investors' risk choices, that the index funds are available at a low cost, and that the low cost of index funds means that a combination of index funds is likely to outperform an active fund of similar risk...why select an actively managed fund?"[19] Obviously, only an overconfident hope in alpha, but at least today there's an alternative, whereas, from a practical perspective, you could not get a low-cost, diversified portfolio before 1975 without paying some delusional or duplicitous manager to take extra gambles with your money.

By year-end 2007, in the United States, assets in Exchange Traded Funds (ETFs) and index mutual funds reached more than $1.4 trillion, and these indexed products have increased more than eightfold over the past 10 years.[20] Yet as large as this is, it is only 11 percent of the total assets managed by all registered investment companies. ETFs and index funds are available in most other broad asset classes but, to date, have attracted less investor interest than those tied to indexes of large-blend domestic equity.

Now, at some level this is not a big opportunity, because for investors, it merely offered one a modestly better Sharpe ratio on average (say from 0.4 to 0.5), but one without a chance for arbitrage that drives a lot of investing. Yet the aggregate savings to investors was much larger than the wealth created by the convexity trade between Eurodollar futures and swaps. Furthermore, people did get rich off this idea, such as the innovators Bogle, McQuown, and Sinquefeld, who are all fabulously wealthy as a result of their pioneering efforts in these domains. Certainly many other executives and owners who were part of these efforts made successful careers targeting this unconventional tactic. As with a lot of alpha, the big rewards are not in passive application or discovery, but active marketing, ownership, and implementation. Those who were able to parlay this into yachts, remains the brokers, which should tell you something about trying to become rich as a retail investor.

CONVERTIBLE BONDS

A convertible bond is basically a bond with a long-term call option attached.[21] For decades, these bonds presented a superior return to straight bonds of similar credit quality. Consider first what a good Sharpe ratio is. The equity premium puzzle is that the apparent return over Treasuries for U.S. equities has historically been around 6 percent. When combined with an annualized volatility of around 17 percent, this implies a Sharpe ratio of 0.35. In the early development of the CAPM, maximizing the Sharpe ratio was the underlying objective, what investors should do, and what they implicitly were doing. A Sharpe of 0.35 is anomalously high relative to alternatives, and so, represents a good benchmark of what a great Sharpe ratio is for an investor.

For Convertible Bond Arbitrage, the idea is that a hedge fund buys convertible bonds, hedges the interest rate risk with bond futures, and the equity risk through short positions on the equity aligned with the convertible bond, thereby isolating only the convertible part of the position. This kind of strategy is really only available to hedge funds, because only a hedge fund could go long and short such different products, and so hedge funds were the primary purchasers of convertible bonds. Most mutual funds are constrained to be only long, and cannot hedge their equity risk, or interest rate risk, so they were at a relative disadvantage as purchasers of this asset. The returns from January 1994 through May 2003 listed in Table 11.1 are quite impressive.

This was the return after fees, which in hedge funds averaged about 2 percent of assets, and 20 percent of profits. Often, this was after paying the portfolio manager 10 percent of the profits of his portfolio. Thus, the returns were making everyone in this space very wealthy, and the growth of an asset class is primarily driven by making not the investors rich, but the managers rich. A Sharpe above 1.0 is a very good return, especially on an asset class as scalable as convertible bonds, and so, investors had no complaints even after paying the managers a large chunk. Clearly, this strategy had a huge amount of alpha. Princeton Newport, the hedge fund operated by *Beat the Dealer* legend Edward Thorpe, and Citidel Investments, a fund giant built by Ken Griffith, both built a good deal of their strategy focusing on convertible bonds, and the rise in funds targeting convertible bonds rose dramatically throughout the 1990s.[22]

How could this be?

TABLE 11.1 Convertible Bond Arbitrage: January 1994 through May 2003

	Hennessee	CS/Tremont	SPX
Annual Return	10.08%	10.36%	10.71%
Annual Standard Deviation	4.20%	4.83%	16.00%
Sharpe	1.30	1.19	0.38

On the supply side, issuers loved them because they exploited the fact that underpricing an option is part of a very subtle moral hazard. A company essentially gets a lower rate on its debt through the value of the option the bondholder gets, because a convert is a portfolio, and while the option is in general undervalued, it is not worth zero:

$$\text{Straight Bond} + \text{Option} = \text{Convert Bond}$$

The positive value of the option implies the convertible bond's bond has a lower yield and lower price, than if they issued a straight bond without an option. A lower interest rate makes the CFO look good, because it is a directly measurable expense. Now, if the stock price subsequently falls, the bondholder will not exercise the option, and the CFO can point to how he saved the company interest expense at no explicit cost, because the option expired as worthless; if the stock price rises, equity holders are usually sufficiently happy to not worry about any dilution from the convertibles.

While a convertible bond is like a bond plus a call option on the equity, it is actually considerably more complicated. A convertible bond is usually callable, so one has to account for the situation that issuers can call bonds back as their credit rating improves, or as interest rates decline. Also, converting the bond into equity extinguishes the bond. Interest rates, credit spreads, and equity prices are not independent of each other, as for example, a much higher stock price in the future will be associated with a lower credit spread. Thus, you need a model that captures the statistical nature of these processes in a way that captures some of the correlations we know exist, but are difficult to quantify. Then, there are an infinite number of combinations of yields and implied option volatilities on the warrants that correspond to its current price, because it could have a yield of 8 percent, and an option vol of 30 percent, or a yield of 9 percent, and an option vol of 20 percent. You have two unknown inputs to the model (volatility and spread), and one observed variable (the price). As it is very difficult to reverse engineer the value implicitly assigned to the option in the convertible bond, it is rare the CFO is held accountable for selling it at too low an implied volatility or too high a credit spread, because the credit spread will necessarily be less than the spread on a straight bond, and there is no unambiguous vol that the convertible bond was sold at, only an implicit vol, and the company rarely goes out of its way to advertise this.

In 2001, I joined a hedge fund in Minneapolis, and one of my first charges was to try to make sense of the prices and volatilities in the convertible bond portfolio. I found that on average, the implied volatilities of these convertibles was about 9 vols (for example, a 30 percent implied annualized volatility for the equity, as opposed to a 39 percent in their comparable straight options) lower than on comparable options or historical volatilities, while the spread on the bonds taking this option value into account was about 2 percent higher (that is, 200 basis points higher). A different convertible bond model, or assumptions, may change those relative numbers, but the bottom line was that convertible bonds gave an investor cheap options, and relatively higher yield, on the same underlying assets. The board and shareholders rarely had the information, nor were they interested in getting it, allowing the management to exploit this issue.

Why this could be so for the demand side was easy given the complexity of the problem. Most credit analysts do not like evaluating option values of equities. If you are a credit specialist, selling your alpha in the credit space, then doing a joint problem such as convertible bonds either meant you would be getting into an area where you did not have a lot of confidence, or sharing the profits with someone else. The same held for option experts. Convertible bonds were a hybrid product that investors generally did not appreciate being aggregated. Issuers persisted because of the perverse incentives to the CFOs and the limited information given to the Board and investors. This situation allowed the product to be underpriced for years, and people like Edward Thorpe, who was a pioneer on option pricing, had the confidence in their ability to value warrants, make some modest assumption about the credit, and diversify. It was easy money for decades.

But around 2002, many investment banks started to roll out pricing models online that made it easier to see what a great deal this was. These pricing tools basically made it easier for someone good at options, or credit, to jump into converts, deferring to the defaults for the stuff he was ignorant on (credit or options, as the case may be). The models were sufficiently well understood, that the presentation was done well, and the default assumptions of the investment bank were not bad. Furthermore, they started trading credit default swaps on these bonds, and also had instruments to strip out the volatility, or credit risk, so one could buy only the optionality on the convertible bond, or only its credit risk. As this market grew, arbitrage basically whittled the premium in convertible bonds away, because hedge funds and the investment banks, were buying the straight debt, or straight options, and selling the pure debt or pure optionality of the same issuer through a derivative on the convertible bond. Traders could avoid worrying about things they did not know, such as credit, or volatility, and take advantage of their specialty. The market disaggregated a product that was fundamentally not appreciated for its aggregation by investors.

TABLE 11.2 Convertible Bond Arbitrage: June 2004–December 2008

	CS/Tremont	Hedge Fund Research HFX	SPX
Annual Return	−2.54%	−3.80%	1.14%
Annual Standard Deviation	8.84%	9.62%	12.94%
Sharpe	−0.64	−0.72	−0.15

Source: Credit Suisse/Tremont Convertible Bond Index, Hedge Fund Research Convertible Bond index.

This all came to a head in the summer of 2003, when the increase in entry ended this game, as it usually does, with a terrible drawdown. Since then, the Sharpe ratio has been less than zero, as shown in Table 11.2. It could be too early to call, but I think the salad days of convertible bonds are now a historical artifact, and you can see this if you try to back into volatilities and spreads given current prices. That is, actual returns since 2003 have been negative in this strategy (it should be beta neutral), and this makes sense given the new tactics used by investors, allowing entry and driving down returns. Unlike pairs trading, there is a way to see if the juice is in the trade given current parameters, and it is gone.

LONG AND SHORT EQUITY HEDGE FUNDS

Hedge funds cover investment strategies so diverse, they are more different than they are alike. Their essence is they can buy or sell anything, unlike mutual funds that are constrained to be long only, in a particular asset, often of a particular type (such as small cap growth funds). But they generally target a volatility slightly below the S&P500, about a 12 percent annualized volatility, even though leverage is a choice variable, and so could easily generate higher volatility and returns.

Hedge funds have typically received 2 percent of assets, and 20 percent of profits for their efforts. The Credit Suisse/Tremont Fund Index shows an average return of 10 percent from 1994 through August 2008, compared to the S&P's 9 percent annualized return over that same period. The beta with the S&P was about 0.25. Now, many people look at the average expense ratio of active (that is, non-index) mutual funds, at 1.0 percent to seem cheaper. But looking deeper at the numbers, the hedge funds appear to be a much cheaper way of accessing equity alpha.

Assume that returns for equity mutual funds are generated through a combination of a passive investment in the benchmark, and then layers on an active portfolio. This generates a process

$$r_p = w_A r_A + (1 - w_A) r_I$$

Where the weighting on the active portfolio is w_A, r_A is the return on the active portfolio, r_I is the return on the index, and r_p is the return on the total portfolio. In this case, the R^2 between the mutual fund and the index would be

$$R^2 = \frac{(1 - w_A)^2 \, \sigma_I^2}{\sigma_P^2}$$

Thus, one can take R^2s and estimate the implicit active picks by the fund manager. Applying this to 152 large cap funds, Ross Miller estimates about 15 percent of the portfolio is actively managed.[23]

This implies an investor can replicate the risk-and-return characteristics of the fund by placing 85 percent of her assets in an index fund that tracks the S&P500 and the remaining 15 percent in an appropriately chosen market-neutral investment. Assuming 20 basis points as the expense ratio for the passive component of a fund (about the same ratio as large index funds), the average fund expense ratio of about 120 basis points can be seen as "overcharging" investors by 100 basis points on the passive component of its portfolio. If we assess those 100 basis points against the 15 percent of the portfolio that is actively managed, we would find that annual expenses account for 6.66 percent of those funds, in addition to the 1.20 percent, for a total of 7.86 percent. That is, if you are paying for alpha, he is charging 7.86 percent of assets for those alpha picks—implying his picks have to return 7.86 percent above the benchmark to justify his fees, which is highly improbable.

A hedge fund that charges the standard annual fee of 2 percent of funds under management plus 20 percent, assuming it made about 10 percent annually, cost 4 percent per dollar invested. Given the average beta of the hedge fund universe was about 0.25, this means that only 75 percent of the equity was truly active. 4 percent divided by 0.75, gives a number of 5.3 percent for the cost of alpha dollars invested.

If you are paying for alpha, active mutual funds are an expensive way to target a dollar of capital applied directly to managerial alpha. Indeed, the average hedge fund has a positive Sharpe ratio, even after accounting for beta exposure.[24] In contrast, the average fund is estimated to slightly underperform or equally perform the index, suggesting negative alpha among those managers. Targeting equity alpha is cheaper in hedge funds, and generally alpha is positive in hedge funds, in contrast to equity funds.

Thus, with funds, innovations can arise at both ends of the superficial expense spectrum. In one, low fees with an explicit goal of matching an index. In another, high fees but highly uncorrelated with the index. Both methods are an improvement over the traditional actively managed mutual fund, and underlies the growth of index and hedge funds over the past decades.

AUTOMATING ACTIVITIES

Finding alpha in the classic sense is like picking up a $20 bill. You make money without hurting anyone. In practice, your idea hurts someone else. Building a better mousetrap puts current mousetrap makers out of business. A common method for generating alpha within institutions is figuring out a cheaper way to do something, usually by eliminating the number of people needed to get something done. In manufacturing or farming, this involves machinery; in finance, it's more likely about computers and statistics.

In banking, scale has been a large part of productivity growth. Back in the bad old days, there were laws designed to keep money in the community, so that every little hamlet was autonomous, an idyllic state for those who hate capital account deficits. The problem is that you then lose out on the free lunch of diversification. In the Great Depression, many of America's thousands of banks failed, and through the uncertainty and self-fulfilling prophecies of a bank run (and, of course other factors), many more failed. Thus, in the United States, 9,000 banks failed in the 1930s, while similarly situated Canada had zero failures. The United States had around 30,000 banks compared to Canada's 10 back then, so the key difference was the greater diversification of Canadian bank portfolios.[25]

The elimination of *unit banking*—where a bank would have one branch only—and the elimination of laws in the 1990s that prohibited interstate banking, have allowed banks to diversify their asset base, taking advantage of the one free lunch in economics.

Another major scale innovation in banking was in the credit underwriting of consumers. In the old days, if a person, not a business, wanted a loan for a car, house, or some other thing, a loan officer would size you up the way people size up potential dates: qualitative, gossipy, and incomparable. I have a bunch of old credit evaluations of consumers from the 1930s that I stumbled into at KeyCorp, historical relics that were being discarded. These are listed in Figure 11.3, where the almost illegible cursive has been written over to allow readability. As seen in Figure 11.3 they make observations

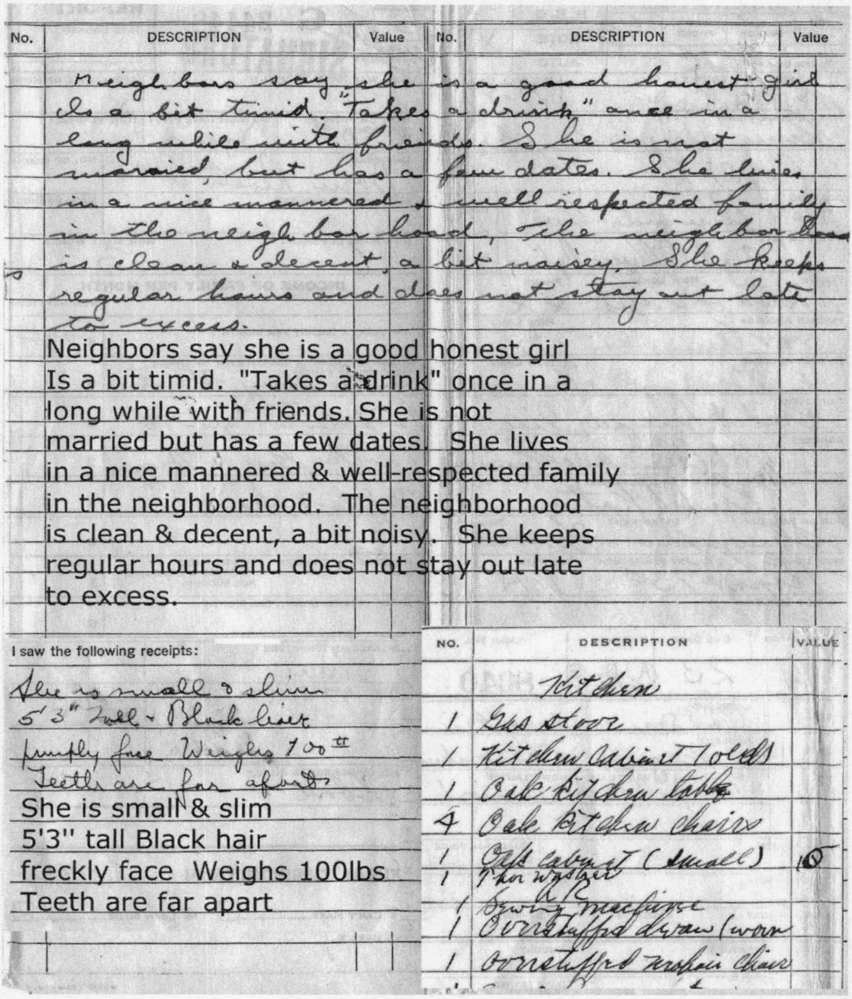

No.	DESCRIPTION	Value	No.	DESCRIPTION	Value

Neighbors say she is a good honest girl
Is a bit timid. "Takes a drink" once in a
long while with friends. She is not
married but has a few dates. She lives
in a nice mannered & well-respected family
in the neighborhood. The neighborhood
is clean & decent, a bit noisy. She keeps
regular hours and does not stay out late
to excess.

I saw the following receipts:

She is small & slim
5'3" tall Black hair
freckly face Weighs 100lbs
Teeth are far apart

NO.	DESCRIPTION	VALUE
	Kitchen	
1	Gas stove	
1	Kitchen cabinet 1 old	
1	Oak kitchen table	
4	Oak kitchen chairs	
1	Oak cabinet (small)	
1	Sewing machine	
1	Overstuffed divan (worn)	
1	Overstuffed armchair	

FIGURE 11.3 Credit Evaluations from the 1930s

that one typically makes when gossiping with friends, and are probably illegal now:

> *"teeth are far apart"*
> *"takes a drink" once in a while*
> *Not married, but has a few dates*
> *Neighbors say she is a good-hearted girl*

Another shows how the furniture inventory of a homeowner is displayed in a list, written in longhand, with no dollar equivalents. An accompanying paragraph describes, qualitatively, the pros and cons of the creditworthiness of the borrower.

The loan officer would interview neighbors, asking about everything related to the borrower's character. They would survey the neighborhood, remarking on how ordered it was. This process would take at least a day's work. Now, on one hand this is very detailed information, and captures information that while no longer used, is probably relevant to someone's ability and willingness to pay. But on the other hand, such information does not move up the ladder well: a headquarters can hardly compare the loan quality of one branch, or region, to another, given these reports. An outsider would have no way to validate these credits, because they are based on rather subjective assessments, and the data are not organized in a database.

In the 1960s, as people in the United States began to move about, credit cards became popular, and companies sprang up to generate an alternative: the consumer credit score. These evaluations use a very limited set of inputs: payment history, length of history, size of balances, recent credit activity. The neat thing is, they are objective, and simply require that lenders cooperate by reporting balances, inquiries, and late payments to a centralized service. They then charge other lenders who inquire about these data. The net result is a more powerful, and more important, validated, credit score. This means that credit can then be sold off to others, whereas in the old system, a pile of such qualitative assessments is very opaque to outsiders, because outsiders do not know the underwriters personally, and so cannot trust their subjective assessments. Credit score data are objectively meaningful because they are validated on a lot of data over a couple of credit cycles, something that is practically impossible for the old approach. The importance of such transparency in credit markets is highlighted in the current mortgage crisis, because the complexity of the mortgage exposure, combined with changes in underwriting standards, has made it very difficult for an outsider to know the credit risk of these products, which means that when concerns are triggered, there is no easy way to assuage panicked investors.

Experts are generally dominated by statistical algorithms given a sufficient amount of objective information. Loans, which have clear success and fail outcomes, are a perfect example of the kind of activity that is inevitably taken over by computers. The qualitative approach of the personal underwriter emphasizes explanation, narrative, and anecdotes, as opposed to the quantitative focus on prediction, models, and statistics. This would all be a matter of personal preference except that statistics dominates anecdotes for the simple reason that the bottom line is a statistic—a portfolio with lower *average* credit losses, and so the statistical approach is amenable to tinkering at the margin and making improvements, while the other generates few concrete tactics that one can leave to future underwriters.

Empirical evidence in favor of quantitative models versus judgment as applied to lending comes from Libby (1975). He asked 16 loan officers from small banks and 27 loan officers from large banks to judge which 30 of 60 firms would go bankrupt within three years of the financial statements with which they were presented. The loan officers requested five financial ratios on which to base their judgments. While they were correct 74 percent of the time, this was inferior to such simple alternatives as the liabilities and assets ratio.

Outside of lending, there are many examples in which models outperformed the experts, including: evaluating graduate school applicants, future student GPA, future faculty ratings, and radiology diagnostics.[26] Why might this be the case? That is, why might statistical models dominate judgment in prediction? Paul Meehl, in his classic 1954 book, *Clinical versus Statistical Prediction,* reviewed evidence that while humans are good at finding important variables, they are not as good at integrating such diverse information sources optimally.[27]

As part of a study for the CIA (that CIA) Rob Johnston's "Integrating Methodologists into Teams of Substantive Experts" noted:

> *The very method by which one becomes an expert explains why experts are much better at describing, explaining, performing tasks, and problem-solving within their domains than are novices, but, with a few exceptions, are worse at forecasting than actuarial tables based on historical, statistical models.*[28]

As opposed to quantitative models that are judged solely on their calibration and power, human analysis is also focused upon presenting a compelling explanation, and focuses more deeply on explaining individual assessments as opposed to broad statistical judgments in a statistical manner, it would be unsurprising if their judgment was not optimized to statistical objectives. Improving inductive reasoning requires continual feedback, and unfortunately in most lending institutions such feedback is anecdotal, not statistical.[29]

Thus, today a consumer loan is more powerfully analyzed, with greater transparency, and may take only 10 minutes, based on verifying you are who you say you are, and matching you with a credit score provided by one of the three national credit bureaus, and costs the institution less than an hour's cost of a credit analyst's time. This is an example of the powers of scale within a field, and those on the cutting edge had alpha by way of a lower cost, and greater flexibility to sell or finance their assets because outsiders could be confident in the credit quality. The credit underwriting is not so much more powerful—after all, interviewing your neighbors probably gives a much deeper picture of one's credit—but rather, cheap and transparent, and harder to game.

Similarly, I was part of a team at Moody's responding to the challenge presented by KMV, a company that sold a commercial credit model based on Merton's model of default, which essentially looked at equity as the call option on the value of the firm, with the value of liabilities as the strike price.[30] Unlike previous statistical models, such as Altman's seminal credit model that was calibrated on a mere 33 defaulting and nondefaulting companies, this model was calibrated with 1,000 defaults, and it is this inevitable advantage as information is warehoused in a useful database, that dooms any human expertise.[31] KMV insisted their models were more powerful than Agency ratings, and even though Moody's eventually acquired KMV, they have maintained this assertion, though given the large amount of revenue from their traditional credit ratings, they downplay the relevance of this by saying that traditional ratings have a different purpose.

I led the development of the private firm model for evaluating company credit when there was no equity information. Given Moody's brand name and existing relationships with banks, we had an advantage in creating a database needed to build, test, and validate such a model, and the Original RiskCalc[TM] model that I created in 2000 dominated alternatives because of this advantage.[32] The model was robust and successful because I had seen credit models that worked while I was the head of Capital Allocations at KeyCorp. These models were actually used for making credit decisions, not merely discussed in academic publications as Altman's original corporate credit model was. A useful model is generally too parochial for academics, who emphasize elegant, general models in academic journals. That is, previous models were too enamored with impressing the wrong people, mainly academics, and so emphasized a consistent methodological innovation such as discriminate analysis, neural nets, or ordered probit, models that could be applied, in theory, to an infinite range of things. The consumer credit way was to use inputs that had theoretical reasons to be related to default (for example, previous credit delinquencies), and transform these inputs to account for obvious nonlinearities in the distribution of these variables as well as the nonlinear effects of these variables, and then nonparametrically fit these into a multinomial model. The whole process all made sense, but very much a kluge for a particular problem, not a general result so prized by academics. RiskCalc[TM] is now one of Moody's best-selling services, and I imagine it will become like a credit bureau score in the future, replacing CFAs who would write the equivalent of the 1930s consumer credit narrative, filled with data but ultimately not scalable.

A floor of CFAs and MBAs looking at financial statements of companies will, I predict, be an anachronism, just as consumer credit analysts no longer interview neighbors of consumers looking for home equity loans. Productivity is about fewer people doing more, so I suspect hard times for professional underwriters, because we simply have too many people doing work that a computer can do, more cheaply, and more accurately. The key is that the firms that switch first will have a cost advantage, and thus will grow more quickly than their competitors. This is real, financial alpha.

And the same is true for trading stocks. In the old days, you called your broker, and basically gave him the job of trading out of your position. Either he would execute a large block—often at an adverse price to compensate for the risk he generates to the floor trader—or he would trade it through the day. Now we have Value Weighted Average Price algorithms, which spread a trade into little buckets of the day. An algorithm takes a desired amount, say 10,000 shares, and slices it up into 500-share chunks, spitting out trades to buy at the bid. If it is not filled in 1 minute, or if the price move away by 3 cents, it cancels, and waits 100 seconds, but ultimately spits out market orders if it does not get filled in say, 20 minutes. It repeats this all day until the order is done, and does it on hundreds of positions. You can add parameters to speed the process up by being more aggressive; add randomization, or even game-theoretic logic, so the specialist or other computers do not infer your pattern. There is no way a human has the ability to replicate the discipline, the accuracy, and the scale and scope of this program. Invariably, he would puke out an order (sell at the bid, buy at the ask), and then move on to the next one. With algorithms, you can monitor their performance in relation to the average traded price, the open, whatever, and fine-tune your algorithm. Furthermore, letting one less institution in on your trading intentions is always a good idea, especially if you are trading for an institution (that is, big orders).

Scale also works in market making, because instead of having multiple individuals post bid and asks for a small set of stocks, having a computer monitor orders, including the limit orders unfilled on the book, you can create a much more efficient market-making algorithm than any single human could do, because it can integrate relevant information more quickly than any person—looking at patterns in the order flow, behavior of comparable assets in slightly different markets, the behavior of assets that are derivative, or merely correlated.

To give an example, centralizing the portfolios of option traders so they merely have to trade, posting up bids and offers, and not worry about their net position in the underlying (delta), saves a lot of money and allows market makers to focus on their value-add. There are several risk numbers of particular interest to option traders—delta, vega, gamma, theta, adjusting volatility parameters—and with computers, many of these issues can be handled by someone else who is aggregating risk across many different traders. I sat next to someone who managed the risk of a group of such floor traders, and if they would start talking about the Fed, or Apple's newest product, he used to yell over the speakerphone: "Just trade!" That is, he didn't want them to waste time thinking about these things, as a floor trader's opinion on the market's direction is about as useful as a plankton's opinion on the tide.

There is considerable belief that much of the success of Renaissance Technologies is in data mining the minutia of this information and acting as an off-floor market maker. When I was at Deephaven, which was part of the market maker NITE Financial, the process of replacing humans with software was going on, whereby a trader making $500,000 could be replaced by software and do the job better. There are always places for human judgment, but such judgment becomes much more analytical, and less of the traditional trader qualities of mere aggressiveness, and one's Rolodex. For derivative portfolios such as options, you can add the value of consolidating the hedging activities, which greatly lowers costs as well.

The bottom line is that for jobs that have objective measures of success, such as underwriting, trading, and market making, computers enable people to create databases, then build and test models that will dominate any human proficiency. Much of finance is not about constructing investment portfolios, but trading, underwriting, and other activities. The alpha generated here is no less real than that found in traditional arbitrage as in Andy Redleaf arbitraging put-call parity in the 1970s, or in fund creation, merely because it focuses on costs and benefits, and technologies, as opposed to Sharpe ratios. The emphasis of finding a better way, given one's knowledge of costs and statistics, is the common theme in alpha finding within finance, much more so than any conception of a priced-risk factor combined with mean-variance optimization.

CONCLUSION

Even if you are not an alpha creator, you need to understand what alpha looks like so you can sell, or manage, more efficiently. Generally, alpha is created by people with the moxie to implement an idea and a thorough knowledge of current prices, as well as the nature of the product's complements and substitutes. The hardest part is that one usually needs two things: unusual access and an idea.

There are always opportunities in markets, and while ephemeral, they last from a year to decades. Any arbitrage takes some intelligence, but these ideas are pretty straightforward once you understand them. Most opportunities would have been very difficult for a retail trader, paying commissions, and the bid-ask, and having the extra hurdle of seeing price quotes with a lag to what those on the exchange see. For example, many of the successful traders outlined in Jack Schwager's *Market Wizards* had floor access, allowing them to make money off the bid-ask spread and other ways (front running), that your average retail investor pays.[33] To ignore this extra edge gives the false impression that it is feasible to become wealthy trading at home in one's pajamas, which merely encourages excessive risk taking in financial markets. Finance is a well-trodden field with many smart people looking at the same data. The most probable avenue to generate alpha is to be on the lookout for ideas, but also to put yourself into a position so that you can implement these ideas, which implies doing something as a vocation, or not doing it at all. Investing can be fun, seeing your portfolio move up and down while watching CNBC, but as competition it is less like golf and more like boxing, where dilettantes do not get handicaps—they get beat up.

CHAPTER 12

Alpha Games

Every pretext needs a principle, and in finance that principle is invariably alpha. When someone says her job "is all about risk management," it's rarely about risk management, properly understood. This creates a massive disconnect, as entrants become cynical about the games being played. You need to be aware of signaling, misdirection, coalitions, and cooperation necessary to understand alpha. Any science dealing with people, not particles, needs to address this. The story of the fish that does not understand what water is underscores that the most obvious, ubiquitous, important realities are often the ones that are the hardest to see and talk about. Alpha deception is a *prima facie* example. It is ubiquitous, and it must be done. You cannot avoid it, and you cannot talk about it explicitly with those you interact with. But humans are social creatures, and after adolescence the Ayn Rand fantasy of being financially and socially rewarded for objective excellence without playing politics, or of science being about disinterestedly observing facts and testing theories, or public servants designing laws to maximize social welfare, all gives way to the fact that you have to compete and persuade in a world of uncertainty, coalitions, and duplicity.

Alpha is ephemeral. It is also takes many guises, combining products such as in convertible arb, or patterns as in pairs, or concepts like volatility, as in the dispersion trade, or finding better ways for investors to tap into equity analysis. Furthermore, exploiting it is very rare for someone without institutional access to markets, so one must find partners. But another important point about alpha is that it is generally intentionally concealed and misrepresented. Understanding this is essential, because as an investor, most opportunities will involve a crucial partnership with someone who has something you need to actually implement your idea. Alternatively, most of those with alpha would be foolish to reveal it fully to their capital providers; the equilibrium is a compromise between two parties who need each other but recognize the self-interest of the other party, not a victory for one side over the other. As the latest book on Warren Buffett notes, the Buffett-Munger approach is to "invert, always invert. Look at it backward. What's in it for the other guy?"[1]

Because alpha is generally recognized as something that is righteously deserving of profits, almost every profit center stresses the alpha component of their revenues that is usually based on an individual *je ne sais quoi*. Thus if you ask a specialist on the NYSE, who has monopoly access to retail flow and loses money at most a handful of days a year, if he makes money off his monopoly control, he will strenuously object, noting he is maintaining an orderly market, providing liquidity to an otherwise highly volatile marketplace through deft risk management.

Alpha can only exist because there are not enough people who are arbitraging it out of the market. Thus, either people are good at keeping secrets, or people do not believe the alpha vendor when they pitch their strategy. The more conventional the alpha, the more similar it is to some previously successful alpha, the easier it will be to sell, but then the more secrecy needed. That is, with high frequency data, if you have a sure money maker you can prove this in short order, so the issue of getting support is not as important as keeping your potential partners from stealing your idea. A really unconventional idea without high frequency data, in contrast, no matter how simple, is often viewed skeptically merely because it is unconventional, as this is true risk, doing what others are not doing, and is not *obviously* feasible as evidenced by the lack of other people doing it.

The essence of Hayek's prophetic critique of socialist economies turned out to be in his paper "The Use of Knowledge in Society," which noted that information needed to run an economy is necessarily dispersed.[2] Socialist economist Oscar Lange argued in the 1930s debate with Ludwig von Mises that a socialist economy could elicit this information through trial and error looking at surpluses and shortages. While von Mises focused on the absence of a price for capital making this impossible, Hayek argued that you cannot compare a competitive outcome to a command-and-control outcome, assuming they have the same information, because only in a competitive system will those with the parochial information about supply and demand be motivated to get this information into resource allocation, and quite indirectly. In the end, information is never fully revealed to any one person. The profits implied by a moment's constellation of prices, situations in an unimaginable set of situations, sets in motion many actors, uncoordinated, whose net effect is the fabled Invisible Hand. Simply seeing the resulting shortages in razor blades and bread is not sufficient because the dispersed information in an economy is not then acting efficiently to the various supply and demand elasticities for the many input and substitutes to these final items. That is, is the shortage because of a lack of alternatives?

Input shortages? Which inputs? Without market prices all along the chain, reverse engineering this problem is impossible.

Similarly, alpha is essentially dispersed, and assuming it is available for a final, top-down algorithm such as in mean-variance analysis, is just as misguided as assuming a politburo in Moscow has the information to run an economy. Getting information from the diverse sources takes a recognition that alpha is ultimately private information, never revealed like a table available for mass readership.

The key thing you need to understand is that dishonesty, like gossip, is a part of life. These things are often portrayed as mere vices, yet in moderation are necessary and serve a purpose, and to think otherwise is naïve. The lies in business made out of a calculated self-interest that serve no greater good are the prominent lies we understand and universally loathe. These include the use of pretexts masking as principle, such as when liquor store owners support legislation that would allow the sale of wine and beer in grocery stores (competitors) using rhetoric from teetotalers. But the fact is that many times they are successful pretexts, and so groups can eventually truly take their pretexts as principle, such is the ability of people to rationalize their self-interest.

Another business lie is more of a lie-to-children type lie, where the idea is that the audience is not quite ready for the truth, such as when you tell children "The stork brought you." The problem here is that those outside the circle of trust need the lies-to-children version of the truth—they may not actually be children, but they're not going to grasp the full complexity, or while they may understand, they may not hold this information with the proper discretion. This process attenuates as we leave childhood, but never really disappears, as every field likes to omit certain unattractive features, exaggerating the charitable aspects of one's industry, as when corporations spend a good deal of advertising on the compulsory United Way activities of their employees (for example, "*Giving back* is a large part of what we do here at Amalgamated Financial Derivatives"). It is a sad fact that over 200 years after Adam Smith, admitting that, say, most companies, and their employees, are primarily self-interested, is a breach of protocol even among the most libertarian of companies.

Unfortunately, this creates the sort of cynicism resonant in *Catcher in the Rye*, where Holden Caulfield is so frustrated when he discovers, as all adolescents do, the intrinsic phoniness of so many adults. It underlies the book *Liar's Poker*, where the author Michael Lewis, who worked on Wall Street for a mere three years while in his twenties, presents the major actors as big phonies, merely aggressive alpha males, dishonest and ignorant. If you have worked in a field for more than 10 years, you know how little you understood when you had only a few years' experience. The impressions of a young Caulfield, or a young Michael Lewis, highlight that to a really self-aware person who does not see the bigger picture, the whole process looks like a big scam and horribly suboptimal. Successful people seem merely better at irrelevancies, and *everything* is a pretext for self-interest. This is because they precociously see through the pretexts and sense the deception, but because they are ignorant of the alternatives, the value of coalitions versus raw intelligence, do not see any greater good. It is a hard thing for a young, thoughtful person to grudgingly acknowledge the realistic optimum from a system built on the unintended effects of moral and intellectual inferiors who perhaps never so intended it.

These people truly "can't handle the truth," because they don't see the bigger picture. It's like if you plopped an earnest young, progressive person back into the Middle Ages, and had them lecture everyone on how the Church is just an institution for perpetuating myths to maintain an unjust hegemony by a patriarchal squirearchy. Well, kind of, but it also tends to be an efficient structure given the state of ethics and technology at that time. Simply removing all the myths and misconceptions does not take one in one giant leap to Sweden in 2009, but rather, back to anarchy. The ethics of business implies a willingness to compromise, to flatter and lie, and patience for fools. In a large organization, motivating a productive effort involves a certain amount of cognitive dissonance, because if everyone were brutally aware of their value and purpose in the group, there would be incessant squabbles over rights and responsibilities because many would find themselves insufficiently appreciated, if not cheated. These practicalities are remote from the ideals of youth. Business naïfs are often prigs about the truth, and this hurts them in large organizations. I know I do not have the ability to fake sincerity sufficiently to lead a large public corporation, given the inevitably large amount of incompetent middle managers one needs to placate.

The Marxist Stephen Marglin wrote a much-discussed piece in 1974 titled "What Do Bosses Do?," in which he argued bosses basically withheld information from workers so they could appropriate more of the profit for the owners. The popularity of Marglin's piece came from the fact that there's some truth to this, where bosses are often sneaky and think of themselves first. The problem with Marglin's piece is that it goes too far. Bosses don't *merely* conceal information, but instruct, motivate, strategize, prioritize, solve personnel problems, and so forth. Nonetheless, bosses, like everyone engaged in alpha deception, do conceal, from employees, customers, investors, and their bosses.

Most of the profits in finance involve a significant amount of alpha deception, where people are generally trying to convince you their profits are due to good old-fashioned Yankee ingenuity. But even within alpha, very little is from more efficient pricing, but rather from standard issues of intermediation: selling customers that a certain product fits their needs, bundling services together, taking advantage of the scale of their enterprise, their brand, and the barrier to entry their alpha deception creates. And the problem with selling something simple is that it is too easy to copy, so there will always be someone willing to do it for a little less. The key is to keep competitors confused as to what you actually do, and make customers think you do more than you actually do.

Think about the value you would receive as a U.S. resident trying to make a phone call in Europe, with their differing country and city codes. It is terribly confusing if you have no experience with it. It would be very valuable for a U.S. resident to be able to pay $5 and have someone say, "These are the rules, you silly foreigner." Two-minute conversation. But the seller then needs a brand name so the buyer knows he is getting correct information, and sellers will compete not on cost but auxiliary features, pointing out they also can tell you where coffee shops are. But the bottom line is, if there's a value to something pretty simple—informing ignorant foreigners about regional phone protocols—any service that addresses it will inevitably be much more complex than it should be.

The fact is that every profit opportunity presented at a parochial level is identified, at some point, by an individual. So every profit opportunity needs two things: One person to see the opportunity, and the resources to take advantage of the opportunity. The person who sees the opportunity needs to conceal a little bit of her insights so as to retain her interest in the alpha, because if she merely tells those with resources about it, she may as well be working for free. Consider telling a sophisticated investor about pairs in the early 1990s, a strategy very easy to explain, simple, and highly profitable. How does one communicate the idea so that it is both convincing, yet is not fully revealed? I have known several firms that use interviews with potential fund managers primarily to generate ideas they then investigate; free R&D. Other firms hire quantitative portfolio managers and understandably ask for a full detail of the model that will be exposing their firm's capital to risk. Once they become sufficiently confident they understand the model, they then make life uncomfortable for him, he leaves, and they no longer have to pay him for the strategy. Indeed, everyone in the field seems to acknowledge this occurs, but everyone also always stresses *her firm* would never do such a thing (beware anyone who stresses their integrity on these issues).

Most financial companies, even successful ones, are infused with petty politics about alpha, and much of one's day is involved not in deriving alpha, but the politics around it. Consider the alpha described in the previous chapter. The essence of the alpha is explainable in a couple of minutes to perhaps a few days, depending on your understanding of statistics and the markets. If John Bogle discovered the index fund back in 1975, it would be unfair to say that he has done nothing since, even if there has been little change in his company's product menu. The key to office politics in finance, is that it plays off alpha. Without alpha, people are fighting over nothing. With alpha, the politics complicates to a different dimension because of the gains from reciprocal altruism in a corporate environment.

BENIGN DECEPTION

Honesty, like all virtues, is good only in moderation. For example, you don't tell your friend his daughter is homely, or tell your customer that you are asking her about her weekend merely because you want to sell her more copying equipment, even if true. At a deep level, a lot of small talk is disingenuous, but that gets into semantics. Base and higher motives are often consistent, as with the famous Invisible Hand where selfishness leads to a social optimum, even if the base motive is the true driver. Being brutally honest is often just an excuse to be cruel.

There are opportunities opened up by ambiguity, allowing people to make proposals they can then rescind, or make commands that would otherwise flout some interpersonal norms. For example, Steve Pinker writes about the use of indirect speech, and how being indirect or vague is helpful for a number of reasons. Given that there are three major social relationship structures—dominance, communal, and reciprocal—indirect requests allow someone to respond without bringing dominance into play ("If you could pass the guacamole, that would be awesome"). Also, in cases where the speakers are not sure of each other's values or intentions, it allows space for negotiation without offense being taken, like asking a date if she would like to come in and see your etchings. People's speech and actions are rarely straightforward, and it is this tricky intentionality that many of those with Asperger's Syndrome, who have a hard time empathizing, find so unsettling in humans, and so comforting in animals that lack this attribute.[3]

To be persuasive, you need to be an advocate, not a judge, and advocates are selectively interested in the truth. Truth underlies the real data, and it helps tremendously to have the data on your side, but it is not essential, especially in the short run. Deliberate deception takes considerable effort, because one then has to consciously suppress the truth. To reduce the tension of such a mindset, good persuaders tend to make themselves believe what they are saying. Self-deception does not require people to sit down and decide they are going to lie to themselves. It usually happens subtly instead, without the person even being aware of it, as they tendentiously ignore some information and highlight other information to rationalize something in their self-interest. This does not have to be monetary, and many people have principles or theories they consider righteous and just, and not merely true, such as that all men are created equal, or their religion. These bigger picture truths then force less important theories and facts to be consistent, because to do otherwise would invalidate their bigger idea.

A glass of red wine a day is a tonic, but too much will destroy your liver. The key is that just as poison is a function of dosage, so are the bad effects of deception and ignorance. A common alpha deceptor is merely blithely deluded about their role. Consider the signature players in the market whose pictures are on the front page of the business section when the market has a big day, the floor traders who make money off the bid-ask spread from customers, who think that they are excellent speculators. Or economists who are paid to do PR, but think they are paid to figure out where interest rates are going. One of the biggest things people do is persuade others; and to be a good persuader, it helps to truly believe in what you are selling.

Navin Johnson best sums it up in the economic primer *The Jerk,* starring Steve Martin, where Navin is lamenting his poor skills as an amusement park weight guesser:

Navin: Frosty, I'm no good at this.
Frosty: Aw, come on Navin, you're doing fine.
Navin: I've already given away eight pencils, two hula dolls and an ashtray, and I've only taken in 15 dollars.
Frosty: Navin, you have taken in 15 dollars and given away 50 cents worth of crap, which gives us a net profit of 14 dollars and 50 cents.
Navin: Ah! It's a profit deal!

Navin probably got more customers because his enthusiastic, delusional belief that he was trying to be a good weight guesser, and when you won and he grimaced, that was the real payoff, not the pencils. A cynical guy who knew it was just a scam would not seem so engaged and would be much less fun, and people are all about putting meaning into things that have very little importance in the big picture. As Ghandi said, "Almost everything you do will be insignificant, but it is very important you do it." There are a lot of weight guessers out there, whose actual task is doing something that is, unknown to them, slightly deceptive in its true purpose.

Consider that market makers spend most of their time looking at current price changes, and the changes of prices related to what they are making markets in. They often have explicit models that figure out the price of their assets based on the movements in these other prices, as in the obvious case of an options trader looking at the change in the underlying stock, and using Black-Scholes to adjust his option prices; or it could be a trader in a stock moving his bid-ask spread up as the S&P500 moves, even though nothing has changed in the order book for his specific stock. The main thing the market maker has to do is keep his model inputs fresh, post prices to potential buyers and sellers, fill market orders, and pick off stale limit orders. Quickness is the key, which is why these guys tend to be young and aggressive (they also tend to be male). Customers generally have access to older prices, and in a situation where the current price moves every second, this clearly puts a trader at an informational advantage, which is why it can be such a lucrative field.

Market makers generate most of their money by their seat, the franchise value of being attached to a well-known institution, and the implied contacts. Many of the most highly paid traders in the 1990s were merely those fortunate to be a market maker for a popular stock like Microsoft. Their profit was pretty much volume times the bid-ask spread, and as the ask-bid was about 1/8 for most stocks in the 1990s, and the daily volume on Microsoft about $10 billion per year, assuming a 10 percent of profits bonus, this created many millionaire "traders," who would then regale their friends and neighbors about their financial insights.

Yet, much of being a trader is encouraging trading activity from a hesitant broker, or giving insights that the broker will pass on to a hesitant client, and so many traders are quite adept at presenting themselves as more than middlemen, but also men with an angle or a story. A good trader is probably truly delusional about his prognostic abilities because this allows him to appear sincere in his sales pitch for the latest trade idea; those who don't believe their own stories make weak sales pitches.[4] Most of these traders are certain they could make money without their customer flow, merely reading the tape, because the same self-deception that serves them well chatting up brokers or impressing their boss generates delusions of strategic grandeur. Supreme self-assurance, even if undeserved, just as much as knowing your Greeks, makes for a good trader. A manager of traders might well find encouraging their delusions a benign myth. Indeed, I have known such market makers, and worked with several such organizations. I would say many—especially in the 1990s before computers made this less apparent—sincerely believed they were primarily good at what they do because of their alpha, their ability to read the tape and anticipate market changes, as opposed to their privileged access to customer orders.

Or consider the fundamental analyst. Most of their value is in their ability to excite readers into thinking their familiarity with a trend or concept means they have an edge investing in various industries. Henry Blodget worked for two years as a journalist and came to Wall Street with a degree in English and a little financial journalism. In the Internet bubble, he boldly stated that Amazon would rise to $400 when it was trading at only $240, which was already quite high, and it hit that target in a few weeks. All the sudden, everyone wanted to hear his opinion on everything, though his experience in equity research, as well as Internet technology, was objectively limited. He was very valuable to his employer, and if you read his writings, you see he is a witty, thoughtful guy. He was not good at what his explicit job was—identifying which stocks to buy—but he was good at writing and speaking in a way that people find engaging and persuasive. His actual alpha was in generating retail trading, his purported alpha was in stock picking.

There are many products that are sold with a little misdirection. The classic is the razor, which is sold at a low price. The replacement blades, however, designed for this specific razor, are quite pricey. The razor is the hook, and should be priced low, because if he buys that, you have a lot of money coming it. Lots of products are built on this misdirection, usually lowballing an up-front investment, hoping the impatient and greedy consumer is preoccupied by their great deal on some more immediate bauble. I had a summer job in high school selling magazine subscriptions door to door, and if I did not want to deal with someone, the easiest way to avoid an involvement is to state the bald truth "Do you want to buy some magazine subscriptions?" A certain "no," was the response, but this closed them off to listening to our highly convoluted sales pitch, which many found appealing.

Unlike naïve ignorance, this is a little more calculated, a little less salutary. After all, you are taking advantage of people's impatience. To the extent you play upon people's behavioral biases, you are manipulating them in an adverse way. But then again, if you did not do it, someone else would, and at the end the day, you do have the best razor available. Being brutally honest can work in some areas, at some levels, but sales necessitate a pitch that is misleading on some level.

Of course, not all delusional alpha has a trade-off. Going back to the delusional market makers and traders, those who did not realize they are mainly there to make money off of volume may have been a useful myth. Yet, in the long run, to the extent this myth deeply pervaded a trading operation, it discouraged the development of systems that would allow them to compete going forward. Many trading operations of various sorts have been automated to some degree, and so those organizations that truly understood their alpha were in a better position to create computer systems that are now making markets. But this is anticipating a regime change, and so one can imagine many groups, fighting to maintain their status as traders and speculators, receiving fat bonuses until a merger occurs, and their trade flow is routed to the new group that has the automated system. Relegated to trading without flow, their edge mysteriously disappears, and they retire into other fields.

To the extent someone believes he has an edge where he really does not can be merely wasteful. Before 1997, within an interstate bank, each state bank was managed somewhat independently for regulatory reasons. First Interstate and KeyCorp, where I both worked, for a long time had little asset and liability committees that would take independent interest rate bets, based partially on their state bank's need to hit an earnings number in their annual "plan." If one state was running low on loan volume and needed more earnings to meet this year's earning target, the one that triggers executive bonuses, how could the ALCO committee hit the target? One way was to put on some yield curve trade that basically generates positive cash flow up front in exchange for negative cash flows further out—these swap trades are zero-sum. This was also done in reverse during good times, like burying nuts for the winter. Alternatively, an easier way was to exploit the large amount of securities not marked to market, kept at historical cost in the banking book, that you can strategically sell to realize gains, or losses, as needed. It is so easy to do this that to this day I ignore income statement data from financial institutions. I regularly attended such meetings in asset and liability committee meetings many times, and this was never an explicitly stated tactic, but such is cognitive dissonance.

Top down, this was inefficient, because the multistate bank has, say, 20 different banks plying many offsetting interest rate bets that just generate excess commissions to Wall Street, and if you pay your group based on their profit and loss, you basically pay out a large bonus on Utah, which made $10 million betting on interest rates, and received nothing back on the loss by Colorado of the same amount, meaning, the corporation lost money on the trade, after commissions and bonus. Also, interpreting your profit and loss from your divisions is complicated because they are a distraction to how they are doing at their core business. After deregulation ended the need to keep state banks separate, and the disastrous yield curve trades of 1994 (when rates rose, exposing many of these income-smoothing trades), these multiple inconsistent asset and liability committees went the way of the office ashtray. This alpha delusion had little benefit and large costs.

THE FAVOR BANK

The "Favor Bank" was coined by Tom Wolfe in his work *The Bonfire of the Vanities*.

> *Everything…operates on favors. Everyone does favors for everybody else.…If you make a mistake, you can be in a whole lotta trouble, and you're going to need a whole lotta help in a hurry.…But if you've been making your regular deposits in the Favor Bank, then you're in a position to make contracts. That's why they call big favors, contracts.*[5]

The quid pro quos of finance are often quite complicated, but highlight an important point. Finance is mainly about being a middle man, intermediation, providing business with savings, and consumers with investments. When you play intermediator, you are not doing one deal; you are managing a set of relationships and a sequence of deals. Furthermore, in a large financial institution, many of your customers and suppliers are within your own company. You need to manage these relationships, often without the benefit of explicit payment. Having alpha in this area means seeing the big picture, how you act cascades in a web of favors, and how you can make trades that are not obvious.

An infamous case exemplifying the complexity of Wall Street's incentive structure, and its inherent combination with alpha deception, was Jack Grubman, an Institutional Investor all star. People hung on his every utterance. Salomon Smith Barney's army of nearly 13,000 brokers shared his picks with clients. When Grubman's e-mail updates hit the newswires, they'd be immediately picked up on CNBC. And when he spoke, stocks moved. On January 20, 2000, after he raised his price target on fiber-optic networker Level 3, its stock rose 12 percent, pumping up its market value by $4.9 billion. Telecom equity underwritings peaked in 2000 at $74 billion, while debt issuance topped out in 2001 at $116 billion. Grubman's firm raked in $1.8 billion in telecom fees in just four years. Looking at his picks in February 1999, they suffered a subsequent 75 percent loss.[6]

His investment prescience was just as lousy as everyone else's, but what is so amusing, is that he had such credibility, when the essence of at least one of his opinions is part of a labyrinth of favors more complex than the Krebs Cycle. In 1999, Grubman was the father of 2-year-old twins, and sought the help of Sanford Weill, Citigroup's co-chair of the board, in placing his children at the prestigious 92nd Street Y Nursery School. Grubman had raised his rating of stock in AT&T from unfavorable to favorable as a favor to Weill. Citigroup, in the meantime, pledged to donate a million dollars to the Y, and Weill did some lobbying for Grubman with the school's board. Grubman wanted a more favorable rating for AT&T because AT&T was about to issue stock for their wireless subsidiary that would have meant about $65 million in fees for Citi, and he wanted the vote of AT&T Chairman Michael Armstrong, who was also on the board at Citigroup, so he could outflank Weill's nettlesome co-chair of the board, John Reed. This is shown in Figure 12.1.

The key is that often, for various reasons, explicit payment between parties in a position to do each other favors is impossible, either because it is illegal, or too blatantly self-serving relative to the group they officially represent. Thus, like in barter economies, where you need to get around the infrequent double coincidence of wants (when the butcher wants shoes, and the shoemaker wants meat), you get highly convoluted transactions,

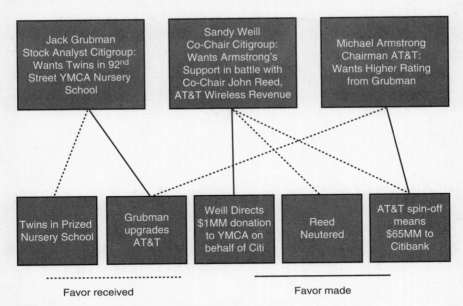

FIGURE 12.1 Corporate Favor Trading Can Be Complicated

as when the butcher wants shoes, the shoemaker wants a new wagon, and the carpenter wants meat. When money is not the medium of exchange, you have to find multiple parties to engage in a profitable transaction. These transactions all need pretexts consistent with their regular course of business, making them seem insanely complicated, but in actuality these kinds of exchanges occur all the time in high school (Cindy lets Britney have her seat in study hall because she likes Jake whose friend Adrian likes Cindy who . . .).

The most famous research adviser was esteemed by everyone for a decade, as a supposed fount of fundamental wisdom on business. Instead, he was merely an articulate, but indiscriminate cheerleader, who would promote any company as a part of a constellation of favors one could not fathom. This is not as bizarre as it sounds, because senior government officials are often given plumb senior positions at financial institutions with no financial background and make millions. For example, Jamie Gorelick was a lifetime lawyer, a deputy attorney general in the Clinton Administration from 1994 to 1997. With no experience in banking, she became a top executive at Fannie Mae, pulling in $26 million over the 1997-to-2003 period. Lifelong political organizer and Clinton White House adviser Rahm Emanuel took three years off from government to make $18 million as an investment banker for Dresdner Klienwort Wasserstein. I knew a finance executive who hired a prominent consulting firm for many projects, and when he was let go, the consulting firm hired him so that he would retain an aura of respectability in his job hunt. When he got his new executive position, the consulting firm now had a new big customer. Many banks hire ex-regulators into senior risk management positions, and the regulators anticipate this. Thus, senior positions, those people making the big decisions in financial institutions, are often not chosen for their trenchant understanding of interest rates, derivatives, or the nature of the product being financed, but rather, access and influence with people who are in a position to trade favors, where financial transactions are merely a single payment in a sequence of people with very different objectives, who all need each other. Evaluating a single financial transaction in isolation, through its stated objective, often reveals a pretext based on some kind of value creation, often misleading colleagues as much as outsiders. Many highly paid financial executives are well paid precisely because they can help in exchanging favors, all the while emphasizing maximizing shareholder value via their alpha.

The favor bank in alpha environments can be very fertile for creating complex barriers of entry. For example, assume you are a trader with zero alpha, but your boss does not fully understand your role—what the average commissions are, does not monitor price impact, does not have appropriate benchmarks, and so forth. Because it's a large desk, he pays you $500K a year, that is, as if you do have alpha. You need to show some alpha to your boss. So you transfer $250K a year to a broker by overpaying on commissions. He then gives you access to initial public offerings (IPOs). The IPO game is basically a way for brokers to capture the one-day pop in IPO prices. Generally, IPOs generate 12 percent return on their first day of trading, and most IPO investors sell in the first couple of days (though, of course, their broker discourages this, to little avail).

For the broker issuing the IPO, by giving these only to clients who pay extra commissions, that first-day return is all capturable. Generally, in 2001, a hedge fund might have paid two cents a share for bare bones trading, and five cents a share for trading bundled with research and trade ideas. Of course, this research is worthless on average and the hedge fund knows it, but it leads to getting on the IPO list. Thus, you capture the one-day pop through the implicit overcharge on commissions to get access to the IPO. To summarize: The investment bank captures the 12 percent one-day spike in the IPO price through overpriced research sold to a fund, which is needed because the issuing firm would not appreciate paying the broker an 8 percent fee plus giving them the benefit of the first-day pop. The hedge fund trades commission dollars for the one-day return from IPOs to help fool his boss. The portfolio manager benefits because this zero-sum trade makes him look good to his boss, as his boss does not notice that commissions are higher than otherwise but does see the IPO gains—explained as deft selection of new issues. A final benefit is achieved by helping the broker, who can be among the best headhunters when a portfolio manager is out of work. Both are better off, and the capital provider and his representatives are basically clueless. The favor bank is complicated, but a very useful tool, and the pretext in this game is always alpha at every step. To the extent someone is using alpha as a pretext for trading favors, they are basically taking advantage of some informational advantage to the detriment of others. Regardless of one's situation, it is useful to understand the true reason transactions are made, because they are rarely one-off decisions made in isolation, and these reasons are rarely explicitly discussed.

MANAGERIAL ALPHA

The most numerous successful players in finance are managers, not quants. Jamie Dimon, Charles Schwab, Walter Wriston. There is a skill to managing people, and this is something most pure innovators are not good at. The key to managing efficiently is understanding where the power in the organization comes from, which in finance means, where the alpha originates. Furthermore, it means understanding not merely where the alpha comes from, but the best way to approach this with customers, bosses, and underlings, each of whom has different interests and incentives.

For example, if you are an executive at Fannie Mae, making millions for your access to legislators and their continued support of your government support, you need to keep the current board of directors and other executives fresh with recent government officials who still have many contacts in government. You also need to understand that this kind of alpha is not something your clients or the public should know, so you mention the value of the mission of encouraging home ownership in PR campaigns, and downplay your executive focus on lobbying Congress for special status. The mission becomes like the lie in the Soviet states that their purpose was all about "the people," as no one in power would even privately admit the truth while they enjoyed their country dachas.

Assume you run a trade floor for a premier investment bank. Your alpha is from making markets, by your brand name and set of connections. That is, you do not speculate, or try to make money off predicting future changes in prices. You should not mention this too much to your boss, because emphasizing it only highlights how your value is perhaps not worth 10 percent of the revenue. Indeed, mentioning this too much to your boss might signal you mention this too much to his boss, which might make him look bad depending on how your boss presents himself to his boss. Highlight to your customers your existing set of other customers, because this merely increases your value to them—they are coming to you because they think you hear all the latest gossip, the latest trade information. You should understand that good traders are worth a piece of their profits, but not too much. The more a senior manager knows about what is involved in trading bonds, or swaps, or swaptions, the less the company has to pay its employees out of ignorance of the alpha generated from those writing the trade tickets. You pay someone 50 percent-plus of profits if you think she did it by sheer foresight, while you would pay her a salary of $50K if you thought she was merely taking orders. The reality is somewhere in between, and this is where having knowledgeable managers helps, because when people are wildly overpaid, such people have great incentives to misrepresent their activities and block information, and this is a cancer in an organization.

The key is the more you know about the essence of alpha in your organization, the more relevant you can be. If you understand that everyone has different incentives, and not everyone needs to be in on every strategy, and some simple white lies are good.

The good news for most people is that management is not just a comparative advantage, but an absolute advantage to those who are not really smart. It is very difficult for someone to feign interest in the activities of someone more than two, if not one, standard deviations in intelligence below them, and so the smarter the person is, the greater their inability to really connect with the large mass of workers who inevitably make up the core of a large organization. One can try, but this is often unsuccessful, because there are all sort of nonverbal *tells* that signal a listener is really uninterested, if not dismissive, about what is being said. For this reason, people do not like working for someone *much* more intelligent or proficient, because these people often do not appreciate, and cannot even pretend to appreciate, their work. Stress is not so much caused by bad times, but by working where you feel your talents are being underappreciated. For a similar reason, salesmen who are too smart are not good salesmen, because they appear to be sneering at their average client's ignorant questions and observations. Someone who sincerely notes that the boss will be very interested in a client's banal suggestion (for example, that they measure risk only by looking at the downside volatility) makes this client feel important and appreciated.

Large organizations are invariably hierarchical in some respect, and a prominent characteristic of human civilization. Strangely, this has been a U-shaped pattern in our evolution. Dominance hierarchies are characteristic of all nonhuman hominid societies, an extreme example being the tiny-testicled, alpha-male gorilla lording it over his band, and are found in many other species of animal—as in the proverbial pecking order among chickens, dogs, seals, and so on. Likewise, dominance hierarchies are a defining characteristic—in fact, an overwhelming feature—of every known civilization before modern times. But dominance hierarchies are rare in the ethnographic literature describing hunting-and-gathering societies—and thus, presumably, also rare in hunting-and-gathering societies as they existed during much of our common evolutionary past. We started in dominance hierarchies, lost it, and regained it.

To account for this fact, an anthropologist at UCLA named Christopher Boehm proposed the idea of a reverse dominance hierarchy. The gist of his idea is that a love of dominance was so bred into the human species during their long, shared hominid past, that they developed an innate distaste of being dominated by others. "All men seek to *rule,* but if they cannot rule they prefer to remain equal," says Harold Schneider, an insight consistent with the relative risk utility function.[7] Without weapons, the biggest and strongest can dominate others by hand-to-hand combat and other intimidations. With weapons, however, even the smallest can have a say in matters. Thus, a gorilla has to manually fight the dominant male to take over his harem of females, and sucker punching the alpha Silverback male who has proven himself in combat, is a highly risky career move. However, humans and our ancestors, with their ability to hunt big game, can easily use a spear and kill even the most powerful man in his sleep. With weapons, a simple conspiracy makes the homicide of a lone, powerful male relatively easy, and is why in simple human societies a strong man, without a coalition, cannot dominate his tribe.

The mechanisms used to enforce equality in these simple hunter-gatherer tribes are based on an innate set of morals that shame hubris, bragging, and personal dominance, and promote ideals like generosity and immodesty. In societies where the gains from a wise leader are small, the leader is mainly chosen for his tact, generosity, ability to serve as an even-handed mediator, and oratory skills that make everyone feel appreciated. The tribe defines the ideal society in a way such that no main political actor gets to dominate another. Then they see to it, as a group, that anyone who tries to infringe on this rule is himself dominated, at first by subtle tactics like gossip, then outright ridicule, but leading to ostracism and even execution. This leader is really a puppet—though one with some selfish satisfaction in his figurehead role—merely articulating a consensus once he recognizes it, as opposed to actually making key decisions. Thus, in these simple societies, the hierarchy is in reverse, because those who are superficially being ruled, are actually dominating the ruler.

In more complex societies, where a leader's decisiveness and strategic vision has a first-order effect on the success of the group, these altruistic skills are still important, but there is now a greater trade-off, because the success of the group also needs strategic vision and tactical know-how, skills that are independent, if not in opposition, to those other skills. Furthermore, in modern civilization people's assets are large and stationary, meaning that, unlike the hunter-gatherer, they have something valuable to steal. The politics of any large organization thus necessitates that leaders are a mix of those attributes that lead to the successful direction of the group, such as decisiveness and wisdom, but yet are balanced by qualities that give the leader support, such as modesty and generosity that does not threaten the more numerous subordinates. They need to sufficiently tax those who have more than the more numerous masses, yet not so much that these wealthier people conspire against the leader. Individuals trying to maximize their success in businesses must engage in coalitions, pretexts, and favor bank trades. It is not sufficient to merely be wise about business strategy because individuals will withhold support for a wise man who appears to not appreciate their efforts. For a middle manager, no amount of wisdom or efficacy by the big boss compensates for being moved down the hierarchy. The tension between needing someone smart and decisive enough to make good decisions, versus needing a leader who makes his workers feel appreciated, creates the common leader who is good at doing both, but in fact is mainly good at this game: *appearing* to do both. Thus, we should not expect the boss to be the smartest man in the room, either in IQ, or knowledge of the product, but rather to pull this off successfully, the boss should be blithely ignorant about the inconsistent objectives articulated to the team, such as trying to simultaneously prioritize innovation and tradition, a meritocracy that recognizes everyone, or a strong sexual harassment policy and a fun Christmas party. People who are really good at logical puzzles, who excel at finding alpha in quantitative finance, are often not very good at managing people, because they cannot, or will not, empathize well with the most people. Thus, in spite of conspicuous examples where the highest-IQ person is both an idea generator and the boss, such as Larry Ellison or Bill Gates, in general the functions involve different skill sets. For that reason, your average person doesn't envy those really smart guys; he thinks they are like idiot savants, smart in one dimension but clueless in what is really important, such as leading a large organization or having lots of sex (alas, adolescent sexual activity and IQ are inversely correlated for IQs above 100).[8] The result is a leader in a modern reverse dominance hierarchy, somewhere between the dominating male silverback gorilla, and the submissive chief of the foraging tribe.

THE ALPHA IN RISK MANAGEMENT

Around 1994, coming out of graduate school, I had an interview to work with JPMorgan in their risk management group. It was all very intimidating as I grew up in a pretty modest middle class background, and at the age of 28 never pulled a salary greater than $21K per year. I was intimidated by their small talk about which ski resorts had the best powder—didn't anyone go camping? At JPMorgan, all the furniture was mahogany, and everyone I met had a nice suit and a fresh haircut. It is reasonable to give a rich person the benefit of the doubt because presumably they are getting paid a lot of money because they have some kind of alpha.

One of the guys I met was a senior risk management executive, who told me that at JPMorgan, they did not eliminate, or even minimize risk, rather, they got paid to *take on risk*. The implication was that risk management was the gatekeeper for strategies and tactics, filtering in the good risks, and out the bad. This was meant to be profound statement. They understood risk as risk managers better than others, that was their alpha, their edge, why all the guys had $50 ties and mahogany desks. It sounded intriguing, and indeed, I had seen it previously at a local brokerage I worked at in Chicago. They offered some simple investments, and had a glossy brochure that noted they were experts at managing the risk of their investments. This was explained mainly by a neat graphic in classic mean-variance space that had a fade effect between the light corner near the origin of zero risk–zero return, and the dark space where risk and returns were infinite ("thar be dragons"), with a little dot implying "we are here" in the middle, usually strictly dominating the S&P in both return and risk space, which is placed there to give a transparent exhibit of a risk-return relation, such as an equity index (see Figure 12.2). The discussions always excluded any concrete definition of what risk was, specifically, because we all know that while equities are riskier than T-bills, sophisticates know this is not merely volatility or beta.

The idea is ubiquitous in finance: The experts, who make a lot of money, can manage risk better than our competitors. Risk is such a slippery concept that is a perfect pretext for managers, because by conflating idiosyncratic risk, or risk of default, with a risk factor that is correlated with expected (that is, average over the cycle) returns, you can work in specific examples that make sense (high yield bonds have higher risk and higher yields) and yet still avoid inconsistencies (high yield bonds have higher risk and equal returns), merely by switching the subject at convenient junctures (such as when the higher stated yield on higher defaulting securities is presented as evidence of risk begetting return). Most people miss the sleight of hand involved. Getting into discussions about expected returns, in contrast, invites much greater audience participation, and potentially, skepticism.

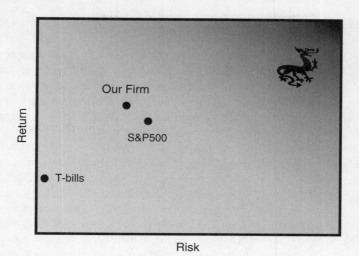

FIGURE 12.2 Promotional Risk and Return "Explanation"

It was an attractive idea, and I had been contemplating risk for a long time, and I was very interested in seeing the practical advantage of understanding risk better than others. Of course, I had no idea *exactly* what they meant, but I had been used to that listening to Minsky talk about how risk is the Most Important Thing, and also indefinable. Like learning to meditate, or knowing God, or true love, something I had not experienced but clearly many others had, and one day I would just "get it." I knew risk was a slippery subject, so I was indulgent with their vagueness, and eagerly wanted to join the guild of people who made money off risk. I figured, they were living this difference.

The neat thing about risk management was it played into my skill set of math, computers, and statistics, but was also universally praised as the essence of finance. Everything came down to risk management, it seemed, at least publicly. Many much better-paid executives, who certainly didn't wish to switch places with my career, would on occasion remark to the press, or in meetings, that they "considered themselves fundamentally a risk manager."

But then, in practice they did not seem to venerate risk management as I understood it. Our CEO, who supposedly had a bond trading background from the 1970s, was rather indifferent to the duration or convexity risk in the bank's balance sheet. Some of the managers were incredibly ignorant of the products and services they were providing. We had one executive ask, since we were making so much money on one asset, but losing on the hedge, why don't we get rid of the hedge? The very basics of financial risk management, from a pure risk management perspective, were foreign to a good percentage of senior executives.

I remember Ron Dembo, the founder of the risk management software Algorithmics, coming by, and talking about how his software would help you see risk, and manage it by having some neat 3-D graphics on exposures to factors such as delta, theta, gamma, whatever is relevant to your trading group. That is, his vision was you would have a large screen, with real-time visualization of our current risk exposure in various dimensions, perhaps on several screens, and throughout the day we could see this information, and use it offensively. Indeed, people in risk management are always talking about turning risk management into a proactive business tool, not just a measure of risk. It was a neat vision. There was no interest in this by the traders. Many other risk managers told of knowing some company where risk managers had the power to reverse a trader's exposure if they decided he was taking too much risk, so for example, in the Risk Management Star Chamber, you would see Trader Number Seven having a long futures position in Treasury bonds, and you would short this position in a different account unbeknownst to him, saving the firm.

What you soon learn as a risk manager is that most business lines are more than happy with existing risk metrics or hedging tools, because these are not the first-order impacts on their bonus. Indeed, several times I worked hard on developing algorithms to show how various trading desks could derive a more efficient hedging algorithm, using some of their actual data, and they responded with a shrug at best. They saw me as trying to muscle in on their bonus pool, if not their job, and as market makers had Sharpe ratios well above 10, so who cares about minimizing the volatility by 5 percent? As for the lending lines, their business was mainly about selling more product, not estimating risk better. If the business of selling car loans made sense at a portfolio size of $10 million, it made sense at $1 billion, so given that their business model worked—that is, the amortized losses imputed into pricing made the profit positive after a capital charge—getting the expected loss correct to the next decimal was not interesting to them. Rather, they were interested merely in getting more business. Most of finance does not involve buying assets traded on secondary markets and warehousing them, it is originating deals to new buyers; supply is not constrained by risk appetite so much as your ability to sell.

I later became a portfolio manager, and would occasionally be presented with unsolicited advice by the risk manager, and as a former risk manager myself, was sympathetic. These were usually innocuous, but often, when they really tried to help, they were irrelevant or worse. They would often make blatant mistakes because they were unfamiliar with my particular data and how they were warehoused, or they would get excited about some intraday measurement that in theory would be really cool, but in practice involved a huge amount of effort for insignificant benefit, usually some plan to centralize data, or create some new tool that would allow them real time monitoring of various positions.

No matter how clueless a financial executive, they were all smart enough to know that saying you made money off *risk* sounded a lot better than the truth. Making money off rich and lazy customers who come to you because of your brand name, and then selling them something almost identical to what 10 other banks are selling, hardly makes a good signal to customers, your underlings, investors, or your boss. Making money by risk management magic, that's nontransferable alpha, and the beautiful thing about risk is that when someone asks for specifics, you can look back incredulously, and say, that's a silly question: in *practice* risk is highly mathematical *and* undefinable, like the Trinity in its apparent inconsistency and importance.

There is truth in their elevation of risk management as a concept, just not in how it is usually understood. The key is that risk management as a separate silo in any organization is necessary because of the incentives offered to those on the front line. Their independent monitoring is essential, because a business line that is usually paid a bonus based on annual revenues has an incentive to take more risk than the firm wants. If he is gambling with someone else's capital, especially when payoffs are often very asymmetric (such as positive during expansions, negative only during recessions), his incentive is to take as much risk as possible. If he loses, he goes to a new firm, and blames the mess on someone else, and outsiders are rarely able to sort this out. Financial institutions are especially prone to this problem because they are highly leveraged, and some businesses can buy an infinite amount of exposure, whereas, say, a media lending business, can sell only so many loans.

The primary need of risk management is to make sure business lines did not do anything stupid or fraudulent, and so risk management's main role is independence, not accuracy. They are necessary to make sure businesses within the corporation do not commit fraud or violate agreed-upon risk limits. In practice, risk management is like an audit, only in real time. Most of the blowups of the past 20 years are what are known as *operational risks,* which is jargon for something that would never have been done if management knew the risk they were taking, such as Orange County betting on interest rates, or a rogue trader who loses billions. Before the fact, no one putatively in charge knew these risks were being taken. The key job of risk managers is monitoring the acknowledged, known risks, so that their underlings do not take them, preventing operational risk.

In practice, risk management's practicalities are rather boring, like transfer pricing—a cost that is essential and not obvious, but still, just something to monitor and minimize. A risk manager estimates this cost objectively, without any skin in the game, and his independent view is valuable to a system where the business line has better information about these risks, yet is self-interested in understating them—at least to the degree he is short-sighted (common enough). In some sense, a risk manager is like the cop in the bank branch who carries a pistol and supposedly puts his life on the line, but his mere presence is sufficient to dissuade most troublemakers, so you are mainly paying them to stand there. Traders, and business lines, can wreck a company very quickly, so they need monitoring. Risk management as a separate business line obviously do their job better, and are more satisfied with their job, if they feel appreciated, and so everyone talking about the importance of risk management has the additional benefit of making these groups feel important.

A SINGULAR RISK MANAGEMENT DECISION

But the viability of a firm, or a business group, depends on risk management of a very different type. The business heads are the judges of the ultimate risks, and risk management very rarely has much influence over these strategic decisions. Consider the recent subprime housing disaster. In the bad old days, one needed a 20 percent down payment, a good credit rating and proof of employment to get a mortgage. In 1989, Congress amended the Home Mortgage Disclosure Act to force banks to collect race data on mortgage applicants. It showed that blacks were rejected at higher rates than whites, which is not surprising because on average blacks have lower incomes, wealth, and credit scores than whites. Several newspapers mined this data, and won Pulitzer prizes based on simple statistics showing blacks getting disproportionate rejections. A 1992 study commissioned by the Boston Fed, led by its president, Richard Syron, argued that even after controlling for credit risk, minorities were rejected at a higher rate. Of course, the databases did not "control for credit risk" but rather just income—as highlighted by the fact that default rates for both races was the same, suggesting fairness—but many in a position to legislate and regulate had seen enough.[9] "This study is definitive," said a spokewoman for the Office of the Comptroller of the Currency.[10] "I don't think you need a lot more studies like this," said Richard Syron.

The study implied that simple racial discrimination was prevalent among mortgage lenders, and the Boston Fed warned the mortgage lenders they regulated: "Discrimination may be observed when a lender's underwriting policies contain arbitrary or outdated criteria that effectively disqualify many urban or lower-income minority applicants."[11] Such "outdated" criteria included having a credit history, income verification, or a significant down payment. In 1993 the Justice Department head Janet Reno noted that eliminating mortgage lending bias (read disparities) was a priority, and issued various actions against banks accused of discriminatory lending.[12] In the 1990s Fannie Mae and Freddie Mac, under the direction of the U.S. Department of Housing and Urban Development, developed quotas for lending to lower-income borrowers that were continually increased. With the government now mandating such lending, government regulators who might otherwise have warned against such lending, based on inadequate down payments or other underwriting criteria, found themselves having to encourage such lending innovations. Like slowly boiling a frog, underwriting standards degraded over a period with increasing housing prices and no one noticed the effect on default risk, so that as of 2006 everyone still thought "mortgage risk" merely referred to anticipating the complex prepayment option.

Dick Syron was made the CEO of Freddie Mac, in large part because he was a forceful advocate for the pretext need to get support from legislators in maintaining their monopoly: helping increase home ownership by the poor, especially minorities (note the complex nature of the favor bank). Freddie Mac's chief risk officer, David A. Andrukonis, told Syron in mid-2004, that the company was buying bad loans that "would likely pose an enormous financial and reputational risk to the company and the country."[13] Yet at that time, these government-sponsored enterprises that guarantee a large amount of mortgages, Fannie Mae and Freddie Mac, were under criticism for an unrelated accounting fraud issue. An embattled Fannie and Freddie emphasized their mission to financing low-income and affordable housing, and after a long battle, in 2005, new legislation designed to curb Fannie and Freddie's power was killed in the Senate's Committee on Banking, Housing, and Urban Affairs.[14,15]

While these underwriting standards are theoretically related to defaults in obvious ways, as these adjustments were made throughout the decade and a half before 2006, the effect of these changes on aggregate mortgage performance was negligible, mainly because the increase in housing prices meant borrower credit was irrelevant because the collateral was increasing in value. Stan Liebowitz, who had written criticisms of the initial Boston Fed studies to little effect in the 1990s, noted that no one highlighted the pernicious credit risks of these changes before 2006.[16,17] Other large mortgage lenders adjusted to the government-sponsored enterprise's lead, and new entrants and existing lenders like Countrywide explicitly targeted these new loans, and rating agencies, like everyone else, were cowed by the theory that the old criteria were arbitrary and racist in effect, as well as the data: No increase in losses appeared.[18] Thus, Moody's and the S&P did not alter the loss assumptions that underlay the complex of derivatives built upon mortgage pools: mortgage-backed securities, credit default swaps based on these securities, or collateralized debt obligations based on these securities. It all started with a lack of adjustment in expected losses to changes in underwriting, something that in the context seemed not just empirically true, but morally right. Andrukonis left Freddie Mac to teach in 2004, while Syron personally pocketed a total of $38 million before Freddie was taken over by the government in September 2008.

The key risk driver in the upcoming debacle was that a relaxation of underwriting criteria would stand as a levee in times of adversity, such as when housing prices decline. In a financial institution, a risk manager bucking the collective wisdom of the business line (who benefits from excessive risk with firm capital), regulators, academia, investors (who had no qualms before 2007) and our largest home loan underwriter or their CEO, in the absence of any actual loss data, is powerless to seriously question such mortgage innovations.[19] To have argued against this in real time, you would have suffered the fate of Andrukonis versus the success of Syron. And this difference was not constrained to greedy businessmen. Alicia Munnell's flawed 1992 piece on mortgage discrimination led this erstwhile Federal Reserve vice president to go become, among economists, wildly successful: Her paper became published in the *American Economic Review,* the leading publication of economists, member of the National Bureau of Economic Research, part of the Council of Economic Advisors to the President, and is a full professor at Boston College.[20] Meanwhile, Liebowitz's rebuttal of Munnell only made the *Economic Inquiry,* a good journal, ranked thirty-sixth in one study, and is doing good work at the University of Texas at Dallas, yet clearly was less rewarded.[21]

There are a lot of books on valuing derivatives based on mortgages, managing things like the prepayments, interest rates, and credit losses. These are complicated problems, and it takes many months to program algorithms that can capture these structures correctly. The default risk was historically a third-order risk for mortgages, and housing prices in aggregate had never had significant year-over-year declines since World War II. As earlier calls from the 1990s that underwriting adjustments would be disastrous did not materialize, by the time of the Bush administration, concerns about default risk were overwhelmed by a phalanx of policies that conspired to increase mortgage production under the pretext of increasing home ownership and removing discrimination. The motives of the players in this complex of nonmonetary favors (banks trying to appease regulators, who were bucking for promotions into the gold mine patronage jobs at Fannie, who were supporting congressmen, who helped mortgage companies, who made charitable contributions to community activists, and so on) meant that with only theory and no data of losses, the full-time risk manager was powerless to prevent this.

This is a signature case of how risk management does not have the authority, in practice, to overrule the major risks that affect a business. Clearly this debacle represents an extreme case, yet in the same way, a full-time risk manager does not have the power to affect most strategic decisions of a large institution, which are usually more a function of the firm's mission statement than some specific risk score. That a risk manager's work will, with hindsight, appear tendentious, biased, and incomplete and is a consequence of this reality.

Risk management as a separate line of business is about catching logical mistakes, fraud, violations of agreed-upon limits by renegade subunits. They enforce rules, help modify them in nonthreatening ways, but they do not create the most important of those rules. As those in charge knew the right answer, they merely had to find those risk managers who would generate the analysis to support their conclusions (for example, in 2006 UBS risk managers applied a 10-day value at risk based on data from the benign 2000–2005 period in traded residential mortgage-backed securities, vastly underestimating their risk). Yet, blaming the risk manager is misplaced, because this was outside the scope of her authority. In the subprime boom, regulators, the federal government, nonprofits, community activists, legislators, and not least investors all wanted more mortgages for people without the ability to pay them back using the standard underwriting criteria.[22]

Indeed, the subprime crisis highlights an additional insight of the relative risk approach. If everyone is doing something, people feel it would be risky not to do it, and as bank acquirers touted ever larger CRA lending targets, opting out of this mania would have implied that those drinking the Kool-Aid such as Countrywide or Washington Mutual would have acquired your bank in short order. CRA commitments skyrocketed under George W. Bush, as during 2003–2004 bank acquirers pledged over $2 trillion in new loans for traditionally underserved communities, a number so large it could only create a large, deep web of enablers and advocates, and disastrous new tactics, such as no income documentation or down payments, necessary to meet these targets. Not playing the game in 2005 and 2006 would have implied you were asking to be taken over.

RISK MANAGEMENT LIKE AUDIT

In the 1990s, I was on the leading edge in capital allocations in financial institutions after leading a consulting project by First Manhattan to institute a comprehensive risk capital allocation mechanism within KeyCorp, which was about the eighth largest U.S. bank at the time. I was talking to Robert Mark at a risk conference, and he was often speaking on risk management and economic capital allocations. He and his team were doing one of the better jobs of capital allocations at CIBC, a large bank based in Toronto. In the late 1990s, he noted in one of his talks, "It's funny this is not reflected in our stock price." Yet, over the subsequent 10 years, CIBC has been hurt just as much as any other bank in the subsequent banking problems. This is because the risk management he was talking about, and doing such a good job at, was merely measuring better what we see on the books that everyone agrees is a risk that should be minimized. Measuring that kind of risk better is good, just like having great Internet security is good, but that won't affect your company's P/E ratio. It is much less important than the job of making strategic decisions that could be wrong, and are thus risky, which is rarely the subject of extended analytical study, because it so parochial.

The business heads who have the real power, who make decisions about where to expand, new sales incentives, or pricing plans, are the ones making the really risky decisions within a bank. Such decisions, however, are not up for a general debate by their subordinates, and especially those underneath them. To placate these people, risk management is something they can all agree is important and that they all work on. This allows the business heads to retain power, which is important because business hierarchies purport to be meritocracies that work for shareholders, but anyone in charge does not want to be like an NFL player having to prove himself in spring training every year. Thus, the subordinates are basically excluded from the strategic debates among the real alpha males in the organization, though not so explicitly that they then withhold support for these same individuals.

So, in one sense, the risk manager at JPMorgan was correct. His company does make or lose money for its shareholders to the extent that it manages risk. But he was either really good at playing the game, or deluded, to think that risk management as a separate line of business was managing those risks. Every financial executive is fundamentally a risk manager, and evaluates strategies based on analogies to the past as well as the behavior of their peers. Such an executive encourages hundreds, if not thousands within his organization to offer opinions and solutions in their limited domain, not emphasizing its second-order effect on the business. The really intelligent workers of risk management, who are not as good at creating coalitions, but who excel in the complex issues of derivatives and pricing models, are satisfied, and those at the top who are often quite clueless of some of these basic issues, stay in charge. Businesses are far from perfect, but they have to play in a game populated by highly imperfect people. Given the distribution of talents, and the relatively poor managerial skills of the quants, and the way businesses play off of access and reputation, this probably does serve the overall company well, a greater good. Given the average amount of intelligence, integrity, greed, people skills, envy, and intellectual courage, it is not an absurd state of affairs.

OVERPAID ALPHA DECEPTORS

The problem is usually based on someone being vastly overpaid for doing something without a lot of management responsibility. A "Head of Global Equity Derivatives," or "Chief Investment Officer," is often in a position where she can receive an unnecessary zero and the end of her annual bonus. This is a classic moral hazard in that it encourages bad behavior from otherwise good people. They become like Gollum in *The Lord of the Rings,* seduced by power and turned into something paranoid, greedy, and pathetic.

If you are getting vastly overpaid, you have a problem. Someone might find out you really are not worth $1 million a year. Your firm could hire someone to do it for $200K, just as well. How do you keep your bosses from figuring this out? Well, first, if one is being vastly overpaid, then they probably are also working for someone who really does not understand what they are doing. If they did, they would not be paying him so much more than they should. Thus, given the boss is ignorant about how this desk generates its profit—that is, its alpha—one needs to perpetuate this misconception. This involves not being helpful with your risk managers and misrepresenting yourself to your boss, mainly by not volunteering information. The best lies are lies of omission, because no one can prosecute you for not volunteering information; mistruths are damnable evidence.

Second, you need to make sure no one very smart and experienced is hired in your group. If your second-in-command is clearly a close substitute and you throw your weekly temper tantrum, you may get fired, and never make that much money again. Thus, hire demonstrably inferior people, and avoid giving any responsibility to anyone bright you may have inherited. I saw this once, and thought it was a particularly insecure person, but then I saw it a couple of more times. In two of the cases, the person actually articulated this goal to me or to people I knew: to hire someone who would not be so good as to be a potential replacement. Whenever someone is insecure, as overpaid millionaires tend to be, he deliberately made sure his lieutenant, the guy who would step in for him when he was out on vacation or sick, was tangibly inferior. As long as the Number Two was demonstrably inferior, Number One was safe.

These people are especially cancerous in that they generally are head of a group making a lot of revenue. This gives them a lot of power. Their habits carry over to other areas, because if you can convince people your group does not need some extra risk assessment, it should not be applied to others, either. Overpaid people do not respect those they trust, and do not trust those they respect. In a sort of reverse catch-22, the only people who understand the futility of their situation working for these people are anxious to escape it, leaving a circle of ignorant and deluded co-conspirators.

Consider the extreme, where alpha is not present, but exists merely from the position. For example, a seat on the NYSE costs about $1 million to buy. This is because, if you are on the exchange floor, that space is worth $1 million to the average, marginal trader—lots of retail flow and the bid-ask spread. If you have alpha on the exchange floor, you should buy this seat, because you can make more than $1 million in present-value terms. In this case, the seat is a proxy for monopoly value, like a taxi cab medallion in NYC, something with a quota, that prevents entry that would drive profits to zero, and within organizations, there are often seats like this, positions that many earnest and smart people could do, but alas only one is chosen and makes the big bucks. But such value need not be an explicit monopoly. Many big organizations are profitable because of their brand name and their existing network of buyers and suppliers, or their government-approved monopoly.

I once reviewed a currency trading desk early in my career as a risk manager, when I had little clout or any real understanding of the alpha, the essence of the net revenue of various groups within a bank. I proudly printed out a sheet with my preliminary estimate of the Value-at-Risk for the desk, about $50K per day for a 95 percent event, based on all of their day-to-day positions. The manager of the desk then tore into me, getting very upset about my abuse of protocol, in that he supposed he should have been involved in this estimate from the very beginning, as I was potentially spreading misinformation on his group within the company.

I was dumbfounded, because I merely took their end-of-day positions, aggregated the exposures to the various currencies and yield curves, and applied the newfangled RiskMetrics algorithm to the desk. As part of risk management, I was privy to their end-of-day positions. I figured he would be very happy I estimated his risk to be so low. What I did not realize was that for a desk making $10 million a year, this made it quite obvious that they were not alpha magicians, because this would imply a Sharpe ratio of about 25, so outside the range of plausible it screams, "Market maker."

Thus, you had a case where a desk head presents his group's function as deft speculators, not market makers, because this inflates their alpha, and justifies their bonuses as a percentage of profits. There are many similar desks on the trading floor, and all of them tell the same story. This basically allows insiders to exploit their information advantage to keep proportionately more of the revenue. I once sat in a meeting where our head of trading noted proudly to the bank CEO that his group made money on a day the stock market fell precipitously. This was really misleading, because they didn't have any significant net positions per course of regular business—they were market makers, and they didn't even trade equities. The CEO nodded in approval. This is really bad because keeping the CEO ignorant of the genesis of alpha in various business lines clearly disserves the shareholders, but it also disserves the public, because the CEO cannot meet his customers' needs better with a solution than might actually not protect the fiefdom of the "Head of Global Default Swaps."

In another case, I witnessed a group that was creating an automated version of a trader. That is, using the electronic feeds, you have a book of limit orders just like the specialists on the floor of the NYSE have. You can adjust your bid and ask, just as a human can. Being a specialist—posting offers to buy and sell at modest quantities—is highly amenable to an algorithm. But to really make money off this within the company, it helps to sell one's algorithm as not merely as something so straightforward, but crucially integrating a proprietary factor model that layered in a directional bet on the equities being traded. While theoretically, there is a case for adding a 1-ish Sharpe factor model to a 5-ish Sharpe market-making algorithm applied to retail flow, I also knew the specifics of how the algorithm worked. The marginal effect of a long-term drift factor was negligible on actual transaction criteria. But the boss did not know this, and so this guy was able to arrogate more of the profits for himself, through his insinuation that much of the profit was not from a straightforward market-making model—and certainly not from the retail trade flow—but a "market-making cum algorithmic-trading model" that suggests the touch of a Buffett or a Lynch.

The costs are more than how much someone is being overpaid. The cost is the senior management does not understand the essence of the profits being generated. They might reallocate their capital, or adjust their product offering, if they understood exactly what their clients were paying for. The alpha deception of the traders means those with the capital are not optimizing its use, because they do not understand where alpha is being generated.

INVESTOR MEETS ALPHA

In theory, equity earns all the profits. Labor and debt earn fixed payments that basically cover their opportunity costs—no abnormal returns there (this was the theme of Frank Knight's *Risk, Uncertainty, and Profit,* published in 1921). Equity is defined as the residual claimant, and he receives the residual revenue, which includes the alpha. Practice is quite different. For example, in Lowenstein's book *While America Aged,* General Motors poured $55 billion into its workers' pension plan over a 15-year stretch ending in 2006, compared to only $13 billion that it paid out in dividends.[23] As retired union workers voted, one could say that GM was not run by shareholders, not by its current union members, but by its ex-union members.

The key is that any written agreement is not worth merely as much as the implicit power of the agents in real time, because most contracts are not renegotiation proof. For example, if A and B write a contract, where B gets 10 percent of the profit, A receives 90 percent, and both are necessary, it is easy for B to renegotiate. He can threaten to walk away, or not try as hard as he could for the duration of the contract. To the extent B is able and willing to withhold his effort, he can negotiate a higher percentage, because A's 90 percent of nothing is worse than 50 percent of something. Profits of all sorts are a function of power and negotiating, because the law and contracts are merely one of many tools used by all claimants to reconcile a power differential.

Looking at alpha, we should see that the investor also does not receive anywhere near the entire alpha in the investment. Look at employee expense as a percent of profits to shareholders at investment banks. Goldman Sachs earned $14.6 billion and $17.6 billion in 2006 and 2007, respectively. They paid out $16.4 billion and $20.2 billion in bonuses in those two years, suggesting that those on the ground, making the deals, are able to get about half of the profit. Note that Goldman has a lot of insider ownership, so I do not think this is a simple capital-management agency problem, where the employees have outnegotiated the shareholders. Alternatively, look at hedge funds. If one assumes that hedge funds make only 2 percent of assets and 20 percent of profits, then over the glory years of convertible bonds from 1994 through 2003, when they returned 10 percent to investors, this implies hedge funds raked in about 5.5 percent of assets in profits for themselves, while investors received about 4.5 percent in annual returns above the LIBOR. As one might expect when you have two inputs, equally necessary, the split seems to be near 50–50.

The one with the idea has to get capital, or partners. If his strategy is a variation on a theme well-known to investors, this is usually quite straightforward. Indeed, the best pitch for an investment strategy is to note a highly successful, comparable strategy, just as for almost any new product. But then, to the extent it is obviously attractive, one then must retain some secrets so that the capital provider does not merely take it the idea, say, "No thanks" to the alpha pitch, and implement it himself. The listeners usually think they *completely* understand the idea, and they can make it even better by adding some personal touches—making it easy in their mind to think it is really their idea—and cut out the potential middleman. Good ideas that are easy to understand will be misrepresented more because to do otherwise is foolish.

Another reason to misrepresent ideas is that people tend to distrust simplicity. It is a fact that more data gives people the illusion that something works better. Barber and Odean claim that when people are given more information on which to base a decision, their confidence increases. This is true even when the information is actually meaningless, but related.[24] Basically, our minds are like naïve statisticians that try to maximize the R^2 by mindless data mining, confusing explanation with predictive ability, hurting out-of-sample performance. In other words, a model of arbitrage based on one factor will generally appear inferior to one based on several, a key point if you are selling a strategy, because you can often accomplish two necessary goals in one swoop, by adding irrelevant factors: It both disguises the strategy and serves to make it look better to the average investor.

Unconventional strategies that are not so obvious, no matter how simple and true, take a lot more work. As John Bogle showed, it was not until he was the CEO of a fund complex that he could implement his idea for a retail index fund, and even then he dealt with a skeptical board, and relied heavily on authority figures like Paul Samuelson. Imagine if he were a bright-eyed young kid with merely a PowerPoint presentation and his own data.

Capital providers need to understand the essence of alpha, and generally all they really understand are two things: a track record and pedigree. Thus, a good degree from a good school is good, especially the Ivy league. A couple years of audited financials is good. A recommendation from someone the investor trusts, be it his uncle or George Soros, is good. Whether the idea makes sense, based on the logic and empirical evidence, has a tertiary effect on its actual probability of being implemented. Most look at arguments for your pet alpha project as advocacy, suspect because of the obvious self-interest involved. People have preconceptions, and if something cleverly articulates or extends their preconceptions, they think it is genius. If it is something outside their preconceptions, they find it uninteresting. If it is contrary to their preconceptions, it is wrong. People are generally not very good at evaluating alpha of the sort that is unconventional, unfamiliar by definition. You can sleep well knowing the logic of your unconventional idea, if true, will be obvious to posterity because the truth does, eventually, get out (though validation from the wild success of those who were fortunate enough to have wealthy relatives, has its downside). But truth is still important to the inventor, because getting started is only a part of the battle, your idea does have to work, and the idea generator will lose the most in terms of opportunity cost if the venture is a dead end.

The more you know, the more efficient you can be in structuring incentives so that your alpha is successful. An investor seeking alpha needs to understand the incentives facing the alpha producer. She needs to get her hands dirty with unconventional, idiosyncratic pitches. To the extent she has some knowledge of the market, she can assess these claims not merely on their track record, or the college of the manager, but on the logic and data in the proposal. For example, if an equity portfolio manager promises you a 10 percent return above the S&P500 investing in equities, you have reason to be very skeptical, indeed, dismissive. This is because the historical data of the S&P500 and mutual fund managers suggests this to be implausible. If you knew nothing about the market, or other data, however, you might believe it is true, based on her anecdotes and testimonials, and irrelevant signaling such as having a nice resume and a pleasant demeanor. This same kind of approach is useful in other domains, although involves a much more detailed level of product knowledge. If you know what the average default rates for B-rated bonds, and the average power of models that predict defaults, how they relate to state-of-the-art alternatives, you know that a manager predicting 4 percent annualized excess returns by going long the correct subset of B-rated bonds is a fraud or a fool. But if the manager shows how one can make money, and actually uses a set of assumptions that are consistent with broader data, and reflects a deep knowledge of the product space, that can be very compelling. The effort, and wisdom, required of an investor looking for alpha is very hands on, and quite contrary to the view of sitting down, looking at means and covariances, and generating portfolio weights.

The fact that alpha is private information makes the search for alpha much different from if we assume that alpha can be assumed. Knowing that as an investor, you are joining forces with someone who needs you, and whom you need in return. The information transfer is fraught with danger for both sides. This is where the rubber hits the road, in terms of benefiting from being smart, educated, hardworking, having integrity, but also not being too trusting. Investing wisely is a lot more about negotiating and understanding a product space than optimizing. That is, to the extent you are passively accepting information on returns and volatilities, your odds of actually finding alpha are about the same as those from investing with a mutual fund manager.

CHAPTER 13

Alpha Seeking Applications

This book presents evidence that risk, in general, is not related to return. Assets on the extreme ends of the risk spectrum, however, those with hope and certainty, have lower-than-average returns. These results are a consequence of our benchmarking our wealth against our peers, of valuing opportunities that provide hope, and needing some amount of certainty as insurance. This implies that investors should focus on the expected returns, which includes anticipating the infrequent lean times, and ignore any nuance to the discount rate—which is pretty much what most investors do in practice. Furthermore, alpha is fundamentally private information, and so the main issues in finding alpha relate to the various issues that arise in negotiating with someone whose incentives are not directly aligned with yours, and of ascertaining the value of something most other people have dismissed.

There are two general areas one can apply these insights to that generate strategies and tactics that are unconventional. The first is avoiding assets with a large hope premium added into their price. To the extent one is benchmarking against the market, going long only assets without huge upside means that you are selling hope relative to the market. If you are long only boring assets that have little chance of doubling, your relative performance is enhanced to the extent the hope assets underperform, as they historically have. These are generally strategies that presume no alpha on one level, but like buying index funds versus active funds, they generate superior returns, with less risk however measured. A second set of recommendations comes from useful rules once we recognize the incentives and information asymmetries in alpha. As our intuition about risk and return comes from a rule that applies mainly to people finding their comparative advantage in life, our understanding of alpha informs our efforts to find our comparative advantage. Indeed, one could say a synonym for alpha is comparative advantage, because what you can do, better than anyone else, is where you have alpha.

MINIMUM VOLATILITY PORTFOLIO

The first, most obvious investing implication is to arbitrage the lack of a positive risk and return relation. Risk may be impossible to define academically, but it seems like less volatility should be preferred to more, as was supposed in the Dark Ages before we found out the CAPM did not work. If you can trade your envy for greed, you should prefer a higher Sharpe ratio, and targeting low volatility stocks is the easiest way to do this.

After finishing my dissertation in 1994 documenting the slight negative relation between volatility and returns, I was eager to apply this in an investment vehicle. The basic idea was simple: Buy low volatility assets, make the same return if not slightly better than the indexes, and generate a higher Sharpe ratio. I figured the attractiveness of this idea was like sliced bread. I went to work at KeyCorp, primarily because of the opportunity to work with the asset management group there, which I was certain would be very excited about this great idea. In short order, I found no enthusiasm, because it was a little too unconventional. People were not interested in pitching a strategy that promised not so much higher returns within an asset class, but mainly lower risk. In the context of relative risk, and how people in general define themselves relative to a benchmark, this makes sense. That is, as described in Chapter 9, investors tend to think of risk as tracking error, deviating from the S&P500 or any relevant index is risk, regardless of whether the total volatility, or covariances with the market, or the business cycle. An equity investor with less volatility, but a tracking error with the benchmarks, is riskier to most investors.

I think a strong case can be made that while people measure risk relative to benchmarks, they *should* measure it more objectively, relative to volatility. The origin of the CAPM is incorrect as a description of reality, but it is a good guide as to how one ought to invest. In the long run, a higher Sharpe ratio implies that one can take on equivalent volatility and generate higher returns, and all that benchmark risk is idiosyncratic: over time it washes away through time diversification. Thus, over a long period, the Sharpe ratio should be the primary metric for developed country equity investing because in general these portfolios have relatively symmetric distributions (unlike debt or options).

While I managed my personal situation by becoming a risk manager, I also set up a fund with a couple of hundred thousand dollars, primarily my parents' money, and set up an S-Corp called the Falken Fund to invest the money. I would invest the money, generate audited returns, and this I thought would help my efforts to someday land a job implementing the strategy. Like so many, I added to the basic idea, in my case by targeting low volatility stocks another factor, taking low volatility stocks that had high momentum, which in the 1990s was a relatively new anomaly that seemed promising. As I had a rather limited amount of funds, I could buy only about 30 stocks, which implied considerable idiosyncratic risk remained in the portfolio, but I was hoping the momentum and low volatility focus would generate higher returns at low risk. I rebalanced this every 6 to 12 months, implementing a very simple filter rule that took little time, and did this on the side while working on risk management issues for KeyCorp and Moody's (I got okays from senior management at those institutions, noting it involved no real outside money and none of my daily time at work). I stopped doing it once I got into a situation to be a *real* portfolio manager at Deephaven, because I wanted to focus then on my directly competing day job.

The strategy performed very well, basically by outperforming in the tech bubble period of 2000 to 2002. From December 1996 through July 2002, it generated a 16 percent annualized return, with a beta of 0.8, versus a 3.8 percent return for the S&P500 over that same period.

I mention this not to brag, but because it highlights that the idea that focusing on low volatility is truly an out-of-sample result. In addition to my dissertation, I actively implemented a strategy fundamentally based on this insight. I am not looking at the past 10 years of data with hindsight, the recent literature on the latest anomaly, and making a grand statement. It is based on a pattern in the historical data, going back to 1926, which I discovered in 1992, and emphasized continually since. Furthermore, I was involved in litigation for almost two years, where one of the demands by my former employer was that I not use volatility as a factor in evaluating stocks, as this was asserted as being *necessarily* derived from my work at this hedge fund. I discovered, wrote about, and implemented this idea well prior to any work I did after 2003. None of this originated, nor was derived from any ex-employer's trade secrets or confidential information. While I currently work in equities implementing long and short equity strategies, the basic idea of my 1990s Falken Fund was an edge based on the superior Sharpe to low volatility equities. This insight, however, is not suited toward hedge funds, where the desired Sharpe ratio is above a 1.0. Thus, it is not like pairs, but rather more like index investing, a modest improvement but highly scalable, long-only approach.

Researchers have investigated minimum variance funds since Haugen and Baker in 1991.[1] All document that a straightforward variance minimization algorithm applied to a large set of stocks, including a no-short-sales constraint, generates about a 30 percent reduction in volatility compared to common U.S. indexes without diminishing returns. These studies had issues, in that only an obscure unpublished piece by Tal Schwartz used a set of stocks that underlay the indexes, which complicates the analysis because it is possible that using a broader set of data to compare to an index create a low volatility portfolio spanning a different set of risk factors, making it an apples-and-oranges comparison.

The long-only, minimum-variance portfolio is an attractive target because it makes no assumptions about returns, merely portfolio volatility. If traditional measures of risk are unrelated to returns, this should be a straightforward way to increase a Sharpe ratio. Curiously, all the papers that examined minimizing index volatility also found that returns were actually higher than the benchmarks. In each case, the higher return was unremarked, as if it had to be some sort of mistake, merely emphasizing the lower volatility feasible in a minimum variance focus.

I denote these long-only, low volatility portfolios MVPs, for Minimum Variance Portfolios. New index weights are calculated for each on January 1 and July 1 based on the prior year's daily returns, using a minimum variance minimization algorithm on the factors and factor loadings from Chris Jones's heteroskedasticity-consistent version of Connor and Korajczyk's principal components procedure.[2] Index weights are then constant for the next six months using a total return index, so there is no rebalancing bias due to equal-weighting daily returns of portfolio constituents.[3] There is no survivorship bias because I use stocks in the indexes at the beginning of the performance period, transaction costs are low, and liquidity issues should be minor because we are only going long stocks within the major equity indexes. Thus, unlike the Fama-French size (SMB) portfolio, with its many illiquid stocks and shorted securities, the January returns for the MVPs are actually slightly less than their sample average, suggesting there are no significant institutional issues due to end-of-year tax strategies that show up in illiquid securities.

Minimum Variance Portfolios are prominent in advanced textbooks on portfolio theory, because they form the leftmost point in the convex hull representing the set of feasible returns in risk-return space. Theoretically, they include long and short positions in stocks. The long-only approach of an MVP is attractive because many obvious stocks we all wish to short (for example, Palm in the 3M spin-off of 1999) in practice cannot be shorted, or have a negative rebate (that is, instead of earning interest on the short sale proceed; you pay a fee on the money you generate). Rebate schedules and impossible-to-borrow lists are difficult to accurately recreate because these are over-the-counter markets.[4] Furthermore, in many developed markets, one can short only 40 percent of the stocks, and proportionately more of the weak stocks everyone wishes to short (for example, in January 2009 highly liquid General Motors was basically impossible to short for retail investors). This makes results difficult to interpret, because one can never be certain it was feasible to implement the short side of a portfolio-minimizing algorithm. Jagannathan and Ma (2003) show that in constructing a global minimum variance portfolio, a no-short-sales constraint actually helps out-of-sample performance because in an unconstrained approach, recommended shorts usually have very high covariances with other stocks. Stocks that have extremely high covariances with other stocks tend to receive negative portfolio weights, and the no-short-sales constraint is equivalent to capping the sample covariances at reasonable level (alternatively, one can think of it as applying a Bayesian base rate to a covariance estimate that mitigates extreme correlations in sample). Hence, to the extent that high estimated covariances are more likely to be caused by upward-biased estimation error, imposing the nonnegativity constraint on position weights reduces the sampling error, and so a no-short-sales restriction is in practice a modest constraint in constructing a minimum variance portfolio, and makes the result something eminently feasible.

Looking at the past 10 years of data for the S&P500, eight years of data for the Nikkei and FTSE, and seven years for the MSCI-Euro Index, Table 13.1 shows that annualized volatility can be reduced by 30 to 45 percent within these indexes by simply reweighting the constituents in a way that minimizes the historical volatility, but is then applied to the out-of-sample returns. Furthermore, in each case, the numerator of the Sharpe ratio was also significantly higher. The FTSE, Nikkei, S&P500, and MSCI-Euro index would need annualized return increases of several percentage points to

TABLE 13.1 Summary Statistics of Minimum Variance Portfolios versus Their Indexes

	FTSE-MVP	FTSE	Nikkei-MVP	Nikkei	SP500-MVP	SP500	MSCI-Euro-MVP	MSCI-Euro
AnnRet	5.28%	−3.82%	1.53%	−4.35%	6.58%	−0.58%	−0.30%	−5.39%
AnnStdev	15.45%	21.11%	16.90%	25.37%	14.47%	20.91%	14.09%	23.38%
Beta	0.67	1.00	0.57	1.00	0.55	1.00	0.52	1.00
Sharpe	0.04	−0.40	0.07	−0.18	0.19	−0.21	−0.19	−0.36

SP500-MVP, Nikkei-MVP, MSCI-MVP, and FTSE-MVP are the Minimum Variance Portfolios of the S&P500, Nikkei 225, MSCI-Euro, and FTSE 100 indexes. Each index is formed at the end of June and December using a long-only subset of the corresponding index, where portfolio weights minimize the portfolio volatility over the prior year's daily returns. Beta is from regressing the daily returns of the MVP on its respective index. The Nikkei and Nikkei-MVP, FTSE, and FTSE-MVP use daily data from January 1 to December 31, 2008, while the SP500-MVP and S&P500 use daily data from January 1, 1998, to December 31, 2008, and the MSCI-related indexes are from January 2, 2002, to December 31, 2008. The Sharpe ratio subtracts the average one-month LIBOR rate for each currency from the annual return, divided by the annualized volatility of returns.

equalize the Sharpe ratios of their relevant MVPs. For example, the S&P500 has an annualized geometric return of almost zero, −0.6% percent, over the past 10 years, whereas the minimum variance subset portfolio generated a 6.58 percent annualized return over that same period. As the volatility of the S&P is about 21 percent versus 14 percent for the MVP, in a Sharpe ratio perspective, the S&P return would have to be about 10 percent higher, annually, to be comparable to the minimum variance portfolio for your mean-variance maximizing investor. Betas of the MVPs range from 0.52 to 0.67. Thus, as index funds dominate actively managed funds primarily because of their 1 percent cost advantage, the relevant advantage here is several orders of magnitudes higher.

The returns in these samples are for geometric returns, and about 2 percent lower than the returns generated from an arithmetic averaging of the monthly returns. This is appropriate, I would argue, because this kind of strategy is a long-run strategy, not a market timing one, and so, the idea is over a long period of time, say 10 years, what were the returns. But the results are qualitatively similar using arithmetic returns. Looking at Figure 13.1, we see that the total return to the average of all the MVPs since

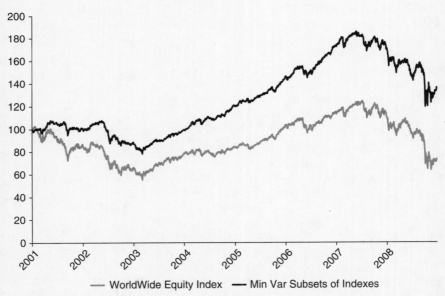

FIGURE 13.1 WorldWide Equity Index versus Minimum Variance Subsets of Indexes
Note: Total return data are averages of index, and minimum variance portfolios described in Table 13.1.

2001 versus the average of the indexes shows the obvious domination of this approach: higher return, at lower volatility, lower cyclicality.

This type of return dominance is especially obvious if one uses the harsh criterion of Second Order Stochastic Domination (SOSD). This criterion was highlighted in the early 1970s, when high-brow theorists like Rothschild and Stiglitz were defining just what, exactly, was risk.[5] One idea was that it was broader than mere standard deviation, as obviously returns with fatter tails, or more negative skew, might be perceived differently from assets with less. Standard deviation is often criticized for being incomplete, as if finance is ignorant that tail risk is important. Yet economists have known of this for decades, and indeed the Rothschild and Stiglitz work in this area tried to come up with better, broader risk measures (that they did not really take off highlights that these more accurate measures have problems, mainly they have too many dimensions and are unintuitive). But all you need to know is that the SOSD metric requires a strictly increasing utility function and global risk aversion, that is, utility is everywhere increasing and concave, two standard assumptions that underlie most risk models.[6] Every risk-averse agent prefers an asset that SOSD another, in this framework. To put this idea in more concrete terms, see Table 13.2. Note the first, fifth, tenth percentiles, and the worst drawdown, for the MVPs are all higher than for their respective indexes. This means that the extreme bad days tend to be much worse for the indexes than for the MVPs. This is tail risk, something that is occluded by a metric like standard deviation that is sufficient only for normal distributions.

If the most widely used equity indexes can be significantly dominated by simply applying the idea that risk is not rewarded using its very constituents, this suggests the failure of the CAPM and its extensions is not a mere academic finding in an abstruse statistical test, but something tangible to regular investors. For those demanding concrete proof that their standard approach works, in general, they should explain the Minimum Volatility Portfolio anomalies, because forming a portfolio based on the most conspicuous, and earliest, metrics of risk, is not data mining the way book-market

TABLE 13.2 Extreme Drawdown for Minimum Variance Portfolios and Their Indexes

	FTSE	FTSE-MVP	MSCI-Eur	MSCI-MVP	Nikkei	Nikkei-MVP	S&P500	S&P500-MVP
0.01	−4.08%	−3.08%	−4.61%	−2.72%	−4.34%	−3.05%	−3.45%	−2.46%
0.05	−1.94%	−1.43%	−2.32%	−1.31%	−2.39%	−1.59%	−1.98%	−1.29%
0.1	−1.36%	−0.95%	−1.53%	−0.86%	−1.82%	−1.11%	−1.42%	−0.91%
MaxDraw	−48.11%	−36.05%	−53.84%	−41.61%	−57.91%	−43.68%	−51.07%	−37.61%

or momentum might be—these are stock characteristics that should sit at the top of one's list of things to measure against returns. The returns to these seemingly low risk portfolios is above the indexes, and for those who are skeptical of alpha and appreciative of relatively small edges, this move should be most attractive to index investors. In Europe, Robeco and Unigestion have recently created funds explicitly targeting low volatility equities, and the only reason for them to not grow, would be if investors truly cannot trade their envy for greed.[7] That is, those who can appreciate index funds relative to active mutual funds, should be able to appreciate MVPs.

BETA ARBITRAGE

It was mentioned in Chapter 4 that stock returns are negatively related to betas against the market index, and perhaps the best evidence of this is that no academic, who must withstand the barbs of conventional wisdom, presents beta-sorted portfolios for benchmarking because the cognitive dissonance would be too great. This is because beta at some level is positively correlated with risk, and the higher return to the low beta portfolio over the high beta portfolio would seem to imply some kind of error in the data. This is wishful thinking. In addition to the total absence of a positive beta-return relationship after controlling for size, consider all the things that would artificially increase the returns to beta that were generally unremarked, because no one likes to pick on a weak theory: the effect of variance on geometric returns, which biases high beta returns upward, or the biased effect of delisting return omissions on highly volatile stocks. Were the bias obstructing the CAPM, they would certainly be first-order adjustments, but as they merely make matters worse, these adjustments are rarely made. Another incidental confirmation of the negative return to beta, is that most anomalies in the literature—accruals, momentum, value—have lower betas on the higher returning stocks. Supposedly, to the extent the higher returning stocks have some risk, such risk is inversely correlated to beta. Again, there is little made of this, because "no guts, no glory—on average" is a pillar of finance that is seemingly impervious to empirical rejection for those currently in academia who made their career writing papers infused with this basic principle.

The investment implications of the failure of beta are fairly straightforward. Assume there exists an equity return above the risk-free rate. For a trader without alpha, this is presumably a necessary condition for investing in equity markets, with their higher volatility and covariance with the business cycle. Assume also that the traditional CAPM, with betas formed against the market return, does not work. Given these assumptions, you can generate the same return as the market, with zero beta.

Consider:

- Expected equity risk premium (above the risk-free rate): 3 percent
- Beta for longs: 0.5
- Beta for shorts: 1.5
- $R_\beta = R_m$ for all β

With these assumptions for what is available in the market, we can generate the exact same return as the market, yet without any beta risk. Just go long 1.5 units of the low beta portfolio (for example, beta 0.5), and go short 0.5 units of the high beta portfolio (beta 1.5). The net result is zero beta (dollar beta of the long and short side are both 0.75). Note that this employs 2.0 units of stock, thus nicely fitting into Reg T, an U.S. regulatory rule that prevents retail investors from having the gross amount of longs and shorts more than twice one's capital. Perhaps someone, someday, will invent a high beta and low beta ETF (as opposed to leveraging the S&P500), and this trade will be made much easier.

What makes this trade even better, is that on average the low volatility longs have a higher-than-average return, and the high volatility shorts have a lower-than-average return, which means that one should expect a higher-than-market return, with zero beta.

I implemented a similar strategy in the United States over the past 10 years, investing in low beta stocks, hedging with high beta stocks such that one is long one unit of stock at zero beta:

$$p_l - p_s = 1 \qquad \text{net long 1 unit}$$

$$p_l \beta_l - p_s \beta_s = 0 \quad \text{zero beta}$$

$$\Rightarrow \; p_s = \frac{\beta_l}{\beta_s - \beta_l}, \; p_l = 1 + p_s$$

p_l = position in long portfolio

p_s = position in short portfolio

β_l = beta of long portfolio

β_s = beta of short portfolio

With these mathematical conditions, we estimate the beta of the portfolio using a rolling estimate of the past year's returns on the low and high beta portfolio returns (that is, using only data prior to date t, for implementation on date t). The beta portfolios are constructed every six months, looking for the lowest and highest beta equities (100 stocks) in the United

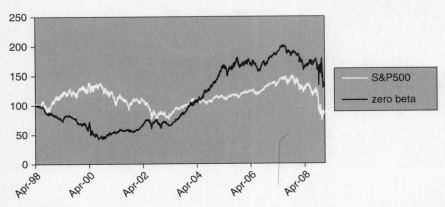

FIGURE 13.2 Total Return to S&P500 and Zero-Beta, Dollar Long, Long/Short Portfolio

States that had over $1 billion market cap, where beta was estimated over the prior year's daily returns. Thus, this is an out-of-sample performance of the basic strategy outlined: long a unit of stock (for example, a dollar), at zero beta, by going short a sufficient amount of the high beta stock to make the portfolio's total beta zero, while having one unit of stock long. The results are shown in Figure 13.2 and Table 13.3.

We can see that if you want $1 million exposure to the market, but with a zero beta, you actually do generate a higher return by about 4 percent, with a lower standard deviation than the market. Plus, you have zero beta, which most investors consider a good thing (back in the 1970s, some would call this riskless investing). The total return chart for the S&P500 versus this alternative is shown, and the relative outperformance seems to be when it is appreciated most, when the market is tanking.

TABLE 13.3 Summary Statistics for Beta Arbitrage Strategy, April 1998–December 2008

	S&P500	Zero-Beta/ Long-Market
Annual Return	1.10%	4.30%
Annual Standard Deviation	21.27%	17.40%
GeoRet	−1.19%	2.92%
Sharpe	−0.21	−0.02
Beta	1.0	0.0

The beta arbitrage portfolio seems like a no-brainer for anyone who appreciates the statistics of mean-variance optimization. It takes no special insight, just recognizing that the CAPM should work, but doesn't.

There are many ways to take advantage of the absence of a beta relation with returns, because for a rational, nonenvious investor, the fact that the CAPM does not work is more interesting than if it did. An alternative is a strategy that directly targets a 1.0 beta, but avoids the high-beta assets that tend to have low returns. This also closely matches the beta of the overall market, and so plays into investor preferences to match the market.

Using data on all stocks above the median market capitalization since July 1962 to ensure an investable sample, I calculated betas to form a portfolio with a target 1.0 beta, by using those 100 stocks with betas most near 1.0. I call this the Trimmed Beta 1.0 portfolio, because it trims off those stocks with very high and very low betas. The mean return to this approach, from 1962–2007, is 14.0 percent, 2.8 percent above the value-weighted market return over that period (see Table 13.4). In comparison, the well-known value portfolio constructed and maintained by Kenneth French, applied to stocks with above-the-median market cap, generated a 14.6 percent annual return.

From an institutional perspective, a Trimmed Beta 1.0 portfolio is attractive if we put it into context. Many institutions have targeted index funds because they generate a cost savings relative to actively managed funds, and this cost savings is slightly less than 1.0 percent in annualized return, yet still approximating the market. Many funds tilt toward things like size and value to achieve an extra 2 to 4 percent lift while being consistent with the market return. In contrast, this strategy takes no bets on value or size, and thus has very little tracking error, and merely plays on the fact that hope and safety stocks generate lower-than-average returns. Clearly, I consider this an attractive investment because of the simultaneous higher return, but target on the market (low benchmark risk), which is something investors really like. Looking at Figure 13.4, we see the outperformance of the value portfolio and the Trimmed Beta 1.0 portfolio, and note that the Trimmed

TABLE 13.4 Returns from 1962 to 2007

	Large-Cap Value	Trimmed Beta 1.0	Value-Weighted Market
Annual Return	14.6%	14.0%	11.2%
Annual Standard Deviation	15.1%	16.8%	15.0%
Beta	0.86	1.03	1.00

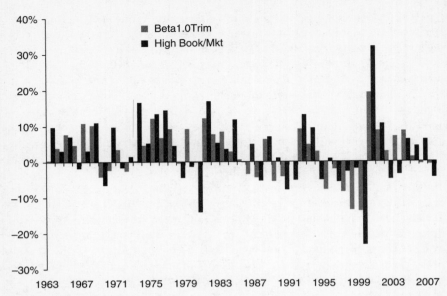

FIGURE 13.3   Return to Trimmed Beta 1.0 and Value Portfolios, 1963–2007

Beta portfolio has fewer extreme periods of underperformance. Further, it tends to underperform when the market is booming, such as in 1998 and 1999, while outperforming in periods of market declines, like 1981 and 2000. Thus, it is somewhat countercyclical. I have a patent pending.

INVESTING IN ANOMALIES

It may be thought that if risk is not, in general, positively associated with returns, then all the prominent anomalies are free lunches: higher return with no more risk. The problem, however, is that most anomalies are artifacts of the publication process, and not really there. Remember that when Bill Schwert wrote on the new size effect back in 1983, he mentioned the other prominent anomalies of his day, the calendar anomalies, specifically the weekend effect and the January effect. These have disappeared, as the findings were primarily a result of low-priced stocks that are large in number, and generate really large returns (for example, moving from one-half to three-fourths in price is a huge percentage move). In practice, these effects cannot be captured, because one actually pays the same large spread that underlies the apparent returns. That is, the bid-ask bounce in these low-priced stocks is a big part of their apparently large returns, but also, their cost to investors. In the 1980s, low-priced stock funds were introduced with the same vigor as small-sized stock funds, but these have disappeared as it became apparent that low price does not reflect a factor or investor bias so much as measurement error.

Consider that for almost a decade, a prominent anomaly was documented by De Bondt and Thaler in 1985, showing that for each year since 1933, going long a portfolio of extreme losers over the previous three years, and short extreme winners over the previous three years, would generate an 8 percent annualized return over the next three years. This was published in the *Journal of Finance,* the leading finance journal, and followed up in 1987 with more results.[8] It seemed like investors were engaging in a simple case of overextrapolation of recent times. Alas, in 1993, Conrad and Kaul (1993) demonstrated that if you did not arithmetically average the returns, the result disappeared, highlighting that this too was a result of low-priced stocks, and their tendency to bias results by moving from their bid to ask price.[9] Indeed, the more prominent "past return anomaly" is actually the opposite of mean-reversion—momentum, first documented in 1992, so it appears that if anything, this theme would have generated low returns if actually implemented.

So, for an investor not plugged in to the latest research, one could easily imagine buying stocks based on flawed research, in that it usually takes 5 to 10 years for the academy to find the problem, and then another five years for this to become conventional wisdom. Currently, an investment bank distributes a monthly review of quant strategies, and lists about 30 different approaches: dividend yield, percent off 52-week high, recommendation changes, and so on. There is always much discussion about the factor rotation, as the latest hot factor approach is always different, which one would expect if most of these are random groupings. On average this is a total waste. As most anomalies do not stand up to scrutiny, this means, on average, you will be wasting resources in a bad investment.

Now, some anomalies, specifically value and size, are so common in theory and practice, one might exempt them. Indeed, the value effect was initially articulated by famous value investor Benjamin Graham in the 1930s, later discussed often by his most famous disciple, Warren Buffett, and lastly, the academics started referencing this effect, starting with Sanjoy Basu in 1977. It has been known for a long time, and seems to be pretty consistent in the data, generating a higher return with no obviously higher risk. But while some investors have become very famous plying this strategy, value funds have not been more successful than growth funds since records of this distinction were made. Houge and Loughran report that small cap value funds realized insignificantly lower annual returns than small cap growth funds: 14.1 percent versus 14.5 percent over the 1975-to-2002 period. Value managers, as a group, were identical with growth-oriented funds, on average.[10]

The original Standard & Poor's 500–Barra value index (Now Standard & Poor's 500–Citigroup index) has generated about the same returns as their growth index over the period from January 1975 through September 2008, which has been about the same as for the S&P500 (9.7 percent, 10.0 percent, and 9.8 percent, annualized, respectively).[11] Furthermore, this index was created around 1990, and they reached backward to build a historical track record for the data. As this took a lot of work, they decided to go back only to 1975, in part because they knew that the value effect was strong in the late 1970s but not early 1970s, implying a look-back bias to this index. Thus, in practice, the value effect is subject to the selection biases all anomalies face.

I believe there are patterns that are useful for statistical equity investing, but as noted in the discussion of alpha, one must have good reason to suspect one's own alpha is complementary to these issues. Just as the main problem with taking advice is knowing what advice to take, knowing which anomalies are good requires almost as much skill as those who document them. Even the most prominent anomalies, ex post, are not all that prominent; ex ante your odds are pretty close to 50–50. If you have data and like to analyze it statistically, understanding the various parochial issues involved, it can be rewarding (it is something I do); however, as a *general* rule, jumping on anomalies in a diversified portfolio is a waste of time.

SAFETY INVESTING

It makes sense for someone to wish that some of their investment portfolio be as close to zero volatility in real terms as possible. Many traders, who are big risk takers, put much of their savings in extremely safe investments, and this makes sense because their careers are so highly correlated with the market that their savings actually constitute a small part of their aggregate wealth. One of the principles of the Kelly Criterion for maximizing the logarithm of one's long-term wealth is that the probability of going into default should be zero. This can be thought of as the negative infinite utility payoff, or the bankruptcy state. If you continuously have access to your account, this means you bet less and less as the market volatility increases. Alternatively, it means you never bet your entire savings. Thus, if having 10 or 30 percent in riskless assets satisfies this basic need, it seems a reasonable objective.

But it can be overdone. People crave certainty, and risk is evaluated on a log scale, so people generally assume it must be the least risky thing possible.

Yet only a modest deviation from the most risky asset generates a sizable lift of 50–100 basis points. Now, when considering reaching for this lift, it is a matter of perspective. Consider the following moves:

Super Safe Investment	Slightly Less Safe Alternative	Average Return Lift
AAA bonds	BBB bonds	1.2%[12]
3-Month U.S. T-bill	1-Year U.S. T-bill	1.04%[13]

Are these worth the risk? With assets this safe, their variability is so low that demonstrating assets in these classes is like proving you are very good at evaluating your skills at forecasting earthquakes. As these happen infrequently, it takes many years to accumulate data that would allow one to see if one is truly good, because the mode signal for everyone, good and bad, is the same. Playing the yield curve from 3 months to 12 months in maturity for a cash account, or from an AAA bond to a BBB bond, the signal-to-noise ratio on any market timing is so low, at annual frequencies, as to be nonexistent. The time needed to even make a reasonable argument that one has alpha in picking among A-rated bonds is probably longer than one's working life.

It is all, the question of whether 100 basis points in annual return is worth the extra uncertainty, quantified as higher volatility, or the size of the negative downside (asymmetric tail risk), classic quantitative risk preferences. The lift in question is not insignificant, but not life changing. I think this choice does fall into the strict mean-variance optimization problem that underlies Modern Portfolio Theory, applicable because there is no alpha here, just a statistical trade-off.

In addition to having some rock-solid investments, and perhaps minor stretches in risk from these (for example, going from overnight to 12-month risk on cash balance), having exposure to broadly diversified, low-cost asset classes also fulfills a fundamental investor desire. By being equally weighted among conventional assets, you mitigate your benchmark risk. Thus, having some money in real estate (their home), and the stock market, is a good idea, because everyone else has their money there too, and broadly speaking, you need to consider your relative risk. Consider if you lived in Southern California in the early 1970s, and decided to rent instead of buy real estate, because the Sharpe ratios on the perceived equity premium puzzle (you identified decades before Mehra and Prescott) suggested equity investing was optimal. You may not be able to retire there because of the massive increase in the value of property over the next 40 years. For those who bought property, this was no big deal, but sadly, not everyone who grew up there owned real estate. The absolute return lift, if implemented with an eye toward low costs (that is, low trading, low fees) should probably generate a modest return above riskless assets, but more importantly, will keep one in company with one's peers, as these assets can trend wildly above historical norms over decades.

HOPE INVESTING

It is easy to say, "Do not gamble" because this has a poor average return. But many people gamble anyway, either out of ignorance, or a real preference for taking on risks that promise extraordinary returns. At the very least, understand that investing in an asset hoping for some life-changing largess, you should have some reason to think you know better than everyone else why, say, a certain asset is undervalued. The riskier the asset considered, the lower your return, because on average, such assets have very low returns. So, you need alpha, to see which advice is good. Now, you might think you have a high IQ, or an MBA, which combined with this advice, makes for wise investing. This too is an insufficient reason, because these same professionals, from good schools, with high IQs, are average stock pickers.

As mentioned, I believe hope is a very useful motivation, but I think it should always guide some effort to get one's hands dirty building a strategy, or choosing a career. Finding alpha passively, by applying statistics to a set of returns, is highly improbable, and should be discouraged or channeled into something else. Thus, I offer the following salve for those who need a little hope in their passive portfolios.

Group all your investing that is done without a general long-term strategy, but has high putative returns, as investing on hope. People have a need for hopeful investments the way we need trace elements called vitamins. So, one might wish to allocate a small portion of one's portfolio to this. Thus, to the extent one should passively invest in dreams of winning it big, the cheapest way is probably the lottery. You can still dream of the fantastic new life you will have if luck smiles upon you. If you only invest once a week, it's merely $52 a year. The odds are really irrelevant, you are paying to dream, and your dreams are not impossible, just so improbable, your intuition does not notice the extra zeros. Our lives are sufficiently short that an investment with a probability of 1 in 100,000, when played weekly, is observationally equivalent to one with odds of 1 in 100 million.

The problem with allocating part of a portfolio to *passive* hope investing in financial markets is that the upside is a *mere* 50 to 200 percent; you need to allocate 30 to 50 percent of your wealth for this to materially change your spending habits, to play into your dreams, and that is too much. Losing

3 percent annually on the 30 percent of your wealth is much more expensive than a weekly lotto ticket.

That means, understand the odds are highly against you in the following:

- Options, especially out-of-the-money options
- Junk bonds
- Highly volatile, beta, stocks
- Highly leveraged company stocks
- Stocks with junk bond ratings

These are classic hope assets that have lower-than-average returns for their class. You are paying for dreams, and it is too costly relative to lotteries because while the returns to these are better than the lottery, the opportunity cost is much greater. And as all you are buying are dreams, and these are passive dreams, not dreams possibly related to some individual alpha, the actual returns do not matter, just having a positive probability of reaching them.

RELATIVE RISK AND BUBBLES

It is common for people to state that bubbles exist, and financial theorists have good models of them. It has been variously suggested that financial bubbles may be endogenous, yet to date, there is no widely accepted theory to explain their occurrence. Take the famous Hyman Minsky Financial Instability Hypothesis: At first, people invest based on the cash flow of the investment, and are able to pay back their investment with principal and interest. Later, the investors still invest only in positive net present value investments, but need to use, in effect, interest-only loans. Lastly, they are engaged in financing by the "greater fool theory," and need fresh stupid investors to cash them out, though at any time the scam will come crashing down. The problem is that these later investors seem to be quite irrational. They either cannot calculate a net present value, or are willing to assume that another fool greater than themselves will come in after them (as in classic pyramid or Ponzi schemes).

There is a large literature on these models, which attempt to generate the famous bubbles we observe in history—the tulip bubble, the South Sea bubble, the Internet bubble—but fundamentally contain someone making a dumb investment at the near-end of the cycle.[14] Modeling bubbles is a highly difficult problem, because invariably one sets up a specific information structure so that agents have bounded rationality. If they had rational expectations and infinite horizons, then the minute an asset went above its fundamental value, such agents would short the asset. When agents are merely selfish, as opposed to mainly envious, one has to put large blinders on them to generate bubbles.

In the recent subprime boom, many investment banks were buying mortgages, in part because they learned these activities generated large profits for others. If you work for UBS, and tell your boss you have a great way to make money, and that JPMorgan, Citigroup, and Bear Stearns are doing it, you are halfway there. As Keynes noted, "Worldly wisdom teaches that it is better for reputation to fail conventionally than to succeed unconventionally."

In a world of relative risk, the impetus can be much more straightforward and intuitive. If an asset is becoming popular, it may reach a stage where it creates a feedback loop, as greater popularity makes it desirable for investors who consider deviations from the consensus to be risky. Thus, popularity implies lower risk by itself, and people will demand more of it, which increases its popularity, starting even more people adding it to their portfolio as they try to emulate the benchmarks. Think of the case of Internet in the late 1990s, when as absurd as the Internet stock's valuation was, many investors were simply afraid of missing the boat, and got in just before the bubble burst. The later stages of the bubble were filled with investors who were investing merely to avoid missing out, because their relative performance was lagging even as the market in general was doing well on an absolute basis. The mechanism, though irrational for an investor with a classic utility function, with a relative utility function, it is rational.

CAPITAL FINDING ALPHA STRATEGIES

If your job is to find strategies with alpha, the first thing you need to know are the basic properties of assets you are potentially investing in. Most investment pitches can be eliminated because they are hardly feasible given base rate information on the asset in question. For example, you should know what the average returns are among the assets in question, their average annualized volatilities, and the cyclicality of a product. The equity risk premium puzzle is that if the return on equities is 5 percent above the risk-free rate, this implies a return that is too high relative to its volatility of around 17 percent on average, and thus a major theoretical puzzle, and empirical outlier (I think it's actually a lot of measurement error, but that is a different issue). Therefore, a Sharpe ratio of 0.35 is *very good*. The average Sharpe ratio in alternative investments in their glory years, like convertible bond arbitrage, generated Sharpes above 1 but below 2. Thus, the odds any investment strategy has a prospective Sharpe above 2 are minute.

Just knowing this fact is very useful. I have met several hedge fund personnel, who seemingly have important jobs and large responsibilities, who want only strategies with Sharpe ratios above 2, or even above 3. This is like demanding your equity portfolio manager outperform the S&P500 by 10 percent a year. The only strategies they seed are those with backtests or testimonials that appear to have such success. Now, backtests are easy to game. If you have the data, you should know how to get the right answer, and rationalizing a successful backtest is usually rather easy. But any strategy that generates such a Sharpe ratio is invariably overfit, meaning it used accidental correlations that are not stable merely because one has to do this to generate such returns. Accepting strategies based on this standard are doomed to fail because overfit or fraudulent strategies do not work well out of sample.

Consider bonds, where there is a lot of foolish investing because the constraints are well documented, but it remains a perennial area of hope unconnected to reality. If one proposes that they have 4 percent return alpha through knowledge of credit risk within high yield corporate bonds, I am highly dubious. How can their edge be 4 percent annually, if the default rate among B-rated bonds is only 6 percent annually, implying that the expected loss rate among B-rated bonds is only 3 percent annually? If you bought only bonds that never defaulted, over the cycle you would have a 3 percent annual edge. Furthermore, transaction costs would be at least 1 percent. While a high yield edge of 2 percent can be levered, this just increases the return and standard deviation, not changing the Sharpe.

Thus, knowing some basic facts about the asset class's properties generates a filter one can apply to potential strategies. Yet this was a crude filter, assuming that an investor can only be perfect, so the constraint is pretty generous. What about something more realistic? This is where the subtlety of having a deeper knowledge of the field really helps, because the more you know, the more you can dismiss bad ideas, and most new ideas are bad ideas.

I worked on bond models at Moody's and therefore developed a sense as to the power of a Moody's rating, in terms of predicting default, and also the power of a quantitative model. As mentioned, statistically, your average model that includes some measure of market leverage (market cap to debt) and equity volatility, will outperform a standard agency rating (for example, Aaa, B) when applied to nonfinancial companies. My current default model is a function of several variables, mainly a Merton distance-to-default measure, a measure of profitability, and a measure of leverage (available at defprob.com). It was fit to the data being presented here because prospectively, I want to use all the information I have. Now, comparing apples to apples and focusing on only bonds with agency ratings between B− and BBB+, we have data from 1997 through 2005, 1,892 companies and about

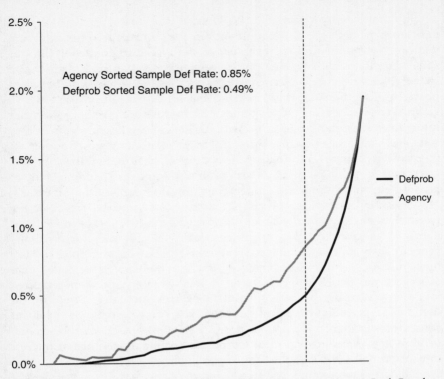

FIGURE 13.4 Power of In-Sample Model versus Agency Ratings on Junk Bonds

330 defaults. Looking at Figure 13.4, one can see that my model generates a lower default rate in the remaining pool of high yield bonds, when using the risk metric to exclude companies, based on an ordinal ranked, reflecting the greater power of my model, compared to the agency rating. In Figure 13.4, each point on the line is the default rate of the sample, annualized, if one excludes various proportions of the sample based on the default model in question. For example, the little straight dotted lines show that if you exclude the worst 20 percent of bonds rated between BBB and B, using both models, the average annual default rate over the next two years, using my Defprob metric generates a 0.49 percent default rate, whereas S&P ratings generates a higher 0.85 percent default rate.

The default rate of the included group starts at zero percent, because initially, only the very best from both models are included, and these rarely default. But then the default rate for both models rise to 1.93 percent, because when we include the entire sample, for both models, it must be identical.

Along the way, the difference in the default rate between the two default indicators maxes out at around 0.36 percent. Thus, there is about a 0.36 percent edge in my model, which was fit in this sample, and so should be somewhat of an upper bound.[15] This is a much smaller bound to apply to a strategy, because it implies that a really smart investor in corporate high yield bonds has at best a slight 0.36 percent edge in default rates over the cycle. As recovery rates average 50 percent, this implies a 0.18 percent annual loss rate. I think my default model is very good, but like credit scoring, mainly in being easy, cheap, transparent, scalable, and as good as it gets, not because it generates preternatural default forecast ability.

I have received calls many times from people starting funds, hoping to generate a good Sharpe ratio, going long and short debt within high yield. Now, if an in-sample fit to a model generates a 0.18 percent loss difference relative to a realistic benchmark (the rating agencies), annualized, this is hardly a pillar of a investment strategy, as it is too slim an edge to really generate the kind of returns hedge fund investors are looking for. How one turns this into a 0.5+ Sharpe strategy, I would be interested in seeing, but at least at the outset I could say to the pitchman, what is your perceived long-only return advantage in long-only high-yield investing? Note that this useful information is very parochial. It involves having access to difficult-to-construct default information, and would probably never make a textbook because it is not a general idea: Corporate default models are of interest to a very small set of people. This again highlights that in practice, if you are evaluating or creating alpha, your valuable edge will be something not found in, or derived from, some fundamental financial principle, but rather, a specific knowledge in a very narrow area.

Many of the high yield arbitrage strategies I have seen are not well thought-out plans, and the players anticipated this (it was sincere delusion). In all the cases, I discovered that people pitching such performance were closet long-only strategists. That is, they would say they do capital structure arbitrage, seemingly buying senior subordinated medium-term notes, hedging with unsubordinated floating rate callable bonds in a similar sector. But in practice they merely went long bonds their buddies were selling; hedging a little, but only a little. In good times (90 percent of the time) it works great; over the cycle, it is a marginal strategy, meant for a long-only vehicle, not a hedge fund.

Another way to see the futility of using debt to create equity-like returns is to consider the average returns to AAA bonds is about 1 percent below BBB bonds. This is the credit spread puzzle most academics consider. The other puzzle, that the average return to a BBB bond portfolio has about the same return as for B bond portfolio over the cycle, before transaction costs, is usually unremarked. The return over Treasuries for BBB- to B-rated bonds

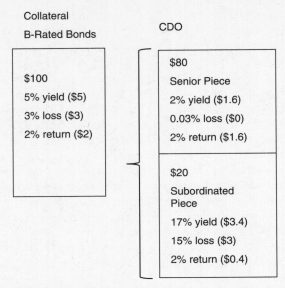

FIGURE 13.5 Slicing B-Rated Collateral Into AAA and Subordinated Bonds

is about 2 percent annualized. Now, say you have $100 worth of B-rated bonds. You can turn them into AAA-rated bonds plus equity in various proportions given the magic of a collateralized default obligation (CDO). The much-maligned rating agencies make mistakes, but they are not stupid. They demand that the average loss rate, over a long period (about 10 years) is the same for the same rating, regardless of whether it is a tranche of the CDO, or part of the pool of securities that makes up the CDO.

The mathematics of the rating agencies demands that the expected loss for the senior, AAA-rated tranche in the CDO, have a 0.03 percent expected annual loss rate, basically zero. This is the first constraint in the exercise: How much subordination is feasible such that the senior piece has a 3-in-10,000 chance of defaulting? As bonds have only downside, this is very important, and it sets the stage for the next set of assumptions. What kind of yields, losses, and implied returns does this generate for the subordinated piece? Looking at Figure 13.5, we can see how the returns and losses must be transferred. If you have $100 worth of collateral in the underlying pool, you can get a decent estimate of the stated yield, the expected losses, and expected return for the B-rated bond, though yields vary considerably over the cycle. Assume the risk-free rate is zero to highlight the math needed to evaluate this structure. We know that the losses will annualize out at

3 percent per year for a B-rated bond portfolio, so we should subtract that from the stated yield to get the return expected. Thus, we have dollar amounts that mathematically must be allocated to the various tranches in the collateralized debt obligation that sits on top of it. Note that the AAA return for asset-backed securities such as CDOs is considerably higher than for corporate AAA bonds, and so with this we can assume that the total return, on average, is independent of the default risk (again, no risk-return relation on average; see Chapter 4).

Now, the senior piece is usually rated AAA, which has a zero expected loss rate (they can and do make mistakes, but this is the expectation). So, all the losses have to be put into the subordinated tranche. We see that given a 20 percent subordinated piece, the loss rate would be 15 percent in this case! Thus, to generate a 2 percent return for these assets, it would need a 17 percent stated yield on the subordinated piece. As defaults are highly concentrated in stressful periods such as 1970, 1990, and 2001, this stress is exacerbated on high yield portfolios because the spreads on non-defaulted bonds increase too, making the downturns much worse than the increase in default. Therefore, looking at returns on high yield bonds, one must take pains to differentiate the mean from the mode, which is one of the most common, and most costly mistake investors make. Only a fool would look at a 17 percent stated yield in debt, and think they would generate a 17 percent return, given data on the returns to high yield and distressed debt over the past 30 years.

Alas, the nature of large organizations involves a lot of fools. American Express invested in subordinated CDO tranches, backed by high yield debt (then yielding about 3 to 4 percent above Treasuries) that had yields of 15 percent in the late 1990s, and these returns were expected by the company, prospectively. In other words, they made a huge bet based on the premise that a 15 percent return in high yield was feasible alpha. They later had to write down losses of more than $1 billion, as Chief Executive Officer Kenneth Chenault noted that "it is now apparent that our analysis of the portfolio did not fully comprehend the risk underlying these structures during a period of persistently high default rates."[16] As average market return for B- and BBB-rated securities is similar, the market offers no method to make water into wine here. The 15 percent expected return was a clear indication that they confused a stated yield with a return; thinking they were picking either the part of the business cycle, or subset of B-rated bonds, impervious to losses, both highly dubious claims. The failure in risk estimation was not in the discount rate, merely the default rate.

In the current subprime crisis, it appears that many investment banks had large portfolios of asset-backed securities of various kinds on their books, basically involved in attempts at fixed-income arbitrage. There are small niches within the ABS universe that offer, I think, dominating returns (for example, mezzanine tranches on unrated commercial debt, because the adjustment factor for not having an agency rating actually penalizes them for having the more powerful, if nontraditional rating model applied to them!). But most of this universe should be held in long-only accounts at mutual fund complexes and pension funds. People who try to get rich on debt don't realize that with the slim margins in this class, alpha can generate only a certain level of outperformance, and is insufficient for being attractive within a public corporation like a bank, or a hedge fund that promises 2 and 20 fees.

That almost all of the major financial institutions were exposed to mortgages that appear to be backed by highly imprudent lending standards, highlights two effects going on that are discussed in this book. First, by benchmarking against others, these investments appeared to be prudent risk-averse portfolio tactics, to keep up with the consensus to which they were compared. Second, the nature of alpha is such that many investors make assumptions that are validated by the behavior of others. Few people actually work through the math, and check the business model on their own, and instead defer to a track record or a comparable strategy's historical performance. This is because those in charge of the business lines tend to be leaders, meaning, they are not the smartest people, but rather, the best at making people feel appreciated, and even if they were highly detail-oriented in their youth, they have not worked through a complex problem on their own in perhaps decades. They have, for their leadership position, an essential skill, but it leads to problems like the bubbles we observe.

The financial crisis of 2008 involved a situation where many large financial institutions were unable to demonstrate to investors that they were solvent. There were no financial institutions that tried to calm investor fears by giving a complete and thorough overview of all the mortgage exposures that were of concern by investors. It appears that they were all unable to value these securities from the bottom up. That is, mortgages have various characteristics like loan-to-value, FICO score, original balances, current balances. Securities built on these mortgage pools have characteristics like overcollateralization, and one needs to add these up. Now, if you own more than a billion dollars worth of these securities, it seems reasonable to have a group that can independently value these securities. That is, based on the performance of the underlying mortgages, what the value of your claims on those pools should be. This is complicated, but there should be people working full-time on this within the institution, and you can break the problem down in such a way that your average Wall Street analyst can gain comfort your estimates are correct to within, say, 10 percent. Instead, it seems no one did this, all comforted by the fact that everyone else was doing the same thing, and in the panic many outside investors assumed large portions of bank portfolios were worth near zero. One would think that if it were at all possible to generate information on a bank's exposures, outsiders could have been comforted. Yet it seems the leaders of these institutions did not have the ability to generate such basic information. A smarter approach would be to work out the math, and apply it, using standard stress tests, such as what happens when collateral prices go down as much as they went up over the past two years, hardly an unreasonable assumption (after all, anything that can go up X percent can go down X percent too).

Consider, in contrast, having been presented with the opportunity to invest in convertible arbitrage in the 1990s. One could actually do the math, looking at the implied credit spreads and volatility in the convertible bonds, comparing it to their long-term options and straight debt, and see that there is extra juice there. The only way to explain the prices of convertible bonds was to assume considerably more spread on the bond, or conversely considerably undervalued options. When hedged correctly against equity movements and interest rates, one could isolate this alpha, and reap the abnormal return with a modest volatility. The difference between the convertible bond arbitrage portfolio generating a 15 percent return and the CDO tranche generating 15 percent, is that one works, given a straightforward application of reasonable assumptions (in the case of convertibles, implied volatilities on long-term options, and spreads on their straight debt). This takes a very thorough knowledge of the assets class, because as Ed Thorpe discovered, his expertise in option pricing allowed him to be comfortable with valuing convertible bonds to a degree your average investor could not be.

Someone with a strategy will not be totally forthcoming, nor should you expect them to be. The only person who is going to give you alpha is someone who has not succeeded in convincing others he has alpha. The onus always comes back to you, however, and Bernie Madoff's case highlights that those not willing to apply due diligence are ripe for fraud. When investing in alpha, remember that *your* alpha should be complimentary to what you are investing in. Oil does not have alpha. It has alpha only if oil futures, say, are a tactic, within an overall strategy of finding patterns, or evaluating people who find patterns, and this should be demonstrable by disciplined self-evaluation. If you are merely taking someone's word for it, based on the person's current wealth and status, you are a passive investor, and should expect people to take advantage of your ignorance.

Ex-professional athletes often lose their nest eggs because the combination of wealth, high testosterone, and modest intelligence makes them sheep to be shorn. Higher levels of testosterone are associated with higher risk taking, but this does not lead them to higher average returns as implied by the CAPM, but rather, merely implies some wily con artist gets them to invest in either Ponzi schemes, trades where the mode is presented as the mean (the mode is positive, the mean zero), or simply a low-probability investment with a large payout that is mainly a way for the promoter to try to get rich quick using other people's money, something that blows up. Generating good returns is not merely a function of luck and risk tolerance, rather luck, effort and intelligence. If you deviate from the consensus in your portfolio and take risk, you need to understand a lot about the specific assets or strategies you are considering, because you will otherwise adversely select strategies based on your ignorance. In investing, there are usually some asset classes with alpha, but these do not have bright seals of approval, and they are hidden, in plain sight, among many other opportunities that look similar but are merely gambles in a period of fortunate returns.

The only thing harder than finding strategies with alpha, alas, is finding capital when you have alpha. A really original good idea is rarely stolen, but rather has to be crammed down people's throats. Most proposed ideas about alpha are like most books, songs, and movies: they stink. Thus, the skepticism you face is merely an accurately calibrated Bayesian predisposition, and you have to overcome this. To the degree the idea is straightforward, the more one says, the less attractive it appears, because simple strategies are not very convincing. Further, they can listen to your pitch, say, "No thanks," and then develop the idea internally: Why buy the cow when you can get the milk for free? An alpha discoverer, looking for an investor, faces both skepticism and duplicity.

Given all the pitfalls, it highlights the importance of having trust, which means having good contacts, and a reputation for integrity. Building these attributes is just as important as any analytical work, because ideas do not succeed on their own.

SEARCH FOR ALPHA

Alpha is about finding a comparative advantage. Something you do, relatively, better than other people, to the best that you can. One must define alpha broadly, because most of us do not have daily profit-and-loss statements like portfolio managers do. For example, some can only recognize alpha, not create it; but then, at another level, that too is alpha. A person who selects portfolio managers, or edits a journal, or publishes books, has a useful and singular skill as an evaluator of alpha. It is important to know alpha comes in many forms, because most of us do not end up in classic creative roles such as being an artist, or running your own portfolio, but creativity is essential for almost any job, which is why one cannot automate so many jobs that, to outsiders, seem insanely dull.

This is important because self-awareness is very important in making choices that maximize your potential. As most people will not discover Sharpe 1-plus strategies, they should focus on the little edge they do have. In general, you should approach risk taking mainly in nonfinancial avenues, in your career, in strategy, not in buying risky assets, per se. The best advice in this domain was probably noted by Casey Kasem in his weekly Top 40 countdown when I was a teenager: "Keep your feet on the ground, but keep reaching for the stars."

It's essential to have dreams, but not delusions. Dreams make us happy, and motivate us to excel. Do not forfeit your dreams merely because when you act on them, you are generally wrong; just be realistic. This means stick to things you are good at, things you like doing, because those are the things where making that extra effort is costless because it is something you like doing. This is the risk taking that leads to greater returns.

On average, risk taking loses money after transaction costs when looked at in isolation, for example, actively managed mutual funds underperform the S&P500. One could say the same thing for people who spend time learning to write poetry: most waste everyone's time, mostly theirs. But the option value in risk taking is outside the act alone, so look at risk taking as a meta strategy. How do you learn you are good at post-production processing of TV shows? By becoming a cameraman while trying to progress into a job as a writer. You try a bunch of things to find that career where you are worth the most. The return of your investment is never the direct payoff of any one thing, but from the self-knowledge and connections gained by getting one's hands dirty. Much of success is dreaming about finding gold, and then discovering you can get rich selling shovels to gold miners. There are many examples of businesses founded on unique business selling points that, with hindsight, were wrong. This is the one thing ignorant but ambitious young people have that their more knowledgeable and older colleagues are envious of. Young people have the time and energy to discover that older people do not, but this assumes one actually invests this time and energy doing things, and does not just talk about them. In searching for alpha, you often have dreams that are often ill-founded, but they can actually be beneficial, because they offset the general underappreciation of the option value of trying things and then learning an incidental skill that introduces you to new opportunities.

You have niches in the world, most where you make $100K a year, a few where you make $150K a year, the latter being the ones where you have alpha. The present value of finding that niche, discounted at 5 percent per year, is about $1 million, so if you spend a lot of money and time trying things that do not work out, it still makes sense. You should take some risk in this dimension, rather than stick with the first opportunity offered to you, if only because it is unlikely this would have your optimal alpha. As you get older the length of your future career shortens, and your opportunity cost increases because your salary presumably increases, so one should take less risk as one gets older.

If you have a job where you perceive no alpha for yourself, now or in the future, well, hopefully you have avocations or family experiences to compensate. Such a job is the classic toil that merely pays the bills. Most people, at least initially in their careers, aspire to much more. Psychologist Martin Seligman writes that the search for meaning is a person's greatest driver, and by this he means, knowing your signature strengths, using them in service of something larger than you, something good. Hitting a tennis ball or playing the piano, is extremely satisfying if you are good, as the process just flows and gives you continual reassurance that you are good. Such a feeling is possible for many when they make the right career choice, though clearly the feedback loop is slower. Signature strengths are a comparative advantage, where you have the most alpha. Applying these in a market economy means you are involved in a web of transactions larger than yourself. Assuming your efforts are part of a system you find morally good (as opposed to, say, developing better ways to distribute spam e-mails), maximizing your alpha should provide you with not merely a way to maximize your income, but give you the greatest satisfaction, and the most meaning, in your life.

CHAPTER 14

Conclusion

Science is a great many things, ... but in the end they all return to this: science is the acceptance of what works and the rejection of what does not. That needs more courage than we might think.

Jacob Bronkowski

There have been many cases where success seems just around the corner, but *almost* is just as close in science as in a mathematical proof. Any field is populated by thousands of really smart individuals who work very hard, and would love to solve an outstanding puzzle. The easiest way to get published, get a job, is to empirically validate a popular theory—everyone in the field welcomes it. Thus, any 40-year-old unsolved puzzle is not the result of insufficient time like how long it took to find the first million digits of Pi; it is the result of an insoluble problem. Think about early thoughts that we were close to finding a cure for war, cancer, or poverty.

In 1942, Paul A. Samuelson laid down the gauntlet and showed economists the way it was going to be in his seminal *Foundations of Economic Analysis*. Unlike psychology or sociology, economists would use a common mathematical structure underlying multiple branches of economics from two basic principles: optimizing behavior of agents and stability of equilibrium as to economic systems. The emphasis on stability was quickly forgotten, but the optimizing and equilibrium is exactly what the founders of Modern Portfolio Theory were doing, following Samuelson's playbook precisely in terms of how to do good economic science. The problem is, their utility functions were wrong in a very fundamental way, emphasizing absolute wealth over relative wealth, or, more prosaically, ignoring that all professionals benchmark their returns, but by the time this became apparent it was too late for economics or finance to merely adjust theory to the data because there was too much path dependence. Thus, we have risk aversion, risk neutrality, and risk loving, all highly mathematically elaborate as having all sorts of consistent insights, but when used

selectively, depending on the data presented, all the theory on which it is
built is rather pointless. The theory is a framework, and frameworks are
lousy theories. This is why economists are not becoming like dentists fixing
cavities as Keynes envisaged, but rather, like someone studying postmodern literary theory, explaining everything, predicting nothing. There are
very few issues in economics that have been accepted as fact merely by
theory, as opposed to their obvious empirical reality, suggesting that the
wonderful, powerful, maximization principles expounded in Samuelson's
Foundations invariably are merely rationalizations. The original exposi-
tions of risk are now seen as incredibly naïve, because volatility of stock
wealth is clearly not helpful in explaining risk premiums. The resulting extension is useful within academic finance, and helpful at keeping those who
aren't economists out of the conversation, but hardly useful at what theory
should do.

Again and again, the bright thought has occurred,

*If we can only define our terms, if we can only find the basic unit, if
we can spot the right "indicators," we can then measure and reason
flawlessly, we shall have created one more science.*
                                                                                      Jacques Barzun

It is tempting to think that the essence of risk is an objective number
that, combined with our risk aversion preferences, tells us what to do. That
these are both so mathematical and precise gives us the illusion of science
and progress, like finding the next element on the periodic table. Yet the
malleability of both risk factors and preferences means that the conventional framework is something ignored at no cost. It is customary to note
that risk is extremely difficult to quantify in practice, but rarely is it acknowledged to be a highly misleading way to approach a successful career
in finance. It is clearly self-serving for economists to presume that their
comparative advantage at looking at investments—portfolio mathematics,
covariance factors—is the essence of finance, yet one must remember that
most investors, even Warren Buffett, do not use equations to make investment decisions and use simple unvarying discount rates. The standard theory
has some useful insights and tools for finding alpha, but it is neither sufficient nor necessary, which is why most successful finance professionals do
not spend much time calculating covariances.

No group of full-time hairsplitters appreciates being told they are splitting hairs. They will roll their eyes, say, "You just don't get it," and take
comfort in continued conversation among themselves. But the facts don't

change, so if you care about the future of your ideas it's good to have them on your side. No one wants to be like a Marxist professor, retiring in 1989 after decades extolling the superiority of East Germany, finding the data now too overwhelming to support his primary intellectual argument. Intellectually, that has to be the most devastating realization possible, which is why people like Noam Chomsky simply reinterpret their earlier position so that they were right all along. Science is done by actual people, after all.

The explosion of complexity in asset pricing in the face of more data is symptomatic of a bad theory. More and better data generally increase confidence in good theories as opposed to making them incredibly more convoluted, and refinements to good theories are merely made to capture second and third order discrepancies, such as in physics when things approach the speed of light. The Arbitrage Pricing Theory and the Stochastic Discount Factor approaches are not extending a theory to fit selective anomalies in the data; they are trying to generate a model that looks good from 30,000 feet. Currently, only someone on the moon thinks that the standard theories work well as an approximation, mainly because the general idea that risk, properly defined, is unpleasant, and so should require compensation, just seems to make sense.

People do not approach finance assuming assets have merely some objective mean and covariance numbers that ignores their search for alpha. To the extent assets are consistent with alpha, traditional risk metrics are generally negatively correlated with expected returns, as investors try to find their comparative advantage in the quickest and most productive way, by taking a big swing. Assets and ideas have alpha, but it takes negotiating skills to capture them, and highly parochial knowledge of a product space to separate the illusory alpha from that which is feasible.

If there were only one thing wrong with our current theory, it would probably have been fixed long ago, yet when there are multiple errors, any one solution is incomplete, and therefore just as wrong, so the existing paradigm maintains its position. Remember, the heliocentric alternative to the geocentric picture of the solar system only became better in an empirical sense when you combined heliocentrism with elliptical orbits and the conservation of angular momentum; just moving the sun to the center of the universe, but leaving the other laws the same, necessitated about the same number of epicycles. The transition needed three things to be an empirical improvement, which is why a long time between Ptolemy and Kepler was needed.

As the nature of argument in the academy is to present articles that address one thing at a time—one asset class, one general adjustment to a utility function—the problems with the existing financial theory have been stuck in a local maximum through a local hill-climbing algorithm that takes too many small steps.

The evidence for the absence of a risk-return relation on average comes from looking at the scope of evidence, and seeing four basic facts:

1. For most assets, the rate of return is unrelated to its volatility, or correlation with various prominent time series.
2. Really safe assets such as short-term T-bills have lower than average return.
3. Really volatile assets such as out-of-the-money options, long shots at racetracks, or high beta stocks, have lower-than-average returns.
4. People trade too much and diversify too little.

The explanation of these disparate observations is not one uber-theory (a framework), but rather, the following somewhat disparate set of three ideas:

1. People are more envious than greedy.
2. People take some risks in all aspects of their life to find their alpha, based on a lot of unfounded hope.
3. People save some money in supersafe assets so that wealth cannot go to zero in financial panics when correlations and volatilities seem to go to extremes.

Now, a framework that fits these three ideas into one general utility function, is not helpful, but the standards of argumentation in academics rather demands that an innovation involving three steps be mushed into one, and a new empirical finding be presented one at a time. Thus, you often see papers like "A Unified Theory of Ten Financial Puzzles,"(answer: tail risk) as opposed to a paper that argued "Three new assumptions that explain four financial puzzles."[1] Isn't the former obviously better? Simplicity and elegance are good things, but we must remember Einstein's dictum to make things as simple as possible, not more so. This simplicity bias necessarily prevents one from seeing the problem, or a solution, because the empirical problem is created by patterns in vastly different areas that have different signs (volatility bad in T-bills, irrelevant in T-bonds, good in stocks); and the theory as to why people take risks based on hope, is quite different from why they benchmark with their peers and not zero or last year. As someone used to kludgy but useful models in default forecasting, I think an observation, and an explanation with a handful of parts is neither overfit nor in need of simplification.

The importance of a relative utility function leads to benchmarking against the consensus in investments, and leads to a symmetry in risk taking—too much or too little relative to the consensus—that leads to a zero risk-return trade-off. We are not so much greedy as power hungry, and power is about our relative wealth in our tribe. The first-order effect of any gain or loss I experience affects my absolute and relative position similarly, so standard implications are maintained: I dislike random volatility, risks from accidents, I like wealth, and so on. Yet in some areas, such as investments or policy preferences, the relativity of the decision is important in explaining behavior. People will never totally embrace selfish individualism because we have an instinct for egalitarianism in that we hate to be dominated, and the domination of one invites the scorn of many that one needs if one works in a large organization. Yet envy, like greed, has a societal silver lining, because if you are indifferent to the envy of others, you are indifferent to a lot of suffering that without context is mere whining.

The grand scope of the risk-return failure in all of the risk proxies, in spite of a massive search for 50 years, suggests a large amount of delusional hope among academics not unlike that of those silly investors in out-of-the-money options. The higher returns of minimum variance portfolios, portfolios with lower volatility and covariance with everything, can only be riskier in the Alice-in-Wonderland world where low volatility, lower tail risk, and low correlation with both the aggregate market and the business cycle, is risky.

The implications of the absolute risk aversion assumption embodied in the CAPM and its extensions are logical, powerful, and slightly surprising, things one wants in a theory, but it also empirically vacuous. The anomalies to the high risk–high return assumption are not exceptions to a general tendency. There is no general tendency within a variety of investments: equities, options, bonds, mutual funds, commodities, movies, lottery tickets, or horse races, among others. This irrelevance of risk to return is implied by a status-conscious investor benchmarking himself against others, and holds in both a utility and arbitrage argument. The standard assumption that relevant volatility is absolute, not relative, may be a good normative theory—that is, what you should do—but a preference for status generates a more accurate positive theory, and its assumption—caring only about relative status—is at least as plausible as assuming people care only about absolute wealth. In light of the severe underdiversification of most portfolios, the higher expected returns that drive them, and the common method of allocating assets to standard categories, this seems to be a more realistic description of the investing process in practice than the CAPM assumption that people invest on the basis of a target beta between their household wealth and the market.

In seeking alpha, we are looking for good ideas that play off our individual talents, so that when we succeed, it implies an ability for us to capture rents via our contacts or reputation. The really important part of any edge is our unique insight into an expected value, combined with efficient ability to implement it. Understanding risk, in terms of estimating the over-the-cycle losses of the venture, is essential. Understanding risk in terms of a particular discount rate is irrelevant.

Notes

CHAPTER 1   Risk Uncorrelated with Returns

1. Eric N. Berg, "Market Place; A Study Shakes Confidence in the Volatile-Stock Theory," *New York Times,* February 18, 1992.
2. Eugene Fama and Kenneth French, "The Cross-Section of Expected Stock Returns, *Journal of Finance* 47 (2) (1992): 427–465.
3. Robert L. Heilbroner, *The Worldly Philosophers: The Lives, Times, and Ideas of the Great Economic Thinkers* (New York: Simon & Schuster, 1999).
4. Barry Nalebuff and Ian Ayres, *Why Not?: How to Use Everyday Ingenuity to Solve Problems Big and Small* (Boston: Harvard Business School Press, 2003); Steven Levitt and Stephen J. Dubner, *Freakonomics: A Rogue Economist Explores the Hidden Side of Everything* (New York: HarperCollins, 2006).
5. Peter L. Bernstein, *Capital Ideas Evolving,* 2nd ed. (Hoboken, NJ: John Wiley & Sons, 2007).
6. Marvin Minsky, *The Emotion Machine: Commonsense Thinking, Artificial Intelligence, and the Future of the Human Mind* (New York: Simon & Schuster, 2007).

CHAPTER 2   The Creation of the Standard Risk-Return Model

1. Peter L. Bernstein, *Capital Ideas Evolving,* 2nd ed. (Hoboken, NJ: John Wiley & Sons, 2007).
2. Peter L. Bernstein, *Against the Gods: The Remarkable Story of Risk* (New York: John Wiley & Sons, 1998), 1.
3. David Silverman, "The Case of Stock Splits: When One Plus One Equals More Than Two," *Smart Money,* August 2, 2005.
4. The Miller-Modigliani Theorem states that the value of a firm is independent of the way it is financed, that is, the debt-equity proportion does not affect the sum value of the debt plus equity.
5. Frank H. Knight, *Risk, Uncertainty and Profit* (Boston: Houghton Mifflin, 1921), 213.
6. Knight, 224.

7. Milton Friedman and Leonard J. Savage, "The Utility Analysis of Choices Involving Risk," *The Journal of Political Economy* 56 (4) (1948): 279.
8. Ecclesiastes 11:2; William Shakespeare, in *The Merchant of Venice,* Act I, Scene I.
9. Harry M. Markowitz. Nobel Prize Speech (1990).
10. James Tobin, "Liquidity Preference as Behavior Towards Risk." *Review of Economic Studies* 25 (2) (1958): 65–86.
11. Jack Treynor, "Toward a Theory of Market Value of Risky Assets." Unpublished Manuscript (1962); William Sharpe, "Capital Asset Prices: A Theory of Market Equilibrium under Conditions of Risk," *Journal of Finance* 19 (3) (1964): 425–442; John Lintner, "The Valuation of Risk Assets and the Selection of Risky Investments in Stock Portfolios and Capital Budgets," *Review of Economics and Statistics* 47 (1) (1965): 13–37; Jan Mossin, "Equilibrium in a Capital Asset Market," *Econometrica* 34 (4) (1966): 768–783.
12. Stephen A. Ross, "The Arbitrage Pricing Theory of Capital Asset Pricing," *Journal of Economic Theory* 13 (3) (1976): 341–360.
13. Eugene Fama, "Efficient Capital Markets," *Journal of Finance* 46 (1991): 1575–1617.
14. Robert C. Merton, "Optimum Consumption and Portfolio Rules in a Continuous-Time Model," *Journal of Economic Theory* 3 (4) (1971): 373–413; Robert Lucas, "Asset Prices in an Exchange Economy," *Econometrica* 46 (6) (1978): 1429–1445; John C. Cox, Jonathan E. Ingersoll, and Stephen A. Ross, "An Intertemporal General Equilibrium Model of Asset Prices," *Econometrica* 53 (2) (1985): 363–384.
15. Philip R.P. Coelho and James E. McClure, "The Market for Lemmas: Evidence that Complex Models Rarely Operate in Our World," *Econ Journal Watch* 5 (1) (2008): 78–90.
16. Michael Harrison and David Kreps, "Martingales and Arbitrage in Multiperiod Securities Markets," *Journal of Economic Theory* 20 (1979): 381–408.
17. $E(e^x) = e^{\mu + 0.5\sigma^2}$
18. Benoit B. Mandelbrot, "The Variation of Certain Speculative Prices," *Journal of Business* 36 (4) (1963): 394.
19. Benoit B. Mandelbrot, *Fractals and Scaling in Finance: Discontinuity, Concentration, Risk: Selecta Volume E* (Berlin: Springer, 1997); Benoit B. Mandelbrot and Richard L. Hudson, *The (Mis)Behavior of Markets: A Fractal View of Risk, Ruin, and Reward* (New York: Basic Books, 2004).
20. Mark Rubinstein, *A History of the Theory of Investments: My Annotated Bibliography* (Hoboken, NJ: John Wiley & Sons, 2006).
21. Hyman P. Minsky, *John Maynard Keynes* (New York: Columbia University Press, 1975).
22. John Maynard Keynes, *The Collected Writings of John Maynard Keynes: Volume 8, A Treatise on Probability* (Cambridge: Cambridge University Press, 1990).
23. John Maynard Keynes, "The General Theory of Employment," *The Quarterly Journal of Economics* 14 (1937): 114–115.

CHAPTER 3 An Empirical Arc

1. Peter L. Bernstein, *Capital Ideas: The Improbable Origins of Modern Wall Street* (New York: Free Press, 1992), 189.
2. William F. Sharpe, "Mutual Fund Performance," *Journal of Business* 39(1) (1966): 119–138; Jack L. Treynor and Kay K. Mazuy, "Can Mutual Funds Outguess the Market?" *Harvard Business Review* 44 (4) (1966): 131–136; Michael C. Jensen, "The Performance of Mutual Funds in the Period 1945–1964," *Journal of Finance* 23 (2) (1967): 389–416.
3. George Douglas, "Risk in the Equity Markets: An Empirical Appraisal of Market Efficiency," *Yale Economic Essays* 9 (1) (1969): 3–45.
4. This unpublished work by John Lintner was noted by Douglas in his paper.
5. Merton H. Miller and Myron Scholes, "Rates of Return in Relation to Risk: A Re-examination of Some Recent Findings," *Studies in the Theory of Capital Markets* (1972): 47–78.
6. The analysis of quirky events that allow one to isolate an effect is a theme of *Freakonomics*, as when they found that given the arbitrary age cutoffs for soccer players in Europe, those born in January did better than those in December, the key being that the hypothesis could not be examined without the arbitrary age cutoff in youth soccer leagues.
7. Fischer Black, Michael C. Jensen, and Myron Scholes, "The Capital Asset Pricing Model: Some Empirical Tests," *Studies in the Theory of Capital Markets* 81 (1972): 79–121; Eugene F. Fama and James D. MacBeth, "Risk, Return, and Equilibrium: Empirical Tests," *Journal of Political Economy* 81 (3) (1973): 607.
8. Jay Shanken, "Multivariate Tests of the Zero-Beta CAPM," *Journal of Financial Economics* 14 (3) (1985): 327–348; Michael R. Gibbons, "Multivariate Tests of Financial Models—A New Approach," *Journal of Financial Economics* 10 (1) (1982): 3–27; Michael R. Gibbons, Stephen A. Ross, and Jay Shanken, "A Test of the Efficiency of a Given Portfolio," *Econometrica* 57 (5) (1989): 1121–1152.
9. Richard Roll, "A Critique of the Asset Pricing Theory's Tests: Part I: On Past and Potential Testability of the Theory," *Journal of Financial Economics* 4 (2) (1977): 129–176.
10. Robert F. Stambaugh, "On the Exclusion of Assets from Tests of the 2-Parameter Model—A Sensitivity Analysis," *Journal of Financial Economics* 10 (3) (1982): 237–268.
11. Jay Shanken, "Multivariate Proxies and Asset Pricing Relations: Living with the Roll Critique," *Journal of Financial Economics* 18 (1) (1987): 91–110.
12. Richard Roll and Stephen A. Ross, "On the Cross-Sectional Relation Between Expected Returns and Betas," *Journal of Finance* 49 (1) (1994): 101–121; Shmuel Kandel and Robert F. Stambaugh, "Portfolio Inefficiency and the Cross-Section of Expected Returns," *Journal of Finance* 50 (1995): 185–224.
13. James Maxwell said, "The true logic of this world is in the calculus of probabilities," in Richard Phillips Feynman, *The Feynman Lectures on Physics 1. Mainly Mechanics, Radiation, and Heat* (Reading, MA: Addison-Wesley, 1970), while Frank Knight noted that "practically all decisions as to conduct in real life

rest upon opinions . . . easily resolve themselves into opinions of a probability." Frank H. Knight, *Risk, Uncertainty and Profit* (Boston: Houghton Mifflin, 1921), 237.

14. Rolf W. Banz, "The Relationship Between Return and Market Value of Common Stocks," *Journal of Financial Economics* 9 (1) (1981): 3–18; Marc R. Reinganum, "Misspecification of Capital Asset Pricing: Empirical Anomalies Based on Earnings Yields and Market Values," *Journal of Financial Economics* 9 (1) (1981): 19–46.

15. "Symposium on Size Effect," *Journal of Financial Economics* 12 (1983).

16. Marshall E. Blume and Robert F. Stambaugh, "An Application to the Size Effect," *Journal of Financial Economics* 12 (1983): 387–404.

17. Tyler Shumway, "The Delisting Bias in CRSP Data," *Journal of Finance* 52 (1997): 327–340.

18. Peter J. Knez and Mark J. Ready, "On the Robustness of Size and Book-to-Market in Cross-Sectional Regressions," *Journal of Finance* 52 (1997): 1355–1382.

19. S. Basu, "Investment Performance of Common Stocks in Relation to Their Price-Earnings Ratios: A Test of the Efficient Market Hypothesis," *Journal of Finance* 32 (3) (1977): 663–682.

20. Laxmi C. Bhandari, "Debt/Equity Ratio and Expected Common Stock Returns: Empirical Evidence," *Journal of Finance* 43 (2) (1988): 507–528.

21. Dennis Stattman, "Book Values and Stock Returns," *The Chicago MBA: A Journal of Selected Papers* 4 (1980): 25–45.

22. G. William Schwert, "Size and Stock Returns, and Other Empirical Regularities," *Journal of Financial Economics*, 12 (1983): 3–12.

23. Werner F.M. De Bondt and Richard H. Thaler, "Does the Stock Market Overreact?" *Journal of Finance* 40 (3) (1985): 793–805; Werner F.M. De Bondt and Richard H. Thaler, "Further Evidence on Investor Overreaction and Stock Market Seasonality," *Journal of Finance* 42 (1987): 557–581; Fischer Black, "Estimating Expected Return," *Financial Analysts Journal* 49 (1995): 169.

24. Peter Bernstein, "Most Nobel Minds," *CFA Magazine*, November-December 2005.

25. Barr Rosenberg, "Extra-Market Components of Covariance in Security Returns," *Journal of Financial and Quantitative Analysis* 9 (2) (1974): 263–273.

26. Nai Fu Chen, Richard Roll, and Stephen A. Ross, "Economic Forces and the Stock Market," *Journal of Business* 59 (3) (1986): 383–403.

27. Christopher S. Jones, "Extracting Factors from Heteroskedastic Asset Returns," *Journal of Financial Economics* 62 (2) (2001): 293–325.

28. The value-weighted index was used by Eugene F. Fama and Kenneth French, "Common Risk Factors in the Returns on Stocks and Bonds," *Journal of Financial Economics* 33 (1) (1993): 3–56; Eugene F. Fama and Kenneth French, "Size and Book-to-Market Factors in Earnings and Returns," *Journal of Finance* 50 (1995): 131; Eugene Fama and Kenneth French, "The Cross-Section of Expected Stock Returns," *Journal of Finance* 47 (1992): 427–67, and Narasimhan Jegadeesh and Sheridan Titman, "Returns to Buying Winners and Selling Losers:

Implications for Stock Market Efficiency," *Journal of Finance* 48 (1) (1993): 65–91. The equal-weighted market proxy was used by Navin Chopra, Josef Lakonishok, and Jay Ritter, "Measuring Abnormal Performance: Do Stocks Overreact?" *Journal of Financial Economics* 31 (1992) 235–268, and Steven L. Jones, "Another Look at Time-Varying Risk and Return in a Long-Horizon Contrarian Strategy," *Journal of Financial Economics* 33 (1) (1993): 119–144. Some used both, such as S. P. Kothari, Jay Shanken, and Richard G. Sloan, "Another Look at the Cross-Section of Expected Stock Returns," *Journal of Finance* 50 (1995): 185–224.

29. Stephen A. Ross, *Is Beta Useful? The CAPM Controversy: Policy and Strategy Implications for Investment Management* (Charlottesville, VA: American Institute for Management and Research, 1993), 11–15.

30. Kent Daniel and Sheridan Titman, "Characteristics or Covariances? (Digest Summary)," *Journal of Portfolio Management* 24 (4) (1998): 24–33.

31. Eugene Fama, Kenneth French, and James Davis, "Characteristics, Covariances and Average Returns 1929–1997," *Journal of Finance* 55 (1) (2000): 389–406.

32. Tim Loughran and Todd Houge,"Do Investors Capture the Value Premium?" *Financial Management* 35 (2) (2006).

33. Josef Lakonishok, Andrei Shleifer, and Robert Vishny, "Contrarian Investment, Extrapolation, and Risk," *Journal of Finance* 49 (5) (1994): 1541–1578.

34. Vineet Agarwal and Richard Taffler, "The Distress Factor Effect in Equity Returns: Market Mispricing or Omitted Variable?" *Staff Research Seminar Series, Manchester School of Accounting and Finance* (Manchester, U.K., February 2003); John M. Griffin and Michael L. Lemmon, "Book-to-Market Equity, Distress Risk, and Stock Returns," *The Journal of Finance* 57 (5) (2002): 2317–2336; Maria Vassalou and Yuhang Xing, "Default Risk in Equity Returns," *The Journal of Finance* 59 (2) (2004): 831–868, document some evidence that distress risk as measured by a Merton model explains returns in size and value, but it does not explain either the size or value effect in their opinion.

35. Tim C. Opler and Sheridan Titman, "Financial Distress and Corporate Performance," *Journal of Finance* 49 (1994): 1015–1040.

36. Robert A. Haugen and Nardin L. Baker, "Commonality in the Determinants of Expected Stock Returns," *Journal of Financial Economics* 41 (3) (1996): 401–439.

37. Jegadeesh and Titman, 1992.

38. Mark M. Carhart, "On Persistence in Mutual Fund Performance," *Journal of Finance* 52 (1997): 57–82.

39. The SDF likes to use the generalized method of moments, whereas APT tests are more visual, looking at spreads of portfolios.

40. Nai Fu Chen, Richard Roll, and Stephen A. Ross, "Economic Forces and the Stock Market," *Journal of Business* 59 (3) (1986): 383; Gregory Connor and Robert A. Korajczyk, "A Test for the Number of Factors in an Approximate Factor Model," *Journal of Finance* 48 (1993): 1263–1291; William F. Sharpe, "Asset Allocation: Management Style and Performance Measurement," *Journal of Portfolio Management* 18 (2) (1992): 7–19.

41. Ravi Jagannathan, Zhenyu Wang, and Federal Reserve Bank of Minneapolis, *The CAPM is Alive and Well* (Federal Reserve Bank of Minneapolis, Research Dept., 1993); Ravi Jagannathan and Zhenyu Wang, "The Conditional CAPM and the Cross-Section of Expected Returns," *Journal of Finance* 51 (1) (1996): 3–53.

42. Martin Lettau and Sydney Ludvigson, "Consumption, Aggregate Wealth, and Expected Stock Returns," *The Journal of Finance* 56 (3) (2001): 815–849.

43. Kris Jacobs and Kevin Q. Wang, "Idiosyncratic Consumption Risk and the Cross-Section of Asset Returns," *The Journal of Finance* 59 (5) (2004); Ravi Jagannathan and Zhenyu Wang, "Lazy Investors, Discretionary Consumption, and the Cross-Section of Stock Returns," *The Journal of Finance* 62 (4) (2007): 1623–1661.

44. Campbell Harvey and Akhtar Siddique, "Autoregressive Conditional Skewness," *Journal of Financial and Quantitative Analysis* 34 (4) (1999): 465–488.

45. Andrew Ang, Joseph Chen, and Yuhang Xing, "Downside Risk," *Review of Financial Studies* 19 (4) (2006): 1191–1239.

46. Robert Engle and Abhishek Mistry, "Priced Risk and Asymmetric Volatility in the Cross-Section of Skewness." Working Paper (2007).

47. Rachel Campbell, Kees Koedijk, and Paul Kofman, "Increased Correlation in Bear Markets," *Financial Analysts Journal* 58 (1) (2002): 87–94 on skewness correlations.

48. Alan Kraus and Robert H. Litzenberger, "Skewness Preference and Valuation of Risk Assets," *Journal of Finance* 31 (4) (1976): 1085–1100; Thierry Post and Pim van Vliet, "Conditional Downside Risk and the CAPM," *ERIM Research Series, ERS-2004–2048-F&A*, Social Science Research Network abstract 797286 (2004).

49. Mark Rubinstein, "The Theorem of Parameter-Preference Security Valuation," *Journal of Financial and Quantitative Analysis* 8 (1) (1973): 61–69.

50. Lawrence Fisher and James H. Lorie, "Rates of Return on Investments in Common Stocks," *Journal of Business* 37 (1964): 1–21.

51. Peter Tanous, *Investment Gurus* (Upper Saddle River, NJ: Prentice-Hall/New York: New York Institute of Finance, 1997).

52. Erik Lundberg, Nobel Prize Presentation Speech (1984).

53. Paul A. Samuelson, "Interactions Between the Multiplier Analysis and the Principle of Acceleration," *Review of Economic Statistics* 21 (2) (1939): 75–78.

54. Christopher A. Sims, "Macroeconomics and Reality," *Econometrica* 48 (1) (1989): 1–48.

55. See James H. Stock and Mark W. Watson, *New Indexes of Coincident and Leading Economic Indicators* (National Bureau of Economic Research, Macroeconomic Annual, 1989), 351–393.

56. Robert Hall, American Economic Association presidential address, May 1993.

57. James H. Stock and Mark W. Watson, *Has the Business Cycle Changed and Why?* (National Bureau of Economic Research, Inc.: NBER Working Papers 9127, 2002).

58. Emanuel Derman, "What Quants Don't Learn in College," *Risk* 16 (7) (2003).

CHAPTER 4   Volatility, Risk, and Returns

1. Eric Falkenstein, "Mutual Funds, Idiosyncratic Variance, and Asset Returns," Ph.D. Dissertation, Northwestern University (1994).
2. Bruce N. Lehmann, "Residual Risk Revisited," *Journal of Econometrics* 45 (1–2) (1990): 71–97.
3. Richard Roll and Stephen A. Ross, "On the Cross-Sectional Relation Between Expected Returns and Betas," *Journal of Finance* 49 (1) (1994): 101–121.
4. George W. Douglas, "Risk in the Equity Markets: An Empirical Appraisal of Market Efficiency," *Yale Economic Essays,* 9 (1967) 3–45.
5. Eric Falkenstein, "Preferences for Stock Characteristics as Revealed by Mutual Funds," *Journal of Finance* 51 (1) (1996): 111–135.
6. Andrew Ang, Robert Hodrick, Yuhang Xing, and Xiaoyan Zhang, "The Cross-Section of Volatility and Expected Returns," *The Journal of Finance* 61 (1) (2006): 259–299; Andrew Ang, Robert Hodrick, Yuhang Xing, and Xiaoyan Zhang, "High Idiosyncratic Volatility and Low Returns: International and Future U.S. Evidence," *Journal of Financial Economics,* 91 (1) (2009): 1–23.
7. Joshua D. Coval and Tyler Shumway, "Expected Option Returns," *The Journal of Finance* 56 (3) (2001): 983–1009.
8. Sophie X. Ni, *Stock Option Returns: A Puzzle,* Social Science Research Network (January 9, 2007), http://ssrn.com/abstract=959024.
9. Tobias J. Moskowitz and Annette Vissing-Jorgensen, "The Returns to Entrepreneurial Investment: A Private Equity Premium Puzzle?" *American Economic Review* 92 (4) (2002): 745–778.
10. John Heaton and Debra Lucas, "Portfolio Choice and Asset Prices: The Importance of Entrepreneurial Risk," *The Journal of Finance* 55 (3) (2000): 1163–1198.
11. Stephen H. Penman, Scott A. Richardson, and İrem Tuna, "The Book-to-Price Effect in Stock Returns: Accounting for Leverage," *Journal of Accounting Research* 45 (2) (2007): 427–467.
12. Robert A. Haugen and Nardin L. Baker, "Commonality in the Determinants of Expected Stock Returns," *Journal of Financial Economics* 41 (3) (1996): 401–439; Stephen H. Penman, Scott A. Richardson, and İrem Tuna, "The Book-to-Price Effect in Stock Returns: Accounting for Leverage," *Journal of Accounting Research* 45 (2) (2007): 427–467; Judson A. Caskey, John S. Hughes, and Jing Liu, *Leverage, Excess Leverage and Future Stock Returns,* Social Science Research Network (May 28, 2008), http://ssrn.com/abstract=1138082.
13. William F. Sharpe, "Risk Aversion in the Stock-Market—Some Empirical Evidence," *Journal of Finance* 20 (3) (1965): 416–422; Jack L. Treynor and Kay Mazuy, "Can Mutual Funds Outguess the Market?" *Harvard Business Review* 44 (4) (1966): 131–136.
14. Michael C. Jensen, "The Performance of Mutual Funds in the Period 1945–1964," *Journal of Finance* 23 (2) (1968): 389–416.
15. Burton G. Malkiel, "Returns from Investing in Equity Mutual Funds 1971 to 1991," *Journal of Finance* 50 (2) (1995): 549–572.

16. Absence of *proof* is not *proof* of absence. In logic, A→B (A implies B) is not equivalent to ≠A→≠B, (not A implies not B). But in probability theory, absence of *evidence* is always *evidence* of absence. If E is a binary event and P(H|E) > P(H), "seeing E increases the probability of H," then P(H|≠E) < P(H), "failure to observe E decreases the probability of H." P(H) is a weighted mix of P(H|E) and P(H|≠E), and necessarily lies between the two.

17. Mark M. Carhart, "On Persistence in Mutual Fund Performance," *Journal of Finance* 52 (1997): 57–82.

18. Russell Wermers, "Mutual Fund Performance: An Empirical Decomposition into Stock-Picking Talent, Style, Transaction Costs, and Expenses," *The Journal of Finance* 55 (4) (2000): 1655–1703.

19. Fischer Black, "The Pricing of Commodity Contracts," *The Journal of Financial Economics* 3 (1976): 167–179.

20. Claude B. Erb and Campbell R. Harvey, "The Strategic and Tactical Value of Commodity Futures," *Financial Analysts Journal* 62 (2) (2006): 69–97.

21. Gary B. Gorton and K. Geert Rouwenhorst, "Facts and Fantasies About Commodity Futures," *Yale ICF Working Paper No. 04–20* (February 28, 2005).

22. Robert Hodrick, *The Empirical Evidence on the Efficiency of Forward and Futures Foreign Exchange Markets*, vol. 24, in Jacques Lesourne and Hugo Sonnenschein, eds., *Fundamentals of Pure and Applied Economics* (Newark, NJ: Harwood Academic Publishers, 1987).

23. Markus Brunnermeier, Stefan Nagel, and Lasse Pedersen, *Carry Trades and Currency Crashes* (National Bureau of Economic Research, Macroeconomics Annual 23, 2008).

24. Thomas A. Garrett and Nalinaksha Bhattacharyya, *Why People Choose Negative Expected Return Assets—An Empirical Examination of a Utility Theoretic Explanation* (Federal Reserve Bank of St. Louis, 2006).

25. Thomas A. Garrett and Russell S. Sobel, "State Lottery Revenue: The Importance of Game Characteristics," *Public Finance Review* 32 (3) (2004): 313.

26. Arthur S. De Vany, *Hollywood Economics: How Extreme Uncertainty Shapes the Film Industry* (New York: Routledge, 2004).

27. Elroy Dimson, Paul Marsh, and Mike Staunton, "The Worldwide Equity Premium: A Smaller Puzzle," American Finance Association, *New Orleans Meetings Paper* (2008).

28. Claude B. Erb, Harvey Campbell, and Tadas Viskanta, "Country Risk and Global Equity Selection," *Journal of Portfolio Management* 21 (2) (1995): 74–83.

29. Magnus Dahlquist and Ravi Bansal, "Expropriation Risk and Return in Global Equity Markets," European Finance Association, *Berlin Meetings Paper* (2002).

30. Jerome Fons, "Default Risk and Duration Analysis," Ph.D. Dissertation, University of San Diego (1985).

31. Edward I. Altman and Gaurav Bana, "Defaults and Returns on High-Yield Bonds," *Journal of Portfolio Management* (2004); Alexander Kozhemiakin, "The Risk Premium of Corporate Bonds," *Journal of Portfolio Management* (2006).

32. Edward Altman and William Stonberg, "The Market in Defaulted Bonds and Bank Loans," *Journal of Portfolio Management* (2006).

33. Burton G. Malkiel and Atanu Saha, "Hedge Funds: Risk and Return," *Financial Analysts Journal* 61 (6) (2005): 80.

34. Antii Ilmanen, "When Do Bond Markets Reward Investors for Interest Rate Risk?" *Journal of Portfolio Management* (1996), 52–55.

35. Qiang Daia and Kenneth J. Singleton, "Expectation Puzzles, Time-Varying Risk Premia and Affine Models of the Term Structure," *Journal of Financial Economics* 63 (3) (2002): 415–441.

36. Donald B. Hausch, Victor Sy Lo, and William T. Ziemba, *Efficiency of Racetrack Betting Markets* (San Diego: Academic Press, 1994).

37. William T. Ziemba and Donald B. Hausch, *Beat the Racetrack* (San Diego: Harcourt Brace Jovanovich, 1984).

38. Campbell (1987); Robert F. Whitelaw, "Time Variations and Covariations in the Expectation and Volatility of Stock Market Returns," *Journal of Finance* 49 (1994): 515–541. Some find a negative relation: Daniel B. Nelson, "Conditional Heteroskedasticity in Asset Returns: A New Approach," *Econometrica* 59 (2) (1991): 347–370.

39. Gene Amromin and Steven Sharpe, *From the Horse's Mouth: Gauging Conditional Expected Stock Returns from Investor Surveys* (Federal Reserve Board of Chicago and Federal Reserve Board working paper, 2006).

40. Benjamin Graham and Jason Zweig, *The Intelligent Investor: The Definitive Book on Value Investing* (New York: Collins Business, 2003), 84.

41. Martin L. Weitzman, *A Unified Bayesian Theory of Equity "Puzzles"* (Cambridge, MA: Harvard University Press, 2005).

42. A dataset is ergodic if a current large cross-section gives the same result as a large time series of one agent in the limit. Many ensembles, like the human populations, are not ergodic.

43. Lars P. Hansen and Thomas J. Sargent, "Acknowledging Misspecification in Macroeconomic Theory," *Review of Economic Dynamics* 4 (3) (2001): 519–535.

44. Karl B. Diether, Christopher J. Malloy, and Anna Scherbina, "Differences of Opinion and the Cross-Section of Stock Returns," *The Journal of Finance* 57 (5) (2002): 2113–2141.

45. Jay Ritter, IPO Data; http://bear.cba.ufl.edu/ritter/ipodata.htm.

46. See http://bear.cba.ufl.edu/ritter/IPOs2006-5years.pdf.

47. Richard A. Brealey, Stewart C. Myers, and Franklin Allen, *Principles of Corporate Finance* (New York: Irwin/McGraw-Hill, 2003); Burton Malkiel, *A Random Walk Down Wall Street: The Time-Tested Strategy for Successful Investing* (New York: W.W. Norton, 2003).

CHAPTER 5 Investors Do Not Mind Their Utility Functions

1. In Milton Friedman, *Essays in Positive Economics* (Chicago: University of Chicago Press, 1953).

2. Given the simultaneous independent development by John Lintner and Jay Mossin, the development of the CAPM was inevitable.

3. Sanford Grossman and Joseph Stiglitz, "On the Impossibility of Informationally Efficient Markets," *American Economic Review* 70 (1980): 393–408; Albert Kyle, "Continuous Auctions and Insider Trading," *Econometrica* 53 (1985): 1315–1335.

4. William N. Goetzmann and Alok Kumar, *Diversification Decisions of Individual Investors and Asset Prices* (Yale School of Management, Yale School of Management Working Papers, 2004).

5. Mark T. Bradshaw, "The Use of Target Prices to Justify Sell-Side Analysts' Stock Recommendations," *Accounting Horizons* 16 (2002): 27–42, finds "buy" and "strong buy" recommendations from brokerages have an average one-year expected return of 25 percent and 34 percent, respectively.

6. Maureen O'Hara, "Presidential Address: Liquidity and Price Discovery," *The Journal of Finance* 58 (4) (2003): 1335–1354.

7. Kalok Chan, Vicentiu Covrig, and Lilian Ng. "What Determines the Domestic Bias and Foreign Bias? Evidence from Mutual Fund Equity Allocations Worldwide," *Journal of Finance* 60:3 (2005).

8. Paul Samuelson, "Using Full Duality to Show that Simultaneously Additive Direct and Indirect Utilities Implies Unitary Price Elasticity of Demand," *Econometrica* (1965).

9. Matthew Rabin, "Risk Aversion and Expected-utility Theory: A Calibration Theorem," *Econometrica* 68 (2000): 1281–1292.

10. Daniel Kahneman and Amos Tversky, "Prospect Theory: An Analysis of Decision Making Under Risk," *Econometrica* 47 (2) (1979): 263–291.

11. Harry Markowitz, "The Utility of Wealth," *The Journal of Political Economy* 60 (2) (1952): 151.

12. George Stigler, "Specialism: A Dissenting Opinion," (1951) in *The Intellectual and the Market Place and Other Essays* (Cambridge, MA: Harvard University Press, 1984), 10.

13. Richard A. Easterlin, *Does Economic Growth Improve the Human Lot? Some Empirical Evidence* (Nations and Households in Economic Growth: Essays in Honor of Moses Abramovitz, 1974), 89–125.

14. Richard A. Easterlin, *Growth Triumphant: The Twenty-first Century in Historical Perspective, Economics, Cognition, and Society* (Ann Arbor, MI: University of Michigan Press, 1996).

15. European happiness, 1950–1973.

16. Japanese happiness, 1950.

17. Robert W. Fogel, *The Escape from Hunger and Premature Death, 1700–2100: Europe, America, and the Third World* (Cambridge: Cambridge University Press, 2004).

18. Ibid.

19. John Knight, Lina Song, and Ramani Gunatilaka. "Subjective Well-being and its Determinants in Rural China," *China Economic Review* (2008).

20. Robert H. Frank and Cass R. Sunstein, "Cost-Benefit Analysis and Relative Position," *University of Chicago Law Review* 68 (2) (2001): 323–374.

21. Richard A. Easterlin, "Will Raising the Incomes of All Increase the Happiness of All?" *Journal of Economic Behavior and Organization* 27 (1) (1995): 35–47;

Gregg Easterbrook, *The Progress Paradox: How Life Gets Better While People Feel Worse* (New York: Random House, 2003); Bruno S. Frey and Alois Stutzer, *Happiness and Economics* (Princeton and Oxford: Princeton University Press, 2002); Andrew E. Clark and Andrew J. Oswald, "Satisfaction and Comparison Income," *Journal of Public Economics* 61 (3) (1996): 359–381. In contrast, the following find absolute income more important: Betsey Stevenson and Justin Wolfers, *Economic Growth and Subjective Well-Being: Reassessing the Easterlin Paradox* (3rd Annual Conference on Empirical Legal Studies Papers, 2008).

CHAPTER 6 Is The Equity Risk Premium Zero?

1. Rajnish Mehra and Edward C. Prescott, "The Equity Premium: A Puzzle," *Journal of Monetary Economics* 15 (2) (1985): 145–161.
2. From the American Institute for Management and Research conference: Cornell (2.5 percent), Siegel (2.0), Campbell (1.5 percent), Williamson (2.0 percent), Arnott (0 percent), and Ibbotson (4.0 percent).
3. It is sad to note how many times good ideas are ruined by trying to make them even better. "Don't gild the lily," the Bard noted.
4. Marshall E. Blume and Robert F. Stambaugh, "An Application to the Size Effect," *Journal of Financial Economics* 12 (1983): 387–404.
5. Werner F.M. De Bondt and Richard H. Thaler, "Does the Stock Market Overreact?" *Journal of Finance* 40 (3) (1985): 793–805; Werner F.M. De Bondt and Richard H. Thaler, "Further Evidence on Investor Overreaction and Stock Market Seasonality," *Journal of Finance* (1987).
6. Jennifer Conrad and Gautam Kaul, "Long-Term Market Overreaction or Biases in Computed Returns?" *Journal of Finance* 48 (1993): 39–63.
7. 42.8 percent, 40.8 percent, 17.1 percent and –97 percent.
8. Elroy Dimson, Paul Marsh, and Mike Staunton, 2006, *The Worldwide Equity Premium: A Smaller Puzzle* (American Finance Association, *New Orleans Meetings Papers,* 2008); William Poundstone, *Fortune's Formula: The Untold Story of the Scientific Betting System that Beat the Casinos and Wall Street* (New York: Hill and Wang, 2005) discusses this issue in depth.
9. Stephen Brown, William N. Goetzmann, and Stephen A. Ross, "Survival," *Journal of Finance* 50 (1995): 853–873.
10. William N. Goetzmann and Philippe Jorion, "Global Stock Markets in the Twentieth Century," *Journal of Finance* 54 (3) (1999).
11. Thomas A. Rietz, "The Equity Risk Premium: A Solution," *Journal of Monetary Economics* 22 (1) (1988): 117–131.
12. Rajnish Mehra and Edward C. Prescott, "The Equity Risk Premium: A Solution?" *Journal of Monetary Economics* 22 (1) (1988): 133–136.
13. Robert J. Barro, "Rare Disasters and Asset Markets in the Twentieth Century," *The Quarterly Journal of Economics* 121 (3) (2006): 823–866.
14. Eugene Fama and Kenneth French, "The Equity Premium," *The Journal of Finance* 57 (2) (2002): 637–659.

15. Olivier J. Blanchard, "Movements in the Equity Premium," *Brookings Papers on Economic Activity* 2 (1993): 75–118; Ravi Jagannathan, Ellen R. McGrattan, and Anna Scherbina, "The Declining U.S. Equity Premium," *Federal Reserve Bank of Minneapolis Quarterly Review* 24 (4) (2000): 3–19; Eugene Fama and Kenneth French, "The Equity Premium," *The Journal of Finance* 57 (2) (2002): 637–659; and Massimiliano De Santis, "Movements in the Equity Premium: Evidence from a Bayesian Time-Varying VAR," (Social Science Research Network, October 2004).

16. Jeremy Siegel, *Stocks for the Long Run* (New York: McGraw-Hill, 2007).

17. Niall J. Gannon and Michael J. Blum, "After-Tax Returns on Stocks versus Bonds for the High Tax Bracket Investor," *The Journal of Wealth Management* (2006).

18. Brad Barber and Terrance Odean, "Trading is Hazardous to Your Wealth: The Common Stock Investment Performance of Individual Investors," *Journal of Finance,* 55 (2) (2000): 773–806.

19. Tim Loughran and Jay R. Ritter, "The New Issues Puzzle," *Journal of Finance* 50 (1) (1995): 23–51; Malcolm Baker and Jeffrey Wurgler, "The Equity Share in New Issues and Aggregate Stock Returns," *The Journal of Finance* 55 (5) (2000): 2219–2257; David Ikenberry, Josef Lakonishok, and Theo Vermaelen, "Market Underreaction to Open Market Share Repurchases," *Journal of Financial Economics* 39 (2–3) (1995): 181–208.

20. Ilia Dichev, "What Are Stock Investors' Actual Historical Returns? Evidence from Dollar-Weighted Returns," *American Economic Review* 97(1) (2006): 386–401.

21. Ian Domowitz and Henry Yegerman, *ITG Inc. Research Report* (August 2005a).

22. Charles M. Jones, *A Century of Stock Market Liquidity and Trading Costs* (Social Science Research Network, May 2002), http://ssrn.com/abstract=313681.

23. Brad M. Barber and Terrance Odean, "Trading Is Hazardous to Your Wealth: The Common Stock Investment Performance of Individual Investors," *The Journal of Finance* 55 (2) (2000): 773–806; Terrance Odean, "Do Investors Trade Too Much?" *American Economic Review* 89 (1999): 1279–1298.

24. Mark M. Carhart, "On Persistence in Mutual Fund Performance," *Journal of Finance*, American Finance Association, vol. 52(1): 57–82 (1997).

25. Burton G. Malkiel, *A Random Walk Down Wall Street* (New York: WW Norton and Co., 2003).

CHAPTER 7   Undiminished Praise of A Vacuous Theory

1. Eugene Fama and Kenneth French, "The Value Premium and the CAPM," *The Journal of Finance* 61(5) (2006): 2163–2185; and Stephen A. Ross, *Is Beta Useful? The CAPM Controversy: Policy and Strategy Implications for Investment Management* (Charlottesville, VA: Association for Investment Management and Research, 1993), 11–15, respectively.

2. John H. Cochrane, "New Facts in Finance," in *Economic Perspectives,* issue Q III (Chicago: Federal Reserve Bank of Chicago, 1999), 36–58.

3. Paul A. Samuelson and William D. Nordhaus, *Economics,* 15th ed. (New York: McGraw-Hill College, 1995).

4. Mark Rubinstein, "Markowitz's Portfolio Selection: A Fifty-Year Retrospective," *The Journal of Finance* 57 (3) (2002): 1041–1045.

5. Margaret Mead, *Coming of Age in Samoa* (New York: HarperPerennial Modern Classics, 2000) and Alfred C. Kinsey, Wardell B. Pomeroy, and Clyde E. Martin, *Sexual Behavior in the Human Male* (Philadelphia: W.B. Saunders, 1948), have both been found to be highly biased by the authors' preconceptions, although they are often still referenced as seminal works.

6. Ivo Welch, *The Consensus Estimate for the Equity Premium by Academic Financial Economists in December 2007,* Social Science Research Network (January 18, 2008), http://ssrn.com/abstract=1084918.

7. Stephen G. Cecchetti, *Money, Banking, and Financial Markets* (Burr Ridge, IL: Irwin Professional Publishing, 2007).

8. Macaulay quote in Theodore Dalrymple, *In Praise of Prejudice: The Necessity of Preconceived Ideas* (New York: Encounter Books 2007), 9.

9. Abraham Flexner, *Medical Education in the United States and Canada: A Report to the Carnegie Foundation for the Advancement of Teaching* (Stanford, CA: Carnegie Foundation for the Advancement of Teaching, 1910).

10. "I hope to show in this paper that the period 1979 to 1999 has also been a highly productive one. Precisely because the conditions for the existence of a stochastic discount factor are so general, they place almost no restrictions on financial data." John Y. Campbell, "Asset Pricing at the Millennium," *Journal of Finance,* 55 (2000): 1515–1567.

11. Web video at www.thirteen.org/bigideas.

12. John Y. Campbell, "Asset Pricing at the Millenium." *Journal of Finance* 55(4) (2000): 1515–68].

13. Mark Rubinstein, *A History of the Theory of Investments: My Annotated Bibliography* (Hoboken, NJ: John Wiley & Sons, 2006), 172.

CHAPTER 8 Why Relative Utility Generates Zero-Risk Premiums

1. Symmetries are the basis of physical laws about space, time, and angles, implying conservation in momentum, energy, and angular momentum, respectively. Local symmetries play an important role in physics because they form the basis for gauge theories.

2. Peter Tanous, *Investment Gurus* (Upper Saddle River, NJ: Prentice-Hall/New York: New York Institute of Finance, 1997), 102.

3. Kenneth L. Fisher, Jennifer Chou, and Lara W. Hoffmans, *The Only Three Questions That Count: Investing by Knowing What Others Don't* (Hoboken, NJ: John Wiley & Sons, 2007).

4. Tanous, 1998, 227.

5. Eugene F. Fama and Kenneth R. French, "Industry Costs of Equity." *Journal of Financial Economics* 43 (1997): 153–193.

CHAPTER 9 Why We Are Inveterate Benchmarkers

1. Adam Smith, *The Theory of Moral Sentiments* (Oxford: Clarendon Press, 1976).
2. Richard Dawkins, *The Selfish Gene* (Oxford: Oxford University Press, 1976).
3. Charles Darwin, *The Descent of Man* (New York: D. Appleton, 1871).
4. John Tooby and Lida Cosmides, *Conceptual Foundations of Evolutionary Psychology,* in David M. Buss, ed., *The Handbook of Evolutionary Psychology* (Hoboken, NJ: John Wiley & Sons, 2005), 5–67.
5. Thomas R. Insel and Russell D. Fernald, "How the Brain Processes Social Information: Searching for the Social Brain," *Annual Review of Neuroscience* 27 (1) (2004): 697–722.
6. ScienceDaily, "Autism Linked to Mirror Neuron Dysfunction," *ScienceDaily,* April 18, 2005. http://www.sciencedaily.com/releases/2005/04/050411204511 .htm.
7. Animals that pass the mirror test include great apes (including humans over 18 months), bottlenose dolphins, killer whales, elephants, and European magpies.
8. Gordy Slack, "I feel your pain" (Salon, November 5, 2007), http://www.salon. com/news/feature/2007/11/05/mirror_neurons/print.html.
9. Donald E. Brown, *Human Universals* (New York: McGraw-Hill, 1991).
10. Natalie Angier, "Political Animals (Yes, Animals)," *New York Times,* January 22, 2008.
11. Max Weber, ed., *Class, Status and Party* (1924) in Hans Gerth and C. Wright Mills, *Essays from Max Weber* (New York: Routledge and Kegan Paul, 1948).
12. Tom Wolfe, *The Right Stuff* (New York: Farrar, Straus and Giroux, 1983).
13. Thorstein Veblen, *The Theory of the Leisure Class: An Economic Study in the Evolution of Institutions* (London and New York: Macmillan, 1899).
14. Wolfgang Pesendorfer, "Design Innovation and Fashion Cycles," *American Economic Review* 85 (1995): 771–792; Luis Rayo and Gary S. Becker, "Evolutionary Efficiency and Happiness," *Journal of Political Economy* 115 (2) (2007): 302–337.
15. Dan Ariely, *Predictably Irrational* (New York: HarperCollins, 2008).
16. Growth models (Harold L. Cole, George J. Mailath, and Andrew Postlewaite, "Social Norms, Savings Behavior, and Growth," *Journal of Political Economy* 100 (6) (1992), 1092–1125); tax policy (Douglas Bernheim and Laurie Simon Bagwell, "Veblen Effects in a Theory of Conspicuous Consumption," *American Economic Review,* 86 (3) (1996): 349–373); public goods (Robert H. Frank, "The Frame of Reference as a Public Good," *The Economic Journal* 107 (445) (1997): 1832–1847); social norms (Douglas Bernheim, "A Theory of Conformity," *Journal of Political Economy* 102 (5) (1994): 841–877); charity (Robert Cialdini and Melanie Trost, 1998); health insurance (Robin Hanson, "Showing that You Care: The Evolution of Health Altruism," *Medical Hypotheses* 70 (4) (2008): 724–742); and repeated interactions (Joel Sobel, "Interdependent

Preferences and Reciprocity," *Journal of Economic Literature* 43 (2) (2005): 392–436).

17. Philip Brickman and Donald T. Campbell, "Hedonic Relativism and Planning the Good Society," *Adaptation-Level Theory: A Symposium* (1971), 287–302.

18. George M. Constantinides, "Habit Formation: A Resolution of the Equity Premium Puzzle," *Journal of Political Economy* 98 (3) (1990): 519; Andrew B. Abel, "Asset Prices Under Habit Formation and Catching Up with the Joneses," *American Economic Review* 80 (2) (1990): 38–42.

19. This implication for the Nash equilibrium, the prisoner's dilemma, was why Judd Hirsch says to Russell Crowe, "You just turned one hundred fifty years of economics on its head," supposedly because it showed an equilibrium where the Invisible Hand does not lead to a societal optimum. If anyone thought this was a big take-away, the repeated game takes us back to the virtue of the Invisible Hand.

20. Robert Axelrod, *The Evolution of Cooperation* (New York: Basic Books, 1984).

21. Robert L. Trivers, "The Evolution of Reciprocal Altruism," *Quarterly Review of Biology*, 46 (1971): 35–57.

22. Robert H. Frank, *Passions Within Reason* (New York: W.W. Norton, 1988).

23. See Gregg Mankiew's post on Wolfers and Stevenson titled "Never Mind," http://gregmankiw.blogspot.com/2008/04/easterlin-paradox.html; or Will Wilkenson's http://www.willwilkinson.net/flybottle/2008/04/16/maybe-money-does-buy-happiness-after-all/.

CHAPTER 10 Alpha, Risk, and Hope

1. Gustav Theodor Fechner, *Elemente der Psychophysik* (1860).

2. Stanislas Dehaene, Véronique Izard, Elizabeth Spelke, and Pierre Pica, "Log or Linear? Distinct Intuitions of the Number Scale in Western and Amazonian Indigene Cultures." *Science* 320(5880) (2008): 1217–1220.

3. John Maynard Keynes, *The General Theory of Employment, Interest and Money*. (London and New York: Macmillan, 1936), 162. Elsewhere, Keynes makes the observation that "Businessmen play a mixed game of skill and chance, the average results of which to the players are not known by those who take a hand. If human nature felt no temptation to take a chance, no satisfaction (profit apart) in constructing a factor, a railway, a mine or a farm, there might not be much investment merely as a result of cold calculation." (150).

4. Brad M. Barber and Terrance Odean, "Trading Is Hazardous to Your Wealth: The Common Stock Investment Performance of Individual Investors," *The Journal of Finance* 55 (2) (2000): 773–806, documents excessive retail trading, which they relate to overconfidence.

5. Shih-Wei Wu, Johnnie E.V. Johnson, Ming-Chien Sung, "Overconfidence in Judgements: The Evidence, the Implications and the Limitations," *The Journal of Prediction Markets*, 2 (1) (2008): 73–90.

6. Burton G. Malkiel, "Returns from Investing in Equity Mutual Funds 1971 to 1991," *Journal of Finance* 50 (1995): 549–572; Mark M. Carhart, "On

Persistence in Mutual Fund Performance," *Journal of Finance* 52 (1997): 57–82; Russell Wermers, "Mutual Fund Performance: An Empirical Decomposition into Stock-Picking Talent, Style, Transactions Costs, and Expenses," *The Journal of Finance* 55 (4) (2000): 1655–1703. On mutual fund performance, Terrance Odean, "Do Investors Trade Too Much?" *American Economic Review,* 89 (1999): 1279–1298, documents excessive retail trading, which they relate to overconfidence.

7. Luis Santos-Pinto and Joel Sobel, "A Model of Positive Self-Image in Subjective Assessments," *American Economic Review* 95 (5) (2005): 1386–1402.

8. ScienceDaily, "Sticks and Stones: A New Study on Social and Physical Pain," *ScienceDaily* (August 28, 2008), http://www.sciencedaily.com/releases/2008/08/080827164140.htm.

9. Shane Frederick, "Cognitive Reflection and Decision Making," *Journal of Economic Perspectives* 29 (4) (2005): 24–42; Jonathan Guryan and Melissa S. Kearney, "Gambling at Lucky Stores: Empirical Evidence from State Lottery Sales," *American Economic Review* 98 (1) (2008): 458–473.

10. Sarah Lichtenstein, Baruch Fischhoff, and Lawrence D. Phillips, "Calibration of Probabilities: The State of the Art to 1980," in Daniel Kahneman, Paul Slovic, and Amos Tversky, *Judgment Under Uncertainty: Heuristics and Biases* (Cambridge: Cambridge University Press, 1982).

11. Norman Mailer, *The Presidential Papers* (New York: Putnam, 1963), 233.

12. Paul Milgrom and Nancy Stokey, "Information, Trade, and Common Knowledge," *Journal of Economic Theory* 26 (1) (1982): 17–27.

13. Sanford Grossman and Joseph Stiglitz, "On the Impossibility of Informationally Efficient Markets," *American Economic Review* 70 (1980): 393–408; Albert Kyle, "Continuous Auctions and Insider Trading," *Econometrica* 53 (1985): 1315–1335.

14. Enriqueta Aragones, Itzhak Gilboa, Andrew Postlewaite, and David Schmeidler, "Fact-Free Learning," *American Economic Review* 95 (5) (2006).

15. Werner Güth, Rolf Schmittberger, and Bernd Schwarze, "An Experimental Analysis of Ultimatum Bargaining," *Journal of Economic Behavior and Organization* 3 (4) (1982): 367–388.

16. Jonathan Haidt, *The Happiness Hypothesis* (New York: Basic Books, 2006).

17. Walter Gutman, *You Only Have to Get Rich Once* (New York: Dutton, 1961).

18. Charles A. Holt and Susan K. Laury, "Risk Aversion and Incentive Effects," *American Economic Review* 92 (5) (2002): 1644–55.

19. Cary A. Deck, Lee Jungmin, and Javier A. Reyes, *Risk Attitudes in Large Stake Gambles: Evidence from a Game Show* (Social Science Research Network, May 17, 2006).

20. Roel Beetsma and Peter C. Schotman, "Measuring Risk Attitudes in a Natural Experiment: Data from the Television Game Show LINGO," *The Economic Journal* 111 (474) (2001): 821–848.

21. W. Kip Viscusi and William N. Evans, "Utility Functions that Depend on Health Status: Estimates and Economic Implications" *American Economic Review* 80 (3) (1990): 353–374.

22. Laura Schechter, "Risk Aversion and Expected-Utility Theory: A Calibration Exercise," *Journal of Risk and Uncertainty* 35 (1) (2007): 67–76.
23. Peter L. Bossaerts, *The Paradox of Asset Pricing* (Princeton, NJ: Princeton University Press, 2002).

CHAPTER 11 Examples of Alpha

1. Sylvia Nasar, *A Beautiful Mind* (New York: Simon and Schuster, 1998), 71.
2. Robert Laughlin, *A Different Universe* (New York: Basic Books, 2005).
3. Andy Redleaf, "The End of Arbitrage, Part 1," *The Whitebox Advisor* (August 2004).
4. Edward Rombach, "Not So Perfect," *Risk* 4 (9) (1990).
5. Simon Boughey and Margaret Eliott, "Fear and Loathing in the Interdealer Swap Market," *Derivatives Strategy* (February 1997).
6. Mark Grinblatt and Narasimhan Jegadeesh, "Relative Pricing of Eurodollar Futures and Forward Contracts," *Journal of Finance* 51 (1996): 1499–1522; Galen Burghardt and Bill Hoskins, "The Convexity Bias in Eurodollar Futures: Part 1," *Derivatives Quarterly* 1 (3) (1995): 47–55.
7. Christopher Jeffery, "Equity Derivatives: Shedding the Correlation 'Axe,'" *Risk* 17 (5) May 18, 2004, 65–68.
8. Andrew W. Lo and Craig MacKinlay, "Stock Market Prices Do Not Follow Random Walks: Evidence from a Simple Specification Test," *Review of Financial Studies* 1 (1988): 41–66.
9. Evan Gatev, William N. Goetzmann, and K. Geert Rouwenhorst, *Pairs Trading: Performance of a Relative Value Arbitrage Rule* (Yale ICF Working Paper No. 08-03, 1999), http://ssrn.com/abstract=141615.
10. Paul A. Samuelson, "Challenge to Judgment," *Journal of Portfolio Management* (1974).
11. Paul A. Samuelson, "Challenge to Judgment," *Journal of Portfolio Management* (1974); Charles D. Ellis, *Winning the Loser's Game,* 3rd ed. (New York: McGraw-Hill, 1998).
12. Paul A. Samuelson, in *Newsweek,* August 16, 1976.
13. *BusinessWeek,* April 30, 1984, 125.
14. *Forbes,* October 7, 1985, 167–168.
15. Russell Wermers, "Mutual Fund Performance: An Empirical Decomposition into Stock-Picking Talent, Style, Transactions Costs, and Expenses," *The Journal of Finance* 55 (4) (2000): 1655–1703.
16. John C. Bogle, Founder, The Vanguard Group, "What Can Active Managers Learn from Index Funds?" From a speech presented to the Bullseye 2000 Conference in Toronto, Canada, December 4, 2000.
17. Robert D. Arnott, Andrew L. Berkin, and Jia Ye, "How Well Have Taxable Investors Been Served in the 1980s and 1990s?" *Journal of Portfolio Management* 26 (4) (2000): 84–93.

18. Burton Malkiel, "Returns from Investing in Equity Mutual Funds 1971 to 1991," *The Journal of Finance* 50 (2) (1995): 549–572.
19. Edwin J. Elton, Martin J. Gruber, and Christopher R. Blake, "The Persistence of Risk-Adjusted Mutual Fund Performance," *Journal of Business* 69 (2) (1996): 133–157.
20. Investment Company Institute, Investment Company Fact Book (2008).
21. In practice, it's more complicated because the bonds are often callable, and exercising the option extinguishes the bond.
22. Igor Loncarski, Jenke ter Horst, and Chris Veld, *The Rise and Demise of the Convertible Arbitrage Strategy,* Social Science Research Network (2007), http://ssrn.com/abstract=929951.
23. Ross M. Miller, *Measuring the True Cost of Active Management by Mutual Funds,* Social Science Research Network (2005), http://ssrn.com/abstract= 746926.
24. Burton Malkiel and Atanu Saha, "Hedge Funds: Risk and Return," *Financial Analysts Journal* 61 (6) (2005): 80–88; William Goetzman and Stephen A. Ross, "Hedge Funds: Theory and Performance," (2000).
25. "Bank Diversification, Economic Diversification?" (Federal Reserve Bank San Francisco Economic Letter, May 12, 2006).
26. Robyn Dawes and B. Corrigan, "Linear Models in Decision Making," *Psychological Bulletin* (1974): 95–106.
27. Paul E. Meehl, *Clinical versus Statistical Prediction: A Theoretical Analysis and a Review of the Evidence* (Minneapolis: University of Minnesota Press, 1954).
28. Rob Johnston, "Integrating Methodologists into Teams of Substantive Experts," *Central Intelligence Agency, Center for the Study of Intelligence Publications, Studies in Intelligence* 47 (1) (2003): 60.
29. Richard Nisbet, David Krantz, Christopher Jepson, and Geoffrey Fong, *Improving Inductive Inference,* in Daniel Kahneman, Paul Slovic, and Amos Tversky, *Judgment Under Uncertainty: Heuristics and Biases* (Cambridge: Cambridge University Press, 1982).
30. Peter Crosbie and Jeff Bohn, "Modeling Default Risk," Moody's KMV (December 18, 2003).
31. Edward Altman, "Financial Ratios, Discriminant Analysis and the Prediction of Corporate Bankruptcy," *Journal of Finance* 23 (4) (1968): 589–609.
32. Eric Falkenstein, Lea V. Carty, and Andrew Boral, *RiskCalc for Private Companies: Moody's Default Model* (Moody's Investors Service Special Comment, May 2000).
33. Jack Schwager, *Market Wizards* (New York: Simon and Schuster, 1989).

CHAPTER 12   Alpha Games

1. Alice Schroeder, *The Snowball* (New York: Bantam, 2008).
2. Friedrich Hayek, "The Use of Knowledge in Society," *American Economic Review* 35 (4) (1945): 519–530.

3. Temple Grandin with Catherine Johnson, *Animals in Translation: Using the Mysteries of Autism to Decode Animal Behavior* (2005).

4. Robert Trivers, "The Elements of a Scientific Theory of Self-Deception," *Annals of the New York Academy of Sciences* (2000).

5. Kravis–De Roulet Leadership Conference (2007) in Ronald E. Riggio, Susan E. Murphy, and Francis J. Pirozzolo, *Multiple Intelligences and Leadership,* (New York: Lawrence Erlbaum Associates, 1999) and Tom Wolfe, *Bonfire of the Vanities* (New York: Farrar, Straus and Giroux, 1990) 384–385.

6. MarketPerform.com for *Money.*

7. Harold Schneider, *Livestock and Equality in East Africa: The Economic Basis for Social Structure* (Bloomington: Indiana University Press, 1979).

8. Carolyn Tucker Halpern, Kara Joyner, J. Richard Udry, and C. Suchindran. "Smart Teens Don't Have Sex (or Kiss Much Either)." *Journal of Adolescent Health* 26(3) (March 2000): 213–225.

9. Peter Brimelow, *Forbes,* January 3, 1993.

10. Stan J. Liebowitz, "Anatomy of a Train Wreck," *National Review/Digital* (October 20, 2008); Benjamin Powell and Randall Holcomb, eds., *Housing America: Building Out of a Crisis* (New Brunswick, NJ: Transaction Publishers, 2009).

11. Stan Liebowitz, "The Real Scandal," *New York Post,* February 5, 2008.

12. Vern McKinley, "Community Reinvestment Act: Ensuring Credit Adequancy or Enforcing Credit Allocation?" *Regulation* 4 (1994): 25–37.

13. Charles Duhigg, "At Freddie Mac, Chief Discarded Warning Signs," *New York Times,* August 5, 2008.

14. Steve Labaton, "New Agency Proposed to Oversee Freddie Mac and Fannie Mae," *New York Times,* September 11, 2003.

15. S. 190 (109th Congress): Federal Housing Enterprise Regulatory Reform Act of 2005.

16. Liebowitz, 2009.

17. Robert Shiller actually did call the Internet bubble, and on the book jacket of his 2008 book, *The Subprime Solution,* Lawrence Summers blurbed that Shiller called the housing bubble, too. Yet, if you read the revised edition of *Irrational Exuberance,* written in 2005, while he has a chapter on the then-recent run-up in housing prices, it was typical economese: On the one hand prices have risen a lot, but on the other hand they did this earlier without a problem (1948), and so forth. On page 209, he writes, "In cities where prices have gotten so high that many people cannot afford to live there, the price increases may start to slow down, and then to fall. At the same time, it is likely the boom will continue for quite a while in other cities." Hardly the clarion call of warning.

18. Claire Robinson, a 20-year veteran who is in charge of asset-backed finance for Moody's, told Roger Lowenstein, "We aren't loan officers. Our expertise is as statisticians on an aggregate basis. We want to know, of one thousand individuals, based on historical performance, what percent will pay their loans?" in Roger Lowenstein, "Triple-A Failure," *New York Times,* April 27, 2008.

19. Liebowitz, 2009, 7.
20. Alicia H. Munnell, Geoffrey M.B. Tootell, Lynne E. Browne, and James McEneaney, "Mortgage Lending in Boston: Interpreting HMDA Data," *American Economic Review* 86 (1) (1996): 25–53.
21. Stan Liebowitz and Ted Day, "Mortgage Discrimination in Boston: Where's the Bias?" *Economic Inquiry* 36 (1) (January 1998): 1–27.
22. James Bovard, "Bush Profiteering from Housing Defaults," June 11 at LewRockwell.com, http://www.lewrockwell.com/bovard/bovard8.html (2005); Stan J. Liebowitz, "Anatomy of a Train Wreck: Causes of the Mortgage Meltdown," in *Housing America: Building out of a Crisis*, edited by Benjamin Power and Randall Holcomb. (New Brunswick, NJ: Transaction Publishers, 2009.)
23. Roger Lowenstein, *While America Aged* (New York: Penguin Press, 2008).
24. Brad Barber and Terrance Odean, "Do the Slow Die First?" *Review of Financial Studies* 15 (2) (2002) 455–488.

CHAPTER 13   Alpha Seeking Applications

1. Robert A. Haugen and Nardin L. Baker, "The Efficient Market Inefficiency of Capitalization-Weighted Stock Portfolios," *Journal of Portfolio Management* 17 (3) (1991): 35–40; Tal Schwartz, "How to Beat the S&P500 with Portfolio Optimization," (Unpublished Manuscript, 2000); http://www.departments.bucknell.edu/management/apfa/Dundee%20Papers/27Schwartz.pdf; Roger Clarke, Harindra de Silva, and Steven Thorley, "Minimum-Variance Portfolio in the U.S. Equity Market," *Journal of Portfolio Management* (2006); David Blitz and Pim van Vliet, "The Volatility Effect," *Journal of Portfolio Management* (2007), 102–113.
2. Christopher Jones, "Extracting Factors from Heteroskedastic Asset Returns," *Journal of Financial Economics* 62 (2001): 293–325; Gregory Connor and Robert A. Korajczyk, "A Test for the Number of Factors in an Approximate Factor Model," *Journal of Finance* 48 (September 1993), 1263–1291.
3. Marshall E. Blume and Robert Stambaugh, "Biases in Computed Returns," *Journal of Financial Economics* 12: 387–404 (1983).
4. In 2005, regulation SHO in the United States created a much more demanding set of rules for short selling, which has increased the disclosure of short-sell lists, but published lists are often conservative (list distributed to the retail public put more "impossible to borrows" to avoid problems) and incomplete.
5. Michael D. Rothschild and Joseph Stiglitz, "Increasing Risk I: A Definition," *Journal of Economic Theory* 2 (3) (1970): 225–243.
6. Define T(x) as the cumulative area between the CDFs up to a point x, where $T(x) = \int_{-\infty}^{x} CDF\,(A(t)) - CDF\,(B(t))dt$. If T(x)>0 for all x, then B is said to second order stochastically dominate A, and be less risky.
7. Robeco Institutional Conservative Equity Fund (RINCEFD NA), Robeco's Capital Growth European Conservative Equity (ROECIEU LX), and Unigestions Unigest Swiss Minimum Variance (RBSSMVF SW).

8. Werner F.M. De Bondt and Richard H. Thaler, "Further Evidence on Investor Overreaction and Stock Market Seasonality," *Journal of Finance* 42 (1987): 557–581.

9. Jennifer Conrad and Gautam Kaul, "Long-Term Market Overreaction or Biases in Computed Returns?" *Journal of Finance* 48 (1) (1993): 39–63.

10. Tim Loughran and Todd Houge, "Do Investors Capture the Value Premium?" *Financial Management* 35 (2) (2006).

11. SVX, SGX, and SPX indexes.

12. Data from Aaa and Baa indexes in the Federal Reserve Bank of St. Louis, FRED data (1919–2008).

13. U.S. bond and bill data, in total returns, averaged monthly, from data from Board of Governors of the Federal Reserve System, H. 15 report (1977–2008).

14. Jean Tirole, "On the Possibility of Speculation under Rational Expectations," *Econometrica* 50 (1982): 1163–1181; Olivier Blanchard and Mark Watson, "Bubbles, Rational Expectations and Financial Markets," (1982), in Paul Wachtel, ed., *Crises in the Economic and Financial Structure* (Lexington, MA: Lexington Books, 1983); J. Bradford De Long, Andrei Shleifer, Lawrence Summers, and Robert Waldmann, "Positive Feedback Investment Strategies and Destabilizing Rational Speculation," *Journal of Finance* 45 (2) (1990): 374–397.

15. It turns out that the default problem has a flat maximum, so that the basic model converges pretty well after 1,000 or so bad observations. Thus, the in-sample and out-of-sample default model, given sufficient data, are not hugely different; that is, the model outperforms the agency ratings, though not as much.

16. American Express Annual Report (2001).

CHAPTER 14 Conclusion

1. Xavier Gabaix, "A Unified Theory of Ten Financial Puzzles," 9th Annual Texas Finance Festival, Social Science Research Network (January 31, 2006), http://ssrn.com/abstract=976436.

Index